JOHN CATT'S
Which School? for Special Needs
2017/18

26th Edition
Editor: Jonathan Barnes

JOHN CATT EDUCATIONAL LIMITED

Published in 2017 by
John Catt Educational Ltd,
12 Deben Mill Business Centre,
Woodbridge, Suffolk IP12 1BL UK
Tel: 01394 389850   Fax: 01394 386893
Email: enquiries@johncatt.com
Website: www.johncatt.com
© 2015 John Catt Educational Ltd

**A CIP catalogue record for this book is available from the
British Library.**

ISBN: 978 1 911382 14 0

Contacts
Editor
Jonathan Barnes

Advertising and School Profiles
Tel: +44 (0) 1394 389850
Email: sales@johncatt.com

Distribution/Book Sales
Tel: +44 (0) 1394 389863
Email: booksales@johncatt.com

Contents

How to use this guide

Here are some pointers on how to use this guidebook effectively

Which School? for Special Needs is divided into specific sections:

1. Editorial
This includes articles, written by experts in their fields, explaining various aspects of special needs education. There are also case studies and other interesting articles.

2. Profiles
Here the schools and colleges have been given the opportunity to highlight what they feel are their best qualities in order to help you decide whether this is the right school for your child. They are presented in sections according to the needs they specialise in:

- social interaction difficulties (autism, ASD & ASP)
- emotional, behavioural and/or social difficulties.
- learning difficulties (including dyslexia/SPLD)
- sensory or physical impairment

Within these sections, schools and colleges are listed by region in alphabetical order.

3. Directory
Here you will find basic up-to-date information about every independent or non-maintained special needs school and college, and further education colleges, in England, Northern Ireland, Scotland and Wales, giving contact details, size of school and which specific needs are catered for. (You will find a key to the abbreviations at the start of each directory section) The directory is divided into four sections:

- social interaction difficulties (autism, ASD & ASP)
- emotional, behavioural and/or social difficulties.
- learning difficulties (including dyslexia/SPLD)
- sensory or physical impairment

Within these sections, each establishment is listed by region in alphabetical order and those that have entries in the profiles section are cross-referenced to allow you to find further detailed information. Against each entry you will find a number of symbols indicating any SEN speciality, including an icon to indicate if the school is DfE approved.

4. Useful associations and websites
In this section we provide a list of useful organisations and websites relevant to special educational needs, which may be useful to parents looking for specific help or advice.

5. Maintained schools
Here we have included basic details of all maintained special schools in England, Northern Ireland, Scotland and Wales. They are listed according to their Local Authority.

6. Index
Page numbers preceded by a D indicate a school appearing in the directory, those without will be found in the profiles section.

How to use this guide effectively
John Catt's *Which School? for Special Needs* can be used effectively in several ways according to the information you are looking for. For example, are you looking for:

A specific school? If you know the name of the school but are unsure of its location simply go to the index at the back of the guide where you will find all schools listed alphabetically.

A particular type of school? Both the profiles and directories are divided into sections according to the type of provision. **See also the appendix on page 179**, which lists specific special needs and the schools that cater for them.

A school in a certain region? Look first in the relevant directory. This will give you the basic information about the schools in each region, complete with contact details and which specific needs are catered for. More detailed information can be found in the profiles section for those schools who have chosen to include a full entry.

More information on relevant educational organisations? At the end of the directories you will find a list of useful organisations and websites relevant to special educational needs.

Please note: regional divisions
To facilitate the use of this guide, we have included the geographical region 'Central & West'. This is not an officially designated region and has been created solely for the purposes of this publication.

One final thing, on the next page you will find a list of commonly used SEN abbreviations. This list can be found repeated at various points throughout the guide.

Abbreviations – a full glossary can be found at page 319

ACLD	Autism, Communication and Associated Learning Difficulties	HI	Hearing Impairment
ADD	Attention Deficit Disorder	LD	Learning Difficulties
ADHD	Attention Deficit and Hyperactivity Disorder	MLD	Moderate Learning Difficulties
		MSI	Multi-sensory Impairment
ASD	Autistic Spectrum Disorder	OCD	Obsessive Compulsive Disorder
ASP	Asperger Syndrome	PD	Physical Difficulties
AUT	Autism	PH	Physical Impairment
BESD	Behavioural, Emotional and Social Difficulties	Phe	Partially Hearing
		PMLD	Profound and Multiple Learning Difficulties
CCD	Complex Communication Difficulties	PNI	Physical Neurological Impairment
CLD	Complex Learning Difficulties	SCD	Social and Communication Difficulties
CP	Cerebral Palsy	SCLD	Severe to Complex Learning Difficulties
D	Deaf	SEBD	Severe Emotional and Behavioural Difficulties
DYS	Dyslexia		
DYSP	Dyspraxia	SEBN	Social, Emotional and Behavioural Needs
EBD	Emotional and Behavioural Difficulties	SLD	Severe Language Difficulties
EPI	Epilepsy	SLI	Specific Language Impairment
GLD	General Learning Difficulties	SPLD	Specific Learning Difficulties
HA	High Ability	SP&LD	Speech and Language Difficulties
		VIS	Visual Impairment

nasen Live is back for another year – this time at the Birmingham ICC on the **7th July 2017**

The one day event will provide SENCOs, school leaders, teachers and other education professionals with a unique platform to celebrate outstanding practice and provision for children and young people with SEND.

Visitors to the event will have the chance to network and explore the latest developments in the SEND and education sector and will also be able to update their knowledge and learn from evidence-based practice.

Delegates will also have access to leading, award winning exhibitors, as well as several seminars and keynotes during the event, delivered by key figures in the sector.

Professor Stephen Hawking CBE, is to open the annual conference via video and formally launch nasen's upcoming dual and multiple exceptionality (DME) campaign.

Other speakers include: Dr Adam Boddison, Chief Executive at nasen; Ofsted for Special Educational Needs and/or Disabilities; Professor Barry Carpenter, CBE, OBE, PHD; Professor Diane Montgomery PHD; Alison Wilcox, Head of Education at nasen; Dr Fiona Pienaar, Director of Clinical Services at Place2be; Dr Rona Tutt OBE; Stuart Miller, Deputy Director at the Department for Education; Natalie Packer, Independent Education Consultant; Rob Webster from the UCL Institute of Edication; Michael Surr, Education Officer at nasen; and Kate Browning, a former SENCo and local authority school improvement officer for SEND.

nasen.org.uk

To book your place, speak to a member of the team today on **01827 311500** or visit
nasen.org.uk/nasenlive

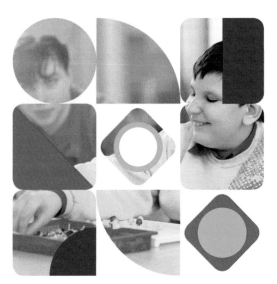

Special needs schools have an important place in the educational landscape

Adam Boddison, chief executive of Nasen, looks at the demand for special school places and how SEND legislation is progressing

I am pleased to have been invited to write the foreword for *Which School? for Special Needs* for the second time. British schools are not only known for their quality provision, but also for their diversity. The modern British education system boasts many different types of school from academies to free schools, from independent schools to faith schools, and from grammar schools to special schools. But with such breadth and choice, it can be a challenge to find the school that best meets the individual needs of a child or young person, particularly in the context of special educational needs and/or disabilities (SEND). I hope this guide proves useful as you navigate this rich and complex educational landscape.

In 2016, the Department for Education published a green paper entitled *Schools that Work for Everyone*, which was primarily focused on increasing the number of grammar schools. However, despite the inclusive title of the green paper, there was no mention about expanding provision for children and young people with SEND. The green paper did not acknowledge the growing national demand for high quality special school places and nor did it acknowledge the contribution that special schools are making to the wider educational system. For example, a number of recent Local Area SEND inspections conducted jointly by Ofsted and the Care Quality Commission have formally recognised the value added when the specialist expertise from special schools is shared with mainstream schools.

This demand for special school places has implications for the recruitment of specialist teachers in terms of both quantity and quality. The Migration Advisory Committee within the Home Office have recently conducted some analysis into teacher shortages in England and their report, published in January 2017, is clear that there is an adequate supply of specialist staff available for teaching in special schools. In addition to this, there have been calls from some special schools

to develop specialist initial teacher training routes for those who know from the outset that they would like to work in special schools. I would argue that one of the best things a school can do for a child with SEND is to provide them with an outstanding teacher and on that basis you need to be a teacher before you become a specialist. Whatever the outcome of this debate, the fact that the discussion is taking place at all demonstrates the importance of special schools as a core feature of our educational system.

There are, of course, some individuals and organisations who argue against the existence of special schools on the basis that if mainstream schools were inclusive enough, special schools would not be needed. This idea of inclusion meaning that all students should be in a mainstream school is now outdated and there is general agreement that inclusion is not a place, but an approach that can work in both specialist and mainstream settings. Mainstream schools can be just as inclusive as special schools if effective SEND provision is knitted into the fabric of the organisation.

The SEND data available from the Department for Education can be useful in determining both regional and national trends. For example, in the school census there is a requirement to report on both the number of children with SEND and their primary area of need. At a regional

> This idea of inclusion meaning that all students should be in a mainstream school is now outdated and there is general agreement that inclusion is not a place, but an approach that can work in both specialist and mainstream settings.

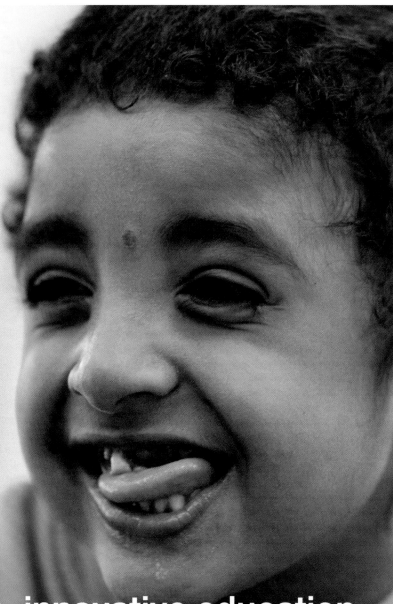

level, this data could be used to identify areas with high levels of particular needs and potentially more targeted local provision to reflect those needs. Alternatively, the same data set might be used to tackle the postcode lottery by identifying areas where competition for specialist provision is reduced. At a national level, the SEND data shows us that despite the changes in the school population over time, the proportion of children with statements or EHCPs (Education, Health and Care Plans) has remained almost constant at 2.8%. Similarly, the data around fixed term and permanent exclusions shows us that in general you are seven times more likely to be excluded if you are a child or young person with SEND compared to those without SEND. This is an area where special schools are making significant progress, since their exclusions are generally much less frequent than in mainstream schools.

2016 and 2017 have seen a number of government consultations including the Fairer Funding Review, the High Needs Funding Review and a consultation on the recommendations of the Rochford Review. The latter is particularly concerned with reviewing the approach to statutory assessment for those children with the most complex learning needs; i.e. those who currently use the p-levels system. The outcome of this consultation will impact on special schools right across England and some mainstream schools too, but only time will tell whether

any new approaches to statutory assessment are more effective or not than current approaches. Lastly,

it has been ten years since the Bercow Report and there have been significant changes to SEND policy and practice during this time, so a follow-up has been commissioned. The Bercow Report: ten years on will consider speech, language and communication provision nationally.

Beyond England, it is worth noting that both Northern Ireland and Wales have consulted on the introduction of revised legislation around SEND and both intend to publish revised codes of practice in the near future. Beyond the UK, the system becomes even more complex and the approach to inclusion is dependent on a number of factors, not least the SEND policies and cultural norms of individual countries.

In conclusion, whilst it is clear that effective SEND provision remains both complex and personalised, the value of both special schools and mainstream schools as part of the wider mix of schools is clear. All schools in England do have a lot to offer, but much like the children who attend them, every school is different. The educational landscape will continue to change, but selecting the right school will constantly remain an important factor in determining outcomes for children and young people with SEND.

For more information about Nasen, visit www.nasen.org.uk

Providing a unique education solution for every pupil

TCES Group schools provide LA funded education for pupils aged 7-18 years whose Social, Emotional or Mental Health (SEMH) needs or Autism Spectrum Condition (ASC) has made it difficult for them to achieve success in a mainstream school. Pupil's co-morbid needs can be complex. Undiagnosed speech, language and communication needs (SLCN), sensory difficulties or learning difficulties can create barriers to learning that must be addressed before the pupil can settle into education. Our integrated approach to education, health and care takes each pupil on an individual journey that encourages a love of learning. We offer two options according to the needs of the pupil:

Option 1 Day School Provision

Tier 1 For pupils with SEMH needs or an ASC for whom the expectation is that they will be able to thrive in and integrate easily into a small group learning environment, which would include an internal induction period as standard. Once in school full time, the pupil would be supported by TCES Group's Team Around the Child approach.

Tier 2 There may be exceptional circumstances where a pupil may need additional support over a specified period to ensure they are able to engage with and thrive in their placement.

Tiers 1 and 2 Services are delivered and managed by the Leadership Teams in each of our schools – Head and Deputy Head Teachers and Inclusion Managers – in conjunction with Head of Clinical Services, Clinical and Therapy Team, School Improvement Team and Contracts and Commissioning Lead.

Option 2 Create Service

Tier 3 For pupils with SEMH or an ASC for whom integration into a class-based school placement is not indicated, which may be for a number of reasons. At best they will need a graduated programme into a small group learning environment. They may need 1:1 support in the medium to long term in tandem with TCES Group's Team Around the Child approach.

Tier 4 Pupils with SEMH or an ASC who either present high risk to themselves or others or who are extremely vulnerable and are therefore at high risk. Pupils' complex and additional needs (across education, health and care) negate their ability to be educated in any group setting.

Tiers 3 and 4 Services are delivered and managed by the Head Teacher and Case Co-ordinators in the Create Service, a parallel service to that of our schools, in conjunction with our Head of Clinical Services, Clinical and Therapy Team, School Improvement Team and Contracts and Commissioning Lead. Therapeutic education, assessment and monitoring is delivered through a highly specialised case co-ordination model. Pupils may attend one of Create's Therapeutic Hubs, be educated in safe community spaces or, in some cases, their own homes.

East London
Independent School

North West London
Independent School

www.tces.org.uk
0208 543 7878

Essex Fresh Start
Independent School

Create Service
Personalised Therapeutic Education

We must highlight the value of special schools amid funding challenges

Claire Dorer, chief executive of The National Association of Independent Schools & Non-Maintained Special Schools (NASS), looks at funding policy

It has been 14 years since Government last focused on special schools. In 2017 we have not one but two policy initiatives which turn the spotlight firmly on the sector.

Whilst planned reforms to school funding have been reported widely in the media, less has been said about the accompanying proposals to reform High Needs Funding. However, the proposed changes will lead to major changes in how local authorities are funded by Government to, in turn, fund special schools. Current allocations are decided by historic factors – mainly how much an authority has spent on High Needs in the past. This means that apparently similar authorities receive very different amounts from Government. The new proposals will move funding to a formula-based system that will determine funding levels on a range of factors ranging from low achievement levels to child deprivation within each authority. The aim is to have a fairer system of funding. On paper, it all sounds very reasonable. However, this is a system of redistribution of funds, meaning whilst some authorities would gain under the new formula, others would lose.

Fortunately, the Government has recognised that it would be unhelpful if any local authority lost funding under the new system. However, the proposed new system assumes that the numbers of children with High Needs will remain static at a time when we are seeing a growth in the number of children with SEND. Effectively, we will be finding ways to make the same amount of money spread across more children and young people and this is a source of worry for both special schools and local authorities. We will all need to work together to find ways of using money as effectively as possible to ensure that children with SEND get access to the right interventions and placements at the right time.

Alongside funding discussions we also have the major review of Residential Special Schools, led by Dame Christine Lenehan, Director of Council for Disabled Children. Dame Christine will be exploring the role these schools play in meeting complex needs and considering outcomes for children.

We know that when money is tight, scrutiny is often closest on those placements that cost the most amount of money – usually those for children and young people with the most complex needs. We spent a lot of time putting together a solid evidence-base for the review to highlight both the value of the sector and the challenge most parents have in accessing it. We had over 300 responses to our parents' survey and although each story is unique but we saw some common themes. For the vast majority of parents, a special school place for their child was an active choice and very much valued. However, many parents noted the struggle they had been through to get their placement and the lack of support they had received early on. Almost half had started tribunal proceedings at some point.

We would like to see parents have easier access to specialist placements and not to have to face such a battle to get them. We hope that Dame Christine's review will affirm the value of our schools and help Government think more strategically about how we support children with complex needs. However, we would also like to see more investment in supporting children in their local areas. As a group of specialist schools, we would love to see better structures for those in the independent and non-maintained sectors to be able to share their expertise with mainstream schools but we think this is something the funding reforms currently miss.

Whilst the Government will report on both the High Needs Funding Reforms and Lenehan Review in 2017, we won't see changes take effect until 2018. That makes the rest of the year a busy time of influencing for those of us working with special schools and local authorities. You can stay in touch with our activities by following us on Twitter @NASSCHOOLS.

For more information about the NASS, visit www.nasschools.org.uk

All that glitters is not gold

Douglas Silas, Principal of Douglas Silas Solicitors, gives an overview of developments in the SEN sector and looks ahead to future developments

As we are now well over halfway through the transitional phase from the old SEN framework to the new SEN framework (which began on 1st September 2014 and is meant to be completed by 1st April 2018), I thought it would be a good time to take stock of where we seem to have got to so far.

Do you remember the long lead up and big fanfare before the introduction of the new SEN framework? There was the Children and Families Act and the new SEND Code of Practice, which both came into effect from 1 September 2014. There were promises of how it was going to be 'the biggest shake-up to SEN for 30 years'. It seems a long time ago now, doesn't it?

The hope was that we could bring in change to allow for a more joined-up approach in terms of providing for children and young people with SEND. Although we now have new names and concepts, such as 'Local Offers', 'Personal Budgets' and, of course, 'Education, Health & Care (or EHC) Plans' and we were told how great the changes would be, it does not necessarily look that way now sometimes.

I think that, generally, most people were pleased to learn that the system would now cater for both children and young people from birth up to 25 years and that Statements of SEN (which only focused on education), would be replaced by EHC plans (which would look also at health and care needs, as well as educational ones). There was also the promise of there being more integration and joint commissioning of education, health and care provision.

Most importantly, we were told that there would now be a greater call for children and young people (and their families) to be put at the heart of the process and that there would be this new concept of 'working together' between parents and professionals tasked with the responsibility and providing for children and young people's needs.

But isn't the idea of 'working together' already what was supposed to be happening anyway?

Has it all really worked out? It seemed from early on that we may be biting off more than we could chew, or trying to do things too quickly and with less, not more (i.e. at a time of funding cuts). Unfortunately, some Local Authorities (LAs) have been unable to comply with the legal timescales for transferring Statements to EHC plans and one of the most immediate problems was nearly every LA having their own versions of the assessment process, or format for EHC plans.

The writing of EHC plans was also criticised individually very early on (particularly by SEND Tribunals) for being often increasingly unworkable documents; for example, often mixing up things like needs, outcomes and provision, or being set out in tabulated or landscape formats, which were very hard to work with. Some of these problems still seem to be with us.

Remember, this change was meant to make everyone's lives easier, but sometimes we seem to have ended up making people's lives harder, no matter which perspective you have or which side of the fence you sit on (i.e. parents, school or LA).

Perhaps it would be better if we focus all of our resources on making things shorter, rather than trying to put everything in. I was ticked off many times in Tribunal hearing for producing working documents of Statements that were 10-12 pages, but I now routinely come across EHC plans which are 30, 40, or even 50 pages long, before an appeal!

Douglas Silas Solicitors

I have heard some LA representatives admitting publicly in the past couple of years that they have been in chaos and things seem to be getting worse, not better. It was supposed to be a 'win-win' situation, but it now sometimes feels as though it has turned into a 'lose-lose' situation.

Take one example, the huge project of transferring some 230,000-odd Statements to EHC plans within prescribed timescales, including those outlined in statutory transfer guidance. At first, these transfers were being attempted properly, but many people found that to do them properly required more time than was being prescribed.

This has led to bizarre situations, where one LA was criticised for not complying with the legal timescales, but was doing the transfers as well as possible and in a way that everyone was happy with the final EHC plan. Whereas another LA was doing it quickly and within the legal timescales, but then not doing a very good job, which would often as not lead to appeals.

This reminds me of the phrase: 'Less haste, more speed'.

As time has gone on, there has been increasing concern that transfers are now at risk of becoming just tick-box exercises, or they stand accused of just being used as a chance to reduce or remove provision, or to make that provision less specific than it was before. There just seem to be too many targets to meet these days and so much focus being put on making people jump through hoops.

Perhaps it would be better if we focus all of our resources on making things shorter, rather than trying to put everything in. For example, remember that EHC plans were supposed to be more accessible and more concise than Statements? I was ticked off many times in Tribunal hearing for producing working documents of Statements that were 10-12 pages, but I now routinely come across EHC plans which are 30, 40, or even 50 pages long, before an appeal!

One of the advantages that we have now that we didn't have a couple of years ago is that we have the benefit of hindsight. They say that hindsight is a wonderful thing and I only wish I had it before!

We can now point to objective evidence with reports such as the Scott report from November 2016, which talks about people's experiences of the new system, or inspections carried out by Ofsted and CQC (the Care Quality Commission), who have jointly been inspecting some local areas to see how well they are discharging their responsibilities to children and young people with SEND.

So, although I have entitled this article 'All That Glitters Is Not Gold' I am definitely not trying to make negative comments about the new SEN framework. I do understand and appreciate how hard everybody has been working and that people working in this area (on all 'sides') can often feel that it is a bit of a thankless task sometimes.

But if you work for a school or LA, you may have already formed a negative or frustrated view of parents or their representatives that you come across, or if you are a parent or representative, you may have already formed a negative or frustrated view of those working for schools or LAs. I know it is never easy but please always try your hardest to give other people the benefit of the doubt if you can.

Go ahead, try it – I bet you will see the difference.

Douglas Silas Solicitors specialise exclusively in SEN, whose website is www.SpecialEducationalNeeds.co.uk

Douglas is also the author of 'A Guide To The SEND Code of Practice (What You Need To Know)' which is available for all eBook readers. For further information visit: www.AGuideToTheSENDCodeOfPractice.co.uk

Help is out there – you are not alone

Melinda Nettleton, head of specialist law firm SEN Legal, shares her story and explains how her firm can help others who were in her situation

As a solicitor with years of experience in most areas of law, I have always been a stickler for preparation. Throughout university, my training contract and early years as a judicial reviewer, I had frequently spent all-night sessions reading up on case law and legislation to make sure I was fully researched and ready for whatever the next day threw at me.

When I fell pregnant with my son in 1989, it didn't take long before I had all the usual 'baby-books' on my shelf too. It wasn't until my child was diagnosed with a severe language disorder and dyspraxia in 1990, however, that I realised that I had nothing at all on Special Educational Needs. It soon proved to be quite a learning curve.

The services I initially expected to help me weren't there, and working out that the people I thought should be able to advise me didn't actually know all the answers either, was an extremely frustrating and time consuming process.

I have always wanted the best for my child, as any parent would, and so took it upon myself to explore options for additional support from his educators. This didn't really get me anywhere. I often remember dropping my son off at the school gates, like other parents, and being met with comments like "it won't get you anywhere", "you'll only be disappointed", "we don't do that here", "no, you won't get that" or similar snippets of soul-destroying so-called 'friendly' advice.

The problem is that some teachers and local authority officers, whether consciously or unconsciously, often give information about their own local authority and NHS policies rather than what the Law and SEN Code of Practice say. You are left wondering, "Have I explained myself clearly enough?". The reality is it's not your communication skills, just the standard disinformation, discouragement and general negativity.

I decided to just get on with it. I ditched the waste-of-time meetings and stopped worrying about what the LA officers and school thought and whether they would be offended.

Consequently, my son went on to receive an education in highly specialist independent settings, funded throughout by my local authority. Now grown up, my son has a first in Philosophy and an MA too. Not bad for a severe language disorder. All that therapy and specialist teaching really does work.

The harsh truth of the matter is that most local authorities are simply balancing their legal obligations with budgetary constraints. To be seen as 'good at

their job', they must deliver within the budget they are allocated. As these budgets are stretched, vital support services are often first to suffer, leaving many children with SEN struggling. However, the current legislation has no "if we can afford it" clause. The law does not allow local authorities to refuse to put provision in place on the ground of cost, if it is evidenced that a child has a specific need.

This situation has left far too many parents in battles against local authorities to secure provisions for their children which the local authorities will be reluctant (to say the least) to pay for.

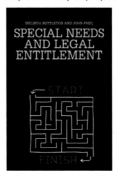

In 2015, Melinda Nettleton and John Friel (specialist Barrister) published 'Special Needs and Legal Entitlement' – a straightforward and comprehensive guide to the legal rights of children and young people with special educational needs. It is availilble for £14.99 on Amazon.

After the experiences I had encountered with my son, I soon realised that I was not alone. I started helping others in their fight against local authorities, with much of this work being conducted from my living room at home in the early days. Fast forward 27 years and I now have a team of 16 people working full time to support those who find themselves in the same desperate situation I did.

SEN Legal was founded on the principle that we don't offer to do for other parents what I couldn't do for mine. Since our incorporation in 2003 we have helped thousands of families in a similar position as I was in, with a success rate consistently, year on year, of over 90%. In the year ending 2016, our success rate was 97%. With such a wealth of specialist experience (personal and professional) in SEND law, we offer a sympathetic approach to families who have been let down and treated wrongly or unfairly, understanding that by the time parents reach us, they are usually at the end of their tether.

We are on your side – whether for simply advice and guidance, or as representatives in your appeals or tribunals. Our objective is always to use our considerable knowledge and experience to achieve the best possible solution for our clients, because when it comes to your child's future, only the best will do.

HESLEY HELPED ME TO HELP MYSELF.

We're one of the UK's leading independent providers of residential services, schools and colleges supporting people with autism and complex needs.

Our highly trained staff provide the highest quality, person-centred approach. Giving those who use our services the support, skills and tools they need to be as independent as possible.

Our unique **Hesley Enhancing Lives Programme (HELP)** is a big part of this.

Combining the latest techniques and practices, HELP is our successful value-based positive behaviour support programme. Based on the principles of Therapeutic Crisis Intervention which is accredited by the British Institute of Learning Disabilities, HELP reduces the need for high-risk interventions by taking an empathic and proactive approach. We focus on how our actions can positively shape the emotional well-being of all those who use our services. It's why all our staff are given HELP training to make sure it works in practice as well as theory.

Find out more about our schools and colleges visit www.hesleygroup.co.uk or call 0800 0556789.

Hesley Group

'Progression, happiness, achievement' – Eleanor's empowering story

The Hesley Group explain how a teenager with complex special needs is fulfilling her potential

Eleanor is a 16-year-old girl with autism, learning difficulties and very complex needs. This includes behaviours that can challenge her, other young people, her support staff and the environment. She spent time living in Italy before moving over to the UK as a young child and lived in various parts of the UK with her adoptive family. Although, at times, it was very difficult and challenging for everyone, she remained in the family home until she was 14 years old, going on 15. Her home life completely broke down at this point with parents no longer being able to safely manage her challenging behaviour. She was placed in a local respite care home full time.

Initially, in the care home, staff there found things very difficult to deal with. Eleanor displayed a very high level of aggressive behaviour towards her care staff and her environment causing extreme levels of damage. Although, support staff at the home did make some progress with Eleanor, she wasn't receiving any positive kind of education and wasn't attending school. Staff were using multiple physical interventions daily to support her when in crisis. She also only had a very limited amount of activities. As the care home knew they could not meet her full needs another placement was sought and she arrived at Fullerton House in April 2016.

Once living at Fullerton, it quickly became apparent Eleanor could not tolerate numerous things in her living environment so a host of moderations were made until her home was right for her to feel comfortable living in.

The behaviour that may challenge being displayed by Eleanor was approached by building positive relationships with her so she would begin to feel safe and contented. This was initially an extremely challenging period; support staff were being hit, having their hair pulled and things thrown at them on a daily basis with Eleanor having upwards of 20 incidents a week. After around 3 months, things had begun to stabilise a little and the number of incidents she was having decreased. Working closely with the support staff that knew her

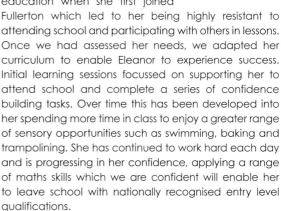

well and the wider MDT, positive changes around her staffing were implemented and have proven to be extremely successful. Eleanor is far more settled, much happier, doing much more and incidents are down significantly. She can go for weeks without having an incident now and even when she does have one, they are nowhere near the severity they were.

Eleanor had experienced a lengthy absence from formal education when she first joined Fullerton which led to her being highly resistant to attending school and participating with others in lessons. Once we had assessed her needs, we adapted her curriculum to enable Eleanor to experience success. Initial learning sessions focussed on supporting her to attend school and complete a series of confidence building tasks. Over time this has been developed into her spending more time in class to enjoy a greater range of sensory opportunities such as swimming, baking and trampolining. She has continued to work hard each day and is progressing in her confidence, applying a range of maths skills which we are confident will enable her to leave school with nationally recognised entry level qualifications.

Life has completely changed for Eleanor. She engages in a wide range of activities now including shopping for groceries and clothing, enjoys trips to the seaside, attends parties and celebrations and interacts with her peers. Considering she only arrived at Fullerton just over 6 months ago, she has made remarkable progress. Her parents are over the moon with Eleanor's achievements, as is everyone at Fullerton.

Fullerton House School is a specialist residential school, offering education and care for 52 weeks per year, for people aged 8 to19. The people we support have complex needs including behaviour that may challenge and a learning disability, often in association with autism. For more information see page 74

For more information about the Hesley Group visit our website at www.hesleygroup.co.uk.

ruskinmill landtrust

ruskinmill
re-imagining potential

Day and residential provision for students 7 - 25 providing specialist Practical Skills Therapeutic Education to young people with complex behaviour, learning difficulties and disabilities including autistic spectrum conditions.
All provisions are rated Good to Outstanding by Ofsted, Estyn, CQC and CSSIW (as of May 2016).

Open days are held regularly. For further details, to request a prospectus or book a place on an open day, please contact our central admissions team, who will guide you through our application process.

Please contact Central Admissions team
01453 837 502   admissions@rmt.org
www.rmt.org

Professional Development & Training

The Ruskin Mill Land Trust, in collaboration with The Field Centre, is pleased to offer a number of innovative professional development opportunities. All programmes braid theory and practice, within the context of a practical skills approach to special education.

MA in Special Education: Practical Skills Transformative Learning
This 3 year part time Masters programme is offered in collaboration with the Inland Norway University of Applied Sciences
For further information, please contact Dr Mandy Nelson
mandy.nelson@thefieldcentre.org.uk

Other programmes offered by Ruskin Mill Land Trust and are delivered on a part time basis over two years, and are aimed at professionals engaged in education who wish to deepen their understanding of the pedagogic potential of the unique educational method of Ruskin Mill Trust, *Practical Skills Therapeutic Education.*
* The Pedagogic Potential of Craftwork
* Teacher Development Programme
* Ruskin Mill Biodynamic Training Programme

For further information, please visit www.thefieldcentre.org.uk

An unexpected journey from tree to chair

Dr Mandy Nelson, Director of Research and Collaboration at Ruskin Mill Trust, joins students on a task – and realises the power of the activity

I was invited to spend a week in a woodland making a chair. This seemed like one of the more unusual and potentially challenging staff development activities that I had ever been offered. As the Director of Research and Collaboration, my role is predominantly office based, and I have spent most of my working career in the comfort of an office.

The idea of making a chair filled me with both excitement and horror. I did wonder if the fact that my Dad was a carpenter would make me pre-disposed to woodwork – as if it would be in my genes. The purpose of making a chair was not so much about skills development for a future career as a chair maker, but was more about the experience. The chair itself was a 'pedagogic decoy'.

Key to my learning was the experience of engaging with the material and tools (cognitively, emotionally and physically), rather than simply making a chair.

Reflecting on my experience of making a chair, not only did it provide useful personal insights but it also showed me that the experience of crafting a chair replicated that of undertaking any project.

My starting point was an idea (to make a chair) and material - a tree trunk, which days earlier had been a living, breathing, growing tree. That was quite a sobering thought. A tree had been cut down for me to make a chair – I guess I had to honour the tree. The first step of the journey was to enter into a process with the material, some tools and with a guide who was going to lead and support me through the process. I started by splitting the logs with an axe. This required a lot of effort, but there was very little to show for it, other than a pile of split logs and aching arms. We were not quite at 'chair stage' yet.

After the axe came the cleaving, splitting the wood. This required consideration of angles of movement and the careful application of pressure – akin to negotiating processes and politics, opportunities and constraints. At times, I had to step back and reflect, and then change my stance (or position) in order to get the wood to split in the direction I needed it to. This required careful consideration, negotiation and re-appraisal of my position and activity. Throughout this process, I had to be mindful of the grain of the wood, its natural patterns and behaviours, and at times, of its tolerances and resistances. We were in this together, and I had to listen to the wood.

As I worked to transform the material from tree to chair, I did so in the company of a guide and fellow traveller on the journey. Sitting in the sunshine on the shaving horse, engaged in conversation and relaxed in the rhythm of the draw saw, the strengths of working together were apparent. At times, the movements were long, arching, slow and effortless. In contrast, there were times for precision and careful measurement. Sometimes there was a need to step back, to respect the grain and work with the material rather than fight its inner nature.

As the chair started to form into recognisable component parts, there was the opportunity for reflection and fine-tuning before assembly. Putting it all together was a task that could not be rushed or completed alone. Like any project, there was a need for a plan, for teamwork, for external support and for all the component parts to assemble in the right place, in the right order and at the right time. It reminded me of project plans long ago completed.

What had been a tree only days earlier now started to resemble a chair – but it was not finished. The legs needed levelling, the seat needed to be woven and the wood needed to be stained. I had not yet completed the chair. Then, after five days of making… there stood a chair. It looked like a chair, a chair that I had made myself. It stood up and didn't wobble. It held my weight. It was a real chair! I was rather pleased with what I had made (as shown by my multiple chair photo posts on social media).

On reflection, I could never have made the chair without starting with an idea and then engaging in a collaborative dialogue with the material (the wood). In addition, the chair would not have emerged without the tools and without the guidance, support and companionship of my colleagues. Like any project, there were challenges, resistance, times I had to start again, and battles (with a knot in an intended chair leg) I could not win, but there was also fun, enjoyment and laugher, companionship and collaboration, and achievement and celebration – and a well-earned sit down on my chair with a cup of tea.

For most of the students at our colleges, young people with autism and other learning disabilities, this kind of outcome is impossible to imagine. Many have been excluded from traditional educational settings and have a huge range of barriers to learning. By transforming the material, they begin to transform themselves. I experienced it myself as I had to learn the nature of the wood and respect its tolerances. As I watched the chair take shape, I made discoveries about myself and in the finished chair was a reflection of me. Engaging with the material gave me a greater sense of myself. To a young person who has spent much of their life labelled and marginalised, this is the greatest lesson we can teach them.

Ruskin Mill Trust operates seven provisions across England and Wales for ages seven and upwards in both day and residential settings. If you're interested in discovering more about the potential of practical skills in education, contact us to enquire about our Masters programme, delivered in collaboration with Inland Norway University of Applied Sciences.

For more informatin on the Ruskin Mill Trust and its schools, see page 53 or visit www.rmt.org

Charlie at LVS Oxford has enjoyed GCSE success and is moving towards a university place at Oxford Brookes.

Building independent futures for young people with autism

Sarah Sherwood, Director of SEN at LVS Hassocks and LVS Oxford, shares the schools' unique approach to preparing autistic students for independent lives

The most important aspect of education for young people with autism is equipping them with the skills they need to live independently as adults. LVS Hassocks and LVS Oxford's approach is focused on educational achievement and building life skills to give young people a greater chance of living independently when they leave at 19 years old.

For many students it is therefore important to offer a wide and ever growing range of academic qualifications, so they can access relevant academic and vocational skills in a vibrant and stimulating environment. We create individual learning plans with defined goals. For some, such as Charlie at LVS Oxford, this is targeted at going on to further education.

LVS Oxford, which only opened in 2014, achieved its first GCSE results in 2016 with all results in the A*-C bracket.

Charlie contributed to those results, and is now studying maths A/S level and a BTEC in ICT, with an offer from Oxford Brookes University to study further education there.

Having been a non-attender who struggled to interact with staff and peers when he joined in 2014, the school's therapists and teachers have empowered him to express himself and find ways to learn effectively, resulting in this success. Staff have done everything to help Charlie achieve; with high anxiety, entering the room where he would take exams was a real issue for him, so LVS Oxford spent several months desensitising him to it prior to his exam. Charlie said: "Exams do make me very anxious, but the school has been very supportive in preparing me for them. I also use relaxation techniques that I've learnt so I feel more in control when I'm sitting exams. I'm definitely more confident as a person".

LVS

Supporting academic qualifications with targeted work experience placements can help young people gain a number of advantages for the future. Enabling students to attend weekly work experience over an extended period of time gives them an opportunity to create independence and build new confidence in a social surrounding. It also shows them what working life is like and gives them the ambition to fulfil their employment dreams. We match students to relevant, achievable yet challenging work experience to give them confidence whilst developing the range of skills that they have. LVS Hassocks and LVS Oxford ensure students are as prepared as possible to go into further training for the job they want when they leave. Amy at LVS Hassocks is a great example. Her ambition is to become a hairdresser so she was supported and helped to apply for placements, and is now taken each week by a Learning Support Assistant to a local hairdresser where she is mentored, learning techniques which will help her gain future employment.

A former LVS Hassocks student, Liam Pope, arrived at the school unable to cook but showed an interest and was supported through cooking qualifications, work experience in a pub kitchen and assisted to find an apprenticeship in catering when he left. Within two years he had become Sodexo Young Chef of the Year and has

made excellent career progress within the company.

These approaches to give students the skills they need to live independently as adults can only take place successfully with an individual-focused approach right from the start, engaging with the students on a one-to-one basis. As many as 60% of our students are school refusers who have often been out of education for as many as three years prior to joining, having been unable to cope with mainstream education.

Craig, 15, spent three years out of education, shutting himself in his bedroom and missing Year 8, Year 9 and all except the first few weeks of Year 7. His mainstream school could not cope with Craig's behaviour which was driven from frustration at being singled out by other children for being different. After attending an open day at LVS Oxford with his mother Debbie, who describes the school as "a lovely place, very peaceful with beautiful grounds and perfect for Craig as he likes to walk and needs a quiet, relaxing environment", a gradual transition began.

This was successfully achieved due to the school therapy staff's commitment to constantly breaking down Craig's barriers, and perseverance in helping him transition at a pace he was comfortable with. This included:

Craig was out of education for three years but is now thriving at LVS Oxford

22

LVS Hassocks' Amy is making great progress at a hairdressing work experience placement

- Home visits to create an initial home/school link
- Initial trips just into the school grounds to develop familiarity with the setting
- Visits to the therapy room, chatting with the therapists to reduce anxiety
- Lunch with the therapists to develop trust
- Transitions into lessons, with phasing out of additional support as Craig grew more confident

This patient, individualised approach has been rewarded, with Craig thriving to such an extent he is now Deputy Head Boy. He is studying qualifications such as a BTEC in Business Studies with his sights set on a career and independent future beyond the school – something he could never have imagined 18 months ago.

All students also learn other skills that will help them to live independently, such as practicing day-to-day tasks like cleaning, washing clothes and cooking, using public transport, handling money and shopping.

For more information about LVS Hassocks see page 67 or for more information about LVS Oxford see page 58. To book an open day visit, go to www.lvs-hassocks.org.uk or www.lvs-oxford.org.uk

Former LVS Hassocks student Liam became Sodexo Young Chef of the Year in 2015

Benefits of hydrotherapy for children with complex needs

By Nicky Pither, Physiotherapist at RNIB Pears Centre for Specialist Learning

Hydrotherapy involves stimulation and gentle exercise in warm water at a constant temperature of 32 degrees Celsius. Hydrotherapy pools tend to be purpose-built with a constant or very gradual water depth of around 1 metre. Pools usually incorporate multi-sensory equipment such as lighting and sound to stimulate the senses.

Hydrotherapy offers tangible benefits to the health and wellbeing of children and young people with a range of disabilities and health conditions:

- The warmth of the water has an effect on the individual neuro-muscular junctions which results in decreased muscle tone and decreased spasticity.

- Buoyancy of the water is used to assist movement of joints - which is either more difficult or painful on dry land.

- Movement in the water and water pressure helps to reduce residual lung capacity for children and young people with chest problems. This enables more efficient lung function and reduces the risk of chest infections developing.

- Creating turbulence around an extremity (i.e. arm or leg) can increase their awareness of the limb and help with mobility - both in the water and later on dry land.

- Multi-sensory environment helps stimulate the senses whilst calming children with sensory and learning difficulties.

At RNIB Pears Centre we offer specialist education, care and therapies to children and young people with complex needs and vision impairment. Additional needs we support include physical disabilities, multi-sensory impairment, significant learning difficulties and disabilities, autistic spectrum disorders, additional medical and health needs (including long-term ventilation or life-threatening or life-limiting conditions) and emotional and behavioural difficulties.

Hydrotherapy has always been part of our provision but until recently we had to go off-site for children to use a hydrotherapy pool at another local school. We were restricted in how often we could access this pool and reliant on minibus drivers being available to take more than one wheelchair user.

Although we worked hard to make hydrotherapy available for everyone that needed it, there were always serious challenges to accessing an external provider's pool which meant that for many, it was just too risky to achieve. Local public baths are too busy and cold and don't have ceiling hoist facilities. Other local hydrotherapy pools tend to be fully booked and only available at inconvenient times.

We wanted to enable our young people with complex needs to access water therapy on a regular basis. In 2015, we launched a fundraising campaign to raise money to build a hydrotherapy pool on our site. Thanks to generous donations from supporters including the Bradbury Foundation, Pears Foundation and local community groups our dream was made a reality and our on-site pool, the Bradbury Hydrotherapy Centre, opened in February 2017.

Since the new hydrotherapy pool has been open for use, the impact on our children and young people has been phenomenal. First and foremost, it's enjoyable and fun! This has had an immediate positive impact on their psychological wellbeing.

Some young people have never been able to use a pool and are now enjoying regular sessions and experiencing the freedom of movement in the pool – whereas on dry land their movements are extremely limited. Also being able to move in the water improves their general physical stamina and lung function.

Others who tend to be in crisis for a lot of the time as they are overloaded by their sensory environment find that after 20 minutes of splashing and moving round in the pool they are a lot calmer and more able to cope in class.

Being able to get to and from the pool easily means that we can respond quickly to changes in young people's fitness to swim. We can be flexible about timing to meet individual health needs, such as medication and therapy programmes. This would never have been possible with

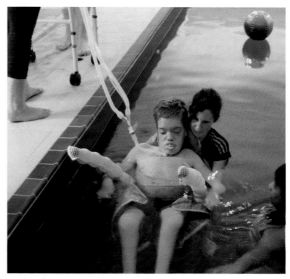

an off-site facility. So, for example, if a young person was initially unable to process the idea of going swimming as they arrive in school but after an hour in class lesson – they felt able to go they could go – whereas before they would have "missed the bus".

All children and young people who are using the hydrotherapy pool have benefitted:

- Young people who are normally in their seating systems in their wheelchair for a lot of the day can experience freedom of movement in the pool.

- Others who don't move much on dry land become active and really enjoy moving round the pool.

- Young people who have very limited movement and struggle to communicate when on dry land are able to vocalise or move their arms to indicate preferences whilst in the water.

- Passive physiotherapy programmes can be difficult to tolerate on dry land but in the water the young people with tight muscles and joints are much happier when their muscle stretches are incorporated into a fun or relaxing time in the pool.

We have been able to extend our outreach service to include hydrotherapy already and this work will develop to a greater extent over time. This allows us to share expertise whilst introducing other children to the opportunities that water therapy offers.

For more information about RNIB Pears Centre and to watch a short film showing the impact of the hydrotherapy pool, visit www.rnib.org.uk/pearscentre
You can also read more about RNIB Pears Centre on page 131

Top tips when choosing a school for your dyslexic child

Deborah Jones, Head of SEN at Bredon School, examines some of the key issues that parents should ask about, or look for, when considering a school

Choosing a school for your child is one of the most important decisions you will ever make.

If your child has a diagnosis of dyslexia, choosing the right school first time, can mean the difference between them being happy and enjoying school, or struggling.

So do you opt for a mainstream school that offers learning support from within, or should you consider opting for a school with a specialist focus?

The qualifications of the teaching staff

If your child needs specialist one-to-one teaching, check to ensure that the staff hold specialist teacher qualifications often referred to as PG. Cert. SpLD or a Diploma in Teaching Learners with Dyslexia (Level 5 or Level 7 equivalent).

These are specific qualifications aligned to teaching students with specific learning difficulties.

Ask what the School's policy is on copying from the board

As strange as it may sound, this is a teaching method which should be banned for dyslexic children!

Copying from the board causes a delay in a dyslexic students' ability to process what they have just read and it will take them even longer to recreate it on their page. It can add unnecessary visual stress and can exacerbate tracking problems.

The distraction of copying-down means that few facts are actually being absorbed or retained.

Handouts

To prevent an over-reliance on copying from the board, it's really important that schools understand that dyslexic students need to have the information given to them on a handout – providing the information they need to help them learn.

Schools should not demand that dyslexic children take their own notes in a lesson, unless they are confident in the use of assistive technology to do so. Instead, a handout should be given at the start of the lesson so that the lesson content is clear and makes sense, the student then doesn't need to worry about trying to record notes as well; they can use their time and their mind to concentrate on listening and understanding.

Assistive technology

Some schools refuse to allow dyslexic students to use a laptop in class, others insist on it.

If your dyslexic child works well on a laptop there are some fantastic assistive technology programmes out there to help them to produce more quality 'written' work.

In an ideal world, a school will embrace these technologies and may even have a specialist assistive technologies teacher on the staff – someone who knows how to use the software to best effect and, importantly, can support both students and staff in implementing its use in class.

Software

Ask whether the school supports the use of other software which is proven to benefit dyslexic students.

Tools to help with planning, such as mind mapping software, are brilliant in supporting a dyslexic student to map their ideas on paper before attempting to write it up.

Teaching ethos

A dyslexic child needs a genuinely multi-sensory teaching approach.

The traditional didactic teaching method of 'chalk and talk' will not maximise the potential of any dyslexic student. But simple methods developed in order to 'hit all senses' such as allowing time to get up and move about, providing visual prompts, incorporating audio sound bites or allowing students the chance to touch something or work with their hands, all increase a dyslexic student's chance of increasing their understanding and improving the retention of information.

Specialist teaching

Specialist teachers should be accustomed to providing structured and cumulative systems for teaching. For example, teachers commit to only delivering one or two new teaching points per lesson, and spend the rest of the time focused on revisiting and reinforcing past teaching. In an ideal world this approach should be embedded through every subject and in all tuition.

A reduced working memory capacity is often a key feature of dyslexia. It is vital that students are not given too much new information at once and that teachers provide information such as key words, scaffolded worksheets and activity timelines to reduce the burden.

When teaching pupils with impaired processing skills or poor working memory, an experienced teacher will always give pupils thinking time before inviting a response, rather than a 'first hand up' approach.

This reduces stress immediately and maximises the time available to think, allowing students to process and reach their conclusion.

Classroom tools

Although there are many, many sophisticated software packages available on the market to aid dyslexic students you don't always necessarily need expensive technologies.

Simple adjustments in the classroom and around school can help a dyslexic child too; from the use of contrasting colours on posters – yellow and blue are reportedly the best contrast for many dyslexics – to the carefully chosen colour of ink in the pens used to record information. These things can make it easier for a dyslexic child to read more clearly.

Black text against a white background is too stark for many dyslexic students and can cause visual stress, so at Bredon School for example, all worksheets/handouts and even staff communications are printed on a softer, buff coloured paper.

Using dyslexia-friendly fonts can help too – traditional fonts such as Times New Roman that use a curly form of the letter 'a' can confuse. Simpler fonts like Comic Sans, which are more akin to printed handwriting, use the more familiar forms of letters. All these simple adjustments can be seen to reduce visual stress for the learner.

Process of checking access arrangements

In many cases, dyslexic students are eligible for additional time in exams or to receive specialist support in the form a reader or scribe.

If a dyslexic student's normal way of working is to type using a laptop or to use assistive technology, an application can often be made for this to be the mode in which they complete 'written' examinations.

It is important that the school knows how to assess students for this additional support and ensures that the appropriate access arrangements are put in place; otherwise students can be at a distinct disadvantage. After all, the purpose of a special access arrangement is to provide a level playing field for all students.

Self esteem

Imagine being in a classroom and working twice as hard as some of your non-dyslexic peers to even just record the date and subject matter of the lesson.

Imagine instead finding that one special area in which, for once, you can be the star pupil – where you can shine and feel your confidence soar as you achieve great things!

To ensure that every dyslexic child has their opportunity to shine, it's vital that a school offers a wide-ranging curriculum enrichment programme. As your child discovers their talent/s, they will grow in self confidence, ability, and in resilience to face challenges and take risks with their learning.

Whether it be a sport, art, music or engineering, the dyslexic child needs to find an area in which to experience success and to excel.

Deborah Jones, PG. Cert. SpLD is Head of SEN at Bredon School in Gloucestershire, a CRESTED-accredited Dyslexia Specialist Provision School and part of the Cavendish Education Group of schools.
For more information about Cavendish Education and its schools, see page 46

Every child is unique – and so is our school

Q&A with Sam Newton, Headteacher of The Children's Trust School

Tell us a bit about yourself

I am Sam Newton and I'm the Headteacher of The Children's Trust School.

I have been teaching for nearly 20 years with over 17 years of experience in complex learning difficulties and special educational needs.

Tell us about The Children's Trust School

The Children's Trust School is a purpose built, non-maintained special school dedicated to education, therapy and care of children and young people between the ages of 3-19.

We support children and young people with a wide range of special educational needs including complex learning difficulties, neurodisability and complex medical needs through day and residential placements.

We are located at The Children's Trust national specialist centre in Tadworth, Surrey admitting children from across the South East of England.

We strive to provide a safe, caring, organised and happy environment where every child's individual needs can be met; we recognise that every child is unique and so provide a personalised approach. In partnership with parents, we aim to enrich each pupil's quality of life by promoting their intellectual, physical, emotional and social development.

Our team consists of specialist teachers and therapists, including occupational therapists, physiotherapists, speech and language therapists, music therapists and health play specialists. We have nurses, on-site doctors and consultants available for those staying here residentially, along with our wonderful care staff; educational psychologists and specialist teaching assistants.

We take a holistic approach to the children and young people's care, education and therapy which is fundamental to our success as a team.

Which curriculum do you follow at The Children's Trust School?

We follow the ImPACTs curriculum which is a highly specialised and developmental based curriculum. We teach our curriculum in an integrated way with our experienced teachers, therapists, specialist teaching assistants and colleagues in care, working holistically together across and throughout the day to support children and young people to reach the next steps in their learning.

Why ImPACTs?

ImPACTs offers a specialised curriculum in five key skill areas:

- Communication, Language & Literacy
- Cognitive skills
- Environmental control technology
- Personal, social and emotional well being
- Physical skills (gross and fine motor)

The development of each key skill includes multi-disciplinary working and the school using the expertise of relevant professionals. Importantly the curriculum recognises and values 'learning via on-going routines' such as eating, drinking and through personal care.

There is a detailed approach to assessment and progress that pupils are making allowing the school to collate meaningful evidence.

The curriculum is non-published to support its ethos that up-to-date research, educational and clinical knowledge is applied on an ongoing basis as research informs.

Tell us about some of the activities you have available for the children and young people who stay residentially at the School

The Children's Trust School is based on a 24-acre site in Tadworth Surrey and shares the site with The Children's Trust charity.

We have great links with community groups and organisations as horse riding for the disabled, scouts, brownies and many more.

We offer state-of-the-art facilities:

- Aquatics therapy pool
- Playground equipment
- Nature trail
- Woodland walk
- Outdoor musical instruments
- Sensory gardens
- Sensory Maze
- Wheelchair-accessible treehouse
- Basketball area
- On-site transportation team

FOCUS: Taddies offers support and opportunities to learn through play

At just 20 months old, Sofia has cerebral palsy and cortical vision, a form of visual impairment. Sofia and her mum Jenny attend Taddies, a parent-child group run by The Children's Trust for young children with complex needs and multiple disabilities.

Jenny said "I had never experienced disability before having Sofia so I have had to learn everything about Sofia's disabilities and needs from scratch. This would have been so much harder without support bases like Taddies."

The group takes place weekly and staff tailor sensory based activities to the child. Taddies staff are experienced working with children with significant developmental impairments or delays, sensory impairments, life-limiting conditions and those who are technology dependant, such as those who might need assistance breathing, for example.

Taddies is free for parents with children under five and often siblings, grandparents and parents who used to come to the group will attend.

"Both Sofia and I benefit from Taddies. It's the only parent-child group that I've been to that runs at Sofia's pace. Sofia gets the chance to meet other children and interact with them like any other child, and I get to meet other parents to talk and make friendships with people who are in the same situation. The teachers work with the children but also educate parents on how to understand their child's needs. Thinking about Sofia's future such as school, and what's next, is not straightforward so having the support from Taddies is really helpful. It's reassuring to know that the teachers

and parents are here for me if I have any questions."

Launa Randles, Deputy Headteacher of The Children's Trust School, said: "Taddies can be really important for families that attend the group. We are able to help parents understand what is appropriate for children, what they can do at home and give advice for what's coming next. It is so important for both the parents and children to have a networking group like this."

What do you have available for early years children with profound and multiple learning difficulties?

We have Taddies, a parent-child group that we run weekly for children from 0–5 years who have additional needs.

Taddies offers a warm, welcome to families and children, and provides support and planned opportunities to learn through play and fun. Our two hour multi-sensory sessions are organised by experienced staff from The Children's Trust School, on an alternate day pattern (Thursday/Friday) for parents/carers to attend with their child. Learning is planned using Early Years Foundation Stage prime areas to develop and promote the following:

- Identity and belonging
- Communication
- Exploring and thinking
- Well-being

Staff engage with the children and parents through a variety of sensory activities including messy play, softplay, musical fun, cooking, water and sand play and regular learning through routines of free flow activities both indoors and outdoors. We record experiences of those who attend to capture the learning and progress that they make. In all of the planned sessions the golden thread of safeguarding is paramount to all experiences and activities.

For more information about The Children's Trust School, see page 129

Supporting young people with psychotherapy

Child and Adolescent Psychotherapist Todd Hinds tells us how psychotherapy supports young people at Dawn House School

Dawn House School is a residential special school for children and young people (5-19) with speech, language and communication needs. All pupils have a speech and language disorder or Asperger's syndrome and associated difficulties which impact on their educational, social and emotional development.

I work at I CAN's Dawn House School as a Child and Adolescent Psychotherapist one day a week as part of the multi-disciplinary therapy team which includes Speech and Language Therapists and Occupational Therapists. I have been working at Dawn House School for four years, prior to this I worked in Child and Adolescent Mental Health Services. As a Child and Adolescent Psychotherapist I am trained to work with children who may present with different communication needs. Some of the children I work with may communicate mostly through non-verbal communication or with the support of play based therapy.

Students with speech, language and communication needs (SLCN) often find it difficult to put into words what they are thinking or how they are feeling. This can be further complicated if the students are also experiencing mental health difficulties. The added dimension of a speech, language or communication difficulty means it's even more crucial that the student's mental health and emotional wellbeing is actively supported by the entire school community. I work closely with teaching staff, care staff and parents and families of pupils in order to continuously monitor the student's mental health and provide advice as to how best to support students with their wellbeing. I run a combination of individual sessions for students, which includes counselling and psychotherapy, along with a range of staff sessions which covers general support, guidance and formal training. As a part of the team at Dawn House, I understand the language needs of the pupils and so can make sure the approach is accessible and relevant e.g. making sure my explanations avoid complex words and concepts, and using visual approaches.

Why a focus on mental health is important for children with SLCN

A focus on mental health support is particularly important for students with SLCN as there are particular challenges they can face during child and adolescent development. An increased desire for greater levels of independence can clash with the anxiety that stems from the desire to interact independently within peer groups and in the wider society. During adolescence, a desire for greater self-determination may also clash with an increased awareness of the levels of support they may still require, which in turn can lead to feelings of over dependence, isolation, loneliness and frustration. Typically, adolescents rely heavily on close peer relationships to navigate this process, but many students with SLCN may have either a very small peer group or none at all and so are limited by who to reach out to for support. This level of isolation can lead to depression and low self-esteem.

Often students with special educational needs have encountered difficulties in previous educational settings. During times of acute stress students can develop depression, mood swings and exhibit high levels of anxiety similar to that seen in post-traumatic stress. Students who move to Dawn House School often arrive with a history that they are still trying to make sense of, and this can trigger social anxiety, prolonged school absence, social isolation and withdrawal. All of this can impact upon adolescent development and complicate their access to opportunities in later life.

The national landscape

In May 2016, the government's Children's Commissioner produced a report that examined access to Mental Health Services in England across 2015. The report highlighted major barriers in terms of access and inconsistent provision of services across England. Figures for the number of referrals made to CAMHS were provided, and highlighted that of all the referrals received in 2015, only 15% were seen immediately, 57% were seen once and then placed on a waiting list, whilst 28% were not seen at all. The picture for the East Midlands, where Dawn House School is situated, is very similar; 14% of referrals were seen immediately, 62%

To find out more about Dawn House School see page 93.

were seen once but then placed on a waiting list and 24% were not seen at all. The report highlights an increase in referrals at a time when services are already under pressure and as a result children are failing to receive the support they need. The implications of this report are that students with complex mental health needs continue to attend school whilst waiting for mental health services. As a consequence there is a need to develop in-house programmes of support for students with these needs.

Dawn House School has a wellbeing team led by full-time staff which means that mental health awareness and support is integrated into the rest of the curriculum. The aim of the team is to promote wellbeing in school, to facilitate access to appropriate external services and provide support to aid emotional literacy, support transitions and manage anxiety. The team monitors the mental health of students and provide in-house support where appropriate. We are looking to develop an in-house referral system, which will allow all staff and parents to raise concerns about a student when concerns arise. Given the pressures facing students with SLCN it is important that we are looking to develop this support in school.

Psychotherapy is a means of better understanding ourselves, which in turn may help us to make the most of the opportunities around us. I generally find that the students I work with become empowered to make some of their own life choices and begin to take notice of the opportunities that are available to them. Supporting students with SLCN with their mental health difficulties is particularly important and can make a huge difference when someone takes the time to listen, understand and provide tools that may help them to communicate how they are feeling. It is particularly inspiring to watch students progress in a short space of time with the support from the entire school.

Does your child feel like a square peg in a round hole at school?

Denise Yates, chief executive of Potential Plus UK, explains the support available for Dual and Multiple Exceptional (DME) children

Does your child have strength in one or more areas; a good vocabulary, a good grasp of words and reading, good problem solving skills? At home, do you often feel that they are able to do things which other children may find more difficult or are they able to take part in discussions at school which cover lots of issues? Do they have a good memory for things they see or hear? Are they very creative especially outside school?

Yet at the same time, are you worried about the difficulties they have at school; difficulties like poor handwriting or spelling, the inability to do tasks which look simple to most people, poor work when they are under pressure? Or do they find it difficult to finish work which has lots of steps or to pay attention? Do small setbacks make them want to give up and do they often feel a failure at school, making them sensitive to criticism, with low self-esteem and a high degree of frustration with

themselves? Do they have poor social skills or feelings of being different from others?

Does all of this affect their behaviour in class or at home? Can they be disruptive; or are they the class 'clown'? Do they seem unmotivated to stick to the task; disorganised, impulsive? Or are they quiet or withdrawn, unable to explain to you what is happening to them?

If any of these characteristics describe your child, have you ever thought that they might be both highly able and have a special education need? These children are called Dual and Multiple Exceptional (or DME) children in the UK (Twice Exceptional or 2e in the USA and elsewhere). According to the Department for Education, about 2 to10 children out of 100 who are highly able also have a Special Education Need.

Potential Plus UK has been working with DME children since 1967. We know that these children come in all

 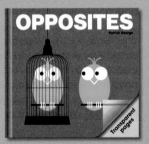 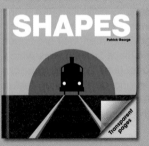 

shapes and sizes with different strengths and weaknesses. We also recognise that it can sometimes be difficult to support DME children. They can seem very able, but they may also find difficulty in what seems to be the most basic of tasks. The difficulties they have depend on their Special Education Need. We believe that it is important that parents and teachers fully understand both the strengths and weaknesses of these children. They can then be supported to develop their self-confidence.

One important issue is to make sure they have friends and feel they can fit in. Sometimes having a special need and high ability can lead to feelings of isolation and even bullying. We also believe it is important to:

- help these DME children to believe in what they can do.

- develop good relationships with these children based on trust and respect. This will help them believe they are valued no matter how "different" they appear to other children.

- guide these children to make sure their expectations are relevant. Sometimes these can be too high or too low.

- give these children the chance to experience real success. This will help to improve their self-esteem.

- encourage these children to be independent.

- help these children to show their frustration and confusion in a positive way.

- guide these children to act less impulsively under stress.

- turn these children's interests into ways of learning.

- help these children make friends with other children who want to achieve success. This can help to motivate DME children.

We believe it is also important to understand the negative behaviour that can come with Dual and Multiple Exceptionality. The children's high ability sometimes helps them to compensate for their special need. However, this means they have to focus their energy on what they are doing or thinking. Sometimes they are unable to do this. For example, when the children are tired it becomes more difficult. On some days, this can make a child appear as if they are 'trying' and on other days they are 'not trying'. This is not the case. They will be trying hard most of the time.

In addition, at school, DME children may well spend a lot of energy just to keep up with their classmates. Having to work so hard just to keep up can be very frustrating for these children. Thinking at a more advanced level makes this even harder. This is because they know what they would like to do, but cannot do it easily.

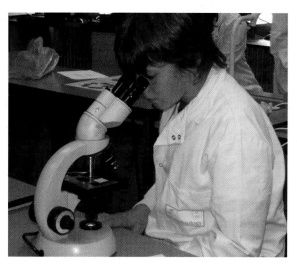

This means that many DME children face daily struggles at school and at home. Parents and teachers must remember this when they support them.

Good relationships between school and home are important. This will help DME children make the most of their learning potential. Parents and teachers need to remember to:

- support both the children's special needs and their high ability.

- challenge the children's high potential. This must be done through work which matches both their Special Educational Needs and their high abilities.

- make sure the child is making progress. This involves setting them the right learning goals.

- ensure that parents are informed about and involved in their child's educational progress.

All of this will help these children to fulfil their high learning potential. DME children need to feel understood and supported. They also need to feel confident and able to ask for further support if needed. Without the right support, we believe that DME children can easily fall into a 'cycle of underachievement'. They can also become increasingly demotivated.

Potential Plus UK is the national charity which supports children and young people with high learning potential, including those with Dual or Multiple Exceptionality. We offer a range of services, including an assessment service; an in-depth helpline for parents, carers and teachers; advice sheets and support for families. We also run a range of training workshops on supporting these children and events for the whole family. For more information see our website www.potentialplusuk.org or contact us via amazingchildren@potentialplusuk.org or on 01908 646433.

Introducing CReSTeD

Exploring the work of the Council for the Registration of Schools Teaching Dyslexic Pupils

Introduction

The Council for the Registration of Schools Teaching Dyslexic Pupils (CReSTeD) is a charity set up to help parents and those who advise them choose schools for children with Specific Learning Difficulties (SpLD) of which the main difficulty is dyslexia. There is however a general recognition that dyslexia rarely exists in isolation and latest research demonstrates a high level of co-occurrence with other difficulties. These include Dyspraxia, Dyscalculia, ADD, as well as Pragmatic and Semantic Language Difficulties.

CReSTeD acts as a source of information which can help parents making a placement decision about a child with SpLD. CReSTeD is a valuable resource for parents, educational advisers and schools.

CReSTeD was established in 1989 and publishes and maintains a list of schools and centres accredited for their SpLD provision - the Register - annually. The schools and centres listed within the Register cover all levels of provision for SpLD pupils and include both state and independent provision. The vast majority of schools on the Register are mainstream, offering a wide range of teaching styles, environment and facilities.

The Register

CReSTeD's main activity is to produce and supply to parents, free of charge, a Register of schools and centres which provide for pupils with one or more SpLD. The levels of provision is divided into six broad categories, five for schools: Dyslexia Specialist Provision (Category DSP), Specialist Provision Schools (Category SPS), Dyslexia Unit (Category DU), Withdrawal System (Category WS) and Maintained Sector (Category MS) and one for centres: Teaching Centres (Category TC). Children have different requirements and personalities; the categories are a way of helping match each child to the type of provision at the school or centre. A report from an Educational Psychologist or a specialist teacher who holds an Assessment Practising Certificate should offer guidance as to the level of provision relevant to the child.

A child at the severe end of the dyslexia spectrum may require a Dyslexia Specialist Provision school, whereas a child with, for example, only some slowness in spelling skills may be suitably provided for in a school from Category Withdrawal System. The categories offer this guidance. Note that the Maintained sector is only open to local authority schools and not to Independent schools.

The Register includes a checklist to help parents decide if a school or centre can meet their child's education needs in relation to SpLD. It also provides a geographical index of schools.

CReSTeD Criteria and Visits

Every school and centre on the CReSTeD list has been independently verified for SpLD provision by CReSTeD consultants which is not the case in all other lists.

The first stage of any registration is for the school to complete the CReSTeD registration form and to provide supporting documentation, such as policies for dyslexia. This form covers staff development, admission policy, organisation of the school week, specific arrangements for SpLD pupils, examination results for the whole school and for SpLD pupils in particular, resources and a list of parents' names so that the Consultant may check parents' feelings about the school or centre.

These criteria include the provision of relevant and high quality information technology resources, Joint Council for Qualifications (JCQ) approved training qualifications for teachers, awareness of the needs of dyslexic pupils by the non-specialist staff, and arrangements to obtain and provide special provision for examinations.

Consultants, who look to see if this information is accurate and that the school or centre meets the criteria set by CReSTeD Council for the particular category, visit the schools.

Schools and centres are visited on a three yearly cycle, with possible earlier visits if there are substantial changes, which should always be swiftly communicated to CReSTeD. If the Head of a CReSTeD school changes, we require the school to inform us and ask the new Head to confirm that the school intends to continue with the SpLD provision in accordance with the criteria set by CReSTeD (at the agreed category level). This enables us to retain the school's details in the Register without the need for an extra visit.

CReSTeD Council will initiate 'responsive' visits if it has any cause for concern about a particular school.

Information

The Register is published annually and is obtainable from the CReSTeD Administrator. To encourage accuracy, Council require schools and centres to inform it of significant changes which impact on provision for SpLD pupils.

The CReSTeD website: www.crested.org.uk contains all the information that is in the Register. It is updated as new information is received, or new schools approved, and contains links to the websites of all registered schools and centres as well as to other websites that may be of assistance to parents of children with one or more SpLD.

CReSTeD Council

Council includes representatives from a wide area of SpLD provision including Dyslexia Action, the British Dyslexia Association, Helen Arkell Dyslexia Centre, the Dyslexia-SpLD Trust and schools.

Categories

Categories are used to explain the type of provision given by a school. One category should not be seen as 'better' than another, but as a guide to the provision required by the student.

There are six categories within our criteria according to the type of provision:

- Dyslexia Specialist Provision (DSP) schools established primarily to teach pupils with Dyslexia.

- Dyslexia Unit (DU) schools offer a designated unit that provides specialist tuition on a small group or individual basis, according to need.

- Maintained Schools (MS) local authority schools able to demonstrate an effective system for identifying pupils with dyslexia.

- Specialist Provision (SPS) schools are specifically established to teach pupils with dyslexia and other related specific learning difficulties.

- Teaching Centre (TC) designated centre providing specialist tuition on a small group or individual basis, according to need.

- Withdrawal System (WS) schools help dyslexic pupils by withdrawing them from appropriately selected lessons for specialist tuition.

Conclusion

CReSTeD was founded to help parents. It has had, and will continue to have, influence on the standards of provision for pupils with SpLD's. Council is grateful for the support of the British Dyslexia Association, Dyslexia Action, Helen Arkell Dyslexia Centre, the Dyslexia-SpLD Trust, the schools on the Register and parents.

For further information contact us via email: admin@crested.org.uk

Or visit our website: www.crested.org.uk

Why have language skills in the classroom deteriorated?

Catherine Routley believes the emphasis of language learning needs to be shifted to the early years

Having been working with both deaf and hearing children with language difficulties for over 30 years, the decline in language skills has increasingly become cause for concern.

Pupils are coming into school with insufficient language, their oral skills not sufficiently developed to support the curriculum.

I am currently seeing children with normal hearing levels needing the type of support and remediation exercises which were once confined to pupils with a hearing loss. Without adequate language skills, listening and reading, speaking and writing are all compromised, resulting in poor academic skills.

Children with poor language skills at age five are significantly more likely to struggle with maths at age 11, a study for Save the Children suggests. For many the economic need to place children in nurseries has meant that much of the pressure is placed on these settings

to develop skills in language access. Nursery teachers agree with anecdotal evidence that children are less verbally advanced than at any time in recent history. "The hard research evidence isn't there as yet because it hasn't been done," says Gill Edelman, of I CAN (a charity concerned with speech and language difficulties in children). "But there is a growing body of opinion among professionals that there are more children than there used to be with communication difficulties – and boys are three times more likely to have problems than girls."

The number of children who have speech and language difficulties at nursery placements is rising in nurseries with little on the horizon to suggest this can be remedied. There has been a suggestion to increase the number of graduate nursery teachers but scant mention of where the funding can be sourced. Poor funding means that training is minimal and combined with frequent staff changes contribute to the perpetuation of the problem.

auditory ⋀ actions

PUPILS WITH LANGUAGE PROCESSING DIFFICULTIES

Do you have a pupil who is not making progress, has difficulty in listening, poor vocabulary, auditory memory, difficulty with following directions but has normal hearing the problem may lie with the processing of language. Auditory processing can exist on its own or with other learning difficulties such as ASD, ADHD and it is often not easy to determine the pupil's main need.

Auditory processing is recognised in the USA as a bona fide disability and here it is becoming increasingly identified in the UK.

Signs of auditory processing, the pupil:

Doesn't speak fluently or articulate clearly
Has poor vocabulary, sentence structure and grammar usage
Uses vague words such as 'thing', 'stuff', 'whatever'
Problems with receptive language
Needs to hear instructions/directions more than once
Appears overwhelmed when there is a lot of auditory activity
Misinterprets verbal messages
Confuses similar words or sounds
Seems distracted or unable to sustain attention when receiving verbal messages
Comprehension of text is poor
Difficulty with phonics

Services provided by Auditory-actions
Assessment ⋀ Advice on the correct strategies for the individual pupil ⋀ Staff and LSA training ⋀ Resources ⋀ 1-1 intervention sessions

The director of Auditory-actions has a wide experience of working with pupils in this area and with other language related difficulties.

Please contact 07904313661 for any further advice
info@auditory-actions.co.uk www.auditory-actions.co.uk

There has also been a shift in the type of pre-school provision provided. Not so long ago they were run by a motherly 'Mrs Brown' in a home from home environment providing many quiet opportunities for language scaffolding. Now they are increasingly part of a large business group, held in acoustically unfavourable settings with story time being slotted in wherever possible It is little wonder that many children have insufficient opportunity to develop oral language competence. Free play is used constantly but without purpose – I was recently at a nursery where poor language was a huge issue. Children played outside for the whole of the afternoon with no stimulating toys and uninterested staff who did very little to aid language development.

Nursery teachers are faced with children who are struggling to develop their vocabulary, cannot speak clearly and have difficulty understanding instructions. They are not going to learn these skills from others and need skilled adult interaction.

Oral language provides the foundation to literacy skills, it cannot be acquired through metamorphosis. It is through listening to adults modelling sentence structure and vocabulary the skills can be transmitted and learned.

Formal language instruction is now needed to assist pupils to achieve the proficiency necessary to become successful learners in the classroom.

I have noticed the lack of that all-important skill – active listening. Everything today is visual with pupils increasingly finding listening a difficult skill to achieve. Active listening provides the key to many skills from simple repeating (auditory memory), and paraphrasing (thinking and reasoning) to reflecting (putting the message in own words). Teachers will attest that a simple request such as 'go to the cupboard and get the pencils' is met with a blank look. If the first stage of listening is providing a challenge, there is little hope for expansion.

There is something of a blame culture with nurseries being seen as not being effective in promoting language. They, in turn, blame the lack of conversation between parent/carers and young children.

Whilst much of the responsibility is apportioned to the nursery, communication begins from birth and despite many initiatives being set up to underline the need for effective communication at home this has not been solved.

Decline in parent child interaction can be attributed to:

- Loss of extended family surrounding babies which means babies and toddlers spending less time engaging with other family members
- Lack of interaction at family regular family routines

All too frequently children from toddler age upwards never eat with the rest of the family; instead they eat on their own while watching television (the National Family and Parenting Institute found this is the case in almost half of the population). A visit to the supermarket will show mother and toddler both on mobile phones. The one-time discussion about what 'shall we have for dinner?' consigned to history.

Within a few years, the wish to communicate via 'techno talk' will become the norm with face-to-face communication becoming consigned to history

Nor is it con fined to social class: often parents who can afford it will opt out from having to interact with their children, preferring instead to provide a whole range of out of school activities, even for very young children. The emergence of early years' speech therapists and settings which specialise specifically in language promotion for young children are evidence of this.

Alan Wells from the Basic Skills Agency found that headteachers believe that, compared with five years ago, fewer pupils now had basic language skills such as speaking audibly and talking voluntarily to others. Less than half of those starting school could recite songs or rhymes.

The 'leave it to the school approach' means schools are the final stop. The school now has to ensure access to a curriculum which requires skills within a range of auditory processing competence: listening, auditory perception, vocabulary, inference, and auditory memory, compounded by reduced funding. Children are being asked to complete tasks in Key Stage 1 for which they do not have the foundation.

This problem will not disappear, needing a shift in emphasis by providing an early years structured language programme.

Catherine Routley is a teacher/consultant in special needs and language skills. She is director of Auditory-Actions. For more information visit www.auditory-actions.co.uk or call 07904 313661

Solving safety and stability issues with special equipment

Alistair Pulling explains some help available for students with poor posture and body awareness

MERU is a specialist charity that offers design and engineering solutions, backed up by input from occupational therapists, to create products where nothing else exists to meet a need.

Schools working with children with disabilities or who exhibit challenging behaviour may find assistive technology created by MERU very helpful. Its design and engineering solutions are backed up by input from occupational therapists, to create products where nothing else exists to meet a need.

As well as working with people with disabilities and parents of disabled children to create bespoke items MERU also offers ready-made products that provide solutions to common issues in schools or organisations.

This includes the Flexzi flexible gadget holder – an adjustable support system for items like buddy buttons, or tablets. Different Flexzis are available with single, double or triple flexible plastic segments that allow perfect positioning of devices. They come with different stability options, including a table-top stand, a lightweight eco-clamp or a heavy duty clamp that's ideal for use with smartphones, cameras or satnavs on off-road wheelchairs.

Children who have difficulty concentrating because poor core strength means they are concerned about slipping down in their chair, or who have tics or tremors that mean they could be unstable in a normal chair could benefit from the special supports for school chairs MERU offers called Rokzi Armz and Legz. These chair supports add extra stability, which offers reassurance and added safety which can mean that fatigue is reduced and concentration improved.

There are several students at Queensmill (a special school for children with Autism Spectrum Disorders) who benefit from using Rokzi Armz and Legz on their school chairs. These adaptations help the students to have improved posture whilst seated and to sit and engage for longer.

The Rokzi Armz provide increased feedback for students who have poor body awareness and tend to lean, slide or get up frequently when using normal school chairs. The Rockzi Legz help to ensure the safety of children who like to rock in their chairs and demonstrate difficulties with balance and limited awareness of danger. This enables students to sit more independently.

Nash College was another educational establishment that came to MERU for help. Nash College is an independent specialist college for learners with moderate to profound learning disabilities. Staff found that some students with behavioural issues were attempting to remove seatbelts when travelling in the college's vehicles, which obviously puts themselves and the other passengers and driver at risk.

MERU responded by creating the Buckle Stopz, a safety device that can stop people putting themselves and other vehicle occupants at risk by releasing safety belts. The Buckle Stopz fits over the seat belt buckle to prevent the seat belt being released, but allows the belt to be released using almost any key, or slim pointed object.

The MERU Buckle Stopz is CE marked as a medical device, and is not intended for use by the general public as a restraint device for children, but by professionals working with people that have conditions that include challenging behaviour, or families who have members with these conditions, only after a full risk assessment. Although with correct use, the Buckle Stopz is intended to increase safety, the device's purpose is to change the method used to release seatbelts, so any driver or carer that is travelling in a vehicle where it is use must be aware of it being present and trained in how it works. Additionally, Buckle Stopz are supplied with a seat belt cutting tool, and a window sticker to inform emergency services that they are in use and how to release them.

If you are considering using a Buckle Stopz a risk assessment to establish whether it is the most appropriate solution, and full training and awareness of how it works to ensure it is used safely are critical, but used correctly it can certainly increase safety

The head of occupational therapy at Nash College commented: "We are very grateful to MERU for developing the Buckle Stopz safety device with us and specifically for one of our students. We made the original referral to MERU after all other devices on the market including some from the U.S. had been tried unsuccessfully as they were either easy to open for this young man with ASD or easily breakable as made of plastic. This meant that our student could not access the community from college on days when his arousal and activity level were very high as we could no longer guarantee his and others safety on minibus transport.

"This was extremely limiting for him and further increased his anxiety and arousal as he could not be as active as he needed to be on such days. The Buckle Stopz has enabled him to stay seated at all times and knowing that it could not be opened or removed helped reassure and calm him and no further incidents were reported. He has since left the college and we have recommended the use of the Buckle Stopz to our colleagues in the community and to his parents to use. Thanks to the minimal cost and extreme durability this is an item that can easily be purchased by families and carers, the instructions are also clear and easy to follow including the safety recommendations.

"We are now using the Buckle Stopz with a variety of young adults with profound or severe learning disabilities and/ or ASD who have been found to open the seatbelts while the vehicle is in motion and may therefore not be safe to travel. We follow a multi-disciplinary assessment process to ensure the best interest is in the heart of any decisions related to safe travel on our transport and always opt for the least restrictive support for the person. The Buckle Stopz is often our first choice."

To find out more, visit www.meru.org.uk or call MERU on 01372 725 203.

School groups

Cavendish Education

14 Waterloo Place,
London SW1Y 4AR
Tel: +44 (0)20 3696 5300
Email: info@cavendisheducation.com
Website: www.cavendisheducation.com

Abingdon House School

Broadley Terrace, London, NW1 6LG
Tel: 020 3750 5526
Email: ahs@abingdonhouseschool.co.uk
Website: www.abingdonhouseschool.co.uk
FOR MORE INFORMATION SEE PAGE 98

Bredon School

Pull Court, Bushley, Tewkesbury, Gloucestershire GL20 6AH
Tel: 01684 293156
Fax: 01684 298008
Email: enquiries@bredonschool.co.uk
Website: www.bredonschool.org
FOR MORE INFORMATION SEE PAGE 90

Gretton School

Manor Farm Road, Girton, Cambridge, Cambridgeshire CB3 0RX
Tel: 01223 277438
Email: info@grettonschool.com
Website: www.grettonschool.com
FOR MORE INFORMATION SEE PAGE 62

The Holmewood School

88 Woodside Park Road
London N12 8SH
Tel: 020 8920 0660
Fax: 020 8445 9678
Email: enquiries@thsl.org.uk
Website: www.thsl.org.uk
FOR MORE INFORMATION SEE PAGE 65

The Independent School (TIS)

23-31 Beavor Lane, Ravenscourt Park,
Hammersmith, London W6 9AR
Tel: 020 3637 7574
Email: admin@tis-london.org
Website: www.tis-london.org
FOR MORE INFORMATION SEE PAGE 99

Hesley Group

**Central Services, Hesley Hall
Tickhill, Doncaster, DH11 9NH
Tel: +44 (0)1302 866906
Fax: +44 (0)1302 861661
Email: enquiries@hesleygroup.co.uk
Website: www.hesleygroup.co.uk**

Fullerton House College

Tickhill Square, Denaby, Doncaster, South Yorkshire DN12 4AR
Tel: 01709 861663
Fax: 01709 869635
Email: enquiries@hesleygroup.co.uk
Website: www.hesleygroup.co.uk
FOR MORE INFORMATION SEE PAGE 75

Fullerton House School

Tickill Square, Denaby, Doncaster, South Yorkshire DN12 4AR
Tel: 01709 861663
Fax: 01709 869635
Email: enquiries@hesleygroup.co.uk
Website: www.fullertonhouseschool.co.uk
FOR MORE INFORMATION SEE PAGE 74

Wilsic Hall College

Wadworth, Doncaster, South Yorkshire DN11 9AG
Tel: 01302 856382
Email: enquiries@hesleygroup.co.uk
Website: www.hesleygroup.co.uk
FOR MORE INFORMATION SEE PAGE 75

Wilsic Hall School

Wadworth, Doncaster, South Yorkshire DN11 9AG
Tel: 01302 856382
Fax: 01302 853608
Email: enquiries@hesleygroup.co.uk
Website: www.wilsichallschool.co.uk
FOR MORE INFORMATION SEE PAGE 77

ICAN

31 Angel Gate (Gate 5), Goswell Road
London EC1V 2PT
Tel: 0845 225 4073
Fax: 0845 225 4072
Email: info@ican.org.uk
Website: www.ican.org.uk

helps children
communicate

I CAN'S Dawn House School

Helmsley Road, Rainworth, Mansfield,
Nottinghamshire NG21 0DQ
Tel: 01623 795361
Fax: 01623 491173
Email: dawnhouse@ican.notts.sch.uk
Website: www.dawnhouseschool.org.uk
FOR MORE INFORMATION SEE PAGE 93

I CAN's Meath School

Brox Road, Ottershaw, Surrey KT16 0LF
Tel: 01932 872302
Fax: 01932 875180
Email: meath@meath-ican.org.uk
Website: www.meathschool.org.uk
FOR MORE INFORMATION SEE PAGE 104

Kisimul

**The Old Vicarage, 61 High Street,
Swinderby, Lincoln, Lincolnshire LN6 9LU
Tel: 01522 868279
Email: enquiries@kisimul.co.uk
Website: www.kisimul.co.uk**

Cruckton Hall

Cruckton, Shrewsbury, Shropshire SY5 8PR
Tel: 01743 860206
Fax: 01743 860941
Email: jo.burdon@cruckton.com
Website: www.cruckton.com
FOR MORE INFORMATION SEE PAGE 70

Kisimul School

The Old Vicarage, 61 High Street, Swinderby,
Lincoln, Lincolnshire LN6 9LU
Tel: 01522 868279
Fax: 01522 866000
Email: admissions@kisimul.co.uk
Website: www.kisimul.co.uk
FOR MORE INFORMATION SEE PAGE 94

Kisimul School – Woodstock House

Woodstock Lane North, Long Ditton, Surbiton, Surrey KT6 5HN
Tel: 020 8335 2570
Fax: 020 8335 2571
Email: admissions@kisimul.co.uk
Website: www.kisimul.co.uk
FOR MORE INFORMATION SEE PAGE 100

Kisimul Upper School

Acacia Hall, Shortwood Lane, Friesthorpe,
Lincoln, Lincolnshire LN3 5AL
Tel: 01673 880022
Fax: 01673 880021
Website: www.kisimul.co.uk

LVS Hassocks
and LVS Oxford
West Sussex and Oxfordshire
Tel: 01344 884440
Email: admissions@lvs-hassocks.org.uk

LVS Hassocks

London Road, Sayers Common, Hassocks, West Sussex BN6 9HT
Tel: 01273 832901
Email: office@lvs-hassocks.org.uk
Website: www.lvs-hassocks.org.uk
FOR MORE INFORMATION SEE PAGE 58

LVS Oxford

Spring Hill Road, Begbroke, Oxfordshire OX5 1RX
Tel: 01865 595170
Email: enquiries@lvs-oxford.org.uk
Website: www.lvs-oxford.org.uk
FOR MORE INFORMATION SEE PAGE 67

NAS

393 City Road
London EC1V 1NG
Tel: +44 (0)20 7833 2299
Fax: +44 (0)20 7833 9666
Email: nas@nas.org.uk
Website: www.nas.org.uk

NAS Anderson School

Luxborough Lane, Chigwell, Essex IG7 5AA
Email: chigwell.school@nas.org.uk
Website: www.andersonschool.org.uk
FOR MORE INFORMATION SEE PAGE 59

NAS Church Lawton School

Cherry Tree Avenue, Church Lawton, Stoke-on-Trent, Staffordshire ST7 3EL
Tel: 01270 877601
Email: churchlawton@nas.org.uk
Website: www.churchlawtonschool.org.uk
FOR MORE INFORMATION SEE PAGE 72

NAS Daldorch House School

Sorn Road, Catrine, East Ayrshire KA5 6NA
Tel: 01290 551666
Fax: 01290 553399
Email: daldorch@nas.org.uk
Website: www.daldorchhouseschool.org.uk
FOR MORE INFORMATION SEE PAGE 78

NAS Daldorch Satellite School

St Leonards, East Kilbride, South Lanarkshire G74
Tel: 01355 246242
Fax: 01290 553399
Email: daldorch@nas.org.uk
Website: www.daldorchhouseschool.org.uk

NAS Helen Allison School

Longfield Road, Meopham, Kent DA13 0EW
Tel: 01474 814878
Fax: 01474 812033
Email: helen.allison@nas.org.uk
Website: www.helenallisonschool.org.uk
FOR MORE INFORMATION SEE PAGE 68

NAS Radlett Lodge School

Harper Lane, Radlett, Hertfordshire WD7 9HW
Tel: 01923 854922
Fax: 01923 859922
Email: radlett.lodge@nas.org.uk
Website: www.radlettlodgeschool.org.uk
FOR MORE INFORMATION SEE PAGE 63

NAS Robert Ogden School

Clayton Lane, Thurnscoe, Rotherham, South Yorkshire S63 0BG
Tel: 01709 874443
Fax: 01709 870701
Email: robert.ogden@nas.org.uk
Website: www.robertogdenschool.org.uk
FOR MORE INFORMATION SEE PAGE 76

NAS Sybil Elgar School

Havelock Road, Southall, Middlesex UB2 4NY
Tel: 020 8813 9168
Fax: 020 8571 7332
Email: sybil.elgar@nas.org.uk
Website: www.sybilelgarschool.org.uk
FOR MORE INFORMATION SEE PAGE 64

NAS Thames Valley School

Conwy Close, Tilehurst, Reading, Berkshire RG30 4BZ
Tel: 0118 9424 750
Email: thames.valley@nas.org.uk
Website: www.thamesvalleyschool.org.uk
FOR MORE INFORMATION SEE PAGE 69

RNIB

105 Judd Street
London WC1H 9NE
Tel: 0303 123 9999
Email: helpline@rnib.org.uk
Website: www.rnib.org.uk

RNIB College Loughborough

Radmoor Road, Loughborough, Leicestershire LE11 3BS

Tel: 01509 611077

Fax: 01509 232013

Email: enquiries@rnibcollege.ac.uk

Website: www.rnibcollege.ac.uk

FOR MORE INFORMATION SEE PAGE123

RNIB Pears Centre for Specialist Learning

Wheelwright Lane, Ash Green, Coventry, West Midlands CV7 9RA

Tel: 024 7636 9500

Fax: 024 7636 9501

Email: pearscentre@rnib.org.uk

Website: www.rnib.org.uk/pearscentre

FOR MORE INFORMATION SEE PAGE 131

RNIB Sunshine House School

33 Dene Road, Northwood, Middlesex HA6 2DD

Tel: 01923 822538

Fax: 01923 826227

Email: sunshinehouse@rnib.org.uk

Website: www.rnib.org.uk/sunshinehouse

FOR MORE INFORMATION SEE PAGE 125

Ruskin Mill

**Old Bristol Road, Nailsworth
Stroud GL6 0LA
Tel: 01453 837 521
Email: enquiries@rmt.org
Website: www.rmt.org**

Argent College

New Standard Works, 43-47 Vittoria Street,
Birmingham, West Midlands B1 3PE
Tel: 01453 837502
Fax: 01384 399401
Email: enquiries@argent.rmt.org
Website: www.rmt.org
FOR MORE INFORMATION SEE PAGE 111

Brantwood Specialist School

1 Kenwood Bank, Nether Edge, Sheffield, South Yorkshire S7 1NU
Tel: 0114 258 9062
Email: enquiries@brantwood.rmt.org
Website: www.rmt.org
FOR MORE INFORMATION SEE PAGE 88

Clervaux Trust

Clow Beck Centre, Jolby Lane, Croft-on-
Tees, North Yorkshire DL2 2TF
Tel: 01325 729860
Email: info@clervaux.org.uk
Website: www.clervaux.org.uk

Coleg Plas Dwbl

Mynachlog-ddu, Clunderwen, Pembrokeshire SA66 7SE
Tel: 01453 837502
Email: enquiries@plasdwbl.rmt.org
Website: www.rmt.org
FOR MORE INFORMATION SEE PAGE 119

Freeman College

Sterling Works, 88 Arundel Street, Sheffield,
South Yorkshire S1 2NG
Tel: 01453 837502
Fax: 0114 252 5996
Email: enquiries@fmc.rmt.org
Website: www.rmt.org
FOR MORE INFORMATION SEE PAGE 114

Glasshouse College

Wollaston Road, Amblecote, Stourbridge, West Midlands DY8 4HF
Tel: 01453 837502
Fax: 01384 399401
Email: enquiries@ghc.rmt.org
Website: www.rmt.org
FOR MORE INFORMATION SEE PAGE 112

Ruskin Mill College

The Fisheries, Horsley, Gloucestershire GL6 0PL
Tel: 01453 837502
Fax: 01453 837506
Email: enquiries@rmc.rmt.org
Website: www.rmt.org
FOR MORE INFORMATION SEE PAGE 91

TCES Group

**Park House, 8 Lombard Road, Wimbledon
London SW19 3TZ
Tel: +44 (0)20 8543 7878
Fax: +44 (0)20 8543 7877
Email: referrals@tces.org.uk
Website: www.tces.org.uk**

East London Independent School (ELIS)

Stratford Marsh, Welfare Road, London E15 4HT

Tel: 020 8555 6737

Custom House, 41 Varley Road, Newham, London, El6 3NR

Tel: 020 7540 9120

Email: referrals@tces.org.uk

Website: www.tces.org.uk

FOR MORE INFORMATION SEE PAGE 81

Essex Fresh Start Independent School (EFS)

Church Street, Witham, Essex CM8 2JL

Tel: 01376 780088

1 Wellesley Road, Clacton, Essex CO15 3PP

Tel: 01255 225204

Email: referrals@tces.org.uk

Website: www.tces.org.uk

FOR MORE INFORMATION SEE PAGE 80

North West London Independent School (NWLIS)

85 Old Oak Common Lane, Acton, London W3 7DD

Tel: 020 8749 5403

Email: referrals@tces.org.uk

Website: www.tces.org.uk

FOR MORE INFORMATION SEE PAGE 82

Create Service London

Romford Therapeutic Hub

23 Victoria Road, Romford RM1 2JT

Tel: 01708 393150

Email: referrals@tces.org.uk

Website: www.tces.org.uk

Barking Therapeutic Hub

3 Queens Road, Barking, Essex IG11 8GD

Tel: 020 8591 8692

Email: referrals@tces.org.uk

Website: www.tces.org.uk

Create Service Essex

Witham

Church Street, Witham CM8 2JL

Tel: 01376 780088

Email: referrals@tces.org.uk

Website: www.tces.org.uk

School profiles

Schools and colleges specialising in social interaction difficulties (Autism, ASD & ASP)

LVS Oxford

PATRON
HM THE QUEEN

LVS Oxford

A unique, positive education for young people
on the autism spectrum

Spring Hill Road, Begbroke,
Oxfordshire OX5 1RX
Tel: 01865 595170
Email: enquiries@lvs-oxford.org.uk
Website: www.lvs-oxford.org.uk

Head Teacher: Mrs Louisa Allison-Bergin
School type:
Coeducational Day & Weekly Boarding
Age range of pupils: 11–19
No. of pupils enrolled as at 01/01/2017: 49

LVS Oxford is an SEN school providing a unique, positive education for young people on the autism spectrum aged 11 to 19.

As students with communication, socialisation and imagination difficulties all have different skills and attributes, we offer a specialist curriculum that recognises young people on the autism spectrum as individuals. Our approach is focused on educational achievement and building life skills to give students a greater chance of living more independently when they leave.

At LVS Oxford our students learn a range of relevant academic and vocational skills in a vibrant and stimulating environment. Supported by their teachers, the ongoing assessment can lead to a range of nationally recognised qualifications.

Opened in 2014, LVS Oxford offers an ever growing range of qualifications including A-level, GCSE, AQA and OCR entry level and BTECs. Five students sat our first ever GCSEs in 2016, with 100% achieving A* – C grades.

Older students and those in weekly residential are given a real focus on developing their independent living skills. They take responsibility for many day-to-day activities from cleaning their bedrooms and doing their own washing to planning and preparing meals.

Supported by excellent pastoral care, we encourage independence, wellbeing and healthy lifestyles, with students learning life skills outside the classroom in a safe and secure environment. There are on-site speech, language and occupational therapists, a school nurse

and a child psychotherapist supporting our students.

We recognise that one of the biggest concerns is what will happen when a young person with a diagnosis on the autism spectrum leaves school at 19. We prepare young people with autism spectrum disorders for life in the workplace, so when students leave us they have the skills and knowledge to get a job and sustain work. They are given the opportunity to engage in work based training either on site, working in the grounds or kitchen, as well as off site for experience in their chosen area, such as Blenheim Palace or the gym.

Whilst we have a criteria and policy for admissions, we also recommend you contact us to discuss the individual's needs or attend one of our open days.

Anderson School

NAS Anderson School
Luxborough Lane, Chigwell, Essex, IG7 5AB
E: chigwell.school@nas.org.uk
www.andersonschool.org.uk

Principal: Gary Simm

School type: mixed free school with day placements for children and young people on the autism spectrum

Catchment area: Essex, East London and neighbouring authorities
Age range: 11-19
Capacity: 78
Established: 2017

Anderson School will be open in September 2017 to children and young people on the autism-spectrum. It will be part of National Autistic Society's Enterprise Campus situated on a 13-acre site, the campus will include an Enterprise Centre and the National Inclusion and Development Centre. This will be in addition to our sixth form centre, workshop and training facilities and indoor and outdoor sports facilities.

Our ambition is to transform the lives of autistic young people with the aspiration that all students leave the school ready for further education, employment or training.

As with all The National Autistic Society schools, the pedagogy of Anderson School is informed by the National Autistic Society's **MyProgress®** methodology. This has been developed through over 50 years' of experience and research to ensure best practice in teaching young autistic people. The school will work in partnership with our other seven schools and the wider organisation to strengthen and develop expertise and innovative thinking.

MyProgress® guarantees that children will use tried and tested approaches that we have developed and used in our network of schools over many years: we know they make a difference. In addition to this we will take opportunities to pilot new and innovative interventions to facilitate the development of social understanding, resilience and independence.

Placements are funded by your local authority.

The National
Autistic Society

"My ultimate aim for this campus is that every child that leaves school will go into meaningful paid employment or other activity."

Mark Lever, CEO, The National Autistic Society

Prior's Court School

(Founded 1999)

Hermitage, Thatcham,
West Berkshire RG18 9NU
Tel: 01635 247202/245914
Fax: 01635 247203
Email: mail@priorscourt.org.uk
Website: www.priorscourt.org.uk
Director of Education and Learning:
Sue Piper

Appointed: September 2011
School type: Independent Special School
Age range of pupils: 5–19
No. of pupils enrolled as at 01/01/2017: 65
Boys: 51 **Girls:** 14 **Sixth Form:** 23
No. of boarders: 60
Fees per annum as at 01/01/2017:
on application

Prior's Court School is an independent special school for students with autism aged from 5 to 19 years. The School offers day, weekly and termly places with 38, 44 and 52 week options. Students are on the autistic spectrum have moderate to severe learning difficulties and complex needs. They may have additional associated diagnoses. Some students exhibit challenging behaviours. All are working within P scales to lower national curriculum levels.

The School was opened in 1999. It is managed by Prior's Court Foundation, a registered, non-profit making charity which also runs a young adult provision and specialist autism training centre on the same site.

As an autism-specific school, Prior's Court is able to focus on meeting the special needs of its students in the most effective and consistent way to support their learning:

• A meaningful and functional curricu-

lum with individualised learning programmes used throughout the waking day is built around students' interests and skills.

• The environment is adapted to meet students' needs – it is highly structured, calm, low-arousal, safe and secure with space and physical exercise a key feature providing opportunities to learn, exercise, socialise and relax onsite. Set in over 50 acres, facilities include a stable yard and paddocks for

est levels of knowledge and expertise. These dedicated staff work closely with families and professionals to create a co-ordinated and consistent programme of education and care whose success is recognised worldwide.

By combining autism expertise and best practice with a person-centred approach, the school aims to achieve the highest level of progress for each individual enabling them to self-manage behaviour, communicate, manage transitions, develop independent living and social skills, make choices and advocate and progress to building vocational skills and undertaking work-placement activities. Skills once taught and practiced onsite can then be generalised and undertaken successfully offsite. Frequent access to the nearby villages, towns and community facilities enable students to work towards inclusion as far as possible.

"The management team leads a culture in which staff strive to understand every child and young person and develop the best means for providing for their needs. Each resident therefore benefits from a personal package of care and many make significant progress as a result." Ofsted for Care Inspection 2015

"I am absolutely delighted with the progress being achieved. Teaching and house staff are superb, broadening our child's skills and experience. Improvement in speech and language has been very impressive, as has the ability to self-manage behaviour."

animal husbandry, a walled garden with greenhouse and polytunnel for horticulture, sensory swimming pool, trampolines, trim trail, zip wire, swings, activity track and outdoor gym.

- The school's strong focus on training means that staff are experienced in using a range of methodologies and strategies to support each individual's needs and development in all settings throughout the waking day.
- A large onsite multi-disciplinary team including Occupational therapy,

Speech & Language therapy, Clinical Psychologists and Nurses as well as dedicated horticulture, animal husbandry, swimming, activities and ICT instructors provide support throughout the school day and in residential settings as well as out in the community where appropriate. All staff (education, residential, night, multi-disciplinary and therapeutic as well as a team of flexible workers who provide cover for absence or injury) are trained from induction onwards ensuring the high-

Gretton School

Manor Farm Road, Girton, Cambridge,
Cambridgeshire CB3 0RX
Tel: 01223 277438
Email: info@grettonschool.com
Website: www.grettonschool.com

Head Teacher: Ms Zoe Kirby
School type:
Coeducational Day & Boarding
Age range of pupils: 5–19

'Where autism makes sense'
Gretton School is a small and friendly school, welcoming boys and girls from 5-19 years old, as weekly boarders or as day students.

Every student at Gretton has a diagnosis of autism or Asperger's syndrome and every student is different. As an NAS-accredited school, we provide a calm and purposeful atmosphere where consistent daily routines and staffing helps to keep anxiety at a minimum and ensures that our students feel safe and confident in their surroundings.

We have a high staff to student ratio and classes are small and personal. We know each of our students really well and employ the best strategies to support them in their everyday school life.

This positive approach, and the value we place on treating each of our students as an individual, means that whatever a child's past experience of education, they will enjoy learning with us.

The curriculum is enriched with real-life opportunities to learn with trips, visits and outings. And learning is extended beyond the National Curriculum through weekly 'Special Interests' sessions. We place an emphasis on the development of life and social skills too, meaning we are able to bring out the best in all our students, and provide them with opportunities to flourish.

Our highly-trained academic, care and therapy teams work together to help students feel supported and encouraged, and so when they are ready to leave us, they do so making the most of all the opportunities ahead of them.

We hope you will visit us to get to know us better.

Radlett Lodge School

NAS Radlett Lodge School
Harper Lane, Radlett, Herts WD7 9HW
T: 01923 854 922 | F: 01923 859 922
E: radlett.lodge@nas.org.uk | www.radlettlodgeschool.org.uk

Principal: Jeremy Keeble

School type: mixed independent school with day, weekly and termly residential placements for children and young people on the autism spectrum

Catchment area: national
Age range: 4-19
Capacity: 55
Established: 1974

At Radlett Lodge School, we are driven by our determination to provide the highest quality education to the children in our care and do the best we can for their families. Ofsted have recognised our pursuit for excellence by rating us Outstanding for both education and care for a number of years.

We get to know every pupil well, ensuring every element of their school life is personalised to them. We use the principles of The National Autistic Society's **MyProgress**® strategy to help your child to learn, develop and prepare for adult life to the very best of their ability – and we celebrate every achievement.

Radlett Lodge School caters for early years, primary, secondary and post-16 pupils. The school and our residential lodge are located on the same site, which supports a close-knit environment and easy transitions. Strong ties with our local community mean pupils apply their learning to the outside world, particularly when approaching adulthood in our post-16 unit. We also offer flexi-boarding to our pupils, and outreach support to external pupils.

In a structured and supportive learning environment and with the help of friendly, approachable staff, students develop social relationships and receive a broad and balanced education.

Placements are funded by your local authority.

The National Autistic Society

"The care and welfare of pupils is at the heart of the school's work."

Ofsted, 2017

Sybil Elgar School

NAS Sybil Elgar School
Havelock Road, Southall, Middlesex, UB2 4NY
T: 020 8813 9168 | F: 020 8571 7332
E: sybil.elgar@nas.org.uk | www.sybilelgarschool.org.uk

Principal: Chloe Phillips

School type: mixed independent school with day, weekly term-time and 52-week residential placements for children and young people on the autism spectrum

Catchment area: national
Age range: 4-19
Capacity: 90
Established: 1965

As the first autism-specific residential school in the world, Sybil Elgar School is a pioneer in autism education. Having paved the way in autism education for over 50 years, we have the knowledge and experience to apply the tailored education and care each young person who learns with us will receive.

We have a highly specialised curriculum, and our dedicated staff closely support the learning of each pupil in communication, social, behavioural,

emotional, sensory, physical and self-help skills. Our extensive performing arts curriculum complements this. Students can discover a new passion or enhance learning in other subjects through music, art and dance. They might play the drums in the school band and even perform at an international arts festival.

Our welcoming environment extends across our three school sites, which include a post-16 department and our year-round children's home, where all staff work together to ensure the

safety, wellbeing and progress of all our students.

We follow the principles of The National Autistic Society's **MyProgress**® strategy to ensure each of our students has an experience with us that is truly personalised to them, their strengths, weaknesses and ambitions. And we recognise every achievement, helping our students value their successes and celebrate them.

Placements are funded by your local authority.

The National Autistic Society

"A school that looks good, has fine facilities and offers excellent care, understanding and education, centred round a core of communication and connectivity with people who understand the world of autism. 'It tastes good here,' said one child, and in the world of autism we doubt there is a higher accolade." **Good Schools Guide 2013**

The Holmewood School

The
Holmewood
School

(Founded 2010)
88 Woodside Park Road, London, N12 8SH
Tel: 020 8920 0660
Fax: 020 8445 9678
Email: enquiries@thsl.org.uk

Website: www.thsl.org.uk
Head Teacher: Lisa Camilleri
School type: Coeducational Day
Age range of pupils: 7–19

'Think differently'

The Holmewood School in North London is a specialist school for boys and girls with high-functioning autism, Asperger Syndrome and other language and communication needs. The school is NAS-accredited and founded on a desire to make a difference and to challenge the way all members of the community think about autism.

Ours is a warm and friendly school where we ensure our students get every opportunity to achieve their full potential in life. This commitment is an intrinsic part of our philosophy and is at the heart of everything we do.

We recognise that every student is different and, in addition to academic achievement, our focus is firmly on their social, emotional and personal development. This is supported by strengthening independence and life skills, which are key to building confidence and self-esteem.

The school offers a diverse range of on-site therapies, from Speech and Language Therapy to Drama Therapy, Lego Therapy and Reflexology. It also benefits from an Occupational Therapy Clinic which through sensory integration, behavioural and developmental support, helps to promote the teaching and learning of essential life skills.

Our curriculum is based on the belief that for an individual to benefit and learn from an activity, they should enjoy it and find it meaningful. Programmes are delivered on a 1:1 basis, in small groups, or as part of larger groups.

The School has recently opened a second site close-by exclusively for its Sixth Form students where they are able to practice their independent travel skills and are able to access further education programmes at local colleges or gain work experience through placements in local companies.

We are immensely proud of our school and our students and we are committed to its continuing success. If you'd like to see The Holmewood School for yourself, please contact us.

West Kirby School and College

WEST KIRBY SCHOOL AND COLLEGE

(Founded 1881)

Meols Drive, West Kirby, Wirral,
Merseyside CH48 5DH
Tel: 0151 632 3201
Fax: 0151 632 0621
Website: www.wkrs.co.uk
Principal: Mr Iain Sim

School type:
Coeducational Day & Weekly Boarding
Age range of pupils: 5–19
No. of pupils enrolled as at 01/01/2017: 87
Fees per annum as at 01/01/2017:
On application

Changing Children's Lives, Building Better Futures

WKS is a Non Maintained Special School for pupils with a wide range of social, communication difficulties often linked with conditions such as Autism and additional complex learning needs.

The school prides itself on being able to help some very complex young people access the National Curriculum and work towards appropriate accreditation in all subjects including Open Awards, GCSEs and AS Levels. Staff are highly skilled in the understanding of the social and emotional needs of the pupils, as well as being able to personalise the academic work accordingly and provide high levels of support.

We believe the views of the pupils are paramount to success and the school offers opportunities for this through School Council, Pupil Voice and individual discussion. Every pupil has an 'individual support plan' which they and staff contribute to. Differentiation and small classes with high levels of adult support have proven successful. We have excellent facilities, particularly for sport, music and other practical subjects.

The school has its own Therapy and Additional Support Services department which provides additional 'therapy' and educational support often necessary for the pupils to access the National Curriculum and fulfil their academic and personal potential. This department consists of: a Clinical Psychologist, Speech and Language Therapists, Occupational Therapist, Behaviour and Reading support specialists/teams, a Learning Mentor, a Family Liaison Officer and Pastoral Care Team.

We have the option of day provision or flexible boarding provision on a termly basis, with pupils staying between one and four nights per week. Residential units include two houses in the locality and all are maintained to a high standard, with individual bedrooms and common areas for dining and recreation. We also offer 52 week options through a newly registered children's home.

We hold the International School Award and have forged strong links with schools in South Africa and China and an orphanage in India, where exchange visits have taken place over a number of years now, real experiences which most of our pupils would have considered beyond their reach.

Post 16 is based off-site. Each pupil has a study programme tailored to their individual needs, involving academic study, vocational and employability skills and further development of social and communication skills. The college has recently established supported Internships to facilitate access to college and work.

Staff are experienced at assisting pupils in the difficult process of transition from school to adult life. All pupils benefit from the strong pastoral ideal that runs through the school, to be aware both of themselves as individuals and within a group, increasing their respect for others, their self-esteem, emotional regulation and self-awareness.

Our staff are well qualified, experienced professionals. Recruitment procedures are rigorous with exemplary professional development available for all. Continued professional development is supported through an extensive range or partnerships with local schools, universities and other agencies.

'This school remains outstanding' (Ofsted 2016).

WKRS is a registered charity no. 207790.

LVS Hassocks

LVS Hassocks

A unique, positive education for young people on the autism spectrum

PATRON
HM THE QUEEN

London Road, Sayers Common, Hassocks, West Sussex BN6 9HT
Tel: 01273 832901
Email: office@lvs-hassocks.org.uk
Website: www.lvs-hassocks.org.uk

Head Teacher: Ms Terry Kelly
School type:
Coeducational Day & Weekly Boarding
Age range of pupils: 8–19
No. of pupils enrolled as at 01/01/2017: 84

LVS Hassocks is an SEN school providing a unique, positive education for young people on the autism spectrum aged 8 to 19.

Our approach is focused on educational achievement and building life skills to give young people a greater chance of living more independently when they leave. Our experience shows that students, parents and supporting local authorities value our specialist care and innovative approach to helping young people reach their full potential.

Academic progress is an important area of development for students, and at LVS Hassocks young people learn a range of relevant academic and vocational skills in a vibrant and stimulating environment. Our accredited qualifications include A-levels, GCSEs, BTECs, NVQs, Functional Skills and ASDAN. In 2016, 100% of learners passed Maths, English Literature and ICT GCSEs, all with A* – E grades.

The spacious and comfortable rooms at LVS Hassocks help residential students to feel safe and secure, and older learners especially are encouraged to develop their independent living skills. They are given responsibility for doing many day-to-day tasks such as washing and cleaning to planning and preparing the group evening meal.

There are on-site speech, language and occupational therapists, a massage therapist, dedicated chefs and practical instructors delivering the vocational skills to help learners develop as individuals. A new sensory room which opened in 2017 provides a further calming impact and gives students the opportunity to regulate themselves.

Real world learning allows all students the opportunity to engage in work-based training either on-site or off-site with work experience placements in their chosen area, such as hairdressing, catering or retail.

One of LVS Hassocks' proudest achievements is our ability to help learners find opportunities beyond school, in further education and full and part-time work after they leave. Our 100% rate of successful placements is testimony to our ethos, helping young people with autism to build positive futures and fulfilled lives within their own communities.

Whilst we have a criteria and policy for admissions, we also recommend you contact us to discuss the individual's needs or attend one of our open days.

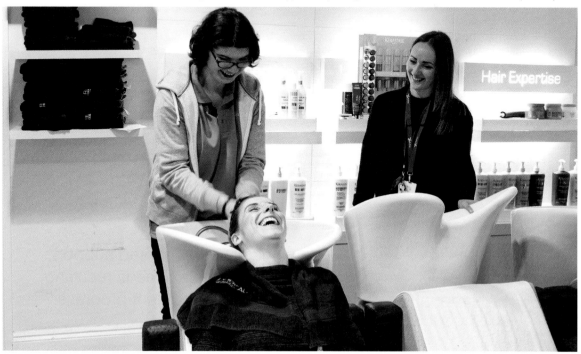

Helen Allison School

NAS Helen Allison School
Longfield Road, Meopham, Kent DA13 0EW
T: 01474 814 878
E: helen.allison@nas.org.uk | www.helenallisonschool.org.uk

Principal: Susan Conway

School type: mixed independent school with day and weekly term-time residential placements for children and young people on the autism spectrum

Catchment area: London, South East and East Anglia
Age range: 5-19
Capacity: 77
Established: 1968

At Helen Allison School we deliver a high quality, relevant and enjoyable education and use our expert knowledge of autism to find the best possible way for each student to learn to the best of their ability.

Following the principles of **MyProgress®**, The National Autistic Society's strategy for working with autistic students, we ensure they get the best start in life with an education tailored to them.

We believe in preparing our students for fulfilling adult lives, so our main curriculum is enhanced with a wide range of social activities and community-based learning.

Through our hub, older students partake in work experience, pursue formal qualifications or might even organise a football tournament with other local schools and colleges.

Rated 'Outstanding' for education, and 'Outstanding' for care under the new Ofsted criteria, we are always pushing for excellence for our students, thinking creatively to adapt to their needs and aspirations.

As one of only a few schools with our own therapeutic team, your child will develop not only academically but foster strong social and communication skills so they can thrive alongside their peers.

Placements are funded by your local authority.

The National Autistic Society

"Through highly personalised support, students with complex needs resulting from autism make excellent progress."
Ofsted, 2015

Thames Valley School

NAS Thames Valley School
Conwy Close, Tilehurst, Reading, Berkshire RG30 4BZ
T: 0118 9424 750 | E: thames.valley@nas.org.uk
www.thamesvalleyschool.org.uk

Principal: David Stewart

School type: mixed free school with day placements for children and young people on the autism spectrum

Catchment area: Reading, Berkshire and neighbouring local authorities
Age range: 5-16
Capacity: 50
Established: 2013

Thames Valley School is a high-achieving specialist school for children and young people on the autism spectrum. Our school has been purpose-built for us, meaning we could design it to be perfectly suitable for our students. We have calming pods where children can relax or read, independent rooms attached to every classroom, outdoor play areas for all ages and a state-of-the-art innovation hub, opening up opportunities for pupils to take on digital projects such as coding, social media and cyber security.

We have high expectations of our pupils, and through delivering the National Curriculum at all key stages, we expect the majority of our students to attain at least the same levels as their mainstream school peers. At age 16 our pupils take national qualifications, and our aim is for most to achieve a wide range of GCSE's at A to C or equivalent vocational qualifications.

Small classes, committed and experienced specialist teachers and a wonderful learning environment all contribute to making our school an exceptional place to be. We follow the principles of The National Autistic Society's **MyProgress®** strategy to give your child an education specific to them, so they can flourish.

Placements are funded by your local authority.

"The school has been the making of my son, he loves coming to school!"
Parent

Cruckton Hall
(part of the Kisimul Group)

(Founded 1981)

Cruckton, Shrewsbury, Shropshire SY5 8PR

Tel: 01743 860206

Fax: 01743 860941

Email: jo.burdon@cruckton.com

Website: www.cruckton.com

Head Teacher: Jo Burdon

School type: Boys' Residential

Age range of boys: 8–19

No. of pupils enrolled as at 01/01/2015: 80

Fees per annum as at 01/01/2015:

On application

Curriculum

All boys at the school have an Individual Pupil Care Plan that sets out their educational and therapeutic needs in addition to care, behavioural or medical information. The curriculum offered to each boy is highly personalised to take these into account. All boys follow a broad curriculum based on the National Curriculum, but then have bespoke activities or interventions built into their timetables. All are taught towards examinations appropriate to their abilities in Maths, English and Science. There are a range of academic options up to GCSE level encompassing humanities, technology and creative subjects. Specialist rooms support the learning in these areas. In addition, we can provide tutoring to A Level where a student is gifted and talented.

Alongside traditional academic subjects, we offer Outdoor Education, including Duke of Edinburgh, our own Forest School, Equine work and a whole range of activities such as Climbing and Cycling with qualified instructors. These support mental and physical well-being and provide opportunities for boys to interact with each other in different groupings and with different adults and the public.

Sessions with Speech and Language therapists, 1-1 interventions for core subjects and work with Assistant Educational Psychologists are built into the individualised timetables as needed.

Assessment and entry requirements

Entry is by interview and assessment. The multi-disciplinary team of professionals will carry out a baseline assessment on each student within the first six weeks

of admission. Cruckton has a visiting consultant child and adolescent psychiatrist who visits the boys on a regular basis, as required. The multi-disciplinary team consists of a consultant educational psychologist, systemic psychotherapist, two speech and language therapists and an occupational therapist. They provide a variety of interventions and therapies to minimise the anxieties and maximise the development of our young people.

The wider environment

The hall is a listed building surrounded by ten acres of gardens that include woods, playing fields and play areas. The site is located within a friendly rural community, in beautiful countryside, four miles from the market town of Shropshire. The Welsh Marches provide a stunning backdrop and a rich source of options for our regular trips and adventures. The town of Shrewsbury offers excellent amenities for the school and is now linked to the motorway network of the West Midlands, greatly improving access.

Residential environment and activities

The structure that provides success for the boys in the classroom environment is replicated in the residential area and boys have a range of recreational activities provided, which reflect their needs and encourage their specialisms. Many boys choose an active leisure programme. This can be provided by activities such as skateboarding, swimming, football and cricket, and in the summer the Adventure Camp encourages team work amongst our student group through activities such as orienteering, mountain biking, rock climbing and raft building. For the more studious, a range of activities from *Warhammer* to chess club are provided. Links with local clubs and societies include the local stables,

local army cadet force, Jiu Jitsu, Laser Quest, bowling alley, street dancing and swimming are well-established. The links between the IEP targets are shared across the 24-hour approach, both in the home and education setting, with a huge variety of enrichment activities and programmes. Forest school, Lego therapy, robotics, stable management, mountain biking, Blists Hill Museum and work experience are all part of the enrichment programme.

Behaviour management

It is accepted that many boys come to Cruckton Hall School exhibiting both difficult and challenging behaviour. The structural consistency of various approaches, combined with a consistent nurturing environment, has a track record of providing the boys with the ability to be accepted within social settings of their choice. The basis of the approach is to foster the following qualities: self-respect, respect for other students, respect for staff,

courtesy, politeness, patience, tolerance and motivation to work. Boys will be encouraged and supported to meet as many of these expectations as is possible. Attendance at school is a non-negotiable requirement of a boy's placement at Cruckton Hall. School uniform is always worn.

Aims and philosophy

Cruckton Hall School aims to provide a warm, structured and caring learning environment in which each boy feels safe and secure, can succeed, is treated as an individual and is able to develop his skills and talents in order that he leaves school as an active participant in, and a positive contributor to, society.

"Cruckton Hall School's new curriculum has had a positive impact on improving and accelerating pupils' progress. Pupils develop the skills they need to learn effectively in lessons and to be prepared for the next stage of their education, training or employment."

"There is provision for pupils' spiritual, moral, social and cultural development by a particular emphasis on improved social skills, respect and tolerance and a better understanding of right and wrong."
Ofsted 2016

Church Lawton School

NAS Church Lawton School, Cherry Tree Avenue, Church Lawton, Stoke-on-Trent, Staffordshire ST7 3EL
T: 01270 877 601 | E: church.lawton@nas.org.uk
www.churchlawtonschool.org.uk

Principal: Paul Scales

School type: mixed free school with day placements for children and young people on the autism spectrum

Catchment area: Cheshire East and surrounding authorities, including Cheshire West, Stoke-on-Trent and Staffordshire

Age range: 4-19
Capacity: 60
Established: 2015

Church Lawton School is The National Autistic Society's second free school providing tailored care for local autistic students. We opened in 2015 and offer a highly specialised learning environment to our pupils on our brand new, purpose-built site.

With large open classrooms and an average class size of six, our pupils have the space and attention they need to reach their full potential.

Combined with well-resourced classrooms our building is equipped for academic excellence, and so we aim for our pupils to perform well in different exam pathways including Entry Level, GCSEs, ASDAN, A Levels and more.

We follow the principles of **MyProgress®**, The National Autistic Society's overall strategy for working with children on the autism spectrum. Systematic and thorough, we work with you and your child to create the best education for them.

We equip pupils with the skills and knowledge to support them as they move into further study and adult life. They get to know their community and, as they move through the school, have the opportunity to take part in work experience or study in local colleges and universities. Above all we are dedicated to making sure every one of our pupils is given the tools they need to thrive.

Placements are funded by your local authority.

The National Autistic Society

"I have never come across a school that is as kind, caring and understanding about its pupils."

A visiting parent

Queen Alexandra College (QAC)
A National College for People with Disabilities

Queen Alexandra College

(Founded 1847)
Court Oak Road, Harborne, Birmingham, West Midlands B17 9TG
Tel: 0121 428 5050
Fax: 0121 428 5048
Email: info@qac.ac.uk

Website: www.qac.ac.uk
Principal: Hugh J Williams
School type:
Coeducational Day & Residential
Age range of pupils: 16+
No. of pupils enrolled as at 01/01/2017: 211

QAC is a friendly Specialist College based in Birmingham. We welcome students who come to our College from all over the country – as well as many who are local to us.

The College has been at its current location since 1903. Our original purpose was to provide education for people who were blind or visually impaired.

Today, in addition to supporting people who have a visual impairment, we offer support and guidance for students on the autistic spectrum (including individuals with Asperger syndrome), those with moderate to severe learning difficulties, students with physical disabilities and those with other needs.

Ultimately, we have a great mix of students which adds to the wonderful atmosphere here in College. Class sizes are small and support levels high.

At QAC your learning is planned around your individual needs, interests and ambitions. Our curriculum covers a wide range of programmes including entry level courses (Preparation for Life) and a range of vocational qualifications. A supported internship study programme could also be followed, which involves spending the majority of time with an employer in a real job role.

The College has a team of specialists on site who are able to support students, including a Visual Impairment Training Officer, Speech and Language Therapists, a Dyslexia Tutor, Healthcare Professionals, Counsellors, Mentors, a Braille Tutor, Mobility and Travel Trainers and a Personal Sex and Health Education Specialist.

Enrichment programmes enhance the curriculum and help to develop self-esteem, confidence and independence. Our residential provision develops essential skills for personal development such as independent living and social skills.

Facilities include new buildings with the latest technology, a fitness centre, state-of-the-art sports hall, sports field, sensory room, onsite travel training area, library and student centre.

For more information please visit www.qac.ac.uk or call 0121 428 5041

Registered charity No. 1065794

Fullerton House School

(Founded 1990)
Tickill Square, Denaby, Doncaster,
South Yorkshire DN12 4AR

Tel: 01709 861663
Fax: 01709 869635
Email: enquiries@hesleygroup.co.uk
Website: www.fullertonhouseschool.co.uk
General Manager: Michael Cavan
Appointed: 2015
Head of Education: Michael Walsh

School type:
Independent Specialist Residential School
Age range of pupils: 8–19
No. of pupils enrolled as at 01/01/2017:
Capacity: 36
Fees per annum as at 01/01/2017:
Available on request

A specialist residential school offering flexible education and care, which can include day and respite provision, for up to 52-weeks-per-year for people aged 8-19, all of whom have complex needs including behaviour that may challenge and a learning disability, often in association with autism.

Fullerton House School is situated in the heart of the village of Denaby Main, near Doncaster. Its central location provides easy access by road, rail or air. Our mission is to enhance the lives of the young people entrusted to us by focusing on their specific needs, capabilities and aspirations.

Education: Each person has a carefully designed Individual Learning Plan based on their specific needs in line with the National Curriculum, which supports their positive progress in a range of areas.

Extended learning: During evenings, weekends and school holidays a wide range of extra-curricular activities are on offer to ensure that people are fully engaged with stimulating and meaningful experiences both on and off-site.

Professional services: A dedicated on-site team including carers, teachers, tutors, communication, behaviour and occupational therapy , psychology and other specialists ensure that people have ready access to the services they require.

High-quality accommodation: Single person and small group occupancy of high-quality accommodation is provided at Fullerton House School. Each person has their own bedroom, the majority of which have en-suite bathrooms. We also have a range of on-site facilities to complement and enrich the lives of those who come to live and learn with us.

Keeping in contact: We understand that while we may offer a very positive option for the person, we may not be on your doorstep. Keeping in touch with loved ones is essential. Everyone has a plan to support optimum contact with family/carers and friends whether this be by phone, letter, email or Skype.

Specialist Colleges

(Founded 2013)

Fullerton House College

Tickhill Square, Denaby, Doncaster, South Yorkshire DN12 4AR

Tel: 01709 861663

Fax: 01709 869635

Wilsic Hall College

Wadworth, Doncaster, South Yorkshire DN11 9AG

Tel: 01302 856382

Fax: 01302 853608

Email: enquiries@hesleygroup.co.uk

Website: www.hesleygroup.co.uk

Head: Richard Webster

Appointed: 2016

School type: Independent Specialist Residential Colleges

Age range of pupils: 18–25

No. of pupils enrolled as at 01/01/2017:

Fullerton House College Capacity: 12

Wilsic Hall College Capacity: 9

Fees per annum as at 01/01/2017:

On request

Specialist residential colleges offering flexible education care and support for up to 52 weeks per year for young people aged 18-25, who have complex needs including behaviour that may challenge and a learning disability, often in association with autism.

At Wilsic Hall College, everyone lives within a beautiful rural setting with ready community access and at Fullerton House College in the heart of the community, in an urban setting with many local facilities including a sports centre, restaurants and shops.

Mission

Our Specialist Colleges support young people with their transition into adult life by focusing on their specific needs, capabilities and aspirations.

Education: Everybody has a highly personalised programme of learning, equipping them with skills they will need for adult life.

Extended learning: During evenings, weekends and college holidays a wide range of extra-curricular activities are on offer to ensure people are fully engaged with stimulating experiences both on and off site providing further, meaningful learning opportunities.

Professional services: A dedicated multi-disciplinary therapeutic team including college tutors, college support workers, consultant clinical psychologist, consultant psychiatrist, applied behaviour analysts, speech and language therapists, occupational therapists, registered manager, care and support staff work together to support each individual's progress.

High quality accommodation: College accommodation includes individualised bedrooms, quality living spaces that promote independence and progressive skills development assisted by the appropriate use of specialist/adaptive technology. We also have a range of on-site and off-site facilities that offer progressive learning opportunities for young people with a range of needs and wishes.

Keeping in contact: We work to develop relationships between staff and families that are strong, positive and mutually respectful. People are supported to be in contact with their friends and family; we welcome visits to the colleges at any time. Everyone has a plan that will include the best means for them to maintain this contact whether by 'phone, letter, email or Skype.

Robert Ogden School

NAS Robert Ogden School
Clayton Lane, Thurnscoe, South Yorkshire S63 0BG
T: 01709 874 443 | F: 01709 807 701
E: robert.ogden@nas.org.uk | www.robertogdenschool.org.uk

Principal: Lorraine Dormand

School type: mixed independent school with day, weekly term-time and 52-week residential placements for children and young people on the autism spectrum

Catchment area: national
Age range: 5-19
Capacity: 127
Established: 1976

One of the largest schools in the UK for autistic children and young people, Robert Ogden School offers an environment where students can feel safe, supported and encouraged to achieve beyond their expectations. Following the principles of **MyProgress®**, The National Autistic Society's strategy for working with your child, we create a tailor-made experience for each student so they reach their full potential.

We are autism experts, with a specialist team dedicated to providing the highest quality care and education to our students. We have two Inclusive Learning Hubs run by a highly skilled group of staff who ensure pupils with particularly complex needs, requiring a non-directive approach, get the individualised curriculum and attention they need to thrive alongside their peers.

With autism-friendly buildings and facilities, your child will comfortably settle into school life. We even have a pottery room, several sensory and soft play rooms, a purpose-built primary unit and a teaching flat for independent living skills. Our students have every opportunity to develop the skills they will need for adult life, which is why we have a student-run café and shop, an award-winning fudge making enterprise project and a partnership with local charity shops. We give our students the help they need to make the best of their strengths and build upon them.

Placements are funded by your local authority.

The National Autistic Society

"You have achieved what many others could not… I am so grateful for Robert Ogden, no wonder so many parents are fighting for a place, it truly is a magnificent school with magnificent staff."

Sarah, parent

Wilsic Hall School

(Founded 1996)
Wadworth, Doncaster,
South Yorkshire DN11 9AG

Tel: 01302 856382
Fax: 01302 853608
Email: enquiries@hesleygroup.co.uk
Website: www.wilsichallschool.co.uk
Head: Geoff Turner
Appointed: 2008

School type:
Independent Specialist Residential School
Age range of pupils: 11–19
No. of pupils enrolled as at 01/01/2017:
Capacity: 31
Fees per annum as at 01/01/2017:
Available on request

A specialist residential school offering flexible education and care, which can include day and respite provision, for up to 52-weeks-per-year for people aged 11-19, all of whom have complex needs including behaviour that may challenge and a learning disability, often in association with autism.

Wilsic Hall School is situated in its own 14-acre site approximately five miles south of Doncaster. Its central location provides easy access by road, rail or air. Our mission is to enhance the lives of the people entrusted to us by focusing on their specific needs, capabilities and aspirations.

Education: Each person has a carefully designed Individual Education Plan based on their specific needs in line with the National Curriculum, which supports their positive progress in a range of areas.

Extended learning: During evenings, weekends and school holidays a wide range of extra-curricular activities are on offer to ensure that people are fully engaged with stimulating and meaningful experiences both on and off-site.

Professional services: A dedicated team including carers, teachers, tutors, behaviour, communication and occupational therapy, psychology and other specialists ensure that each person has ready access to the services they require.

High-quality accommodation: Single person and small group occupancy of high-quality accommodation is provided at Wilsic Hall School. Each person has their own bedroom, the majority of which have en-suite bathrooms. We also have a range of on-site facilities to complement and enrich the lives of those who come to live and learn with us.

Keeping in contact: We understand that while we may offer a very positive option for the person, we may not be on your doorstep. Keeping in touch with loved ones is essential. Everyone has a plan to support optimum contact with family/carers and friends whether this be by phone, letter, email or Skype.

Daldorch House School

NAS Daldorch House School
Sorn Road, Catrine, East Ayrshire, Scotland KA5 6NA
T: 01290 551 666 | F: 01290 553 399
E: daldorch@nas.org.uk | www.daldorchhouseschool.org.uk

Principal: Bernadette Casey

School type: mixed independent school with day, weekly, termly and 52-week residential placements for children and young people on the autism spectrum

Catchment area: national
Age range: 8-21
Capacity: 28 residential
Established: 1998

At Daldorch House School we work compassionately with each of our pupils, while challenging them to achieve to the best of their ability. Our 11 acre site is in a beautiful rural setting, while being only an hour from the bustle of Glasgow city centre.

Our classrooms are designed to suit the needs of all our pupils, and each lesson is arranged according to those learning in it.

Developing communication, social and life skills is at the core of our 24-hour curriculum at Daldorch, and we enrich each pupil's learning by capitalising on their interests and expanding their understanding of the world.

We also have a satellite school in East Kilbride, offering a year-round residential provision for families living in the South Lanarkshire local authority area, meaning your child can live and learn close to home in an area they know well.

Our curriculum is relevant, engaging and designed to develop each child's independence as they mature, our focus on lifelong learning strengthening as they approach adult life. With a blended approach to learning through The National Autistic Society's **MyProgress®** strategy, your child will have an education at Daldorch that is entirely personalised to them.

Placements are funded by your local authority.

The National Autistic Society

"The school has excellent systems for identifying the strengths of young people and the difficulties they face."
Education Scotland

Schools and colleges specialising in emotional, behavioural and/or social difficulties (EBSD)

Essex Fresh Start Independent School (EFS)

Essex Fresh Start
Independent School

(Founded 2007)
Church Street, Witham, Essex CM8 2JL
Tel: 01376 780088
1 Wellesley Road, Clacton, Essex CO15 3PP
Tel: 01255 225204
Email: referrals@tces.org.uk

Website: www.tces.org.uk
Schools' Proprietor: Thomas Keaney
Head Teacher: Cheryl Rutter
Appointed: 2007
School type: Coeducational Day
Age range of pupils: 7–19 years

Essex Fresh Start (EFS) is a TCES Group school, providing LA funded day school education for pupils aged 7-19 years whose social, emotional and mental health needs or Autism Spectrum Condition has made it difficult for them to achieve success in a mainstream school. Our pupils often have additional undiagnosed learning or sensory needs and speech, language and communication needs which create a complex set of barriers that must be addressed before they can settle into education.

Pupils attending EFS often require highly personalised learning programmes, focusing on developing their independent study skills. In addition, our Post-16 programmes of study specialise in developing independence, preparation for adult life and life after school.

We know that it is only when pupils enjoy their school that they make real progress. We offer a structured routine in a safe, comfortable environment, which encourages mutual respect and tolerance.

We nurture each child's ambitions by accrediting them with as many achievements as possible to help them make positive choices for their future careers. As a result, 80% of our leavers happily go straight into work, education or training.

In addition to counselling, nurture groups and art and drama therapy, we offer speech and language intervention from our own Speech and Language Therapists, plus clinical assessments for our more hard-to-reach pupils whose needs may need further assessment.

Pupils who need this bespoke intervention are supported through referral to a Clinical Psychologist and a Paediatrician at Consultant level (a service we retain).

A parallel service to our schools, Create Service offers therapeutic education, delivered through a case co-ordination model, to pupils who present (or are at) significant risk to themselves or others and cannot be educated in a school setting.

At EFS, 'Every Child Really Matters'. We delight in seeing our pupils make progress, gain qualifications and achieve skills they never before thought possible.

To find out more about the school and its facilities please come and visit us! Contact us on referrals@tces.org.uk or 020 8543 7878.

East London Independent School (ELIS)

East London
Independent School

Stratford Marsh, Welfare Road,
London E15 4HT
Tel: 020 8555 6737
Custom House, 41 Varley Road, Newham,
London, El6 3NR
Tel: 020 7540 9120

Email: referrals@tces.org.uk
Website: www.tces.org.uk
Schools' Proprietor: Thomas Keaney
Acting Head Teacher: Simon Cartwright
School type: Coeducational Day
Age range of pupils: 7–19 years

East London Independent School (ELIS) is a TCES Group school, providing LA funded day school education for pupils aged 7-19 years whose social, emotional or mental health (SEMH) needs or Autism Spectrum Condition has made it difficult for them to achieve success in a mainstream school. Pupils will often have additional undiagnosed learning or sensory needs and speech, language and communication needs which create a complex set of barriers to learning that must be addressed before the pupil can settle into education.

The school is situated across two sites: Custom House is ELIS' stand-alone dedicated provision for pupils with an Autism Spectrum Condition whose primary autism needs may be part of a complex array of co-morbid diagnoses.

The Stratford Marsh site educates pupils with SEMH needs.

Pupils attending ELIS often require highly personalised learning programmes and can remain for Post-16 programmes of study; specialising in developing independence, preparation for adult life and life after school (including study at college or preparation for the world of work).

Running as a parallel service to ELIS, TCES Group's Create Service offers therapeutic education, delivered through a case co-ordination model, to pupils who present (or are at) significant risk to themselves or others, meaning they cannot be educated in the school environment.

Our pupils are provided with the opportunities and support necessary to

develop their self-esteem, interpersonal and social skills as well as making positive behaviour choices both in and out of school. We firmly believe our pupils will become successful members of society through the knowledge, values and thinking skills learned in the classroom.

Many of our pupils have experienced difficulties, trauma and rejection in their previous school life. We offer the stability that is a necessary pre-requisite for reflecting on their experience and gaining insight, emotional literacy, resilience and empathy with others so their future can be brighter and happier.

To find out more about the school and its facilities please come and visit us! Contact us on referrals@tces.org.uk or 020 8543 7878.

North West London Independent School (NWLIS)

North West London
Independent School

(Founded 2008)
85 Old Oak Common Lane,
Acton, London W3 7DD
Tel: 020 8749 5403
Email: referrals@tces.org.uk
Website: www.tces.org.uk

Schools' Proprietor: Thomas Keaney
Co-Head Teachers:
Katrina Medley and Kevin Parker
School type: Coeducational Day
Age range of pupils: 7–19 years

TCES Group's North West London Independent School (NWLIS) provides LA funded day-school education for pupils aged 7-19 years whose Social, Emotional or Mental Health needs or Autism Spectrum Condition has made it difficult for them to achieve success in a mainstream school. Pupil's co-morbid needs can be complex. Undiagnosed speech, language and communication needs, sensory or learning difficulties can create barriers to learning that must be addressed before the pupil can settle into education.

Our integrated approach to education, health and care, described by Ofsted (who rated every area of the school as 'Outstanding') as innovative and unique, takes each pupil on an individual journey that encourages a love of learning.

Pupils are taught in groups of up to six to ensure each individual receives an intensive level of support, with a Teacher and TA as minimum. TCES Group's

Inclusion Model is embedded at NWLIS, delivered by the Inclusion Manager and Pastoral Co-Ordinator: tutor support, key work, group process, nurture groups and drama therapy, speech and language intervention and clinical assessments are part of the core offer.

The school delivers TCES Group's 5 Part Curriculum, which includes access to support from the Clinical and Therapy Team on an as-needs basis. SALT, OT, Counselling, Drama and Art Therapy are delivered by our in-house team and access to Clinical Psychology and a Paediatrician at Consultant level can be arranged for pupils whose needs require further investigation. *"Pupils rapidly develop their social skills and resilience to manage their emotions through the school's unique therapeutic approach."* Ofsted 2017

Pupils attending NWLIS often need highly personalised learning programmes and can remain for Post-16 programmes of study.

A parallel service to our schools, TCES Group's Create Service offers therapeutic education, delivered through a case co-ordination model, to pupils who present (or are at) significant risk to themselves or others, who cannot be educated in a school setting.

To find out more about the school and its facilities please visit us! In the first instance contact us on referrals@tces.org.uk or 020 8543 7878.

Early Intervention Works

Therapeutic Care and Education for Younger Children

Appletree
treatment centre
growing & learning together

Appletreetreatmentcentre.co.uk

Over 20 years' experience specialising in therapeutic care and education for girls and boys 6 to 12 years old with emotional, health, social and associated learning difficulties, who have suffered: Trauma, Neglect, Physical, Emotional, Sexual abuse.

Therapy in Action - Not Therapy in a Vacuum

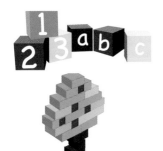

Qualified, Experienced Psychologists and Therapists provide individual therapy for our children, clinical input for each childs' programme, clinical consultation and training for our care, teaching and support teams.

Therapeutic Relationships, Structured 24 hour Programme
Our therapeutically informed teams are skilled at helping our children form healthy attachments, build emotional resilience and confidence, increasing their self-esteem, helping them acquire the skills needed to succeed at home, in life and in school.

Stability and Felt Security are Key to our Children's Success
Once a child is placed with us we will not exclude them, they will only experience planned moves forward. This stability and security helps them develop meaningful relationships, build self esteem and develop resilience.

Successful reintegration to families

After an average of just 2 years and 6 months with us 91% of our leavers in the last 5 years were able to leave residential care/special school provision and return to families or foster families and day schools. The remaining 9% of our leavers continued in residential care to facilitate increased and appropriate contact with their families.

We work alongside adoptive, foster and birth families

All children engage in individual therapy, most continue throughout their stay with us

Close to 100% attendance in education with no unauthorized absence

Appletree

Fell House

Willow Bank

Appletree Treatment Centre has three children's homes

Appletree for up to 12 children

Fell House for up to 8 children

Willow Bank for up to 4 children

We provide high quality therapeutic care and education. We help children who are vulnerable and require a nurturing environment.

Appletree and Fell House each have their own school on site, Willow Bank children attend Appletree school

tel 015395 60253 - Natland, Kendal Cumbria LA9 7QS **- email clair.davies@appletreetc.co.uk**

Everyone within Appletree Treatment Centre has a responsibility for, and is committed to, safeguarding and promoting the welfare of children and young people and for ensuring that they are protected from harm.

Kirby Moor School

Longtown Road, Brampton,
Cumbria CA8 2AB
Tel: 016977 42598
Headteacher: Mrs Catherine Garton

School type: Boys' Residential & Day
Age range of boys: 9–18
No. of pupils enrolled as at 01/01/2017: 40

Kirby Moor School and The Herdley Bank Centre

"Equipping young people to reach their full potential"

Kirby Moor School and The Herdley Bank Centre for pupils aged 9-18 are the two male only school sites owned by North Lakes.

For the past decade North Lakes has succeeded in enabling young people to make above expected progress socially, emotionally and academically. Our schools meet the needs of pupils who face Social, Emotional and Mental Health difficulties. Our 2 school sites specialise in supporting and progressing those who live with: SEMH, Autism spectrum conditions, attachment based disorders and High anxiety.

"The quality of teaching in the nurture group, and pupils' engagement with their learning, are Outstanding...pupils with complex emotional difficulties settle into the expectations of the school in a safe and sheltered environment." – Ofsted Outstanding.

Key Strengths:

- The classroom learning and practical, hands-on activities are underpinned by the content of the National Curriculum.
- The facilities and teaching lead pupils to make outstanding progress academically, socially and in understanding the world around them.
- Individual robust transition programmes help support our pupils for the next stage of their education.
- The location promotes a quiet and calming environment.
- We support pupils who benefit from a highly predictable daily routine, with formal and informal classroom spaces.
- Pupils achieve higher than expected rates of progress.
- Our pupils achieve excellent attendance scores and truly re-engage with

learning – including those with school phobia.

A Word From Our Head:

We work with students who cannot cope in a mainstream school for a variety of reasons, including autism, attachment disorders or anxiety issues. Our aim is to achieve academic, social and emotional progress. We want to prepare our students for future independent lives.

We believe that education is about developing the whole person, by meeting the physical, emotional, spiritual and social, as well as their academic learning needs. We are committed to making a positive impact on young people's lives and helping them to become the person they want to be. Planning engaging activities helps our pupils develop knowledge and skills, resulting in more self-confident pupils ready for more independent futures.

"Pupils make outstanding progress with their learning across a wide range of subjects... Those who remain until the end of Key Stage 4 are well prepared to take up places on a variety of courses in further education. This is a major achievement, given the low starting points with which most enter the school."

Recent Developments:

- Opening the second school site to meet more complex needs
- Adopting a therapeutic model to help support our pupils

Our therapeutic model is based upon the whole brain child approach of Dan Sigal. Staff support pupils adopting the P.A.C.E way of being: Patient, Accepting, Curious and Empathic. A Consultant psychotherapist offers 1:1 play therapy for our young people and staff training. We work in "the here and now". Our approach encourages thinking, aids emotional regulation and helps new choices to be made.

Pupils are supported by individual

programmes and planning. We have developed a very comprehensive assessment and tracking system which ensures that our pupils are always being taught at the level which leads them to thrive. We have an active elected school council, football and cross country teams.

Kirby Moor School gained Outstanding Ofsted in all 4 areas inspected:

Leadership and Management

"...is outstanding ...Subject leaders ensure that pupils have access to appropriate external accreditation at levels suited to their capabilities... pupils aspire to be successful in their education."

Behaviour and Safety of Pupils

"...is outstanding. All enter the school with complex emotional conditions and previous challenging behaviour. Pupils' academic achievements provide outstanding evidence of the improvements in their behaviour over time."

Quality of Teaching

"...is outstanding because it enables pupils to enjoy being in school, to take their work seriously and to achieve outstanding results."

Achievement of Pupils

"...is outstanding. Pupils' progress in English and Mathematics is excellent. They enjoy reading and many demonstrate excellent success in extended writing. Pupils progress rapidly in mathematics and science, and learn to apply a range of skills from their ICT lessons."

Philpots Manor School

(Founded 1959)
West Hoathly, East Grinstead,
West Sussex RH19 4PR
Tel: 01342 810268
Email: info@philpotsmanorschool.co.uk

Website: www.philpotsmanorschool.co.uk
Education Co-ordinator:
Mr Darin Nobes BA (Hons), PGCE, NPQH
School type: Coeducational Boarding
Age range of pupils: 7–19

No. of pupils enrolled as at 01/01/2017: 32
Boys: 21 **Girls:** 11
Fees per annum as at 01/01/2017:
Day: £65,000
Weekly Boarding: £65,000

Founded in 1959 and set in the heart of the Sussex countryside, Philpots Manor School is an independent residential school and training centre offering an academic and social education to children and young adults from 7 to 19 years of age.

The emotional, behavioural, social and communication problems that most of our students display may stem from a learning difficulty, social deprivation, abuse or from a recognised clinical condition, such as epilepsy, a development disorder or autism. Students need to have the potential to function in a social situation. Because of this we do not admit students with severe learning difficulties, severe psychological problems, or with extreme behavioural problems.

Classes usually contain a maximum of six students with one class teacher and at least one class assistant. Our residential units can accommodate either up to six or nine residential students, depending on the size of the unit. We also cater for day students. We offer a 36 week curriculum with residential children returning home at weekends. As well as offering a wide range of academic subjects we also offer horse-riding, pottery, gardening, weaving, art and music. Most pupils are entered for examination at GCSE or Entry Level in English, Maths, Science and Art at a time that is appropriate for each. Up to six GCSE subjects are offered.

OCN courses for Post-16 pupils accredit a wide range of subjects that most pupils study. Continuous assessment by the teachers avoids examinations for those pupils who least benefit from additional stress in their lives. Current courses include stable management and land-based studies.

We have play therapy, counselling, speech, music, Eurythmy and Bothmer Gym as well as a visiting osteopath.

For further information, please visit our website at:

www.philpotsmanorschool.co.uk
or telephone 01342 810268

West Heath School

WEST**HEATH**
REBUILDING LIVES THROUGH EDUCATION

(Founded 1998)

Ashgrove Road, Sevenoaks, Kent TN13 1SR
Tel: 01732 460553
Fax: 01732 456734
Email: admissions@westheathschool.com
Website: www.westheathschool.com
Principal: Mr James Nunns
Appointed: September 2016

School type:
Coeducational Day & Boarding
Age range of pupils: 10–20
No. of pupils enrolled as at 01/01/2017: 135
Fees per annum as at 01/01/2017:
Day: £52,500
Residential supplement: £35,000

Who we are
West Heath is an Ofsted Outstanding and award-winning charity set up specifically to support vulnerable children for whom maintained SEN and mainstream schools were unable to meet needs. The school designation of Social, Emotional and Mental Heath only goes a short way to describing the complexity of need of our students. We have 130 places, 26 of which are residential, therapeutic centre and training facilities, all based on our 32 acre site in Sevenoaks, Kent.

Who we support
Students being referred to us will have seen their mainstream provision break down, some having worked their way through a number of specialist providers unable to meet need or effectively engage with the young person. Others may have come from the Health sector, having been resident in a mental health institution, with limited experiences of a formal learning environment. The SEN diagnosis of our student group is varied, many have a diagnosis of an Austism Spectrum Condition; all our students face challenges with their social communication and interaction with the social world in which they live.

How we support
Our focus is on education, both in terms of academic and personal development. Barriers to learning and the challenges our students face are met rather than avoided, with strategies put in place to support ongoing development. We have a range of therapies on site, working directly with students to meet needs identified from professionals. Therapy is embedded into our curriculum, with Speech and Language and Self Science lessons forming part of the weekly timetable. We have created a number of different learning environments and approaches to education to enable students to successfully access provision and to make learning possible.

What can you study?
We follow the National Curriculum and have a range of options in Key Stage 4. Our facilities are extensive including a professional catering kitchen, sports facilities including tennis courts and swimming pool, expressive arts, including a studio and textiles room. We also offer options including Duke of Edinburgh, animal-based studies and Princes Trust. Study is not limited to the subjects we offer on site, students work toward studying at college with support before finally making the transition to independent study.

The environment
Our school has a number of study environments. All our class sizes are small, with a maximum of six per class in Key Stage 3 and ten in Key Stage 4. Students whom are unable to meet the challenges of a general school structure and require a higher level of support and will be based within our Therapeutic Centre, some of our students are unable to keep themselves safe and therefore will study with our offsite team until they are able to meet the challenges of their daily lives.

After West Heath
We are pleased to say that the majority of our learners have positive and successful outcomes. These may include returning to study in a mainstream environment, gaining full time employment or simply being better placed to meet the personal challenges that had previously been barriers to their becoming active members of society.

The **Roaches** School

The Roaches School

- Children Aged from 7 to 16
- Trained to support social, emotional and behavioural difficulties
- Based on two sites;
- Lower School - Roach End Farm, nestling in the Peak District
- Upper School - Satis House, located in Biddulph to support boys and girls with complex social difficulties.

Therapeutic Centre

- 24 hour therapeutic placement
- Staff are trained to meet young people's therapeutic needs.
- A member of the Community of Communities
- Young People's needs are identified and guided by qualified Psychotherapists
- Individual key workers are allocated to ensure that your child's needs are being addressed.

Testimonial

"My son has been attending the Roaches School for four years. During this time he has been in full time education where previously he had been excluded from two mainstream schools. His self esteem and confidence were very low and he had attempted suicide at 7 years old and often stated he wished he was dead. Since attending The Roaches his confidence has excelled, his behaviour has improved dramatically and he is much happier within himself. This wouldn't have happened without the Roaches staff who give regular feedback, and offer outstanding support to my son and to us as a family. I would recommend the Roaches School to any family who have a child who requires a lot of extra support with their education and their social/ emotional needs and general wellbeing."

The Roaches School has been graded as "Outstanding" by Ofsted since Oct 2010.

Brantwood Specialist School

1 Kenwood Bank, Nether Edge, Sheffield, South Yorkshire S7 1NU
Tel: 0114 258 9062
Email: enquiries@brantwood.rmt.org
Website: www.rmt.org

Headteacher: Christine Haylett
School type: Independent Coeducational Day & Residential
Age range of pupils: 7–19

Brantwood is an independent specialist school for children and young people aged 7-19 with complex difficulties, particularly Autistic Spectrum Condition, including Asperger Syndrome, attachment disorder, PDA (Pathological Demand Avoidance), ADHD and those deemed 'hard to engage'. The school offers daytime and residential provision up to 52 weeks and respite care subject to availability. The school is set in a quiet, leafy neighbourhood with secure grounds and has been graded by Ofsted as 'Good' education provision and 'Outstanding' Care provision.

Curriculum

The curriculum has four distinct strands: Steiner Waldorf Education provides a holistic and inclusive approach to the development of the young person, which emphasises the importance of the distinct ways in which humans relate to the world through their intellectual, emotional and physical activity.

Practical Skills Therapeutic Education (PSTE) enables people to develop transferable skills through real-life purposeful activities, gain confidence through achievement in school, engage in the wider community and achieve a wide range of qualifications according to their interests and skills.

The National Curriculum ensures that students can achieve appropriate nationally-recognised qualifications, including NOCN, BTEC, GCSE and A level.

Individual Therapies, such as Speech and Language, Movement (Eurythmy), Massage, Art and Occupational Therapies, are incorporated into each young person's education plan as appropriate. The team of therapists work closely with staff and parents/carers at all times.

Brantwood Specialist School provides:

- Small class sizes and house groups of five students or fewer according to a student's ability and need
- Healthy organic food and nutritional education
- Engagement with the local community and help in planning leisure time and outdoor activities
- Involvement in festivals, other celebrations and social and cultural events
- Opportunities to develop and improve living skills for both day and residential students

Residential

Residential provision is in the school's central location within the local community, providing consistency, warmth and positive role modelling to develop the young person's skills and potential. Students are actively engaged in leisure activities, community participation and planning and cooking a healthy organic diet.

'Skilled teaching, together with sensitive care and therapeutic support, meet pupils' complex social, emotional and behavioral needs well. Pupils are also well supported by teaching assistants and key works. As a result, pupils' behavior, personal development and self-esteem improve markedly during their time here.' Ofsted 2016

Admissions

For enquiries or Admissions, please contact us on 0114 250 0036, or email admissions@brantwood.rmt.org. School placements are available throughout the year.

Brantwood Specialist School Registered No: 373/6002. Children's Home Registered No: SC423753. Ruskin Mill Trust is an educational charity No: 1137167.

Schools and colleges specialising in learning difficulties (including dyslexia/SPLD)

Bredon School

Pull Court, Bushley, Tewkesbury,
Gloucestershire GL20 6AH
Tel: 01684 293156
Fax: 01684 298008
Email: enquiries@bredonschool.co.uk

Website: www.bredonschool.org
Head Teacher: Mr Koen Claeys
School type:
Coeducational Boarding & Day
Age range of pupils: 7–18

'Come Alive & Thrive'

Bredon School in Gloucestershire supports students with dyslexia, dyspraxia and other specific learning needs to achieve their potential in a caring, nurturing environment.

Offering boarding and day facilities, the school is situated in an idyllic 84 acre rural estate and holds CReSTeD 'Dyslexia Specialist Provision' status; an accolade which recognises our outstanding provision for children with dyslexia and dyspraxia – including onsite Speech & Language Therapy, access to assistive technologies and highly qualified specialist staff.

We pride ourselves on our small class sizes and our warm and encouraging atmosphere.

All pupils benefit from multi-sensory teaching, including access to a School Farm where students learn basic animal care and help to feed the livestock and maintain the estate. Younger pupils have the opportunity to learn outdoors also, on the School Farm and in the dedicated woodland classroom, learning basic bush craft skills and understanding more about nature and habitats.

A wide-ranging curriculum includes practical vocational courses such as BTECs in catering & hospitality and engineering, as well as GCSE and A Level choices. Bredon also benefits from having its own onsite CISCO academy which teaches programming and networking skills suited

to those looking for technical ICT careers in the future.

All students make progress in the friendly and supportive environment and as they grow in self confidence and self belief, they are able to achieve impressive academic results.

An array of extra curricular activities, including drama, the arts and music, cookery, outdoor education trips, a Combined Cadet Force, the Duke of Edinburgh award scheme, clay and air rifle shooting, climbing, canoeing and traditional team sports, means every student finds an area in which to shine.

If you'd like to visit us to know more, please do get in touch.

Ruskin Mill College

The Fisheries, Horsley, Gloucestershire
GL6 0PL
Tel: 01453 837502
Fax: 01453 837506
Email: enquiries@rmc.rmt.org

Website: www.rmt.org
Principal: Paul Garnault
School type:
Coeducational Day & Residential
Age range of pupils: 16–25

Ruskin Mill College, a long-standing and successful independent college in Gloucestershire, offers over 100 places to young people with complex learning and behavioural difficulties, mental health issues and autistic spectrum disorders, including Asperger Syndrome.

Practical Skills Therapeutic Education

Set in 140 acres including a biodynamic farm, woodlands and a fishery, the college is operated by Ruskin Mill Trust, whose internationally renowned *Practical Skills Therapeutic Education* method offers young people a unique opportunity to learn and develop transferable skills through meaningful, hands-on, real-life activities and accredited courses.

The college provides an extensive range of nutritional, therapeutic and medical support. Each core element of the educational cycle is designed to establish active and positive relationships with nature, people and the community through a holistic approach to human development and supports three key stages: overcoming barriers to learning, becoming skilled, and being ready to engage and give back to the community.

Integrated Learning for Living and Work

The college offers a personalised pre-entry assessment leading to an individualised learning and development programme to work towards agreed outcomes. A rich and varied curriculum offers exciting opportunities to develop communication, social, work and living skills, leading to increased independence. Activities include practical land-based and traditional craft activities including animal husbandry, fish farming, woodland management, horticulture, catering, drama and art, with communication and functional skills embedded throughout the day and residential provision. At Gables Farm and the market garden, students help to grow and harvest

healthy biodynamic food and prepare meals in the college canteens, café and households.

Accreditation and Transition

Courses are accredited through the Regulated Qualifications Framework and students will also prepare for work competency through a wide range of internal and external work experience. Qualifications include NVQs and BTECs. The college's cultural programme offers students further opportunities to develop their social and work skills. Throughout their placement, students work with a dedicated transition team and engage with their acquired transferable skills to prepare for life after college.

Residential Provision

Students live in family or team houses in the local community which offer the

consistency, warmth and positive role modelling that some young adults need to develop their living skills, achieve greater independence and re-imagine their potential. Students can progress onto placements in training flats or semi-independent living, where they have the opportunity to take greater responsibility for themselves. Ruskin Mill College takes referrals throughout the year and offers up to 52-week placements.

Admissions

For all initial enquiries please contact the Admissions Team on 01453 837502 or by email: admissions@rmc.rmt.org

Ruskin Mill Trust is an educational charity and draws its inspiration from the insights of Rudolf Steiner, John Ruskin and William Morris. Charity No: 1137167.

The Unicorn School

(Founded 1991)

20 Marcham Road, Abingdon, Oxfordshire OX14 1AA
Tel: 01235 530222
Email: info@unicornoxford.co.uk
Website: www.unicornoxford.co.uk
Headteacher: Mr. Andrew Day BEd (Hons) University of Wales (Cardiff)

School type: Coeducational Day
Age range of pupils: 6–16
No. of pupils enrolled as at 01/01/2017: 75
Fees per annum as at 01/01/2017:
Information on application.

The Unicorn School is a leading, specialist day school for pupils aged 6 years and up, who have dyslexia, dyspraxia, dyscalculia, or who need support with Speech and Language. The school introduced GCSE education in September 2016, making us unique as the only dyslexia-specialist day school in Oxfordshire to provide GCSE education. The Unicorn School has a proven record of providing specialist education for both girls and boys from Year 2 and above, and pupils now have the opportunity to complete their secondary education at our school.

The Unicorn School provides a nurturing environment in which every pupil is helped to build self-confidence, appreciate their learning difficulties and develop their own personal learning style. Our teachers are specialists in working with dyslexia and related difficulties, equipping our pupils with the strategies for learning that will enable them to succeed in their future education and beyond.

We warmly welcome you to visit us at The Unicorn School to discuss how we can support your child's needs. To join us at our upcoming open mornings, or to book an individual visit please contact our Registrar on 01235 530222, or registrar@unicornoxford.co.uk.

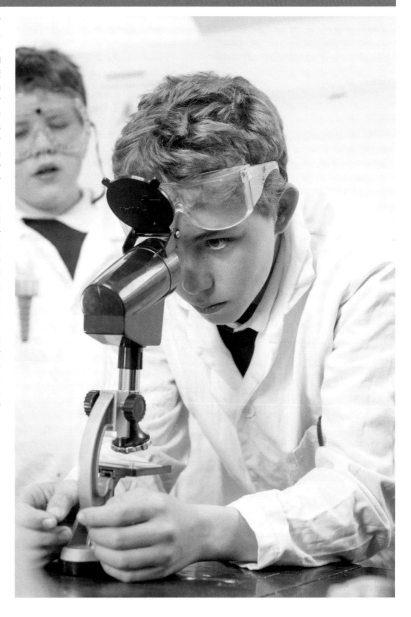

I CAN'S Dawn House School

helps children communicate

(Founded 1974)

Helmsley Road, Rainworth, Mansfield, Nottinghamshire NG21 0DQ
Tel: 01623 795361
Fax: 01623 491173
Email: dawnhouse@ican.notts.sch.uk
Website: www.dawnhouseschool.org.uk
Principal: Jenny McConnell

School type:
Coeducational Day & Residential
Age range of pupils: 5–19
No. of pupils enrolled as at 01/01/2017: 79
Fees per annum as at 01/01/2017:
On request

I CAN's Dawn House School is a specialist speech, language and communication school for children and young people aged 5-19 years. We are committed to the highest quality education, therapy and care for pupils with speech and language disorder or Asperger's Syndrome and associated difficulties.

At Dawn House School the pupils receive the specialist intensive support that they need. We are able to cater for a number of other difficulties which are commonly associated with communication difficulties, including: learning difficulties, behavioural difficulties, problems with attention and memory, motor dyspraxia, sensory difficulties, autistic spectrum difficulties and emotional problems.

Pupils' individual needs are assessed and addressed through curriculum planning and assessment and IEP planning. Speech and language therapists and teachers plan lessons that meet two sets of targets: curriculum learning objectives and specific speech and/or language aims. For pupils who need more specific focused work to develop their speech and language skills, individual or small group sessions are timetabled during the school day.

Our school makes use of Makaton to support children's learning. The school also promotes the use of a range of voice output devices to support individual pupil's communication.

A full-time Occupational Therapist and OT assistants work within some lessons and with individual pupils on more focused, intensive work where necessary. The Family and Community Liaison Worker supports pupils' families and is a key link between home and school.

Residential Care at Dawn House School aims to ensure the emotional and physical well-being of our boarding pupils through an extended curriculum. The school can provide opportunities for non-residential young people to benefit from extended days and overnight stays. The care staff organise a range of activities out of school hours.

Dawn House was rated as an 'Outstanding' school by Ofsted in March 2014 and January 2015, its residential care inspection also gained an 'Outstanding' rating in February 2016. The inspectors found pupils at the school achieve exceptionally well and all pupils make outstanding progress whatever their individual needs or disabilities.

The Further Education department caters for students (16-19 years) who have a communication difficulty or Asperger's Syndrome. The provision is based at the Dawn House site but has very close partnerships with Vision West Notts and Portland two local FE colleges, local employers and training providers.

Dawn House School is part of I CAN, the children's communication charity (www.ican.org.uk).

Kisimul School

(Founded 1977)

The Old Vicarage, 61 High Street,
Swinderby, Lincoln, Lincolnshire LN6 9LU
Tel: 01522 868279
Fax: 01522 866000
Email: admissions@kisimul.co.uk
Website: www.kisimul.co.uk
Director of Education:

Mr Danny Carter BA(Hons), MA, MEd
School type: Coeducational
Independent Residential Special School
Age range of pupils: 8–19
No. of pupils enrolled as at 01/01/2017: 60
Fees per annum as at 01/01/2017:
On application

Kisimul School is one of the UK's leading independent residential special schools, offering a homely and safe environment for children who have severe learning difficulties, challenging behaviour, autism and global developmental delay.

Kisimul School offers residential education, care and leisure programmes at both our upper and lower school, for up to 52 weeks of the year, for pupils aged 8 to 19 years. The school is registered with the Department for Education and Ofsted. Limited day placements are also offered at both school sites.

The name Kisimul, pronounced 'kishmul', was taken from Kisimul Castle, which overlooks one of the safest harbours in the British Isles. Like its namesake, Kisimul School offers a safe haven, providing care and protection for its pupils whilst preparing them for the journey ahead into adulthood.

Kisimul School was founded in 1977 in a comfortable Georgian house (known today as the Old Vicarage) set in four acres within the small Lincolnshire village of Swinderby. Facilities at the Old Vicarage include an indoor heated swimming pool, large playground, soft play areas with ball pool and multi-sensory rooms for relaxation and stimulation.

In 2003, our upper school, Acacia Hall opened, offering the same standard of exceptional care and education within grounds adapted and utilised in a way to reflect the older age group. Acacia Hall offers riding stables, an adventure playground, collection of small farm animals and an area dedicated to horticulture.

Kisimul School has opened an additional school, Woodstock House, in Long Ditton, Surrey. Woodstock House received its first pupils in April 2008, and

again offers the same quality of care and education for pupils aged 8 to 19 years. Kisimul School has developed this site to be a mirror image of its existing school operations, using the same teaching methods and ethos.

Kisimul School's mission is to continuously strive for excellence in the care and education of its pupils, with a vision to have the best assisted living environment.

The school provides a caring, consistent, safe and supportive environment in which its young people can flourish and develop their skills in order to fully realise their individual potential. Residential and school staff work closely together to enable the pupils to progress in their personal development and learning. The 24-hour approach incorporates a wide range of activities to enrich the learning experiences of all pupils, helping them to learn to communicate and cooperate more effectively with others and enabling them to grow in confidence, self-esteem and independence.

The highly structured school curriculum aims to address the very specific needs of our pupils, by providing every opportunity for them to enjoy their education and develop their skills, knowledge and understanding through practical and functional learning experiences.

Classes are small and matched to learning profiles alongside the dynamics of peers. There is a high staffing ratio which reflects the complex needs of learners. The curriculum incorporates the National Curriculum (lower school) and an accreditation based vocational learning model is a feature at the upper school. An integrated therapeutic programme includes Psychology, Speech and Language, Music Therapy and Occupational Therapy (Sensory

Integration) is part of the core provision of the school.

A key priority is to develop our pupils' communication skills and since many are non-verbal we teach the alternative and augmentative systems of Makaton signing and PECS (Picture Exchange Communication System) alongside vocalisations and speech.

External accreditation is gained through a wide variety of ASDAN 'Towards Independence' programmes and the Duke of Edinburgh's Award Scheme.

Kisimul School works closely with the parents, carers and professionals from its placing authorities to ensure the highest possible standards of care and education.

Kisimul School is committed to the view that all people are entitled to equality of opportunity regardless of ability or disability, gender or chosen gender, age, status, religion, belief, nationality, ethnic origins or sexual orientation.

For further information, including exciting job opportunities within Kisimul School, please visit our website at www.kisimul.co.uk or contact us at the address above.

Pield Heath House School

Pield Heath House School

(Founded 1901)

Pield Heath Road, Uxbridge,
Middlesex UB8 3NW
Tel: 01895 258507
Fax: 01895 256497
Email: admin@pieldheathschool.org.uk
Website: pieldheathschool.org.uk
Executive Principal: Sister Julie Rose

School type: Co-educational Day and
Short Break/Residential
Age range of pupils: 7–19
No. of pupils enrolled as at 01/01/2017: 96
Fees per annum as at 01/01/2017:
Upon application

Pield Heath House is a non-maintained school in West London for young people aged 7-19. Judged 'Outstanding' by Ofsted at our last three inspections we offer day, residential and short break provision for those with moderate to severe learning difficulties, complex learning and behavioural needs, including autistic spectrum disorders and associated speech, language and communication difficulties.

Each of our students has a personalised education programme which addresses their specific needs to live a fulfilled life in a challenging and changing world. Our multi-disciplinary team facilitates the learning process both in classroom settings and in the home environment for those who are resident.

Therapies: our therapeutic service includes Music, Dance, Speech and OT and the team of experienced therapists work alongside educational and residential staff in supporting the development of each individual student.

Curriculum: a comprehensive programme based on the National Curriculum is offered at Key Stage 2 and 3. Small class groups, with a high level of staff support, enable our students to access a suitably individualised curriculum. Statutory requirements at Key Stage 4 include the core subjects of English, Maths, ICT, RE, Citizenship and Science.

For students aged 14-19, the curriculum is structured to enable them to acquire the necessary skills to develop independence in their adult lives. Programmes are designed to promote their personal, social and vocational skills, and they have the opportunity to access nationally accredited programmes including ASDAN, OCR , NOCN and Btec qualifications. Performing Arts is a key element of the post 16 curriculum offer.

Inclusion Hub: for those students who are unable to access learning in a classroom environment we have an Inclusion Hub which provides individual spaces for learning. Each student is supported with a highly personalised timetable and follows an individualised curriculum, closely related to their interests and abilities. Here staff provide support to develop the skills to allow the student to reintegrate, over time, back into the classroom.

Thrive: we are proud to be a Thrive accredited school and follow its principles to help support the emotional and social development of our students. Our Inclusion Support Team works with staff, therapists and parents to deliver a programme for each student to help improve their confidence, behaviour and social interactions.

Pield Heath House accommodates a wide range of learning requirements; the provision is flexible and tailored to optimise individual rates of progress and attainment. This encourages the development of confident, well adjusted, sensitive and independent young people able to live life to the full.

The Link Primary School

(Founded 1964)
138 Croydon Road, Beddington,
Croydon, Surrey CR0 4PG
Tel: 020 8688 5239
Fax: 020 8667 0828
Email: office@linkprim.co.uk

Website: www.linkprim.co.uk
Head Teacher: Mrs Sandy Turner
School type: Coeducational Day
Age range of pupils: 4–11
No. of pupils enrolled as at 01/01/2017: 50

The Link Primary School provides specialist teaching and therapy for up to 50 children aged 4 to 11 years whose primary need is speech, language and communication. Some pupils may also have additional learning, sensory or physical needs. The School has been recognised by Ofsted as 'outstanding' since 2008 and draws upon over 50 years of experience.

The School has a warm, safe, friendly and nurturing environment which helps children to learn, express their ideas, communicate, develop friendships and become confident citizens. Small classes with high adult to child ratio enable children to settle quickly, move confidently around the school and learn the daily routines which form an integral part of school life.

Children enjoy a wide range of school facilities including an ICT suite, library, fully equipped hall, food technology room, art room and music room. During playtime they have access to climbing frames, sandpit, trikes and other outdoor toys and games.

A brand new teaching block with facilities for enhanced therapy was completed in September 2015 and also provides the children with larger classrooms and additional outdoor learning opportunities including a sensory garden and kitchen allotment.

We foster close relationships with our local community to enable our children to gain valuable life experiences and encourage children to play an active role in extra-curricular activities such as dance and athletics club. A range of off-site activities are available including horse riding and for the older children the opportunity to experience a residential educational visit.

Establishing and developing relationships with parents and carers is a central part of our philosophy. Children learn best when the school and parents work together and we value the contribution that parents make to our school and endeavour to provide many opportunities where parents are involved in school life.

Abingdon House School

Abingdon
House School

(Founded 2005)
Broadley Terrace, London, NW1 6LG
Tel: 020 3750 5526
Email: ahs@abingdonhouseschool.co.uk
Website: www.abingdonhouseschool.co.uk

Head Teacher: Mr Roy English
Appointed: 2013
School type: Coeducational Day
Age range of pupils: 5–16

'Expanding unique talents'
Abingdon House School is an independent day school for students with specific learning difficulties including dyslexia, dyspraxia, speech and language needs and autistic spectrum conditions and is CReSTeD-accredited as a 'Specialist Provision' school.

We deliver a bespoke education developing and expanding the unique talents of each and every one of our students, whilst at the same time addressing any educational challenges that they may face. These challenges may cause many problems, but they can be overcome. Once at Abingdon, the change in a student's self esteem is marked. As they achieve in academic and creative areas, a belief in their own abilities grows and fuels further success.

Our environment is based on understanding a student's individual needs, nurturing their academic and social development and caring for their well being. We understand the importance of discipline and boundaries and the school fosters a sense of pride and belonging.

The school has a team of Speech and Language Therapists, Occupational Therapists, Physiotherapists and Music and Play Therapists. Together with specialist Literacy and Maths teachers, these staff make up the 'Special Provision Team'. Therapy is integrated into the school day, with therapists working alongside teaching staff within classrooms and also at lunch and break times. We also offer therapy on a need-led basis in small group, paired and individual sessions.

Our teaching style is multi-sensory and the school day is organised around a regular routine, with plenty of opportunity for outdoor time, access to the arts and the opportunity to perform and take part in sports and fitness activities.

"The children (are) completely involved in their own learning and given ample opportunity to give their opinion and to record their work in a variety of ways. Above all... a sense of enjoyment and fun". CReSTeD inspector.

The Independent School (TIS)

THE
INDEPENDENT
SCHOOL

23-31 Beavor Lane, Ravenscourt Park,
Hammersmith, London W6 9AR
Tel: 020 3637 7574
Email: admin@tis-london.org

Website: www.tis-london.org
Principal: Ms Tanya Moran
School type: Coeducational Day
Age range of pupils: 11–16

'Independence of thought, independence of mind, independence of learning… achieving independence beyond our doors'.

The Independent School, London, is a small, friendly, mainstream secondary school for boys and girls aged 11-16 years old.

The School offers a close-knit community and the opportunity to learn in a modern, bright and inspiring environment. We have a staff-to-student ratio of 1:4 and a maximum class size of 8 students. This ensures that each individual's needs are catered for and that their progress is carefully monitored.

We welcome students with mild specific learning needs such as dyslexia and dyspraxia, together with those who perform better in a more individualised environment. We believe that learning differences should never be seen as a barrier to academic success.

Through individually tailored teaching, together with the TIS Enriched Skills Programme, the School aims to equip every student, regardless of learning style, with the confidence, skills and self-belief necessary to fulfil their potential at GCSE and beyond.

We provide guidance and support with personal organisation skills, such as touch typing, study skills and time management, and each student benefits from a designated teacher mentor that they meet with regularly to reflect on their learning, set targets and importantly, to ensure that their time at The Independent School is happy and productive.

We have a strong focus on the development of Information Technology (IT) skills, making the curriculum more accessible and engaging. Students are linked to our IT structure via their own individual tablet, enabling us to draw on the best IT educational resources available.

We help all our students build the confidence, skills and self belief necessary to achieve independence beyond our doors.

If you'd like to find out more, we'd love to hear from you.

Kisimul School – Woodstock House

(Opened 2008)

Woodstock Lane North, Long Ditton,
Surbiton, Surrey KT6 5HN
Tel: 020 8335 2570
Fax: 020 8335 2571
Email: admissions@kisimul.co.uk
Website: www.kisimul.co.uk
Director of Education:

Mr Danny Carter BA(Hons), MA, MEd
School type: Coeducational
Independent Residential Special School
Age range of pupils: 8–19
No. of pupils enrolled as at 01/01/2017: 40
Fees per annum as at 01/01/2017:
On application

Kisimul School is one of the UK's leading independent residential special schools, offering a homely and safe environment for children who have severe learning difficulties, challenging behaviour, autism and global developmental delay.

Kisimul School offers residential education, care and leisure programmes at both our upper and lower school, for up to 52 weeks of the year, for pupils aged 8 to 19 years. The school is registered with the Department for Education and Ofsted. Limited day placements are also offered at both school sites.

The name Kisimul, pronounced 'kishmul', was taken from Kisimul Castle, which overlooks one of the safest harbours in the British Isles. Like its namesake, Kisimul School offers a safe haven, providing care and protection for its pupils whilst preparing them for the journey ahead into adulthood.

The original Kisimul School was founded in 1977 in a comfortable Georgian house (known today as the Old Vicarage) set in four acres within the small Lincolnshire village of Swinderby. Facilities at the Old Vicarage include an indoor heated swimming pool, large playground, soft play areas with ball pool and multi-sensory rooms for relaxation and stimulation.

In 2003, our upper school, Acacia Hall opened, offering the same standard of exceptional care and education within grounds adapted and utilised in a way to reflect the older age group. Acacia Hall offers riding stables, an adventure playground, collection of small farm animals and an area dedicated to horticulture.

Woodstock House received its first pupils in April 2008, and again offers the same quality of care and education for pupils aged 8 to 19 years. Kisimul School has developed this site to be a mirror image of its existing school operations, using the same teaching methods and ethos.

Woodstock House is situated within 8.1 acres of tranquil countryside, offering space to develop in a safe and secure environment. Woodstock House is within easy access from the M25 via the A3.

Kisimul School's mission is to continuously strive for excellence in the care and education of its pupils, with a vision to have the best assisted living environment.

The school provides a caring, consistent, safe and supportive environment in which its young people can flourish and develop their skills in order to fully realise their individual potential. Residential and school staff work closely together to enable the pupils to progress in their personal development and learning. The 24-hour approach incorporates a wide range of activities to enrich the learning experiences of all pupils, helping them to learn to communicate and cooperate more effectively with others and enabling them to grow in confidence, self-esteem and independence.

The highly structured school curriculum aims to address the very specific needs of our pupils, by providing every opportunity for them to enjoy their education and develop their skills, knowledge and understanding through practical and functional learning experiences.

Classes are small and matched to learning profiles alongside the dynamics of peers. There is a high staffing ratio which reflects the complex needs of learners. The curriculum incorporates the National Curriculum (lower school) and an accreditation based vocational learning model is a feature at the upper school. An integrated therapeutic programme includes Psychology, Speech and Language, Music Therapy and Occupational Therapy (Sensory Integration) is part of the core provision of the school.

A key priority is to develop our pupils' communication skills and since many are non-verbal we teach the alternative and augmentative systems of Makaton signing and PECS (Picture Exchange Communication System) alongside vocalisations and speech.

External accreditation is gained through a wide variety of ASDAN 'Towards Independence' programmes and the Duke of Edinburgh's Award Scheme.

Kisimul School works closely with the parents, carers and professionals from its placing authorities to ensure the highest possible standards of care and education.

Kisimul School is committed to the view that all people are entitled to equality of opportunity regardless of ability or disability, gender or chosen gender, age, status, religion, belief, nationality, ethnic origins or sexual orientation.

For further information, including exciting job opportunities within Kisimul School, please visit our website at www. kisimul.co.uk or contact us at the address above.

Moor House School & College

(Founded 1947)

Mill Lane, Hurst Green, Oxted, Surrey RH8 9AQ
Tel: 01883 712271
Fax: 01883 716722
Email: admissionsteam@
moorhouseschool.co.uk;
info@moorhouseschool.co.uk
Website: www.moorhouseschool.co.uk

Principal: Mrs H A Middleton
School type:
Coeducational Day & Residential
Age range of pupils: 7–19
No. of pupils enrolled as at 01/01/2017: 129
Fees per annum as at 01/01/2017:
On request

Our vision is of a society where speech and language disabilities do not prevent a young person from achieving his or her learning and communication potential, building an independent life and contributing positively to society.
"Quality of teaching: Outstanding" – Ofsted 2014

Moor House is a non-maintained Special Needs School and College, a registered charity and a world class centre of excellence, providing specialist education, therapy and residential care for children and young people aged 7-19 with language and related communication difficulties.

The School provides a nurturing environment where the holistic educational needs of each individual child can be met. Our core service is to provide integrated teaching, therapy and residential care services for students with the most complex and severe speech and language impairments. One-to-one assessments, small class sizes, highly specific and bespoke therapy, and an extended curriculum in a therapeutic environment, not only enable children and young people to attain their highest educational and communication potential whilst at Moor House, but also develop much higher levels of independent living skills, self-expression, and self-esteem for the rest of their lives.

At the time of its establishment in 1947, Moor House was the only school of its type in the UK that offered a pioneering range of specialised therapeutic and educational techniques for children with severe speech and language disorders, and many techniques currently used, both in this country and abroad, originated at Moor House School & College. Innovative

work in many areas of speech and language therapy and in teaching methods continues to place the School & College at the forefront of research, development and practice in the education of children and young people with communication disorders.

Learning

Students are taught in small classes by teachers with experience working with children and young people with language difficulties. Adapted language and specialist visual approaches are used so that children can understand and develop the language that they need for learning.

Speech and language therapists work closely with teachers to understand and support each child's difficulties and strengths. Teachers plan and deliver lessons collaboratively with speech and language therapists, and work together

to help students develop curriculum language.

Curriculum

An adapted National Curriculum is taught at Moor House and learning is tailored to the students' strengths while helping them with areas of difficulty, and there is a particular emphasis on development of language, literacy, life and social skills.

Progress and Qualifications

Our results show that overall our students make excellent progress. Many students take GCSE qualifications, which we offer in English Language, English Literature, Mathematics, Science, ICT, History, Fine Art and Ceramics. We also offer Functional Skills qualifications in English and Maths, vocational qualifications such as Home Cooking Skills at Levels 1 and 2, the AQA Unit Award Scheme in Science, and Entry Level qualifications in subjects such as English, Maths, ICT, DT and Music.

The College's objective is to support each student to gain vocational qualifications, make confident and appropriate life choices and to be prepared for the next stage of their adult life.

Outcomes for students in the sixth form provision are outstanding with many achieving level 2 and 3 vocational qualifications.

Speech and Language Therapy

Speech and language therapy is an essential part of a student's week at Moor House and is integrated throughout their day. The speech and language therapists work with students individually, in groups, as well as in the classroom where lessons such as English are jointly planned and delivered.

Each therapist has a small caseload of students. The intensive therapy programme may focus on learning skills, developing strategies to communicate, as well as supporting the student to understand their own strengths and difficulties. Skills for talking in everyday situations, language for lessons, social skills, friendship skills and independence skills are all key parts of a student's programme.

At Moor House, we use specialist methods where appropriate such as Electropalatography (EPG), Shape Coding by Susan Ebbels ® and signing. The department strives to keep up to date with new research and the team is continually developing therapy methods.

Occupational Therapy

At Moor House, Occupational Therapy (OT) is provided to help students with important skills needed in everyday life to maximise potential for learning and independence. These include fine and gross motor skills, visual perceptual skills, visual motor skills, alertness and sensory processing skills, as well as organisational skills and independence and life skills. OTs work on these skills to help students at Moor House to develop their independence in activities of daily living such as handwriting, touch typing, doing up a tie or shoe laces, travel or cooking skills. Strategies are provided to develop sensory processing in lessons to manage and improve attention control.

Moor House School & College has a team of OTs and a fully equipped OT suite which includes sensory integration equipment.

Residential Care

Our Residential Care has been classed as Outstanding by Ofsted in each of the last five years, and recent developments have seen the creation of a home from home residential village on campus. The Care team work to provide our students with a homely environment whilst they stay with us. The team also works closely with the teaching and therapy staff to ensure that each child receives the support needed.

Moor House pioneering Research and Development

Our speech and language therapists are engaged in cutting edge research in all areas of speech and language disabilities. We work with Universities and share methods developed at Moor House with other therapists through journals and presentations. Moor House is deservedly held in high regard by academics and specialists in the field. For a list of pioneering and authentic research undertaken by our researchers, please see www.moorhouseschool.co.uk/research.

Moor House Training and Information for the wider community

The professional team of speech and language teachers, therapists and researchers at Moor House also provides a range of outreach, information and training services in speech and language disorders for parents and the wider community.

I CAN's Meath School

I CAN

helps children communicate

(Founded 1982)

Brox Road, Ottershaw, Surrey KT16 0LF
Tel: 01932 872302
Fax: 01932 875180
Email: meath@meath-ican.org.uk
Website: www.meathschool.org.uk
Headteacher: Janet Dunn OBE, MA, AdvDipSpecEduc

Appointed: September 2003
School type:
Coeducational Day & Residential
No. of pupils enrolled as at 01/01/2017: 60
Fees per annum as at 01/01/2017:
On request

I CAN's Meath School is a residential (weekly) and day school providing teaching, therapy and care to children aged 4-11 years with speech and language disorders or Asperger Syndrome and associated difficulties (attention control, fine and gross motor co-ordination problems, mild visual and/or hearing impairments, medical needs and social interaction problems). Meath School is a unique proactive specialised learning community. The school and care settings have been recognised by Ofsted as continuously 'outstanding' since 2008 and are on the Ofsted Outstanding Providers list.

Children with associated difficulties may also benefit from the provision. These include some degree of learning difficulty, attention control, fine and gross motor co-ordination problems, mild visual and/or hearing impairments, medical needs and social interaction problems.

Learning and achieving
All pupils are taught within a dynamic broad, balanced and relevant curriculum, based on the National Primary Curriculum (2014). There is a strong underpinning focus on thinking and learning skills which can be transferred throughout different subjects and into real life situations. Four levels of the curriculum are delivered at a modified pace and are highly differentiated to meet the needs of all pupils with severe and complex language needs. Strong multi-professional processes for assessment, planning, teaching and reviewing ensure that each pupil makes outstanding progress in language skills and learning.

Classes are primarily based on pupils' language comprehension levels, also taking account of curriculum attainments, learning and social needs. In this way

we know behaviour and progress are maximised.

Class groups can include between eight and twelve pupils, across year groups and Key Stages.

Each class has a core team of teacher, speech and language therapist and at least one learning support assistant. The speech and language therapy team and occupational therapist department are a critical and integral part of the pupils' education. Specialist teaching is offered in music, art, craft, design and PE.

Partnership with parents
Meath School staff collaborate closely with parents, sharing successes and helping with any concerns or difficulties at home. The Family Support Worker acts as a link between home and school and will visit families where needed.

The School
Meath School is housed in fine Victorian buildings and the site includes a modern teaching block, gym, music, art and cookery rooms, ICT suite, small swimming pool, school field, activity play areas and a woodland park with bike track. The school has a programme of lunch clubs, after school clubs, trumpet tuition and a summer holiday club.

Meath School is part of I CAN, the children's communication charity (www.ican.org.uk), and is an integral part of the I CAN Centre in Surrey. It belongs to a local confederation of mainstream schools. The Centre offers holistic multi-disciplinary independent two day specialist assessment services, training and outreach programmes.

More House School

(Founded 1939)
Moons Hill, Frensham, Farnham, Surrey

GU10 3AP
Tel: 01252 792303
Fax: 01252 797601
Email:
schooloffice@morehouseschool.co.uk
Website: www.morehouseschool.co.uk
Headmaster: Jonathan Hetherington
BA(Hons), MSc(ed), QTS

School type: Boys' Boarding & Day
Age range of boys: 8–18
No. of pupils enrolled as at 01/01/2017: 470
Fees per annum as at 01/01/2017:
Day: £12,792 – £17,931
Weekly Boarding: £19,938 – £25,764
Full Boarding: £22,029 – £27,906

Founded in 1939, More House School is an independent day and boarding school with more than 460 boys on roll, making it the largest specialist school of its type in the country. Many boys travel long distances to attend the school, which is currently used for placements by 30 local authorities. The school has also been recognised as one of the top 600 schools in the country for GCSE Music by the Incorporated Society of Musicians.

We are dedicated to helping boys with a range of learning difficulties and styles, who require a small, supportive learning environment in which to flourish.

Our aim is to help each boy who joins us, achieve, in the widest possible sense, more than he, or his parents, ever expected. This is accomplished by knowing a great deal about each student – his strengths as well as his difficulties. For his strengths, he must first be helped to identify them and, eventually, change them into a marketable form. His difficulties will not be static. We are mindful that we must be alert to changes caused by a student's own development, those of society and by the curriculum and make sure that each of our students is equipped to meet them.

The Learning Development Centre (LDC) is a purpose-built area, housed centrally in the school, where all therapy is delivered by fully qualified therapists and specialist tutors. Almost all boys in the school attend lessons weekly for between 2 and 8 half hour sessions, with support continuing through GCSE and A level year where necessary. Attendance in the LDC forms part of each boy's timetable, removing any need to miss lessons.

The work of the Learning Development Centre is fully integrated into school life, with many staff being form tutors and mentors. The pooling of shared expertise within the inclusive staff body of the school – highly qualified Speech and Language Therapists, Occupational Therapists, Literacy Therapists, Numeracy Therapists, Cognitive Behavioural Therapist, Adolescent Psychotherapeutic Counsellor, as well as classroom subject-specialist teachers experienced in supporting pupils with a broad range of learning difficulties.

More House School is a transformative experience for the students who attend and also their families, our students' journey's will vary hugely from that of their mainstream peer group, but the end result will be the same. Academic success and a platform with which to move on to the next stage of their lives.

St Catherine's School

St Catherine's School
For Speech, Language and Communication Needs

(Founded 1983)

Grove Road, Ventnor, Isle of Wight PO38 1TT

Tel: 01983 852722

Fax: 01983 857219

Email: general@stcatherines.org.uk

Website: www.stcatherines.org.uk

Principal: Mrs R Weldon

Appointed: September 2016

School type: Coeducational Boarding

Age range of pupils: 7–19

No. of pupils enrolled as at 01/01/2017: 53

Boys: 40 **Girls:** 13 **Sixth Form:** 26

No. of boarders: 30

Fees per annum as at 01/01/2017:

On request

St Catherine's offers specialist education, therapy and residential care to students with **speech, language, communication** and occupational therapy needs, and associated conditions such as **autism, dyspraxia** and **dyslexia**. Our small school provides a nurturing and supportive environment for our students – a mixture of day, weekly and termly boarders – who come from across the UK.

What makes St Catherine's special?

- Our education, therapy and care department provide a tailored package of individualised support for each student.
- Intensive speech, language and occupational therapy is integral to the education and residential care programme.
- We focus not only on academic success but also on each student as a whole. Students take a wide range of qualifications including Entry Level exams, GCSEs and BTEC and we also work to achieve success outside the classroom with a focus on life-relevant learning skills.
- Where required, we provide a Total Communication approach including the use of sign-supported English to aid understanding.
- We support each student with their social development, helping them with relationship management and developing social and emotional resilience.
- We provide a homely experience for our residential students, with each student having their own individual bedrooms and access to personalised extra-curricular activities.
- Our seaside town-centre location means that we are actively involved in the local community, which offers a range of activities and a 'real life' setting for practising essential life-skills such as shopping and independent travel.
- We have two dedicated nurses within St Catherine's, who work closely with the care, teaching and therapy teams.
- We offer a range of work-related experiences including accredited courses at our vocational training unit, work experience and taster courses at the local College.

"Students make outstanding progress in their speech and language, social presentation, personal care and independence. Their self-esteem and confidence blossoms." Ofsted 2015

St John's School & College

St. JOHN'S

EMPOWERING VOICE. ENABLING CHOICE

Business Centre, 17 Walpole Road,
Brighton, East Sussex BN2 0AF
Tel: 01273 244000
Fax: 01273 602243

Email: admissions@st-johns.co.uk
Website: www.st-johns.co.uk
Principal & Chief Executive:
Mr Simon Charleton
Appointed: February 2017
School type:
Coeducational Boarding & Day

Age range of pupils: 7–25
No. of pupils enrolled as at 01/01/2017: 118
Boys: 96 **Girls:** 22
No. of boarders: 47
Fees per annum as at 01/01/2017:
Day: £50,000 approx
Full Boarding: £100,000 approx

St. John's is a non-maintained special school and independent specialist college, working with learners who have complex learning disabilities; including some learners who may have difficulties resulting from social, emotional and mental health needs, Autistic Spectrum Conditions, Asperger's Syndrome and Pathological Demand Avoidance Syndrome.

St. John's is a place where learning is shaped around your hopes and aspirations; where our courses are tailored to meet your goals and where you are supported by a highly skilled staff team who respect your choices and lifestyle.

St. John's innovative curriculum provides a full range of exciting, challenging and meaningful learning experiences (both accredited and non-accredited) that prepare each learner with relevant vocational and personal skills that will significantly impact on their future lives.

Our focus on vocational skills is carried out through real, work based learning, which allows our learners to work within and support the services and functions of our organisation, our own enterprises and community work experience placements.

Maths, English, Communications and ICT are embedded or are timetabled sessions along with PSHE, sport, termly options and community access.

Learners at St. John's have access to a variety of vibrant and age appropriate learning environments that reflect their needs. These include: our cafés providing real work experience, theatre for performing arts, fully equipped music and recording studio, construction workshop, community printing enterprise, IT and project hub and sensory areas.

Throughout their journey at St. John's learners are supported by our qualified and experienced Wellbeing team, who provide communication therapy, occupational therapy, behaviour support, nursing and counselling.

We also have a dedicated transitions team who support learners in visiting potential services for their future lives. The team works closely with the Wellbeing team in preparing learners for life beyond St. John's.

St Joseph's Specialist School & College

Christ in Our Lives
No Limits ... Just Possibilities

(Founded 1950)

Amlets Lane, Cranleigh, Surrey GU6 7DH

Tel: 01483 272449

Fax: 01483 276003

Email: admissions@
st-josephscranleigh.surrey.sch.uk

Website:
www.st-josephscranleigh.surrey.sch.uk

Principal: Mrs Annie Sutton

Appointed: April 2016

School type:
Coeducational Day & Residential

Age range of pupils: 5–19

No. of pupils enrolled as at 01/01/2017: 75

Fees per annum as at 01/01/2017:

Day: £57,905 *Full Boarding:* £83,898

St Joseph's Specialist School & College is recognised by Ofsted as an "Outstanding" well established day school and Children's Home providing care over 52 weeks of the year for children and young people with special needs from ages 5 to 19 years.

Currently with 73% of students on the Autistic Spectrum we also specialise in a range of complex needs including Speech & Language difficulties, moderate to severe learning difficulties, social communication disorders and challenging behaviours. Autism Accredited by the National Autistic Society, St Joseph's is a proven solution for both families and Local Authorities seeking the next step for education, care and therapy.

With Specialisms in Communication Interaction and the Creative Arts, we offer tailor made teaching and learning styles, environment, therapies, and professional standards to meet all the needs of ASD students through personalised learning programmes based on an integrated curriculum, functional communication, visual structure and positive behaviour management. These programmes incorporate a number of methods recognised for working with ASD students: TEACHH, Intensive Interaction, PECS, Social Stories and MAKATON signing and symbols. By focusing on learning and behavioural needs, as well as personal preferences, enabling a truly bespoke and personalised approach is taken to ensure success. Information is carefully gathered from a wide range of sources including: the Statement of Special Educational Needs or Education Health Care Plan; the diagnosis; developmental history; educational records and assessments; medical records; parents, care staff and observations.

The school is situated close to Cranleigh Village, which retains a great sense of 'community' with a range of amenities including a Leisure Centre, library, shops, cafes, Arts Centre, churches, sports and social clubs. With good transport links to both Horsham and Guildford where more leisure and social facilities including cinemas, theatre and indoor bowling can

be found. The school is an active member of the local community and all students are encouraged to take an active part in community life, to maximise their potential and engage with local people.

Strong leadership, teaching, care and therapeutic intervention combine to deliver positive outcomes to meet high expectation and aspirations of

both students and families. A calming environment takes into account a wide variety of complex sensory issues and uses a variety of techniques – photographs, symbols and visual clues – children feel comfortable in their surroundings and cope easily with daily routines.

We specifically adapt the curriculum to meet each child's individual needs and focus on the development of personal social and communication along with independent living skills, especially for

those aged 16+ years.

By maintaining routines within a structured environment and promoting functional communication we enable students to stay motivated, maximise their potential and work towards positive learning outcomes, whilst seeing a reduction in both anxiety and challenging behaviours.

Therapies

We have our own dedicated team of integrated therapists who work within both class and residential settings to enhance and complement the education and care of all students. Our Director of Therapies co-ordinates and leads a department which includes Speech and Language, Occupational Therapy, Music, Arts, Equine and Drama.

We believe communication underpins successful learning, self-esteem, positive behaviour and opportunities for life. All students are assessed and a therapy programme devised based on their individual needs. To ensure learning is transferred to real life situations, our therapists accompany our children and young people into the community on a regular basis to access local facilities and activities.

Residential Options

Registered as a Children's Home, we provide care, education and therapies

for up to 52 weeks a year. Alternatively, we can offer a variety of Residential options to meet the needs of Local Authorities, Students and families, ranging from weekly boarding to 52 week placements.

We offer an environment where each student is supported and able to develop the skills needed to maximise personal independence. Each residential group is staffed on an individual basis and well equipped to give a homely atmosphere. Our last Ofsted Inspection rated the Children's home as "Good". By maintaining a waking day curriculum we believe our students benefit greatly from a consistency of approach.

Fully integrated into our community we ensure all our students' skills are transferred and managed in realistic settings and reflects their levels of need. A Speech and Language therapist also regularly visits all the residential groups to ensure consistency across the day.

Supported Living

We also provide Supported Living for young people aged 19+. Springvale in Cranleigh and Long Barn in Beare Green offer accommodation for adults with learning difficulties where each young person has their own tenancy and is supported by a tailored individual support package reflecting their own lifestyle choices and activities.

Shapwick School

SHAPWICK SCHOOL

(Founded 1974)

Shapwick Manor, Station Road, Shapwick,

Somerset TA7 9NJ
Tel: 01458 210384
Email: office@shapwickschool.com
Website: www.shapwickschool.com
Principal: Mr A Wylie B.Ed, PG Dip, NPQH
Headteacher: Mrs H Lush B.Sc (Hons); GTP
School type:

Coeducational Day & Boarding

Age range of pupils: 8–19 years
No. of pupils enrolled as at 01/01/2017: 84
Fees per annum as at 01/01/2017:
Day: £18,519 – £19,386
Weekly Boarding: £24,258 (Prep)
Full Boarding: £25,560 – £27,858
Flexi Boarding: £50 per night (plus day fees)

Shapwick School in Somerset is one of the few remaining independent schools for young people with specific learning difficulties. The strict admission criteria mean that the school specialises in a niche area of educational need. We believe that our students deserve the best specialist education possible and this being delivered in a conducive and empathetic environment.

Shapwick School is located close to the Avalon Marshes, an area of outstanding natural beauty. The surrounding area provides a wonderful teaching resource and an astounding outdoor classroom especially for Art, Photography and Geography. For every student, we aim to personalise their learning experience. We do not expect our students to fit into the Shapwick educational provision rather we fit the educational provision around the student. This can only be achieved by establishing a thorough understanding of how the specific learning difficulty has impacted upon the individual. Once this has been established, it is then possible to build a personalised programme to include some or all of the following – specialist, in-class teaching with class sizes of 6-8 students, Speech and Language Therapy, Occupational Therapy, Counselling, 1:1 Literacy and Maths support, the use of Assistive Technologies, Sensory Integration, Social Communication.

We see our role as developing our students as independent and confident young people, who will contribute positively to their community on leaving school, as well as seeing them achieve academic success.

The school motto states 'The same road by different steps'. This captures the ethos of the school.

We have high expectations of both students and staff.

We may have to find alternative solutions and think tangentially in order to work with individual students but that makes for a very dynamic and buzzy school environment. The staff team, along with parents, will always work together to find a unique plan for our unique individuals.

Argent College

New Standard Works, 43-47 Vittoria Street,
Birmingham, West Midlands B1 3PE
Tel: 01453 837502
Fax: 01384 399401
Email: enquiries@argent.rmt.org

Website: www.rmt.org
Principal: Oliver Cheney
School type: Coeducational Day
Age range of pupils: 16–25

Argent College was launched in 2015 as a satellite of Glasshouse College (established in 2000 and awarded 'Good' by Ofsted) and based in the centre of Birmingham. Argent College offers up to 60 places to young people with a wide range of complex and comorbid learning, emotional and behavioural difficulties, mental health issues, ASD and Asperger Syndrome.

Practical Skills Therapeutic Education

Set within the heritage Jewellery Quarter of central Birmingham, Argent College is operated by Ruskin Mill Trust, whose internationally renowned Practical Skills Therapeutic Education method offers young people a unique opportunity to learn and develop transferable skills through meaningful real-life activities and accredited courses in both day and residential settings.

The college provides a focused and safe learning environment and is part of the wider educational, vocational and social enterprise schemes at the New Standard Works. It benefits from an extensive range of nutritional, therapeutic and medical support within Glasshouse College. Each core element of the educational cycle is designed to establish active and positive relationships with nature, people and the community through a holistic approach to human development and supports three key stages: overcoming barriers to learning, becoming skilled, and being ready to engage and give back to the community.

Integrated Learning for Living and Work

A personalised pre-entry assessment leads to an individualised learning and development programme. A rich and varied curriculum offers exciting opportunities to develop communication, social, work and living skills. This includes two newly refurbished state-of-the-art

visitor centres at nearby Glasshouse College which offer students exceptional opportunities to develop social and vocational skills in professional and public environments.

Activities at Argent College include jewellery-making, leatherwork, textiles, photography, living skills, catering, horticulture and candle-making, with numeracy, communication, social and functional skills embedded throughout the provision. The development of a roof garden, a bakery, café and cultural programmes at the New Standard Works will offer a wide range of work-based and vocational skills opportunities.

Accreditation and Transition

Argent College delivers a range of BTEC courses within the varied curriculum, which

are accredited through the Regulated Qualifications Framework. Access to work experience is available in the local community and other new businesses as they develop in the local area, and will be expanded upon at the New Standard Works as social enterprises become available. Throughout their placement, students work with a dedicated team to consolidate their transferable skills and prepare for transition.

Admissions

For all initial enquiries, please contact the Admissions Team on 01453 837502 or by email at: admissions@rmt.org.

Ruskin Mill Trust is an educational charity and draws its inspiration from the insights of Rudolf Steiner, John Ruskin and William Morris. Charity No: 1137167.

Glasshouse College

Wollaston Road, Amblecote, Stourbridge, West Midlands DY8 4HF
Tel: 01453 837502
Fax: 01384 399401
Email: enquiries@ghc.rmt.org

Website: www.rmt.org
Executive Principal: Oliver Cheney
School type:
Coeducational Day & Residential
Age range of pupils: 16–25

Glasshouse College, awarded 'Good' by Ofsted and 'Good' by Care Quality Commission, offers over 100 places to young people with a wide range of complex and comorbid learning, emotional and behavioural difficulties, mental health issues, ASD and Asperger Syndrome.

Practical Skills Therapeutic Education

Set within the heritage glassmaking district of Stourbridge, including 46 acres of farm and woodlands, Glasshouse College is operated by Ruskin Mill Trust, whose internationally renowned *Practical Skills Therapeutic Education* method offers young people a unique opportunity to learn and develop transferable skills through meaningful real-life activities and accredited courses in both day and residential settings.

The college provides an extensive range of nutritional, therapeutic and medical support. Each core element of the educational cycle is designed to establish active and positive relationships with nature, people and the community through a holistic approach to human development and supports three key stages: overcoming barriers to learning, becoming skilled, and being ready to engage and give back to the community.

Integrated Learning for Living and Work

A personalised pre-entry assessment leads to an individualised learning and development programme. A rich and varied curriculum offers exciting opportunities to develop communication, social, work and living skills.

Two newly refurbished state-of-the-art visitor centres, the Glasshouse Arts Centre and the Ruskin Glass Centre, offer students exceptional opportunities to develop social and vocational skills in professional and public environments.

Activities include traditional glass-making, jewellery-making, land-based and traditional craft activities, animal husbandry, woodland management, mountain biking, catering, working a narrowboat, music, art and drama, with numeracy, communication and functional skills embedded throughout the day and residential provision. The college's farm and gardens help students to grow and harvest healthy biodynamic food and then prepare meals in our canteens, cafés and households.

Accreditation and Transition

Courses are accredited through the Regulated Qualifications Framework and include OCNs, NVQs, BTECs, and GCSE and AS levels in partnership with local providers. Work competency is gained through a wide range of internal and external work experience. Throughout their placement, students work with a dedicated team to consolidate their transferable skills and prepare for transition.

Residential Provision

Students live in family or team houses in the local community, which offer the consistency, warmth and positive role modelling that some young adults need to develop living skills, achieve greater independence and re-imagine their potential. Training flats offer even more opportunities to take greater responsibility for themselves. Glasshouse College accepts referrals throughout the year and offer up to 52- week placements, as well as respite care.

Admissions

For all initial enquiries, please contact the Admissions Team on 01453 837502 or by email at: admissions@rmt.org.

Ruskin Mill Trust is an educational charity and draws its inspiration from the insights of Rudolf Steiner, John Ruskin and William Morris. Charity No: 1137167.

Overley Hall School

(Founded 1979)
Overley, Wellington, Telford, West
Midlands TF6 5HE
Tel: 01952 740262
Fax: 01952 740875

Email: info@overleyhall.com
Website: www.overleyhall.com
Headteacher: Mrs Beverley Doran
Appointed: September 2013
School type: Coeducational Residential

Age range of pupils: 8–19
No. of pupils enrolled as at 01/01/2017: 20
Boys: 18 **Girls:** 2
No. of boarders: 20

Overley Hall School is an independent, residential special school and Children's Home, providing education and care to children and young adults aged from eight to 19 years who have a wide range of complex needs including autism, epilepsy and severe learning disabilities. The school is committed to offering each child a wide range of good quality experiences; this occurs through partnerships with parents/carers, teachers and therapists in the delivery of a waking day curriculum by a dedicated team.

Our therapy team is comprised of language and communication and occupational therapists.

The school/residential home is set in a quiet, rural location which provides a calm and nurturing learning and living environment for young people in our care. Our school building, alongside the residential house, stands in 13 acres of lawn, walled kitchen garden and woodland.

Other facilities within the campus and grounds include a lifeskills room, indoor sensory hydropool, soft play space, art and craft workshops, sensory lodge, cinema room, farm shop, recreational and relaxation areas.

Our registered 'Forest School' operates within the woodland areas, and is led by qualified practitioners from Overley Hall School; this offers pupils opportunities for multi-sensory outdoor learning and recreation experiences throughout the seasons.

Freeman College

Sterling Works, 88 Arundel Street, Sheffield, South Yorkshire S1 2NG
Tel: 01453 837502
Fax: 0114 252 5996
Email: enquiries@fmc.rmt.org

Website: www.rmt.org
Principal: Perdita Mousley
School type:
Coeducational Day & Residential
Age range of pupils: 16–25

Freeman College, awarded 'Good' by Ofsted, and 'Good' by CQC, offers over 90 places to young people with complex learning and behavioural difficulties, mental health issues and ASD, including Asperger Syndrome.

Practical Skills Therapeutic Education

Based in the illustrious metalworking district of Sheffield, the college is operated by Ruskin Mill Trust, whose internationally renowned *Practical Skills Therapeutic Education* method offers young people a unique opportunity to learn and develop transferable skills through meaningful real-life activities and accredited courses in both the day and residential programmes.

Freeman College provides an extensive range of nutritional, therapeutic and medical support. Each core element of the educational cycle is designed to establish active and positive relationships with nature, people and the community through a holistic approach to human development and supports three key stages: overcoming barriers to learning, becoming skilled, and being ready to engage and give back to the community.

Integrated Learning for Living and Work

A personalised pre-entry assessment leads to an individualised learning and development programme. A rich and varied curriculum is designed to offer opportunities to develop lifelong communication, social, work and living skills. Activities include traditional metal crafts such as spoon forging, copper-work, pewter-work and jewellery, as well as land-based and traditional crafts, animal husbandry, horticulture, catering and hospitality, music, art and drama, with communication and functional skills embedded throughout the day and residential provision. Healthy food is grown and harvested at the college's 9-acre market garden (using the biodynamic method) and prepared with students in the canteens, café and households.

Accreditation and Transition

Courses are accredited through the Regulated Qualifications Framework and include OCNs, NVQs, BTECs, as well as GCSE and AS-levels delivered in partnership with local providers. Work competency is gained through a wide range of internal and external work experience including through its arts and crafts shop, the Academy of Makers, cultural and events programmes, workshops and award-winning café. Throughout their placement, students collaborate with a dedicated transition team to hone their transferable skills and prepare for life after college.

Residential Provision

Students live in family or team houses in the local community, which offer the consistency, warmth and positive role modelling that some young adults need to develop their living skills, achieve greater independence and re-imagine their potential. Students can progress onto placements in training flats where they have the opportunity to take greater responsibility for themselves.

Freeman College takes referrals throughout the year and offers up to 52-week placements.

Admissions

For all initial enquiries please contact the Admissions Team on 01453 837502 or by email: admissions@rmt.org.

Ruskin Mill Trust is an educational charity and draws its inspiration from the insights of Rudolf Steiner, John Ruskin and William Morris. Charity No: 1137167.

Fullerton House School

(Founded 1990)

Tickill Square, Denaby, Doncaster,
South Yorkshire DN12 4AR

Tel: 01709 861663
Fax: 01709 869635
Email: enquiries@hesleygroup.co.uk
Website: www.fullertonhouseschool.co.uk
General Manager: Michael Cavan
Appointed: 2015
Head of Education: Michael Walsh

School type:
Independent Specialist Residential School
Age range of pupils: 8–19
No. of pupils enrolled as at 01/01/2017:
Capacity: 36
Fees per annum as at 01/01/2017:
Available on request

A specialist residential school offering flexible education and care, which can include day and respite provision, for up to 52-weeks-per-year for people aged 8-19, all of whom have complex needs including behaviour that may challenge and a learning disability, often in association with autism.

Fullerton House School is situated in the heart of the village of Denaby Main, near Doncaster. Its central location provides easy access by road, rail or air. Our mission is to enhance the lives of the young people entrusted to us by focusing on their specific needs, capabilities and aspirations.

Education: Each person has a carefully designed Individual Learning Plan based on their specific needs in line with the National Curriculum, which supports their positive progress in a range of areas.

Extended learning: During evenings, weekends and school holidays a wide range of extra-curricular activities are on offer to ensure that people are fully engaged with stimulating and meaningful experiences both on and off-site.

Professional services: A dedicated on-site team including carers, teachers, tutors, communication, behaviour and occupational therapy , psychology and other specialists ensure that people have ready access to the services they require.

High-quality accommodation: Single person and small group occupancy of high-quality accommodation is provided at Fullerton House School. Each person has their own bedroom, the majority of which have en-suite bathrooms. We also have a range of on-site facilities to complement and enrich the lives of those who come to live and learn with us.

Keeping in contact: We understand that while we may offer a very positive option for the person, we may not be on your doorstep. Keeping in touch with loved ones is essential. Everyone has a plan to support optimum contact with family/carers and friends whether this be by phone, letter, email or Skype.

Specialist Colleges

(Founded 2013)

Fullerton House College

Tickhill Square, Denaby, Doncaster, South Yorkshire DN12 4AR

Tel: 01709 861663

Fax: 01709 869635

Wilsic Hall College

Wadworth, Doncaster, South Yorkshire DN11 9AG

Tel: 01302 856382

Fax: 01302 853608

Email: enquiries@hesleygroup.co.uk

Website: www.hesleygroup.co.uk

Head: Richard Webster

Appointed: 2016

School type: Independent Specialist Residential Colleges

Age range of pupils: 18–25

No. of pupils enrolled as at 01/01/2017:

Fullerton House College Capacity: 12

Wilsic Hall College Capacity: 9

Fees per annum as at 01/01/2017:

On request

Specialist residential colleges offering flexible education care and support for up to 52 weeks per year for young people aged 18-25, who have complex needs including behaviour that may challenge and a learning disability, often in association with autism.

At Wilsic Hall College, everyone lives within a beautiful rural setting with ready community access and at Fullerton House College in the heart of the community, in an urban setting with many local facilities including a sports centre, restaurants and shops.

Mission

Our Specialist Colleges support young people with their transition into adult life by focusing on their specific needs, capabilities and aspirations.

Education: Everybody has a highly personalised programme of learning, equipping them with skills they will need for adult life.

Extended learning: During evenings, weekends and college holidays a wide range of extra-curricular activities are on offer to ensure people are fully engaged with stimulating experiences both on and off site providing further, meaningful learning opportunities.

Professional services: A dedicated multi-disciplinary therapeutic team including college tutors, college support workers, consultant clinical psychologist, consultant psychiatrist, applied behaviour analysts, speech and language therapists, occupational therapists, registered manager, care and support staff work together to support each individual's progress.

High quality accommodation: College accommodation includes individualised bedrooms, quality living spaces that promote independence and progressive skills development assisted by the appropriate use of specialist/adaptive technology. We also have a range of on-site and off-site facilities that offer progressive learning opportunities for young people with a range of needs and wishes.

Keeping in contact: We work to develop relationships between staff and families that are strong, positive and mutually respectful. People are supported to be in contact with their friends and family; we welcome visits to the colleges at any time. Everyone has a plan that will include the best means for them to maintain this contact whether by 'phone, letter, email or Skype.

Wilsic Hall School

(Founded 1996)
Wadworth, Doncaster,
South Yorkshire DN11 9AG

Tel: 01302 856382
Fax: 01302 853608
Email: enquiries@hesleygroup.co.uk
Website: www.wilsichallschool.co.uk
Head: Geoff Turner
Appointed: 2008

School type:
Independent Specialist Residential School
Age range of pupils: 11–19
No. of pupils enrolled as at 01/01/2017:
Capacity: 31
Fees per annum as at 01/01/2017:
Available on request

A specialist residential school offering flexible education and care, which can include day and respite provision, for up to 52-weeks-per-year for people aged 11-19, all of whom have complex needs including behaviour that may challenge and a learning disability, often in association with autism.

Wilsic Hall School is situated in its own 14-acre site approximately five miles south of Doncaster. Its central location provides easy access by road, rail or air. Our mission is to enhance the lives of the people entrusted to us by focusing on their specific needs, capabilities and aspirations.

Education: Each person has a carefully designed Individual Education Plan based on their specific needs in line with the National Curriculum, which supports their positive progress in a range of areas.

Extended learning: During evenings, weekends and school holidays a wide range of extra-curricular activities are on offer to ensure that people are fully engaged with stimulating and meaningful experiences both on and off-site.

Professional services: A dedicated team including carers, teachers, tutors, behaviour, communication and occupational therapy, psychology and other specialists ensure that each person has ready access to the services they require.

High-quality accommodation: Single person and small group occupancy of high-quality accommodation is provided at Wilsic Hall School. Each person has their own bedroom, the majority of which have en-suite bathrooms. We also have a range of on-site facilities to complement and enrich the lives of those who come to live and learn with us.

Keeping in contact: We understand that while we may offer a very positive option for the person, we may not be on your doorstep. Keeping in touch with loved ones is essential. Everyone has a plan to support optimum contact with family/carers and friends whether this be by phone, letter, email or Skype.

The New School

BUTTERSTONE

(Founded 1992)

Butterstone, Dunkeld, Perth & Kinross
PH8 0HA
Tel: 01350 724216
Fax: 01350 724283
Email: info@thenewschool.co.uk
Website: www.thenewschool.co.uk
Head of School: Mr Chris Holmes

Appointed: June 2016
School type:
Coeducational Day & Boarding
Age range of pupils: 11–19
No. of pupils enrolled as at 01/01/2017: 25
Boys: 21 **Girls:** 4
Fees per annum: Available on request

Education should be enjoyable and meaningful – we believe all young people are able to develop and achieve their potential. Through a range of educational opportunities across the 24 hour curriculum we help to prepare for life beyond school.

We have clear expectations and the relaxed, flexible and supportive environment of The New School encourages our young people to feel comfortable with who they are, and to flourish as individuals.

We are a Theraputic Learning Community. Our provision is aimed at those young people who find mainstream education difficult to access. The New School specialises in education for fragile learners in general, for young people with

Aspergers/Autistic Spectrum condition, ADHD, Tourette's syndrome and Foetal Alcohol syndrome. Skilled teaching and care staff support young people who have had interrupted learning, dissatisfying school experiences, or simply those who learn differently. We are a truly inclusive school.

The New School curriculum is broad, coherent and highly varied – meeting the different needs of each and every one of our young people. Our classes are small, with an average of five. Our students are encouraged to follow interests – making the learning motivating, relevant and meaningful for them, regardless of academic ability. We deliver a full menu of SQA accredited courses, from Curriculum

for Excellence National 2 up to Higher level in most subjects. ASDAN accreditation system units and courses are offered to some students, helping them to develop independence, skills for work and skills for life. Speech and language therapy is offered to all students, if required. Our sector-leading 'Showcase' eprofile recording system ensures that the student population recognise and celebrate their own achievements – both academic and more broadly throughout their time here, evidence is gathered across the 24-hour curriculum. We are passionate about outdoor learning, and utilise the beautiful school situation to promote this in various ways. Our trained staff deliver full Duke of Edinburgh's Award up to Gold level.

Coleg Plas Dwbl

Mynachlog-ddu, Clunderwen,
Pembrokeshire SA66 7SE
Tel: 01453 837502
Email: enquiries@plasdwbl.rmt.org
Website: www.rmt.org

Principal: Paul Garnault
School type:
Coeducational Day & Residential
Age range of pupils: 16–25

Coleg Plas Dwbl offers places to young people with complex learning and behavioural difficulties, mental health issues and autistic spectrum disorders, including Asperger Syndrome.

Practical Skills Therapeutic Education

Coleg Plas Dwbl is based in 100 acres of biodynamic farm and woodlands. Coleg Plas Dwbl is operated by Ruskin Mill Trust, whose internationally renowned *Practical Skills Therapeutic Education* method offers young people a unique opportunity to learn and develop transferable skills through meaningful real-life activities and accredited courses, helping them to prepare for adulthood. The college provides a range of nutritional and therapeutic support. Each core element of the educational cycle is designed to establish active and positive relationships with nature, people and the community through a holistic approach to human development and supports three key stages: overcoming barriers to learning, becoming skilled, and being ready to engage and give back to the community.

Integrated Learning for Living and Work Programme

Coleg Plas Dwbl offers a personalised pre-entry assessment leading to an individualised learning and development programme. A rich and varied curriculum offers exciting opportunities to develop communication, social, work and living skills. Activities include practical land-based and traditional craft activities, animal husbandry, woodland management, horticulture, catering and drama with social, communication and functional skills embedded throughout the day and residential curriculum. Students help to work the farm producing, harvesting and preparing healthy organic food, and supplying local outlets.

Accreditation and Transition

Courses are accredited through the Regulated Qualifications Framework and students will prepare for work competency through a wide range of internal and external work experience. Qualifications include Agored Cymru, LANTRA Awards and the Welsh Baccalaureate. The curriculum is also supported by additional sessions and activities which help students to understand and explore the culture and history of the area and try local crafts. Throughout their placement, students are supported by staff to focus on transition and engage with the many transferable skills acquired to prepare for life after college.

Residential Provision

Students live in family houses or team houses which offer the consistency, warmth and positive role modelling that some young adults need to develop their living skills, achieve greater independence and re-imagine their potential. When appropriate, students can then progress to placements in training flats where they have the opportunity to take greater responsibility for themselves. Coleg Plas Dwbl takes referrals throughout the year and offers placements for up to 52 weeks.

Admissions

For all initial enquiries please contact the Admissions Team on 01453 837502 or by email at: admissions@rmt.org

Ruskin Mill Trust is an educational charity and draws its inspiration from the insights of Rudolf Steiner, John Ruskin and William Morris. Charity No: 1137167.

Schools and colleges specialising in sensory or physical impairment

The Pace Centre

Specialist education and therapy
for children with motor disorders

(Founded 1990)
Philip Green House, Coventon Road,
Aylesbury, Buckinghamshire HP19 9JL
Tel: 01296 392739
Fax: 01296 334836
Email: info@thepacecentre.org

Website: www.thepacecentre.org
Head Teacher: Mrs Claire Smart
Appointed: September 2016
School type: Independent Special School
Age range of pupils: 0–16
Fees per annum available on request

A specialist school for children with motor disorders

Pace offers a nurturing, stimulating and rich environment to children and young people with a wide range of sensory motor disorders and related communication, educational and medical needs. Our aim is to unlock potential and empower children to live life as independently as possible.

Our highly skilled transdisciplinary team of experts work in close collaboration to deliver an individually tailored curriculum. Drawing on best practice from a range of clinical and educational disciplines, the curriculum is bespoke to each child's abilities and goals and delivers outstanding outcomes. Each class has a minimum ratio of one to one with a specialist leader for each session.

"Pupils make rapid progress against their individual targets. This is because teaching and continuous support from a wide range of professionals accurately meets pupils' needs." – Ofsted 2016

Our model

At the heart of our transdisciplinary approach lies the relationship between postural, movement, sensory and perceptual skills and how these impact on academic learning.

In December 2016, Ofsted rated Pace "Outstanding" for the fifth consecutive inspection.

What we offer

Education
Pre-school
Reception
Key stages 1-4
Dual placements
Community outreach
Commissioned services

Onsite therapy
Occupational therapy
Physiotherapy

Speech and language therapy
Hydrotherapy
Hippotherapy
Rebound therapy

Approaches we use
Conductive education
Sensory integration
Bobath

Communication
Alternative and augmentative communication
British Sign Language

Family support
Early intervention
Assessment and advice
Sleeping
Feeding
Moving and handling

Communication
Parent training and support
Parent partnership

Daily independence programmes
Group and individual programmes to develop sensory registration and processing skills

Specific programmes to develop movement skills, fine motor skills, hand skills, selfcare and independence skills

Wheelchair skills

Group and individual programmes to develop communication skills, including 'high tech' communication aides and ICT user groups

Engagement with the local community through regular citizenship activities.

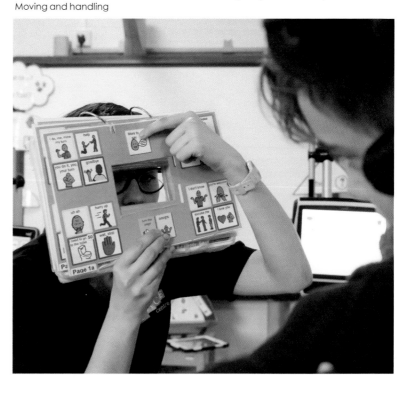

RNIB College Loughborough

**RNIB College
Loughborough**

(Founded 1989)
Radmoor Road, Loughborough,
Leicestershire LE11 3BS
Tel: 01509 611077
Fax: 01509 232013
Email: enquiries@rnibcollege.ac.uk

Website: www.rnibcollege.ac.uk
Principal: June Murray
School type:
Coeducational College and residence
Age range of pupils: 16–65
No. of pupils enrolled as at 01/01/2017: 52

We are a friendly residential college supporting young people and adults with vision impairment and additional disabilities to achieve their goals. Our programmes are designed to develop independence skills for involvement in community life.

Education and skills

Choose us for your Further Education and you'll learn practical skills and gain work experience within our enterprises – our Café, eBay business, Conference Centre, Arts Centre, Shop and Office. You could also choose a course at our partner mainstream college located next door.

If you are a young adult wanting to gain the skills and confidence to progress into independent or supported living, you may want to apply for our Bridge programme. It's a one-year residential programme which will help you to build your independence. You'll be encouraged and supported to do things you've previously had help for, making you ready to move into your own home.

Also on offer is Flexible Futures, our daytime activities programme. You could spend time in each of our different enterprises, providing a vital role in these real businesses and being part of college life. You could also go out and enjoy the local community.

Accommodation

Our Stan Bell Centre offers modern, purpose built, safe accommodation. Learners are encouraged to be as independent as possible; however we recognise that some people will always need a little more support. Our residence is staffed 24 hours a day.

Needs we support

- Vision impairment
- Learning difficulties and disabilities
- Autistic spectrum disorders (ASD)
- Physical disabilities
- Communication difficulties
- Mild hearing problems
- Additional healthcare needs, such as epilepsy
- Additional emotional and behavioural difficulties

Wider services

RNIB offers a wide range of other services for children, young people, their families and the professionals who work with them. Find out more at www.rnib.org.uk/children

Visit us!

The best way to find out more about our college is to come and have a look round. Call us today to arrange your visit!

Royal School for the Deaf Derby

(Founded 1894)
Ashbourne Road, Derby,
Derbyshire DE22 3BH
Tel: 01332 362512
Fax: 01332 299708

Email: enquiries@rsdd.org.uk
Website: www.rsdd.org
Headteacher: Helen Shepherd
School type:
Coeducational Day & Boarding

Age range of pupils: 3–19
No. of pupils enrolled as at 01/01/2017:
Boys: 72 **Girls:** 44
Fees per annum as at 01/01/2017:
Fees set according to individual need

Royal School for the Deaf Derby (RSDD) is a non-maintained residential special school with a nationwide catchment area. There are approximately 120 children and young people on roll aged between 3 and 19. All pupils have Statements of Special Educational Need or Education and Health Care Plans for hearing impairment.

RSDD prides itself on being a warm and inclusive environment which provides both day and week-long residential places. Language is developed using the child's preferred method of communication. Children are listened to, can express their views and are understood. The broad range of subjects offered is delivered using an individualised approach tailored to the language profiles of each child. Pupils are based in small groups, taught by teachers of the deaf with the support of education assistants. Deaf and hearing staff work throughout the school allowing pupils access to a high quality language environment.

An Audiologist and Speech and Language Therapists who specialise in working with deaf children, provide expert support. The Health Centre provides a comprehensive support service to pupils and a 'Complex Needs SENCO' provides additional input where the needs of the child are not straightforward. Children and young people also enjoy close partnership working with external agencies such as National Deaf CAMHS and Sign Health.

We have high expectations of all children and young people and our performance as a school. Teaching and learning is highly differentiated to ensure all children are start from individual starting points and progress on a par with or better than their non-hearing impaired peers and intervene where progress stalls. All subjects at every key stage are formally accredited i.e. GCSE, BTEC British Sign Language, A Level, Driving theory.

Primary pupils develop and grow through learning in a fun and stimulating environment. Pupils take part in the Standard Assessment Tests at the end of each Key Stage. We strive for high academic achievement in the Secondary Department according to individual potential and starting points. Post 16 Department works in partnership with local mainstream providers offering young people the same opportunities and experiences enjoyed by all young people

supported by communication support workers off campus and subject specialist teachers of the deaf whilst on-campus.

Residences offer a rich cultural environment where both BSL and English are valued. Pupils are encouraged to participate in deaf and hearing community activities leading towards their independence. They live in purpose built accommodation which can be personalised to be more homely. Dedicated and qualified social care staff work with them to develop independence skills, promote a sense of belonging and self-esteem.

The School is situated on a green campus within walking distance of the city centre and a few miles from the Peak District. Children and young people enjoy an outdoor gym, sports hall and sports pitch. All key stages have dedicated resources including Early years where children can learn inside or outside in an all-weather area.

For further information please email enquiries@rsdd.org.uk or call us on 01332 362512 or text 07500 878565

Royal School for the Deaf Derby is a Registered Charity (No. 1062507)

RNIB Sunshine House School

Sunshine House School

33 Dene Road, Northwood,
Middlesex HA6 2DD
Tel: 01923 822538
Fax: 01923 826227
Email: sunshinehouse@rnib.org.uk

Website: www.rnib.org.uk/sunshinehouse
Head: Jackie Seaman
School type: Coeducational
Age range of pupils: 2–14

At RNIB Sunshine House School we offer specialist support to blind and partially sighted children with significant learning difficulties and disabilities and their families.

With a range of specialist indoor and outdoor facilities, we provide a safe and supportive environment for children to meet their full potential.

Education and Curriculum

Everyone at Sunshine House is treated as an individual with their own specific needs and learning goals. Working together with parents and specialists we ensure that achievements go beyond the classroom into everyday life.

Our specialist school educates children and young people from two to 14 years who have a range of physical, learning and sensory needs. Children follow an individually tailored curriculum supporting their special education needs. Most children are working between P levels 1 and 8. Each class has no more than eight children with a minimum support ratio of two adults for every three children.

Therapies and Healthcare

Our team of in-house therapists combine their work with a child's learning, making therapies a part of everyday school life. We also have a paediatric community nurse who ensures that all health needs are met.

Family services

We're part of a family of five local special schools with The Eden Academy, working together to offer your child access to an enhanced range of expertise, activities and resources. You can get to know other parents and children and have fun through our thriving family services. Activities include after-school and holiday clubs, family events, sibling support groups, networking and advice for parents.

Needs we support

- Vision impairment
- Multi-sensory impairment and deaf-blindness
- Significant learning difficulties and disabilities
- Physical disabilities
- Communication difficulties
- Additional medical and health needs, including long-term ventilation or life-threatening or life-limiting conditions

Wider services

RNIB offers a wide range of other services for children, young people, their families and the professionals who work with them. Find out more at www.rnib.org.uk/children

Visit us!

The best way to find out more about our school is to come and have a look round. Call us today to arrange your visit!

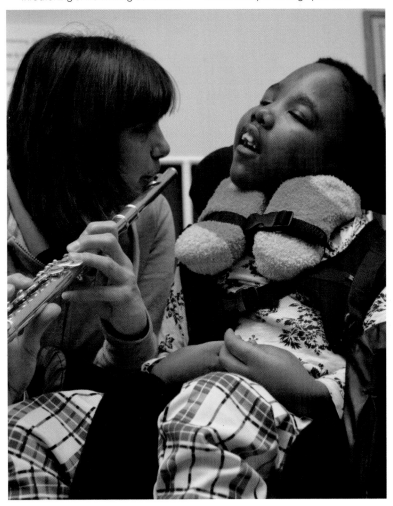

Chailey Heritage School

(Founded 1903)

Haywards Heath Road, North Chailey,

Lewes, East Sussex BN8 4EF

Tel: 01825 724444

Fax: 01825 723773

Email: office@chf.org.uk

Website: www.chf.org.uk

Charity Chief Executive: Helen Hewitt

Headteacher: Simon Yates

Director of Social Care: Denise Banks

School type:

Coeducational Boarding & Day

Age range of pupils: 3–19

No. of pupils enrolled as at 01/01/2017: 85

Fees per annum as at 01/01/2017:

Please contact the school for details

Chailey Heritage School, part of Chailey Heritage Foundation, is a non-maintained special school for children and young people aged 2-19 with a wide range of complex physical, communication, sensory and learning difficulties and health needs. Chailey Heritage School was judged to be 'Outstanding' by Ofsted in October 2014 for a third consecutive time. Chailey Heritage Residential is a registered children's home and offers flexible care packages from short breaks through to 52 weeks of the year.

Meeting children's health and therapy needs

Chailey Heritage School's unique on-site partnership with Chailey Clinical Services, part of Sussex Community NHS Foundation Trust. Working with our expert teachers, the pupils' health and therapy needs are met in a holistic way by a highly skilled team that includes Paediatric Medical Consultants and Doctors, a full range of Therapists, residential Nursing team and Rehabilitation Engineers.

Experts in promoting independence through powered mobility and communication

Every young person has the opportunity to experience appropriate forms of powered mobility. The award-winning Chailey Heritage Foundation engineering team have developed a range of advanced assistive technologies to develop driving skills and allow progression. All pupils at Chailey Heritage School have some level of communication difficulty. We always strive to meet every individual's need and their right to communicate and be listened to. By working closely alongside Speech and Language Therapists, we develop a wide variety of Alternative and Augmentative Communication (AAC) approaches to meet personal needs.

Purposeful learning

Chailey Heritage School has developed its own curriculum driven by the individual learners needs. This means every learner has their own curriculum built specifically for them based on their skills and desired outcomes, it is broad, in that it covers all aspects of their development and it is balanced in that it weighs up, specifically for them, the input that is needed. Above all it is meaningful to each child and their family.

Support for parents and families at every step in any way we can

We work in partnership with parents and families at every step of their Chailey Heritage journey, providing support at difficult times and celebrating achievements together.

Chailey Heritage Residential

Chailey Heritage Residential is a nationally recognised, registered children's home for 3 to 19 year olds with complex physical disabilities and health needs. We offer flexible residential provision ranging from short breaks to 52 weeks a year.

Find out more

We take great pride in and celebrate the achievements of our young people. Whatever your role in our school is or might be – as a parent, potential parent, grandparent, governor, volunteer, fundraiser, supporter – we would be delighted to show you around. Please get in touch now to arrange a visit. We also offer services for under 3 and over 19 year olds see our website for further details.

Chailey Heritage School and Chailey Heritage Residential are part of Chailey Heritage Foundation, registered charity number 1075837, registered in England as a charitable company limited by guarantee No. 3769775

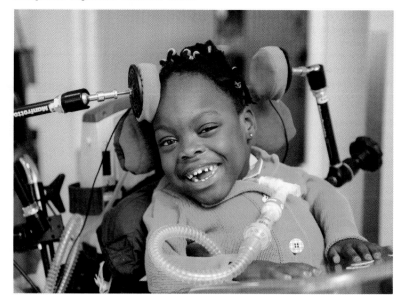

School for Deaf Children 5-16 years

Hamilton Lodge offers a full curriculum to deaf children aged 5-16 years in our school.

We take a "child-centred communication" approach at Hamilton Lodge and we support the development of both English and British Sign Language.

We focus our curriculum development on courses and accreditations that match the needs of individual pupils. We offer a range of GCSE, Entry Level, Functional Skills, Pathways, Unit Award courses and Signature sign language qualifications.

We have a well-established Work Experience Programme and Duke of Edinburgh Award Scheme, both of which focus on individuals being able to build their independence skills, confidence and self-esteem.

Further Education for Deaf Young People 16 -19 years

Hamilton Lodge College provides the right stepping stone into an independent and successful adult life. Based in the heart of a vibrant city, our college students are supported to make the most of the city's facilities.

We provide FE places in partnership with City College Brighton & Hove, Plumpton College, and St John's College.

Students attend lectures at their chosen colleges with the support of Student Support Workers provided by Hamilton Lodge.

Students receive direct teaching from Teachers of the Deaf from Hamilton Lodge to support their chosen courses as well as support with life skills, driving theory courses and English & maths.

New Specialist Provision for Deaf Children with Complex Needs

In 2016, Hamilton Lodge opened this provision to ensure that deaf pupils with more complex needs could access our education.

With support some pupils are able to transition to our core provision but some require a different curriculum and care package to meet their needs.

Our new specialist provision is tailored to meet the needs of those pupils. It is now fully open with a specially adapted residential house and a specialist team to ensure that these pupils have full access to a broad and balanced curriculum at Hamilton Lodge as well as a comprehensive care package.

The provision is based within the school and pupils are well integrated into our school family.

HAMILTON LODGE SCHOOL & COLLEGE
EDUCATION & CARE FOR DEAF STUDENTS FROM PRIMARY TO F.E.

HAMILTON LODGE, WALPOLE ROAD, BRIGHTON, EAST SUSSEX BN2 0LS
Telephone: 01273 682362 Fax 01273 695742 Minicom: 01273 682362 Email: admin@hamiltonlsc.co.uk
www.hamiltonls.co.uk @hamiltonlodge HamiltonLodgeSC hamiltonbrighton
Registered charity in England: Hamilton Lodge (Brighton) no. 307066. Registered in England company no. 544254.

St Mary's School & 6th Form College

(Founded 1922)
Wrestwood Road, Bexhill-on-Sea,
East Sussex TN40 2LU
Tel: 01424 730740
Fax: 01424 733575
Email: admin@stmarysbexhill.org

Website: www.stmarysbexhill.org
Principal: Amanda Clugston
School type:
Coeducational Boarding & Day
Age range of pupils: 7–19
No. of pupils enrolled as at 01/01/2017: 58

We are an inspirational School and 6th Form College for young people aged 7-19 with speech, language and communication disabilities, many of whom have other complex needs. We are committed to providing integrated therapy, education and care tailored to each young person's abilities and aspirations.

The pupils are taught in small groups and follow an exciting broad and balanced curriculum, which is adapted to meet individual needs and is delivered by highly qualified teachers and support staff with the integrated support of therapists for a truly holistic approach.

Children receive individual therapy programmes which may include specialist support from: Speech and Language Therapists, Physiotherapists, Occupational Therapists, Well-being Team and an Educational Psychologist.

Other specialist professionals include an Audiologist, Sign Language Tutors, Child and Family Support Worker, visiting Doctor (GP) and onsite Nursing Team.

Here at St Mary's, we support each child to develop and maximise their communication skills. Parent signing classes are offered on site or via Skype to ensure families can communicate with their child as effectively as possible.

At St Mary's our residences are warm and caring places, creating a 'home from home' feel. In nurturing and stimulating environments we work with our pupils to develop life skills and encourage everyone to learn and live with each other. Opportunities to take part in a wide range of activities are available every day, with children and young people accessing the local community on a regular basis.

Our fantastic facilities include:
- Aspire Vocational Centre
- Sensory Room
- Physiotherapy Room
- Adventure Playground
- Swimming and Hydrotherapy pool
- Sensory Integration Room
- Traversing Wall
- Nature Trail
- Music & Drumming Room
- Outdoor Tennis Courts
- Science Lab
- ICT Suite
- Horticultural area & Polytunnel

The Children's Trust School
Non-Maintained Special School

(Founded 1985)

Tadworth Court, Tadworth,
Surrey KT20 5RU
Tel: 01737 365810
Fax: 01737 365819
Email: school@thechildrenstrust.org.uk
Website:
www.thechildrenstrustschool.org.uk

Head Teacher: Samantha Newton
School type:
Day and Residential to 52 weeks
Age range of pupils: 3–19
Designated number: 44
Fees per annum as at 01/01/2017:
On application

At The Children's Trust School our aim is to provide high quality education and expertise to meet each pupil's individual special educational needs and to celebrate all achievements in a happy, secure environment.

As a non-maintained special school for 3-19 year olds, we pride ourselves on seeing the 'whole' child and delivering education, health and care for children and young people with complex needs in an integrated and holistic approach.

Through day and residential placements (of up to 52 weeks) we focus on personalised planning supporting pupils to improve and develop understanding of the world around them and their functional skills.

We have a skilled team of teachers, classroom and care support staff and nursing and medical staff. We also have an extensive team of therapists, ranging from occupational, physio and speech and language to play, leisure and music therapists. We also offer education, care and therapy to children from the age of three. Our early years pupils are offered age-appropriate education and activities based on our specially-developed curriculum. Taddies is a weekly run parent and child group for children aged 0-5 years old who have additional needs.

Our curriculum focuses on communication, language and literacy, fine and gross motor physical skills, environmental control technology, social, emotional and personal wellbeing and cognitive development.

We provide stimulating educational opportunities, supported by unparalleled expertise delivering significant outcomes for our pupils.

Treloar School

Treloar's
Enabling Education

(Founded 1908)

Holybourne, Alton, Hampshire GU34 4GL
Tel: 01420 547400
Email: admissions@treloar.org.uk
Website: www.treloar.org.uk
Principal: Martin Ingram
School type:
Coeducational Boarding & Day

Religious Denomination: Non-denominational
Age range of pupils: 2–19 yrs
No. of pupils enrolled as at 01/01/2017: 87
Boys: 44 *Girls:* 43 *Sixth Form:* 22
No. of boarders: 45
Fees per annum as at 01/01/2017:
As per assessment

Treloar Nursery and School provide education, care, therapy, medical support and independence training to children and young people from 2 to 19 years of age with complex physical disabilities. Provision is both day and residential and students come from across the UK and overseas. Our residential School provision was rated Outstanding by Ofsted in 2016. Our College is based on the same site and offers continued education and care up to the age of 25 was similarly rated Outstanding by Ofsted in 2017. At Treloar's we prepare students for life after they leave and equipping them with the confidence, independence skills and, where applicable, qualifications they require.

Students also have access to an on-site health centre, occupational, speech and language and physio therapists, educational psychologists, visual impairment and assistive technology specialists plus dieticians and counsellors. Timetables are integrated with classroom and daily living activities to ensure the most beneficial use of a student's time. Our transition team work individually with each student from assessment through to their expected destination to help them reach their goals and aspirations.

Entry Requirement

Admission is considered on the basis of each student's needs following discussion and assessment with education, medical, therapy and care staff. Each student's

programme is constructed to ensure we meet their individual needs. Part-time placements, limited time placements and respite for day students are all available.

Life on Campus

Treloar's is situated in beautiful East Hampshire on the edge of Alton with a good road and rail network. We ensure a varied range of extra-curricular activities including sports, art, drama, clubs and visits off-site utilising our own specialist fleet of vehicles. On-site facilities include a swimming pool, all weather sports facilities, a hydrotherapy pool and social club.

Treloar Trust is a registered charity which supports Treloar School and College (Charity No 1092857).

RNIB Pears Centre for Specialist Learning

RNIB Pears Centre

(Founded 1957)
Wheelwright Lane, Ash Green, Coventry,
West Midlands CV7 9RA
Tel: 024 7636 9500
Fax: 024 7636 9501
Email: pearscentre@rnib.org.uk

Website: www.rnib.org.uk/pearscentre
Headteacher: Angela Farrell
School type: Coeducational day school and Children's Home
Age range of pupils: 2–19
No. of pupils enrolled as at 01/01/2017: 30

At RNIB Pears Centre, we provide a stimulating, creative and purpose-built setting for children and young people with complex needs and vision impairment to live, learn and grow.

We support children to make progress, to develop their independence, and to make their own choices.

Our co-located school and children's home offer flexible packages of support to children and families, depending on what you need:

- Education with up to 52-week residential care
- Education only (if your child lives at home, for example)
- 24-hour residential and/or nursing care only.

This includes therapies and health support, depending on what your child needs.

Education and outreach

If you're looking for a specialist school, our education celebrates a child's abilities and stimulates all of their senses. Our broad, balanced and relevant curriculum is fully personalised to meet individual learning needs.

Ofsted rated our school as 'Outstanding'! This shows that we're very effective in helping children to make progress in their learning and development.

Our national outreach service offers practical support to pupils and educational advice and guidance to professionals and parents. We can also mentor students and provide braille tuition.

Therapies

Our in-house therapy and school team offers specialist expertise in vision impairment, multi-sensory impairment, complex needs and learning disabilities, physiotherapy, speech and language therapy, behaviour management and mobility/habilitation. Hydrotherapy, music therapy, rebound therapy, clinical psychology, occupational therapy and medical led support of health and wellbeing are also part of our provision. Our new hydrotherapy pool is also improving the quality of life and learning experiences for children and young people.

Specialist care and leisure

Sometimes, the chance to share the care of a child can help to relieve pressure on families. Our children's home offers 24-hour care all year round, with waking night staff in spacious bungalows.

Each young person living with us has their own bedroom, which is made safe and personal to them. We support children to access a range of activities and community events, like pop concerts and swimming.

If your child has high health and medical needs, our nursing care offers rehabilitation and a real alternative to long stays in hospital.

Needs we support

- Vision impairment
- Multi-sensory impairment and deaf-blindness
- Significant learning difficulties and disabilities
- Autistic spectrum disorders (ASD)
- Physical disabilities
- Communication difficulties
- Additional medical and health needs, including long-term ventilation or life-threatening or life-limiting conditions
- Additional emotional and behavioural difficulties

Our board of trustees allows us to accommodate a number of children who do not have vision impairment as their primary need.

Wider services

RNIB offers a wide range of other services for children, young people, their families and the professionals who work with them. Find out more at www.rnib.org.uk/children

Visit us!

The best way to find out more about what we offer is to come and have a look round. Call us today to arrange your visit!

St John's Catholic School for the Deaf

St John's
Catholic School for the Deaf
Boston Spa, Yorkshire

(Founded 1870)
Church Street, Boston Spa, Wetherby,
West Yorkshire LS23 6DF

Tel: 01937 842144
Fax: 01937 541471
Email: info@stjohns.org.uk
Website: www.stjohns.org.uk
Headteacher: Mrs A Bradbury BA(Hons), MSc, NPQH

School type:
Coeducational Boarding & Day
Age range of pupils: 4–19
No. of pupils enrolled as at 01/01/2017: 62
Fees per annum as at 01/01/2017:
On application

Special needs catered for

St John's Catholic School is a centre of excellence for sensory and communication needs for pupils aged 4-19. It is a school where spoken language is used, and where every young person communicates equally and successfully with others. We encourage and nurture ambition, self-esteem and confidence in all pupils.

The school offers a broad and balanced curriculum offering the opportunity to take GCSEs, entry level qualifications and a wide range of vocational courses. There is specialist unit for pupils with very complex needs, including multi-sensory impairment

and autism. Older pupils attend the well-established sixth form, where courses are hosted in local FE colleges and pupils are supported by qualified and experienced learning mentors. We accept day and weekly boarding pupils, and welcome pupils of all faiths and denominations.

Specialist facilities

All pupils are taught by teachers with additional qualifications in deafness or multi-sensory impairments. The school classrooms are acoustically treated and benefit from Soundfield technology. There is a resident audiologist and health and medical needs are coordinated by the school nurse and supported by a

programme of personal, social and health education. There are strong links with the local child and adolescent mental health team who specialise in working with deaf young people.

We have a team of highly specialised speech and language therapists who deliver both individual and group therapy sessions to all pupils. The therapists work with staff across the whole school and maintain close contact with parents, so everyone is clear how to maximise pupils' progress.

Primary

Teaching is tailored to pupils' individual needs by specialist teachers and a broad and imaginative curriculum inspires creative and enthusiastic learners. Indoor and outdoor zones provide a vibrant learning environment, and there are sensory and soft play rooms for sensory integration. Primary pupils enjoy regular integration and social opportunities at neighbouring schools and take part in an extensive programme of enrichment activities.

Secondary

There is a high level of personalisation in the curriculum for secondary pupils – more than sixteen subjects can be studied at different levels, from entry level to GCSEs and their equivalent. The development of literacy and numeracy is a key priority, and this is achieved through intensive specialist teaching in small classes. As well as traditional academic subjects, our curriculum provides a strong focus on creative and practical subjects that develop social communication and other essential skills for future adult life.

Sixth form

The sixth form offers our students the opportunity to study a wide range of academic and vocational courses

linked to two local colleges. Students have full time support from learning mentors who are all trained to support the communication needs of deaf people. Linking with mainstream colleges helps students build wider friendship groups and offers new social opportunities.

The sixth form residential setting provides a full life-skills programme which is accessible for young people with a range of additional needs such as visual impairments. By the end of their time at St John's, students have well-developed independence skills for adult life.

Multi-sensory impairment

There is a small specialist unit for pupils who have more complex needs, including multi-sensory impairment (MSI) and autism. These young people are supported by expert staff, and learning concentrates on presenting meaningful experiences that avoid sensory overload. Communication systems are built around the child's preferences, including PECs (Picture Exchange Communication system), Makaton, hand over hand signing and computer aided systems.

Boarding facilities

The residential areas are homely and welcoming. Young people who board live in small family units and are looked after by an experienced and knowledgeable staff team, who help them to form positive relationships and develop negotiation and co-operation skills. There is a full programme of leisure activities, and children have the opportunity to participate in local clubs and sports societies. The school offers weekly or flexi-boarding, and all students go home every weekend.

Home school links

Very close links with families are maintained, with regular updates on progress and achievements. Parents are welcome to visit the school, and are kept up to date with activities by the half termly newsletter.

General environment

The school is within walking distance of the elegant and vibrant Georgian village of Boston Spa, where there are shops, cafés and parks. The extensive buildings are well-equipped and include a gym with specialist fitness equipment, a purpose built theatre and sound recording room, a fully stocked library, an IT suite and a number of sensory rooms. The grounds are perfect for sports and leisure activities, with marked pitches and a newly-developed sensory garden.

Doncaster School for the Deaf

Doncaster School for the Deaf

(Founded 1829)

Leger Way, Doncaster, South Yorkshire
DN2 6AY
Tel: 01302 386733
Fax: 01302 361808
Email: principal@ddt-deaf.org.uk or
secretary@ddt-deaf.org.uk
Website: www.deaf-trust.co.uk

Executive Principal: Mr Alan W Robinson
School type: Non-maintained (Special)
Coeducational Boarding and Day
Age range of pupils: 4–19
No. of pupils enrolled as at 01/01/2017: 32
Boys: 20 *Girls:* 12
Fees per annum as at 01/01/2017:
Fees on request

We offer a broad and balanced curriculum which is accessible to all our pupils, providing smooth progression and continuity through all Key Stages.

The language and communication policy at Doncaster School for the Deaf is a pupil-centred approach, based on their method of preferred communication. We aim to meet the needs of pupils who communicate through British Sign Language (BSL) or English.

The School has a full-time Audiologist, Speech and Language Therapists and a team of Teaching Assistants as well as an on-site fully qualified Nurse. Most teachers are experienced and qualified teachers of the deaf.

Provision for resident pupils is in a modern comfortable house sympathetically converted to provide high standards of living accommodation.

Qualifications include A Levels, AS Levels, GCSE, Entry Level Certificate of Achievement, ASDAN unit Awards and Signature (BSL). The school believes that the school curriculum should be broad, balanced and personalised in order to reflect the needs of each pupil and to nurture a lifelong desire to learn. In addition to curriculum subjects pupils access speech therapy, BSL lessons and Deaf Studies. Some KS4 and KS5 pupils are able to access vocational courses as part of the 14-19 curriculum.

The School works in partnership with Little Learners Day Nursery and Communication Specialist College Doncaster (formerly Doncaster College for the Deaf) which share the same campus.

We have close links with parents, and other professionals.

The school occupies a large, pleasant site. A superb sports hall, heated indoor swimming pool and extensive playing fields. The school welcomes visitors.

The Royal Blind School

ROYAL BLIND
THE ROYAL BLIND SCHOOL

(Founded 1835)
43 Canaan Lane, Edinburgh, EH10 4SG

Tel: 0131 446 3120
Fax: 0131 447 9266
Email: office@royalblindschool.org.uk
Website: www.royalblind.org/education
Head Teacher: Elaine Brackenridge (BEd)

School type: Coeducational,
National Grant Aided Special School
Age range of pupils: 5–19
Fees per annum as at 25/01/2017:
Available on request

The Royal Blind School was founded in 1835. It is run by Scotland's largest vision impairment charity, Royal Blind, and is regulated by Education Scotland and the Care Inspectorate. We are a grant-aided special school supported by the Scottish Government.

The school, situated in Morningside, Edinburgh, is Scotland's only residential school specialising in the care and education of visually impaired young people, including those with complex needs.

Places are paid for through fees from local authorities or privately. We offer 52-week residential or term-time boarding, as well as nightly and weekly boarding. Our residential houses are fully accessible and designed to be a home from home.

We enrol pupils from P1 to S6 and in addition there is a free pre-school playgroup held on Friday mornings during term-time.

The Royal Blind School has a high ratio of staff to pupils and we offer a full curriculum of subjects. Each child follows an individualised education programme underpinned by the Curriculum for Excellence and Getting it Right for Every Child (GIRFEC). We deliver a broad general education and offer qualifications and accreditation by the Scottish Qualifications Authority (SQA), Junior Awards Scheme Scotland, Personal Achievement Awards and ASDAN in the senior phase.

Our approach is inclusive and pupil-centred, providing many opportunities for experience and achievement. We strive to make learning fun, challenging and self-affirming. We deliver independent living skills, building self-confidence and self-esteem by providing a greater awareness of the wider environment through mobility and orientation to ensure that all pupils become as independent as possible.

Pupils in fourth, fifth and sixth year have the opportunity to take part in work experience. Some pupils are involved in a Coffee Shop Enterprise Project. This activity gives young people the opportunity to develop a valuable range of life skills such as social interaction, handling money, planning, shopping and baking.

Outreach Support

We also provide an education outreach service offering support, training, resources and advice to staff in mainstream schools who are working with visually impaired pupils through our Learning Hub, www.royalblind.org/learninghub.

For more information please visit our website www.royalblind.org/education or telephone 0131 446 3120, or email office@royalblindschool.org.uk.

Scottish Charity No. SC 017167.

Directory

Schools and colleges specialising in social interaction difficulties (Autism, ASD & ASP)

Abbreviations

ACLD	Autism, Communication and Associated Learning Difficulties
ADD	Attention Deficit Disorder
ADHD	Attention Deficit and Hyperactive Disorder (Hyperkinetic Disorder)
ASD	Autistic Spectrum Disorder
ASP	Asperger Syndrome
AUT	Autism
BESD	Behavioural, Emotional and Social Difficulties
CCD	Complex Communication Difficulties
CLD	Complex Learning Difficulties
CP	Cerebral Palsy
D	Deaf
DEL	Delicate
DYS	Dyslexia
DYSP	Dyspraxia
EBD	Emotional and Behavioural Difficulties
EBSD	Emotional, Behavioural and/or Social Difficulties
EPI	Epilepsy
GLD	General Learning Difficulties
HA	High Ability
HI	Hearing Impairment
HS	Hospital School
LD	Learning Difficulties
MLD	Moderate Learning Difficulties
MSI	Multi-sensory Impairment
OCD	Obsessive Compulsive Disorder
PD	Physical Difficulties
PH	Physical Impairment
Phe	Partially Hearing
PMLD	Profound and Multiple Learning Difficulties
PNI	Physical Neurological Impairment
PRU	Pupil Referral Unit
SCD	Social and Communication Difficulties
SCLD	Severe and Complex Learning Difficulties
SEBD	Severe Emotional and Behavioural Disorders
SEBN	Social, Emotional and Behavioural Needs
SLD	Severe Learning Difficulties
SLI	Specific Language Impairment
SPLD	Specific Learning Difficulties
SP&LD	Speech and Language Difficulties
SLCN	Speech Language & Communication Needs
VIS	Visually Impaired

Key to Symbols

Type of school:

⚉	Boys' school
⚉	Girls' school
⚉	International school

School offers:

Ⓐ	A levels
⚉	Residential
⑯	Entrance at 16+
⚉	Vocational qualifications
⚉	Learning support
✓	This is a DfE approved independent or non-maintained school under section 41 of the Children and Families Act 2014 or section 342 of the 1996 Education Act

Please note: Unless otherwise indicated, all schools are coeducational day schools. Single-sex and boarding schools will be indicated by the relevant icon.

Central & West

Bath & North-East Somerset

Rookery Radstock
Wells Road, Radstock, Bath, Bath & North-East Somerset BA3 3RS
Tel: 01761 438611
Principal/Manager: Ms Doreen Paisley
Age range: 18–25
No. of pupils: 27
Special needs catered for: ASD, ASP
16 🏫

Bristol

Aurora Hedgeway School
Rookery Lane, Pilning, Bristol BS35 4JN
Tel: 01454 632532
Principal: Ms Kim McConnell
Age range: 8–19
Special needs catered for: AUT
16

Oxfordshire

LVS OXFORD
For further details see p. 58
Spring Hill Road, Begbroke, Oxfordshire OX5 1RX
Tel: 01865 595170
Email: enquiries@lvs-oxford.org.uk
Website: www.lvs-oxford.org.uk
Head Teacher: Mrs Louisa Allison-Bergin
Age range: 11–19
No. of pupils: 49
Special needs catered for: ASD, ASP, AUT
🏫 16

Swalcliffe Park School Trust
Swalcliffe, Banbury, Oxfordshire OX15 5EP
Tel: 01295 780302
Principal: Mr Kiran Hingorani
Age range: B11–19
No. of pupils: 45
Special needs catered for: ADHD, ASD, BESD, DYS, DYSP, MLD, SP&LD
👤 🏫 16 ✓

West Berkshire

PRIOR'S COURT SCHOOL
For further details see p. 60
Hermitage, Thatcham, West Berkshire RG18 9NU
Tel: 01635 247202/245914
Email: mail@priorscourt.org.uk
Website: www.priorscourt.org.uk
Director of Education and Learning: Sue Piper
Age range: 5–19
No. of pupils: 65 VIth23
Special needs catered for: AUT, CLD, EPI, MLD, SCLD
🏫 ✓

Wiltshire

Farleigh Further Education College Swindon
Fairview House, 43 Bath Road, Old Town, Swindon, Wiltshire SN1 4AS
Tel: 01793 719500
Principal/Manager: Mr Martin Bentham
Age range: 16–25
No. of pupils: 63
Special needs catered for: ASP, LD
16 🏫

Stratford Lodge
4 Park Lane, Castle Road, Salisbury, Wiltshire SP1 3NP
Tel: 0800 138 1184
Head: Mr Greg Sorrell
Age range: 16–19
Special needs catered for: ADHD, ASD, ASP
🏫 16

East

Cambridgeshire

GRETTON SCHOOL
For further details see p. 62
Manor Farm Road, Girton, Cambridge, Cambridgeshire CB3 0RX
Tel: 01223 277438
Email: info@grettonschool.com
Website: www.grettonschool.com
Head Teacher: Ms Zoe Kirby
Age range: 5–19
Special needs catered for: ASD, ASP, AUT
🏫 16 ✓

On Track Training Centre
Enterprise House, Old Field Lane, Wisbech, Cambridgeshire PE13 2RJ
Tel: 01945 580898
Headteacher: Mrs Sharon Claydon
Age range: 11–18
Special needs catered for: ADHD, ASP, EBD
16 ✓

Park House
Wisbech Road, Thorney, Peterborough, Cambridgeshire PE6 0SA
Tel: 01733 271187
Head: Mr Alan Crossland
Age range: 4–16
Special needs catered for: AUT
✓

The Beeches Independent School
218 Dogsthorpe Road, Peterborough, Cambridgeshire PE1 3PB
Tel: 01733 344448
Head of Education: Ms Kathryn Black
Age range: G10–18
Special needs catered for: AUT
16

Essex

The Yellow House School
1 Alderford Street, Sible Hedingham, Halstead, Essex CO9 3HX
Tel: 01787 462504
Proprietor: Debbie Pester
Age range: 13–17
No. of pupils: 11
Special needs catered for: ADHD, ASP, EBD
✓

Hertfordshire

NAS RADLETT LODGE SCHOOL
For further details see p. 63
Harper Lane, Radlett, Hertfordshire WD7 9HW
Tel: 01923 854922
Email: radlett.lodge@nas.org.uk
Website: www.radlettlodgeschool.org.uk
Principal: Jeremy Keeble
Age range: 4–19
No. of pupils: 55
Special needs catered for: ASD, ASP, AUT
🏫 16 ✓

Norfolk

Acorn Park School
Mill Road, Banham, Norwich, Norfolk NR16 2HU
Tel: 01953 888656
Head Teacher: Mr John Shaw BEd(Hons), DipEdMan
Age range: 4–19
Special needs catered for: ASD, AUT, CLD, EPI, LD, MLD, SCD, SCLD, SLD, SPLD
🏫 16

East Midlands

Derbyshire

High Grange School
Hospital Lane, Mickleover,
Derby, Derbyshire DE3 0DR
Tel: 01332 412777
Principal: Mr Gavin Spicer
Age range: 8–19
Special needs catered for:
ADHD, ASD, ASP, AUT
(A) (16+) (✓)

Leicestershire

Sketchley School and Forest House
Manor Way, Sketchley, Burbage,
Leicestershire LE10 3HT
Tel: 01455 890 023
Principal: Ms Sarah-Jane Astbury
Age range: 8–19
No. of pupils: 30
Special needs catered for:
ASD, ASP, AUT
(16+) (✓)

Northamptonshire

Alderwood
302 Wellingborough Road,
Rushden, Northamptonshire
NN10 6BB
Tel: 01933 359861
Head: Mrs Jacqueline Wadlow
Special needs catered for: ASD, AUT
(≗) (16+) (✓)

Cambian Potterspury Lodge School
Towcester, Northamptonshire
NN12 7LL
Tel: 0800 138 1184
Executive Head: Ms Lise Sugden
BSc(Hons), PGCE, NPQH
Age range: B8–18
No. of pupils: 40 VIth8
Special needs catered for:
ADD, ADHD, ASD, ASP, AUT,
DYS, DYSP, EBD, SCD, SP&LD
(♟) (≗) (16+) (✓)

Hill Farm College
c/o The Manor House,
Squires Hill, Rothwell,
Northamptonshire NN14 6BQ
Tel: 01536 711111
Principal: Jo Morris
Age range: 14–19
No. of pupils: 12
Special needs catered for:
ADHD, ASD, ASP
(≗) (16+)

Rutland

Wilds Lodge School
Stamford Road, Empingham,
Rutland LE15 8QQ
Tel: 01780 767254
Age range: 5–18
Special needs catered for:
ASD, MLD, SEBD
(16+)

Greater London

Essex

NAS ANDERSON
For further details see p. 59
Luxborough Lane,
Chigwell Essex IG7 5AB
Email: chigwell.
school@nas.org.uk
Website:
www.andersonschool.org.uk
Principal: Gary Simm
Age range: 11–19
No. of pupils: 78
Special needs catered for:
ASD, ASP, AUT
(16+)

Kent

Baston House School
Baston Road, Hayes,
Bromley, Kent BR2 7AB
Tel: 020 8462 1010
Principal: Steve Vincent
Age range: 3–19
Special needs catered for: ASD
(16+) (✓)

Middlesex

NAS SYBIL ELGAR SCHOOL
For further details see p. 64
Havelock Road, Southall,
Middlesex UB2 4NY
Tel: 020 8813 9168
Email: sybil.elgar@nas.org.uk
Website:
www.sybilelgarschool.org.uk
Principal: Chloe Phillips
Age range: 4–19
No. of pupils: 90
Special needs catered for:
ASD, ASP, AUT
(≗) (16+) (✓)

Surrey

Link Secondary Day School
82-86 Croydon Road, Beddington,
Croydon, Surrey CR0 4PD
Tel: 020 8688 7691
Headteacher: Miss P
Ridgwell BEd, NPQH
Age range: 11–19
No. of pupils: 48 VIth9
Special needs catered for:
ASD, ASP, SP&LD, SLI
(✓)

London

North London

Kestrel House School
104 Crouch Hill, London N8 9EA
Tel: 020 8348 8500
Headteacher: Kerry Harris
Age range: 4–16
Special needs catered for: ASP, AUT
(✓)

THE HOLMEWOOD SCHOOL
For further details see p. 65
88 Woodside Park Road,
London N12 8SH
Tel: 020 8920 0660
Email: enquiries@thsl.org.uk
Website: www.thsl.org.uk
Head of School: Head
Teacher Lisa Camilleri
Age range: 7–19
Special needs catered for:
ASD, ASP, AUT, SP&LD
(IB) (16+) (✓)

TreeHouse School
Woodside Avenue, London N10 3JA
Tel: 020 8815 5424
Head: Julie O'Sullivan
Age range: 3–19
No. of pupils: 67
Special needs catered for: ASD, AUT
(16+) (✓)

South-East London

Riverston School
63-69 Eltham Road, Lee
Green, London SE12 8UF
Tel: 020 8318 4327
Headmistress: Mrs S E Salathiel
Age range: 9 months–19 years
No. of pupils: 215
Special needs catered for:
ASD, ASP, AUT, LD
(♿) (£) (✏)

South-West London

Priory Lodge School
Priory Lane, London SW15 5JJ
Tel: 020 8392 4410
Principal: Pancho Martinez
Age range: 5–19
No. of pupils: 40
Special needs catered for:
ADHD, ASD, ASP, AUT, LD
(16+) (✓)

Rainbow School
48 North Side, Wandsworth
Common, London SW18 2SL
Tel: 020 3031 9700
**Head of Upper
School:** David Anthony
Age range: 4–19
Special needs catered for:
ASD, ASP, AUT, SCD
(✓)

**The Chelsea Group
of Children**
The Hall, Waynflete Street,
London SW18 3QG
Tel: 020 8946 8330
Director: Libby Hartman
Age range: 4–8
Special needs catered for: ADHD,
ASP, AUT, LD, MLD, SP&LD, SPLD
✔

North-East

Durham

Hurworth House School
Westfield Drive, Hurworth,
Darlington, Durham DL2 2AD
Tel: 01325 729 080
Principal: Mr John Anderson
Age range: 7–19
No. of pupils: 30
Special needs catered for:
AUT, BESD, EBD
16+

Tyne & Wear

ESPA College
6-7 The Cloisters, Ashbrooke,
Sunderland, Tyne & Wear SR2 7BD
Tel: 0191 510 2600
Principal (Acting): Mrs C Pickup
Age range: 16–25
No. of pupils: 100
Special needs catered for:
ASD, ASP, AUT
♨

Thornhill Park School
21 Thornhill Park, Sunderland,
Tyne & Wear SR2 7LA
Tel: 0191 514 0659
Head Teacher: Margaret Burton
Age range: 4–19
No. of pupils: 74
Fees: Day £33,752–£45,806
FB £117,433–£204,986
Special needs catered for:
ASD, ASP, AUT
♨ 16+ ✔

North-West

Cheshire

Inscape House School
Together Trust Campus,
Schools Hill, Cheadle,
Stockport, Cheshire SK8 1JE
Tel: 0161 283 4750
Head of School: Anne Price
Age range: 5–19
No. of pupils: 100
Special needs catered for:
ASD, ASP, AUT, CLD
16+ ✔

Royal College Manchester
Seashell Trust, Stanley Road,
Cheadle, Cheshire SK8 6RQ
Tel: 01616 100100
Age range: 19–25
No. of pupils: 70
Special needs catered for:
ASD, D, MSI, PD, PMLD, VIS
♨

Royal School Manchester
Seashell Trust, Stanley Road,
Cheadle, Cheshire SK8 6RQ
Tel: 01616 100100
Age range: 2–19
No. of pupils: 45
Special needs catered for:
ASD, D, HI, MSI, PMLD
16+

Cumbria

Lindeth College
Wigton Road, Carlisle,
Cumbria CA2 6LB
Tel: 01228 822649
Principal/Manager: Ms
Shirley Harrison
Age range: 16–25
No. of pupils: 30
Special needs catered for:
MLD, SLD
16+ ♨

Greater Manchester

Fairfield House School
59 Warburton Lane, Partington,
Manchester, Greater
Manchester M31 4NL
Tel: 0161 7762827
Headteacher: Ms Melanie Sproston
Age range: 8–19
Special needs catered for: ASD
16+ ✔

Lancashire

**Aurora Brambles
East School**
Woodlands, Holly Tree Close,
Darwen, Lancashire BB3 2NG
Tel: 01254 706 600
Head Teacher: Sam Clark
Age range: B10–16
Special needs catered for: SEBD

Bracken School
1 Harbour Lane, Warton,
Preston, Lancashire PR4 1YA
Tel: 01772 631531
Headteacher: Paul Addison
Age range: G11–16
No. of pupils: 5
Special needs catered for:
ADHD, DYS, MLD
♿

Oliver House School
Hallgate, Astley Village,
Chorley, Lancashire PR7 1XA
Tel: 01257 220 011
Principal: Ms Wendy Sparling
Age range: 6–19
No. of pupils: 28
Special needs catered for:
ASD, ASP, AUT, LD
♨ 16+ ✔

Red Rose School
28-30 North Promenade,
St Annes on Sea, Lytham St
Annes, Lancashire FY8 2NQ
Tel: 01253 720570
Principal: Colin Lannen
Age range: 5–16
Special needs catered for:
ASD, DEL, SPLD
✔

Rossendale School
Bamford Road, Ramsbottom,
Bury, Lancashire BL0 0RT
Tel: 01706 822779
Headteacher: Mr David Duncan
Age range: 8–18
Special needs catered for:
ADD, ADHD, ASD, ASP, AUT,
BESD, CLD, DYS, DYSP, EBD, EPI,
HA, SCD, SEBD, SLD, SPLD
Ⓐ ♨ ✔

Trax Academy
1 Stuart Road, Bredbury,
Stockport, Lancashire SK6 2SR
Tel: 0161 483 1505
Headteacher: Mr Edward Sloane
Age range: 11–18
No. of pupils: 12
Special needs catered for:
ADHD, EBD
16+ ✔

Westmorland School
Weldbank Lane, Chorley,
Lancashire PR7 3NQ
Tel: 01257 278899
Head Teacher: Mrs S M Asher
BSc (Hons), PGCE, NPQH
Age range: 5–11
No. of pupils: 44
Special needs catered for:
ADHD, ASD, ASP, AUT, BESD,
MLD, SP&LD, SPLD
✔

Merseyside

Arden College
40 Derby Road, Southport,
Merseyside PR9 0TZ
Tel: 01704 534 433
Principal/Manager: Mr
Mark Musselle
Age range: 16–25
No. of pupils: 53
Special needs catered for: ASD, LD
16+ ♨

Lakeside School
Naylors Road, Huyton, Liverpool, Merseyside L27 2YA
Tel: 0151 4877211
Head Teacher: Mrs V I Size BEd(Hons), MEd(Autism)
Age range: 5–13
No. of pupils: 24
Special needs catered for: ADD, ADHD, ASD, ASP, AUT, BESD, CLD, DEL, DYS, DYSP, EPI, HA, HI, LD, MLD, PH, SCD, SP&LD, SPLD, SLI, VIS
✔

Peterhouse School for Pupils with Autism & Asperger's Syndrome
Preston New Road, Southport, Merseyside PR9 8PA
Tel: 01704 506682
Headteacher: Mrs Janet Allan BA (Hons), PGCE, SEN Dipl, NPQH
Age range: 5–19
No. of pupils: 47 VIth23
Fees: Day £38,190 WB £90,896 FB £120,045
Special needs catered for: ASD, ASP, AUT
🏠 16+ ✔

WEST KIRBY SCHOOL AND COLLEGE
For further details see p. 66
Meols Drive, West Kirby, Wirral, Merseyside CH48 5DH
Tel: 0151 632 3201
Website: www.wkrs.co.uk
Principal: Mr Iain Sim
Age range: 5–19
No. of pupils: 87
Special needs catered for: ADHD, ASD, BESD, SCD, SEBD, SLI
🏠 ✔

South-East

Berkshire

Heathermount, The Learning Centre
Devenish Road, Ascot, Berkshire SL5 9PG
Tel: 01344 875101
Headteacher: Ms Ruth Bovill
Age range: 5–19
No. of pupils: 25
Special needs catered for: ASD, ASP, AUT
16+ ✔

NAS THAMES VALLEY SCHOOL
For further details see p. 69
Conwy Close, Tilehurst, Reading, Berkshire RG30 4BZ
Tel: 0118 9424 750
Email: thames.valley@nas.org.uk
Website: www.thames valleyschool.org.uk
Principal: David Stewart
Age range: 5–16
No. of pupils: 50
Special needs catered for: ASP, AUT

East Sussex

Rookery Hove
22-24 Sackville Gardens, Hove, East Sussex BN3 4GH
Tel: 01273 202 520
Principal/Manager: Mr Loz Blume
Age range: 18–35
No. of pupils: 13
Special needs catered for: ASD, ASP
16+ 🏠

Step by Step School for Autistic Children
Neylands Farm, Grinstead Lane, Sharpethorne, East Sussex RH19 4HP
Tel: 01342 811852
Headteacher: Mrs Faye Palmer
Age range: 4–11
No. of pupils: 12
Special needs catered for: AUT
✔

Hampshire

Grateley House School
Pond Lane, Grateley, Andover, Hampshire SP11 8TA
Tel: 0800 138 1184
Head: Mr Greg Sorrell
Age range: 9–19
Special needs catered for: ASD, ASP
🏠 16+ ✔

Hill House School
Rope Hill, Boldre, Lymington, Hampshire SO41 8NE
Tel: 0800 138 1184
Head of School: Ms Kate Landells BSc (open), CertSocSci(open) NVQ3 HSC, PTLLS(L4)
Age range: 11–19
Special needs catered for: ASD, AUT, SCD, SCLD, SLD
🏠 16+ ✔

Southlands School
Vicars Hill, Boldre, Lymington, Hampshire SO41 5QB
Tel: 0800 138 1184
Head: Ms Karen Gittins
Age range: B7–19
Special needs catered for: ASD, ASP
🧍 🏠 16+ ✔

Tadley Court School
Tadley Common Road, Tadley, Basingstoke, Hampshire RG26 3TB
Tel: 0118 981 7720
Principal: Phil Jonas
Age range: 5–19
No. of pupils: 67
Special needs catered for: ASD, ASP, AUT
🏠 16+ ✔

Kent

Blue Skies School
126 Maidstone Road, Chatham, Kent ME4 6DQ
Tel: 01634 357770
Head of School: Mr Jonathan Higgins
Age range: 11–19
No. of pupils: 17
Special needs catered for: ASD, ASP, AUT
16+ ✔

NAS HELEN ALLISON SCHOOL
For further details see p. 68
Longfield Road, Meopham, Kent DA13 0EW
Tel: 01474 814878
Email: helen.allison@nas.org.uk
Website: www.helenallisonschool.org.uk
Principal: Susan Conway
Age range: 5–19
No. of pupils: 77
Special needs catered for: ASD, ASP, AUT
🏠 16+ ✔

The Quest School
Church Farm, Church Road, The Old Stables, Offham, Kent ME19 5NX
Tel: 01732 522700
Headteacher: Mrs Anne Martin
Age range: 4–14
No. of pupils: 8
Special needs catered for: AUT, EBD
✔

Surrey

Eagle House School (Mitcham)
224 London Road, Mitcham, Surrey CR4 3HD
Tel: 020 8687 7050
Head: Katherine Walker ACLD ASC ASD ASP AUT
Age range: 4–11
Special needs catered for: ASD, ASP, AUT, MLD, SCD, SLD
✔

Eagle House School (Sutton)
95 Brighton Road, Sutton, Surrey SM2 5SJ
Tel: 020 8661 1419
Head: Yvonne Gabriel ACDL ASC ASD ASP AUT
Age range: 11–19
Special needs catered for: AUT
16+ ✔

Jigsaw CABAS® School
Building 20, Dunsfold Park, Stovolds Hill, Cranleigh, Surrey GU6 8TB
Tel: 01483 273874
Executive Head: Ms Kate Grant
Age range: 4–19
No. of pupils: VIth17
Fees: Day £49,900–£52,732
Special needs catered for: ASD, AUT
16+ ✔

Papillon House School
Pebble Close, Tadworth, Surrey KT20 7PA
Tel: 01372 363663
Headteacher and Director: Mrs Gillian Hutton
Age range: 4–16
Fees: Day £45,000
Special needs catered for: ASD, AUT
✔

Unsted Park School and Sixth Form
Munstead Heath Road, Godalming, Surrey GU7 1UW
Tel: 01483 892 061
Principal: Mr Steve Dempsey
Age range: 7–19
No. of pupils: 55
Special needs catered for: ASD, ASP, AUT
🏠 16+ ✔

West Sussex

LVS HASSOCKS
For further details see p. 67
London Road, Sayers Common,
Hassocks, West Sussex BN6 9HT
Tel: 01273 832901
Email: office@lvs-
hassocks.org.uk
Website:
www.lvs-hassocks.org.uk
Head Teacher: Ms Terry Kelly
Age range: 8–19
No. of pupils: 84
Special needs catered for:
ASD, ASP, AUT
(16)

South-West

Cornwall

Three Bridges
Education Centre
East Hill, Blackwater, Truro,
Cornwall TR4 8EG
Tel: 01872 561010
Headteacher: Kathleen Hampshire
Age range: 11–19
No. of pupils: 8
Special needs catered for:
ASD, ASP, AUT
(16) (✓)

Devon

Acorn School
Little Oak, Knowstone,
South Molton EX36 4SA
Tel: 01271 859720
Headteacher: Mrs Abbie Heard
Age range: 11–16
Special needs catered for: SEBD

Devon Education and
Children's Services
Bere Alston, Yelverton,
Devon PL20 7EX
Tel: 01822 840379
Principal: Mr John Steward
Age range: 7–19
No. of pupils: 63
Special needs catered for:
ADHD, ASD, ASP, AUT, BESD, CLD,
EBD, GLD, MLD, SCD, SCLD
(⚲) (16) (✓)

Dorset

Cambian Wing College
126 Richmond Park Road,
Bournemouth, Dorset BH8 8TH
Tel: 0800 138 1184
Head: Ms Kim Welsh
Age range: B16–25
Special needs catered for:
ASD, ASP
(♦) (⚲) (16)

Portfield School
Parley Lane, Christchurch,
Dorset BH23 6BP
Tel: 01202 573808
Headteacher: Mr Tyler Collins
Age range: 3–19
No. of pupils: 59
Special needs catered for: ASD, AUT
(⚲) (16) (✓)

Purbeck View School
Northbrook Road, Swanage,
Dorset BH19 1PR
Tel: 0800 138 1184
Head: Ms Sophie Clarke
Age range: 7–19
Special needs catered for: ASD, AUT
(⚲) (16) (✓)

The Forum School
Shillingstone, Blandford
Forum, Dorset DT11 0QS
Tel: 0800 138 1184
Acting Head: Mr David Keeton
Age range: 7–19
Special needs catered for: ASD, AUT
(⚲) (16) (✓)

Somerset

3 Dimensions
Chardleigh House, Chardleigh
Green, Wadeford, Chard,
Somerset TA20 3AJ
Tel: 01460 68055
Education Manager: Ms Nita Ellul
Age range: B11–16
No. of pupils: 5
Special needs catered for:
ADHD, AUT, EBD
(♦) (⚲) (✓)

Farleigh College Mells
Newbury, Nr Mells, Frome,
Somerset BA11 3RG
Tel: 01373 814980
Principal: Ms Sharon Edney
Age range: 11–19
No. of pupils: 52
Special needs catered for: ADD,
ADHD, ASD, ASP, AUT, DYS, DYSP
(⚲) (16) (✓)

Farleigh Further Education
College Frome
North Parade, Frome,
Somerset BA11 2AB
Tel: 01373 475470
Principal/Manager: Mr
Alun Maddocks
Age range: 16–19
No. of pupils: 87
Special needs catered for: ASP, LD
(16) (⚲)

North Hill House School
Fromefield, Frome,
Somerset BA11 2HB
Tel: 01373 466 222
Principal: Ms Sharon Edney
Age range: B6–19
No. of pupils: 62
Special needs catered for:
ADD, ADHD, ASD, ASP, AUT
(♦) (⚲) (16) (✓)

West Midlands

Shropshire

CRUCKTON HALL
For further details see p. 70
Cruckton, Shrewsbury,
Shropshire SY5 8PR
Tel: 01743 860206
Email: jo.burdon@cruckton.com
Website: www.cruckton.com
Head Teacher: Jo Burdon
Age range: B8–19
No. of pupils: 80
Special needs catered for:
ADD, ADHD, ASP, AUT,
DYS, EBD, PMLD, SPLD

Options Higford
Higford Hall, Higford, Shifnal,
Shropshire TF11 9ET
Tel: 01952 630600
Headteacher: Anne Adams
Age range: 8–19
Special needs catered for:
ASD, AUT, CLD, DYS, DYSP, EPI,
GLD, HA, LD, MLD, MSI, PMLD,
SCLD, SLD, SP&LD, SPLD

Staffordshire

NAS CHURCH LAWTON SCHOOL
For further details see p. 72
Cherry Tree Avenue, Church
Lawton, Stoke-on-Trent,
Staffordshire ST7 3EL
Tel: 01270 877601
Email: churchlawton@
nas.org.uk
Website: www.church
lawtonschool.org.uk
Principal: Paul Scales
Age range: 4–19
No. of pupils: 60
Special needs catered for:
ASD, AUT

Priory Highfields
9 & 11 Highfields Road, Chasetown,
Burntwood, Staffordshire WS7 4QR
Tel: 01543 672 173
Principal: Ms Joan Pearson
Age range: 18–25
No. of pupils: 10
Special needs catered for: ASD

Rugeley School
Blithbury Road, Blithbury, Rugeley,
Staffordshire WS15 3JQ
Tel: 01889 504400
Principal: Ms Joan Pearson
Age range: 5–19
No. of pupils: 48
Special needs catered for:
ASD, ASP, AUT, MLD, SLD

Strathmore College
Unit 7 Imex Centre, Technology Park,
Stoke-on-Trent, Staffordshire ST4 8LJ
Tel: 01782 647380
Principal/Manager: Ms Kate Ward
Age range: 16–25
No. of pupils: 37
Special needs catered for: ASD,
ASP, BESD, CLD, GLD, LD, MLD, SLD

Warwickshire

Avon Park School
St John's Avenue, Rugby,
Warwickshire CV22 5HR
Tel: 01788 524448
Head Teacher: Gareth Plant
Age range: 6–16
No. of pupils: 19
Special needs catered for: ADD,
ADHD, ASD, ASP, BESD, CLD,
DYSP, LD, SCD, SEBD, SP&LD

West Midlands

QUEEN ALEXANDRA COLLEGE (QAC)
For further details see p. 73
Court Oak Road,
Harborne, Birmingham,
West Midlands B17 9TG
Tel: 0121 428 5050
Email: info@qac.ac.uk
Website: www.qac.ac.uk
Principal: Hugh J Williams
Age range: 16+
No. of pupils: 211
Special needs catered for:
ADD, ADHD, ASD, ASP, AUT,
BESD, CLD, CP, D, DYS, DYSP,
EBD, EPI, GLD, HA, HI, LD, MLD,
MSI, PD, Phe, PH, PNI, SCD,
SCLD, SLD, SP&LD, SPLD, SLI, VIS

The Island Project School
Diddington Hall, Diddington Lane,
Meriden, West Midlands CV7 7HQ
Tel: 01675 442588
Principal: Sarah Gallagher
Age range: 6–19
Special needs catered for: ASD, AUT

Worcestershire

Options Malvern View
The Rhydd, Hanley Castle,
Worcestershire WR8 0AD
Tel: 01684 312610
Registered Manager: Darren
Goodwin
Age range: 16–25
Special needs catered for: ASD

Yorkshire & Humberside

Lincolnshire

Options Barton
Barrow Road, Barton-upon-
Humber, Lincolnshire DN18 6DA
Tel: 01652 631280
Headteacher: Mark Eames
Age range: 8–19
Special needs catered for: ASD,
ASP, AUT, CLD, DYS, DYSP, GLD, HA,
LD, MLD, MSI, PMLD, SCLD, SLD, SPLD

The Bridge@Barton School
Barrow Road, Barton-upon-
Humber, Lincolnshire DN18 6DA
Tel: 01652 631280
Head of School: Mr Mark Eames
Age range: 8–19
Special needs catered for:

North Lincolnshire

Demeter House School
Bigby Street, Brigg, North
Lincolnshire DN20 8EF
Tel: 01652 654251
Headteacher: Mrs L Wardlaw
Age range: B5–14
No. of pupils: 5
Special needs catered for:
ADD, EBD

Options Roxby House
Winterton Road, Roxby,
Scunthorpe, North
Lincolnshire DN15 0BJ
Tel: 01724 733777
Centre Head: Mr Russell Leese
Age range: 16–30
Special needs catered for: ASD

South Yorkshire

FULLERTON HOUSE COLLEGE
For further details see p. 75
Tickhill Square, Denaby,
Doncaster, South
Yorkshire DN12 4AR
Tel: 01709 861663
Email: enquiries@
hesleygroup.co.uk
Website:
www.hesleygroup.co.uk
Head: Richard Webster
Age range: 18–25
Special needs catered for:
ASD, ASP, AUT, CLD, DYS, DYSP,
GLD, LD, MLD, SCLD, SLD, SPLD

FULLERTON HOUSE SCHOOL
For further details see p. 74
Tickhill Square, Denaby,
Doncaster, South
Yorkshire DN12 4AR
Tel: 01709 861663
Email: enquiries@
hesleygroup.co.uk
Website: www.fullerton
houseschool.co.uk
General Manager: Michael
Cavan
Age range: 8–19
Special needs catered for:
ASD, ASP, AUT, CLD, DYS, DYSP,
GLD, LD, MLD, SCLD, SLD, SPLD

NAS ROBERT OGDEN SCHOOL
For further details see p. 76
Clayton Lane, Thurnscoe,
Rotherham, South
Yorkshire S63 0BG
Tel: 01709 874443
Email: robert.ogden@nas.org.uk
Website:
www.robertogdenschool.org.uk
Principal: Lorraine Dormand
Age range: 5–19
No. of pupils: 127
Special needs catered for:
ASD, ASP, AUT

WILSIC HALL COLLEGE
For further details see p. 75
Wadworth, Doncaster,
South Yorkshire DN11 9AG
Tel: 01302 856382
Head: Geoff Turner
Age range: 19–25
No. of pupils: 3
Special needs catered for:
ASD, ASP, AUT, CLD, DYS, DYSP,
GLD, LD, MLD, SCLD, SLD, SPLD

WILSIC HALL SCHOOL
For further details see p. 77
Wadworth, Doncaster,
South Yorkshire DN11 9AG
Tel: 01302 856382
Email: enquiries@
hesleygroup.co.uk
Website:
www.wilsichallschool.co.uk
Head: Geoff Turner
Age range: 11–19
Special needs catered for:
ASD, ASP, AUT, CLD, DYS, DYSP,
GLD, LD, MLD, SCLD, SLD, SPLD

Scotland

Aberdeenshire

Troup House School
Gamrie, Banff, Aberdeenshire
AB45 3JN
Tel: 01261 851 584
Principal: Mr David McNally
Age range: 8–16+
No. of pupils: 12
Special needs catered for:
AUT, BESD

East Ayrshire

NAS DALDORCH HOUSE SCHOOL
For further details see p. 78
Sorn Road, Catrine, East
Ayrshire KA5 6NA
Tel: 01290 551666
Email: daldorch@nas.org.uk
Website: www.daldorch
houseschool.org.uk
Principal: Bernadette Casey
Age range: 8–21
Special needs catered for:
ASD, ASP, AUT

South Lanarkshire

NAS Daldorch Satellite School
St Leonards, East Kilbride,
South Lanarkshire G74
Tel: 01355 246242
Principal: Shona Pinkerton
Age range: 5–19
No. of pupils: 5
Special needs catered for:
ASD, ASP, AUT

Wales

Carmarthenshire

Coleg Elidyr
Rhandirmwyn, Llandovery,
Carmarthenshire SA20 0NL
Tel: 01550 760400
Age range: 18–25
No. of pupils: 43
Special needs catered for:
ADD, ADHD, ASD, ASP, AUT,
BESD, CLD, DEL, DYSP, EBD, EPI,
GLD, LD, MLD, Phe, SCD, SLD

Flintshire

Options Kinsale
Kinsale Hall, Llanerch-y-Mor,
Holywell, Flintshire CH8 9DX
Tel: 01745 562500
Head of Service: Mr Mark Williams
Age range: 8–19
Special needs catered for:
ASD, AUT, CLD, DYS, DYSP, EPI,
GLD, LD, MLD, MSI, PH, PMLD,
SCLD, SLD, SP&LD, SPLD

Options Ty Ni Cymru
Kinsale Hall, Llanerch-y-mor,
Holywell, Flintshire CH8 9DX
Tel: 01745 562570
Registered Manager: Shian Thomas
Age range: 18+
Special needs catered for: ASD

Torfaen

Priory College South Wales
Coleg Gwent, Pontypool
Campus, Blaendare Road,
Pontypool, Torfaen NP4 5YE
Tel: 01495 762 609
Principal/Manager: Mr Simon Coles
Age range: 16–25
No. of pupils: 11
Special needs catered for:
ASD, ASP, LD

Vale of Glamorgan

Beechwood College
Hayes Road, Penarth, Vale
of Glamorgan CF64 5SE
Tel: 029 2053 2210
Principal: Mr Darren Jackson
Age range: 16+
No. of pupils: 66
Special needs catered for:
ASD, ASP, SLD

Wrexham

Priory College North Wales
Ty Dewi Sant, Rhosddu
Road, Wrexham LL11 0ZX
Tel: 01978 340580
Principal/Manager: Mr Simon Coles
Age range: 16–25
No. of pupils: 5
Special needs catered for:
ASD, ASP, LD

Schools and colleges specialising in emotional, behavioural and/or social difficulties (EBSD)

Abbreviations

ACLD	Autism, Communication and Associated Learning Difficulties
ADD	Attention Deficit Disorder
ADHD	Attention Deficit and Hyperactive Disorder (Hyperkinetic Disorder)
ASD	Autistic Spectrum Disorder
ASP	Asperger Syndrome
AUT	Autism
BESD	Behavioural, Emotional and Social Difficulties
CCD	Complex Communication Difficulties
CLD	Complex Learning Difficulties
CP	Cerebral Palsy
D	Deaf
DEL	Delicate
DYS	Dyslexia
DYSP	Dyspraxia
EBD	Emotional and Behavioural Difficulties
EBSD	Emotional, Behavioural and/or Social Difficulties
EPI	Epilepsy
GLD	General Learning Difficulties
HA	High Ability
HI	Hearing Impairment
HS	Hospital School
LD	Learning Difficulties
MLD	Moderate Learning Difficulties
MSI	Multi-sensory Impairment
OCD	Obsessive Compulsive Disorder
PD	Physical Difficulties
PH	Physical Impairment
Phe	Partially Hearing
PMLD	Profound and Multiple Learning Difficulties
PNI	Physical Neurological Impairment
PRU	Pupil Referral Unit
SCD	Social and Communication Difficulties
SCLD	Severe and Complex Learning Difficulties
SEBD	Severe Emotional and Behavioural Disorders
SEBN	Social, Emotional and Behavioural Needs
SLD	Severe Learning Difficulties
SLI	Specific Language Impairment
SPLD	Specific Learning Difficulties
SP&LD	Speech and Language Difficulties
SLCN	Speech Language & Communication Needs
VIS	Visually Impaired

Key to Symbols

Type of school:

(symbol)	Boys' school
(symbol)	Girls' school
(symbol)	International school

School offers:

(A)	A levels
(symbol)	Residential
(16+)	Entrance at 16+
(symbol)	Vocational qualifications
(symbol)	Learning support
(✓)	This is a DfE approved independent or non-maintained school under section 41 of the Children and Families Act 2014 or section 342 of the 1996 Education Act

Please note: Unless otherwise indicated, all schools are coeducational day schools. Single-sex and boarding schools will be indicated by the relevant icon.

Central & West

Buckinghamshire

Benjamin College
4 Wren Path, Fairford Leys,
Aylesbury, Buckinghamshire
HP19 7AR
Tel: 01296 483584
Principal: Mr Jeremy Yelland
Age range: 12–18
Special needs catered for: BESD
(16) ✔

Gloucestershire

Cotswold Chine School
Box, Stroud, Gloucestershire
GL6 9AG
Tel: 01453 837550
Headteacher: Maureen
Smith MA(Ed), PGCertSpLd,
PGCE, BA(Hons)
Age range: 9–19
No. of pupils: 48
Special needs catered for:
ADD, ADHD, ASP, AUT, DYS,
DYSP, EBD, EPI, MLD, SP&LD
(🕎)(🏛)(✔)

Oxfordshire

Action for Children Parklands Campus
Chardleigh House, Near Appleton,
Abingdon, Oxfordshire OX13 5QB
Tel: 01865 390436
Principal: Mr. Sean Cannon
Age range: 11–19
No. of pupils: 7 VIth2
Fees: Day £50,000 FB £192,000
Special needs catered for: ADD,
ADHD, ASD, ASP, AUT, BESD,
EBD, LD, MLD, SEBD, SPLD
(🏛)(16)(✔)

Chilworth House School
Thame Road, Wheatley, Oxford,
Oxfordshire OX33 1JP
Tel: 01844 339077
Head Teacher: Mr Dave
Willcox BEd (Hons)
Age range: 4–11
No. of pupils: 29
Special needs catered for: ADHD,
ASD, ASP, BESD, EBD, MLD, SCD, SLD
(16)(✔)

Chilworth House Upper School
Grooms Farm, Thame Road,
Wheatley, Oxfordshire OX33 1JP
Tel: 01844 337720
Head Teacher: Mr Kevin
Larsen BEd(Hons), MA,
PGCE ED Management
Age range: 11–16
No. of pupils: 59
Special needs catered for: ADD,
ADHD, ASD, ASP, AUT, BESD,
DEL, GLD, HI, LD, MLD, Phe, SCD,
SCLD, SEBD, SP&LD, SPLD
(✔)

Hillcrest Park School
Southcombe, Chipping Norton,
Oxford, Oxfordshire OX7 5QH
Tel: 01608 644621
Headteacher: David
Davidson MA(Hons), PGCE
Age range: 7–18
Special needs catered for: ADD,
ADHD, ASD, ASP, BESD, DYS, DYSP,
EBD, GLD, MLD, SCD, SEBD
(🏛)(✔)

Mulberry Bush School
Standlake, Witney,
Oxfordshire OX29 7RW
Tel: 01865 300202
Director: John Turberville BSc, MA
Age range: 5–12
No. of pupils: 36
Special needs catered for: EBD
(🏛)(✔)

East

Bedfordshire

Advanced Education – Walnut Tree Lodge School
Avenue Farm, Renhold
Road, Wilden, Bedford,
Bedfordshire MK44 2PY
Tel: 01234 772081
Headteacher: Mr John Boslem
Age range: 11–16
Special needs catered for: EBD
(✔)

Cambridgeshire

Cambian Wisbech School
The Old Sessions House, 32
Somers Road, Wisbech,
Cambridgeshire PE13 1JF
Tel: 0800 138 1184
Head of School: Ms Debra Eason
Age range: 9–17
Special needs catered for:
EBD, SEBD
(16)(✔)

Chartwell House School
Goodens Lane, Newton, Wisbech,
Cambridgeshire PE13 5HQ
Tel: 01945 870793
Head: Mrs D A Wright
No. of pupils: 8
Fees: FB £67,600
Special needs catered for: DYS, EBD
(🕎)(🏛)(✔)

The Old School House
March Road, Friday Bridge,
Wisbech, Cambridgeshire PE14 0HA
Tel: 01945 861114
Manager: Rick Ogle-Welbourn
Age range: B7–13
Special needs catered for: EBD
(🕎)(🏛)(✔)

Essex

Cambian Essex School
Unit 13, Flitch Industrial Estate,
Chelmsford Road, Great
Dunmow, Essex CM6 1XJ
Tel: 0800 138 1184
Head of School: Ms Jane Brand
Age range: 11–19
Special needs catered for: BESD
(16)(✔)

ESSEX FRESH START INDEPENDENT SCHOOL (EFS)
For further details see p. 80
Church Street, Witham,
Essex CM8 2JL
Tel: 01376 780088
Email: referrals@tces.org.uk
Website: www.tces.org.uk
Schools' Proprietor: Thomas
Keaney
Age range: 7–19 years
Special needs catered for:
ASD, AUT, BESD, SP&LD
(16)(✔)

Hopewell School
Harmony House, Baden Powell
Close, Dagenham, Essex RM9 6XN
Tel: 020 8593 6610
Headteacher: Ms Sharina Klaasens
Age range: 5–18
Special needs catered for:
EBD, MLD, SEBD
(16)(✔)

Jacques Hall
Harwich Road, Bradfield,
Manningtree, Essex CO11 2XW
Tel: 01255 870311
Principal: Mr Paul Emmerson
Age range: 11–18
No. of pupils: 21
Special needs catered for:
ADHD, BESD, EBD, MLD, SEBD
(🏛)(16)

The Ryes College & Community
New Road, Aldham,
Colchester, Essex CO6 3PN
Tel: 01787 372 611
Headteacher: Miss Jackies Shanks
Age range: 7–24
Special needs catered for:
ADD, ADHD, ASD, ASP, AUT,
BESD, EBD, SCD, SEBD
(🏛)(16)(✔)

Norfolk

Avocet House
The Old Vicarage, School Lane,
Heckingham, Norfolk NR14 6QP
Tel: 01508 549320
Principal: Mrs Vicki Collings
Age range: B8–16
No. of pupils: 8
Special needs catered for:
EBD, SEBD, SPLD
(🕎)(🏛)(✔)

Future Education
168b Motum Road, Norwich,
Norfolk NR5 8EG
Tel: 01603 250505
Headteacher: Mr Dennis Freeman
Age range: 14–16
Special needs catered for: BESD
(✔)

Sheridan School
Thetford Road, Northwold,
Thetford, Norfolk IP26 5LQ
Tel: 01366 726 040
Interim Principal: Mr John Steward
Age range: 8–17
No. of pupils: 40
Special needs catered for:
ASD, ASP, BESD, SPLD
(🏛)(16)(✔)

Suffolk

Bramfield House
Walpole Road, Bramfield,
Halesworth, Suffolk IP19 9AB
Tel: 01986 784235
Head: Mrs D Jennings
Age range: B10–18
No. of pupils: 51
Special needs catered for:
ADD, ADHD, BESD, DEL, EBD
(†)(血)(✔)

On Track Education Centre (Mildenhall)
82E & F Fred Dannatt Road,
Mildenhall, Suffolk IP28 7RD
Tel: 01638 715555
Headteacher: Mrs Ruth Durrant
Age range: 11–18
Special needs catered for: EBD
(16+)(✔)

East Midlands

Derbyshire

Eastwood Grange School
Milken Lane, Ashover, Chesterfield,
Derbyshire S45 0BA
Tel: 01246 590255
Principal: Mr Ray Scales
Age range: B9–16+
No. of pupils: 34
Special needs catered for: BESD
(†)(血)(✔)

The Linnet Independent Learning Centre
107 Mount Pleasant Road,
Castle Gresley, Swadlincote,
Derbyshire DE11 9JE
Tel: 01283 213989
Head Teacher: Jan Sullivan
Age range: 5–16
No. of pupils: 13
Fees: Day £74,250
Special needs catered for: ADD,
ADHD, ASD, ASP, BESD, CLD,
DEL, DYS, DYSP, EBD, GLD, LD,
MLD, SCD, SEBD, SP&LD, SPLD
(✔)

The Meadows
Beech Lane, Dove Holes,
Derbyshire SK17 8DJ
Tel: 01298 814000
Headteacher: Ms Rachel Dowle
Age range: 11–16
Special needs catered for: EBD
(✔)

Leicestershire

Claybrook Cottage School
Frolesworth Lane, Claybrook
Magna, Lutterworth,
Leicestershire LE17 5DA
Tel: 01455 202049
Headteacher: Mrs
Jennifer Collighan
Age range: 8–16
Special needs catered for: BESD
(✔)

Gryphon School
Quorn Hall, Meynell Road,
Quorn, Leicestershire LE12 8BQ
Tel: 01509 414 338
Headteacher: Miss Christina Church
Age range: 11–17
Special needs catered for: EBD
(✔)

Lewis Charlton School
North Street, Ashby-De-La-
Zouch, Leicestershire LE65 1HU
Tel: 01530 560775
Head: Ms Georgina Pearson
Age range: 11–16
No. of pupils: 20
Special needs catered for: EBD
(血)(✔)

Meadow View Farm School
c/o Brookland Farm House, Kirby
Road, Barwell, Leicestershire LE9 8FT
Tel: 01455 840 825
Headteacher: Mr J Read
Age range: 6–11
Special needs catered for:
ASD, BESD, SCD
(✔)

Oakwood School
20 Main Street, Glenfield,
Leicester, Leicestershire LE3 8DG
Tel: 0116 2876218
Headteacher: Wayne Parkes
Age range: 8–18
No. of pupils: 18
Special needs catered for: EBD
(✔)

Trinity College
Moor Lane, Loughborough,
Leicestershire LE11 1BA
Tel: 01509 218906
Headteacher: Rebecca Goodrich
Age range: 9–16
No. of pupils: 36
Fees: Day £36,075
Special needs catered for:
EBD, MLD
(✔)

Lincolnshire

Broughton House
Brant Broughton,
Lincolnshire LN5 0SL
Tel: 0800 138 1184
Head of Service: Mr
Michael Semilore
Age range: 16–25
Special needs catered for: AUT,
BESD, LD, SCD, SCLD, SEBD, SLD
(16+)(血)

Northamptonshire

Ashmeads School
Buccleuch Farm, Haigham
Hill, Burton Latimer, Kettering,
Northamptonshire NN15 5PH
Tel: 01536 725998
Headteacher: Joyce Kuwazo
Age range: 11–16
No. of pupils: 12
Special needs catered for: EBD
(✔)

Belview Lodge
124b Midland Road,
Wellingborough,
Northamptonshire NN8 1NF
Tel: 01933 441877
Headteacher: Ms Candy Shaw
Age range: 11–17
No. of pupils: 4
Special needs catered for: BESD
(✔)

Cambian Northampton School
67a Queens Park Parade,
Kingsthorpe, Northampton,
Northamptonshire NN2 6LR
Tel: 0800 138 1184
Head of School: Ms Hermione Horn
Age range: 8–18
Special needs catered for:
EBD, MLD
(16+)(✔)

Thornby Hall School
Thornby Hall, Thornby,
Northampton,
Northamptonshire NN6 8SW
Tel: 01604 740001
Director: Ms Rene Kennedy
CertEd, DipArt Therapy
Age range: 12–18
No. of pupils: 20
Fees: FB £106,177
Special needs catered for: EBD
(血)(16+)(✔)

Nottinghamshire

Freyburg School
The Poppies, Greenmile
Lane, Babworth,
Nottinghamshire DN22 8JW
Tel: 01777 709061
Headteacher: Mr David Carr
Age range: B11–16
Special needs catered for: BESD
(†)(✔)

Hope House School
Barnby Road, Newark,
Nottinghamshire NG24 3NE
Tel: 01636 700380
Headteacher: Mrs Teri
Westmoreland
Age range: 4–19
No. of pupils: 3
Fees: Day £135,000–£155,000
FB £160,000–£180,000
Special needs catered for:
ADD, ADHD, ASD, ASP, AUT,
BESD, DEL, EBD, SCD, SEBD
(16+)(✔)

Wings School, Nottinghamshire
Kirklington Hall, Kirklington, Newark,
Nottinghamshire NG22 8NB
Tel: 01636 817430
Principal: Dr John Flint
Age range: 9–17
Special needs catered for:
ADD, ADHD, ASP, BESD, EBD
(血)(✔)

Rutland

The Grange Therapeutic School
Knossington, Oakham,
Rutland LE15 8LY
Tel: 01664 454264
Director: Dr A J Smith MA,
MEd, PhD, CPsychol, AFBPs
Age range: B8–16
No. of pupils: 75
Special needs catered for: EBD
(†)(血)(16+)(✔)

Greater London

Essex

Barnardos
Tanners Lane, Barkingside,
Ilford, Essex IG6 1QG
Tel: 020 8550 8822
Special needs catered for: AUT,
EBD, MLD, PMLD, SLD, SP&LD, SPLD
♿ ⑯

Middlesex

Unity School
62 The Ride, Hounslow,
Middlesex TW8 9LA
Age range: 11–16
No. of pupils: 4
Special needs catered for: EBD
♿

Surrey

Cressey College
Croydon, Surrey CR0 6XJ
Tel: 0208 655 2798
Headteacher: Ms Adrienne Barnes
Age range: 11–17
Special needs catered for:
BESD, EBD, SCD
✔

Kingsdown Secondary School
112 Orchard Road, Sanderstead,
Croydon, Surrey CR2 9LQ
Tel: 020 8657 1200
Principal: Mr Kevin Henry OBE
Age range: 11–16
No. of pupils: 12
Special needs catered for:
ASD, ASP, EBD, SPLD
♗ ✔

London

East London

EAST LONDON INDEPENDENT SCHOOL (ELIS)
For further details see p. 81
Stratford Marsh, Welfare
Road, London E15 4HT
Tel: 020 8555 6737
Email: referrals@tces.org.uk
Website: www.tces.org.uk
Schools' Proprietor: Thomas
Keaney
Age range: 7–19 years
Special needs catered for:
ASD, BESD
⑯ ✔

Leaways School London
Theydon Road, Clapton,
London E5 9NZ
Tel: 020 8815 4030
Headmaster: Richard Gadd
Age range: 10–17
Special needs catered for: SEBD

North-West London

Gloucester House the Tavistock Children's Day Unit
33 Daleham Gardens,
London NW3 5BU
Tel: 0207 794 3353
Headteacher: Ms
Ellenore Nicholson
Age range: B5–12
Special needs catered for: BESD
♗ ✔

South-East London

Cavendish School
58 Hawkstone Road, Southwark
Park, London SE16 2PA
Tel: 020 7394 0088
Headteacher: Mrs Sara Craggs
Age range: 11–16
No. of pupils: 42
Special needs catered for: EBD
✔

Octavia House School, Vauxhall
Vauxhall Primary School, Vauxhall
Street, London SE11 5LG
Tel: 02036 514396 (Option:1)
Executive Head: Mr James Waite
Age range: 5–14
No. of pupils: 65
Special needs catered for: ADD,
ADHD, BESD, EBD, SCD, SEBD

Octavia House School, Walworth
Larcom House, Larcom
Street, London SE17 1RT
Tel: 02036 514396 (Option:2)
Executive Head: Mr James Waite
Special needs catered for: ADD,
ADHD, BESD, EBD, SCD, SEBD

Trinity School
4 Recreation Road, Sydenham,
London SE26 4ST
Headteacher: Mr Philip Lee
Age range: 11–16
Special needs catered for: BESD
✔

West London

Insights Independent School
3-5 Alexandria Road,
Ealing, London W13 0NP
Tel: 020 8840 9099
Headteacher: Ms Barbara Quartey
Age range: 7–18
No. of pupils: 62
Special needs catered for: ADD,
ADHD, ASD, ASP, BESD, DYS,
EBD, GLD, MLD, SCD, SPLD
⑯ ✔

NORTH WEST LONDON INDEPENDENT SCHOOL (NWLIS)
For further details see p. 82
85 Old Oak Common Lane,
Acton, London W3 7DD
Tel: 020 8749 5403
Email: referrals@tces.org.uk
Website: www.tces.org.uk
Schools' Proprietor: Thomas
Keaney
Age range: 7–19 years
Special needs catered for:
ASD, AUT, BESD, SP&LD
⑯ ✔

North-East

Durham

Highcroft School
The Green, Cockfield, Bishop
Auckland, Durham DL13 5AG
Tel: 077 02916189
Headteacher: Mr David Laheney
Age range: 11–16
No. of pupils: 3
Special needs catered for: BESD
✔

Priory Pines House
Middleton St George,
Darlington, Durham DL2 1TS
Tel: 01325 331177
Principal: Mr John Anderson
Age range: 7–16
No. of pupils: 16
Special needs catered for: EBD
♿

East Riding of Yorkshire

Cambian Beverley School
Units 19 & 20, Priory Road
Industrial Estate, Beverley, East
Riding of Yorkshire HU17 0EW
Tel: 0800 138 1184
Head Teacher: Ms Melanie Ellis
Age range: 10–18
Special needs catered for: EBD, LD
⑯ ✔

Hartlepool

Cambian Hartlepool School
Unit E, Sovereign Park, Brenda
Road, Hartlepool TS25 1NN
Tel: 0800 138 1184
Head of School: Mr Paul Barnfather
Age range: 10–18
No. of pupils: 10
Special needs catered for: EBD
⑯ ✔

Northumberland

Cambois House School
Cambois, Blyth,
Northumberland NE24 1SF
Tel: 01670 857689
Headteacher: Mr David Smith
Age range: 11–16
No. of pupils: 8
Special needs catered for:
BESD, EBD
✔

Emotional, behavioural and/or social difficulties (EBSD)

Tyne & Wear

Talbot House School
Hexham Road, Walbottle,
Newcastle upon Tyne,
Tyne & Wear NE15 8HW
Tel: 0191 229 0111
Director of Services: A P James
DAES, BPhil, CRCCYP
Age range: 7–18
No. of pupils: 40
Special needs catered for: ADD,
ADHD, ASD, BESD, EBD, MLD
(✓)

Thornbeck College
14 Thornhill Park, Sunderland,
Tyne & Wear SR2 7LA
Tel: 0191 5102038
Principal: Ms Christine Dempster
Special needs catered for: ASP, AUT

West Yorkshire

Broadwood School
252 Moor End Road, Halifax,
West Yorkshire HX2 0RU
Tel: 01422 355925
Headteacher: Mrs Deborah Nash
Age range: 11–18
No. of pupils: 38
Special needs catered for: EBD
(✓)

Meadowcroft School
24 Bar Lane, Wakefield,
West Yorkshire WF1 4AD
Tel: 01924 366242
Head of School: Miss
Lynette Edwards
Age range: 10–19
Special needs catered for: EBD
(16) (✓)

North-West

Cheshire

Advanced Education – Warrington School
2 Forrest Way, Gatewarth
Industrial Estate, Warrington,
Cheshire WA5 1DF
Tel: 01925 237580
Headteacher: Olufemi Onasanya
Age range: 11–18
No. of pupils: 10
Special needs catered for:
BESD, EBD, SEBD
(16) (✓)

Halton School
33 Main Street, Halton Village,
Runcorn, Cheshire WA7 2AN
Tel: 01928 589810
Headteacher: Emma McAllester
Age range: 7–14
No. of pupils: 14
Special needs catered for: EBD
(✓)

High Peak School
Mudhurst Lane, Higher Disley,
Stockport, Cheshire SK12 2AP
Tel: 01663 721 731
Principal: David Glaves
Age range: 9–19
Special needs catered for: SEBD
(🏛)

Hope Corner Academy
70 Clifton Road, Runcorn,
Cheshire WA7 4TD
Tel: 01928 580860
Head of School: Rev. D Tunningley
Age range: 14–16
Special needs catered for:
ASD, BESD, MLD

Cumbria

APPLETREE SCHOOL
For further details see p. 83
Natland, Kendal,
Cumbria LA9 7QS
Tel: 01539 560253
Email: clair.davies@
appletreeschool.co.uk
Website: www.appletree
treatmentcentre.co.uk
Head of Education: Mr R
Davies BEd, MSpEd
Age range: 6–12
Special needs catered for: ADD,
ADHD, BESD, DEL, DYS, DYSP, EBD,
GLD, HA, LD, MLD, SCD, SEBD
(🏛) (✓)

Cambian Whinfell School
110 Windermere Road,
Kendal, Cumbria LA9 5EZ
Tel: 0800 138 1184
Head: Mr Huw Davies
Age range: B11–19
No. of pupils: 5
Special needs catered for: AUT, EBD
(👤) (🏛) (16) (✓)

Eden Grove School
Bolton, Appleby, Cumbria CA16 6AJ
Tel: 01768 361346
Principal: Mr John McCaffrey
Age range: 8–19
No. of pupils: 65
Special needs catered for:
ADHD, ASP, AUT, BESD, CP, DYS,
EBD, EPI, MLD, PH, SP&LD
(🏛) (16) (✓)

Eden Park Academy
119 Warwick Road, Carlisle,
Cumbria CA1 1JZ
Tel: 01228 537 609
Headteacher: Miss Kerry Maynard
Age range: 11–16
No. of pupils: 6
Special needs catered for: EBD

Fell House School
Grange Fell Road, Grange-
Over-Sands, Cumbria LA11 6AS
Tel: 01539 535926
Headteacher: Mr Rob Davies
Age range: 7–12
No. of pupils: 8
Special needs catered for: EBD
(🏛) (✓)

KIRBY MOOR SCHOOL
For further details see p. 84
Longtown Road, Brampton,
Cumbria CA8 2AB
Tel: 016977 42598
Headteacher: Mrs
Catherine Garton
Age range: B9–18
No. of pupils: 40
Special needs catered for:
ADHD, ASD, BESD
(👤) (🏛) (16) (✓)

Oversands School
Grange-Over-Sands,
Cumbria LA11 6SD
Tel: 01539 552397
Head Teacher: Mr. Robin Adams
Age range: B10–19
No. of pupils: 41
Special needs catered for: ADHD,
ASD, ASP, AUT, BESD, EBD, MLD, SPLD
(👤) (🏛) (✓)

Underley Garden School
Kirkby Lonsdale, Carnforth,
Cumbria LA6 2DZ
Tel: 01524 271569
Headteacher: Ellie Forrest
Age range: 9–19
No. of pupils: 43
Special needs catered for:
ADD, ADHD, ASP, SLD, SP&LD
(🏛) (✓)

Wings School, Cumbria
Whassett, Milnthorpe,
Cumbria LA7 7DN
Tel: 01539 562006
Principal: Donagh McKillop
Age range: 11–17
Special needs catered for:
ADD, ADHD, ASP, BESD, EBD
(🏛) (✓)

Greater Manchester

Acorns School
19b Hilbert Lane, Marple, Stockport,
Greater Manchester SK6 7NN
Tel: 0161 449 5820
Headteacher: Naseem Akhtar
Age range: 5–17
No. of pupils: 40
Special needs catered for: EBD
(✓)

Ashcroft School
Together Trust Campus,
Schools Hill, Cheadle, Greater
Manchester SK8 1JE
Tel: 0161 283 4832
Head of School: Eileen Sheerin
Age range: 8–18
No. of pupils: 81
Special needs catered for:
BESD, EBD, SEBD
(✓)

Cambian Birch House School
98- Birch Lane, Longsight,
Manchester, Greater
Manchester M13 0WN
Tel: 0800 138 1184
Headteacher: Mr Bilal Mahmud
Age range: 11–19
No. of pupils: 22
Special needs catered for:
BESD, EBD, SEBD
(16) (✓)

Lime Meadows
73 Taunton Road, Ashton-Under-
Lyne, Greater Manchester OL7 9DU
Tel: 0161 3399412
Head of School: Mr W Baker
Age range: B14–19
No. of pupils: 5
Special needs catered for: EBD
(👤) (🏛) (16) (✓)

Nugent House School
Carr Mill Road, Billinge, Wigan,
Greater Manchester WN5 7TT
Tel: 01744 892551
Principal: Miss W Sparling
BA(Hons), QTS, MA(SEN),
PG Dip (Autism), NPQH
Age range: B7–19
No. of pupils: 65
Fees: Day £63,036–£84,048
Special needs catered for: EBD
(👤) (🏛) (16) (✓)

St. John Vianney School
Rye Bank Road, Firswood, Stretford,
Greater Manchester M16 0EX
Tel: 0161 881 7843
Age range: 4–19
No. of pupils: 80
Fees: Day £7,155
Special needs catered for: MLD
(16) (✓)

Lancashire

Aurora Brambles School
159 Longmeanygate, Midge Hill, Leyland, Lancashire PR26 7TB
Tel: 01772 454 826
Head Teacher: Mr Dan Creed
Age range: B11–16
Special needs catered for: EBD

Aurora Keyes Barn School
Station Road, Salwick, Preston, Lancashire PR4 0YH
Tel: 01772 673 672
Head Teacher: Ms Diana Denooijer
Age range: 5–12
Special needs catered for: EBD

Belmont School
Haslingden Road, Rawtenstall, Rossendale, Lancashire BB4 6RX
Tel: 01706 221043
Headteacher: Mr M J Stobart
Age range: B10–16
No. of pupils: 70
Special needs catered for: ADD, ADHD, ASD, ASP, AUT, BESD, DEL, EBD, SCD, SEBD

Cedar House School
Bentham, Lancaster, Lancashire LA2 7DD
Tel: 015242 61149
Headteacher: Ms Kathryn Taylor BEd (Hons)
Age range: 7–18
No. of pupils: 63
Special needs catered for: ADD, ADHD, ASD, ASP, BESD, DYSP, EBD, EPI, GLD, LD, MLD, SCD, SEBD, SP&LD, SPLD

Crookhey Hall School
Crookhey Hall, Garstang Road, Cockerham, Lancaster, Lancashire LA2 0HA
Tel: 01524 792618
Headteacher: Mr D P Martin
Age range: B11–16
No. of pupils: 64
Special needs catered for: ADD, ADHD, BESD, DEL, EBD, SCD, SEBD

Cumberland School
Church Road, Bamber Bridge, Preston, Lancashire PR5 6EP
Tel: 01772 284435
Head Teacher: Mr Nigel Hunt BSc (Hons), PGCE (SEN), NPQH
Age range: 11–18
No. of pupils: 57
Special needs catered for: ADHD, ASP, BESD, MLD, SP&LD

Darwen School
3 Sudell Road, Darwen, Lancashire BB3 3HW
Tel: 01254 777154
Headteacher: Mr Sean Naylor
Age range: 7–16
No. of pupils: 10
Special needs catered for: EBD

Elland House School
Unit 7, Roman Road, Royton, Lancashire OL2 5PJ
Tel: 0161 6283600
Headteacher: Mrs Jan Murray
Age range: 11–16
Special needs catered for: BESD

Learn 4 Life
Quarry Bank Community Centre, 364 Ormskirk Road, Tanhouse, Skelmersdale, Lancashire WN8 9AL
Tel: 01695 768960
Head of School: Ms Catherine Briggs
Age range: 11–16
No. of pupils: 4
Special needs catered for: ADD, ADHD, ASD, ASP, AUT, BESD, DYS, EBD, GLD, SCD

Moorlands View Children's Home and School
Manchester Road, Dunnockshaw, Burnley, Lancashire BB11 5PQ
Tel: 01282 431144
Head Teacher: Wayne Carradice
Age range: 11–16
No. of pupils: 12
Special needs catered for: EBD

Roselyn House School
Moss Lane, Off Wigan Road, Leyland, Lancashire PR25 4SE
Tel: 01772 435948
Headteacher: Miss S Damerall
Age range: 11–16
No. of pupils: 21
Special needs catered for: AUT, EBD

The Willows at Oakfield House School
Station Road, Salwick, Preston, Lancashire PR4 0YH
Tel: 01772 672630
Headteacher: June Redhead
Age range: 5–11
No. of pupils: 23
Special needs catered for: EBD, SLD

Waterloo Lodge School
Preston Road, Chorley, Lancashire PR6 7AX
Tel: 01257 230894
Headteacher: Debbie Proctor
Age range: 11–18
No. of pupils: 45
Fees: Day £29,649
Special needs catered for: ADD, ADHD, BESD, DEL, EBD, SCD, SEBD

Merseyside

Clarence High School
West Lane, Freshfield, Merseyside L37 7AS
Tel: 01704 872151
Head: Ms Carol Parkinson
Age range: 7–17
Special needs catered for: EBD

Olsen House School
85-87 Liverpool Rd, GT. Crosby, Liverpool, Merseyside L23 5TD
Tel: 0151 924 0234
Headteacher: Jeremy Keeble
Age range: 9–16
Special needs catered for: SEBD

Warrington

Chaigeley
Thelwall, Warrington WA4 2TE
Tel: 01925 752357
Principal: Mr Antonio Munoz Bailey
Age range: B8–16
No. of pupils: 75
Special needs catered for: ADD, ADHD, ASD, ASP, AUT, BESD, DYS, EBD, GLD, HA, LD, MLD, SCD, SEBD, SLD, SP&LD

Cornerstones
2 Victoria Road, Grappenhall, Warrington WA4 2EN
Tel: 01925 211056
Head: Ms Caron Bethell
Age range: B7–18
No. of pupils: 11
Special needs catered for: AUT, EBD

South-East

Berkshire

Beech Lodge School
13 Home Farm, Honey Lane, Hurley, Berkshire SL6 6TG
Tel: 01628 879384
Headteacher: Lucy Barnes
Special needs catered for: ADHD, BESD, DYS, SEBD

Cressex Lodge (SWAAY)
Terrace Road South, Binfield, Bracknell, Berkshire RG42 4DE
Tel: 01344 862221
Headteacher: Ms Sarah Snape
Age range: B11–16
No. of pupils: 9
Special needs catered for: BESD

High Close School
Wiltshire Road, Wokingham, Berkshire RG40 1TT
Tel: 0118 9785767
Head: Mrs Zoe Lattimer BSc(Hons), PGCE
Age range: 7–18
Special needs catered for: ADHD, ASD, ASP, BESD, EBD, MLD

Buckinghamshire

Unity College
150 West Wycombe Road, High Wycombe, Buckinghamshire HP12 3AE
Tel: 077 02916189
Headteacher: Mrs Lois Hubbard
Age range: 11–16
No. of pupils: 12
Special needs catered for: BESD, MLD, SEBD

East Sussex

Headstart School
Crouch Lane, Ninfield, Battle,
East Sussex TN33 9EG
Tel: 01424 893803
Headteacher: Ms Nicola Dann
Age range: 7–18
Special needs catered for: BESD
(16+) (✔)

Springboard Education Junior
39 Whippingham Road, St
Wilfred\'s Upper Hall, Brighton,
East Sussex BN2 3PS
Tel: 01273 885109
Headteacher: Elizabeth Freeman
Age range: 7–13
Special needs catered for:
ADHD, BESD
(✔)

The Lioncare School
87 Payne Avenue, Hove,
East Sussex BN3 5HD
Tel: 01273 734164
Headteacher: Mrs J Dance
Age range: 7–16
No. of pupils: 9
Special needs catered for: EBD
(✔)

The Mount Camphill Community
Faircrouch Lane, Wadhurst,
East Sussex TN5 6PT
Tel: 01892 782025
Head of Education: Mr Julian Ritchie
Age range: 16–24
No. of pupils: 35
Special needs catered for: ADD,
ADHD, ASD, ASP, AUT, BESD, CLD,
CP, DEL, DYS, DYSP, EBD, EPI, GLD,
HI, LD, MLD, MSI, PD, Phe, PH,
PNI, SCD, SLD, SP&LD, SPLD, SLI
(🏫)

Hampshire

Coxlease Abbeymead
Palace Lane, Beaulieu,
Hampshire SO42 7YG
Tel: 02380 283 633
Principal: Mr Rick Tracey
Age range: 9–16
No. of pupils: 5
Special needs catered for: EBD
(🏫)

Coxlease School
Clay Hill, Lyndhurst,
Hampshire SO43 7DE
Tel: 023 8028 3633
Principal: Mr Rick Tracey
Age range: 9–18
No. of pupils: 55
Special needs catered for: BESD, LD
(🏫) (16+) (✔)

Hillcrest Jubilee School
84-86 Jubilee Road, Waterlooville,
Hampshire PO7 7RE
Tel: 03458 727477
Head of School: Alice Anstee
Age range: 8–16
Special needs catered for:
BESD, SEBD
(🏫) (16+)

St Edward's School
Melchet Court, Sherfield English,
Romsey, Hampshire SO51 6ZR
Tel: 01794 885252
Head: L Bartel BEd(Hons)
Age range: B9–18
No. of pupils: 38
Special needs catered for: ADD,
ADHD, ASD, ASP, AUT, BESD, DYS,
EBD, MLD, SCD, SEBD, SPLD
(🚹) (16+) (✔)

The Serendipity Centre
399 Hinkler Road, Southampton,
Hampshire SO19 6DS
Tel: 023 8042 2255
Head Teacher: Dr. Michele Aldridge
Age range: G9–18
No. of pupils: 15
Special needs catered for: SEBD
(🚺) (✔)

Kent

Brewood School
86 London Road, Deal,
Kent CT14 9TR
Tel: 01304 363000
Head of School: Mr Daniel Radlett
Age range: 11–18
No. of pupils: 12
Fees: Day £23,863
Special needs catered for: ADD,
ADHD, ASD, ASP, AUT, BESD, CLD,
DEL, EBD, EPI, GLD, HA, HI, LD,
MLD, PH, SCD, SLD, SP&LD, SLI
(✔)

Browns School
Cannock House, Hawstead Lane,
Chelsfield, Orpington, Kent BR6 7PH
Tel: 01689 876816
Headteacher: Mr M F Brown
Age range: 7–12
No. of pupils: 32
Special needs catered for:
EBD, SPLD
(✔)

Caldecott Foundation School
Hythe Road, Smeeth,
Ashford, Kent TN25 6PW
Tel: 01303 815678
Acting Head: Mrs Valerie Miller
Age range: 5–18
No. of pupils: 56
Special needs catered for: EBD
(🏫) (16+) (✔)

Esland School
Units 12-13, Oare Gunpowder
Works, Off Bysingwood Road,
Faversham, Kent ME13 7UD
Tel: 01795 531730
Head of School: Mr M Colvin
Age range: 12–17
No. of pupils: 9
Special needs catered for: BESD
(✔)

Greenfields School
Tenterden Road, Biddenden,
Kent TN27 8BS
Tel: 01580 292523
Director: Gary Yexley
Age range: 5–11
No. of pupils: 13
Fees: Day £29,004
Special needs catered for: EBD
(✔)

Heath Farm School
Egerton Road, Charing Heath,
Ashford, Kent TN27 0AX
Tel: 01233 712030
Head: Liz Cornish
Age range: 5–16
No. of pupils: 70
Special needs catered for: EBD
(✔)

Hope View School
Station Approach, Chilham,
Canterbury, Kent CT4 8EG
Tel: 01227 738000
Head of School: Ms Carla Kaushal
Age range: 11–17
No. of pupils: 16
Special needs catered for:
ADD, ADHD, ASD, ASP, BESD
(✔)

Hythe House Education
Power Station Road,
Sheerness, Kent ME12 3AB
Tel: 01795 581006
Headteacher: Mr Robert Duffy
Age range: 11–16
No. of pupils: 20
Special needs catered for: EBD
(✔)

ISP Sittingbourne School
Church Street, Sittingbourne,
Kent ME10 3EG
Tel: 01795 422 044
Headteacher: Craig Walter
Age range: 11–16
Special needs catered for:
BESD, SCD, SEBD
(✔)

Learning Opportunities Centre
Ringwould Road, Ringwould,
Deal, Kent CT14 8DN
Tel: 01304 381906
Headteacher: Mrs Diana Ward
Age range: 11–16
No. of pupils: 40
Special needs catered for: EBD
(🏫) (✔)

Little Acorns School
London Beach Farm,
Ashford Road, St Michael's,
Tenterden, Kent TN30 6SR
Tel: 01233 850422
Headteacher: Alison Neal
and Tony Hollett
Age range: 4–14
No. of pupils: 7
Special needs catered for: EBD
(🏫) (✔)

Meadows School and Meadows 16+
London Road, Southborough,
Kent TN4 0RJ
Tel: 01892 529144
Principal: Mike Price
BEd(Hons), DipSEN, MA
Age range: 11–19
No. of pupils: 45
Special needs catered for: ADHD,
ASP, AUT, DYS, DYSP, EBD, MLD, SEBD
(🏫) (✔)

Ripplevale School
Chapel Lane, Ripple,
Deal, Kent CT14 8JG
Tel: 01304 373866
Principal: Mr Ted Schofield CRSW
Age range: B9–16
No. of pupils: 30
Special needs catered for: ADD,
ADHD, ASD, ASP, AUT, BESD, CLD,
DYS, DYSP, EBD, GLD, HA, LD, MLD,
PMLD, SCD, SCLD, SP&LD, SPLD
(🚹) (🏫) (✔)

Small Haven School
146 Newington Road,
Ramsgate, Kent CT12 6PT
Tel: 01843 597088
Age range: 5–13
No. of pupils: 8
Fees: Day £23,863
Special needs catered for: ADD,
ADHD, ASD, ASP, AUT, BESD, CLD,
DEL, EBD, EPI, GLD, HA, HI, LD,
MLD, PH, SCD, SLD, SP&LD, SLI

The Davenport School
Princess Margaret Avenue,
Ramsgate, Kent CT12 6HX
Tel: 01843 589018
Headteacher: Mr Franklyn Brown
Age range: B7–12
Special needs catered for: EBD
(🚹) (✔)

The Lighthouse School
24 Clarendon Road,
Margate, Kent CT9 2QL
Tel: 01843 482043
Principal: Mr David Wilkinson
Age range: 5–18
No. of pupils: 5
Special needs catered for:
BESD, SEBD
(16+) (✔)

The Old Priory School
Priory Road, Ramsgate,
Kent CT11 9PG
Tel: 01843 599322
Head: Jack Banner
Age range: B10–15
Special needs catered for: EBD
(🚹) (✔)

The Old School
Capel Street, Capel-le-Ferne,
Folkestone, Kent CT18 7EY
Tel: 01303 251116
Headteacher: Martyn Jordan
Age range: B9–17
No. of pupils: 24
Special needs catered for: EBD

WEST HEATH SCHOOL
For further details see p. 86
Ashgrove Road, Sevenoaks,
Kent TN13 1SR
Tel: 01732 460553
Email: admissions@
westheathschool.com
Website:
www.westheathschool.com
Principal: Mr James Nunns
Age range: 10–20
No. of pupils: 135
Fees: Day £52,500
Special needs catered for:
ADD, ADHD, ASD, ASP, BESD,
DEL, EBD, SCD, SP&LD, SPLD

Surrey

Cornfield School
53 Hanworth Road, Redhill,
Surrey RH1 5HS
Tel: 01737 779578
Headteacher: Mrs Jayne Telfer
Age range: G11–18
No. of pupils: 25
Special needs catered for: EBD

Grafham Grange School
Nr Bramley, Guildford,
Surrey GU5 0LH
Tel: 01483 892214
Headteacher: Ms Debra Henderson
Age range: B10–19
Special needs catered for:
ADHD, ASD, BESD, EBD, SP&LD

Tudor Lodge School
92 Foxley Lane, Woodcote,
Purley, Surrey CR8 3NA
Tel: 020 8763 8785
Headteacher: Ms Patricia Lines
Age range: 12–16
No. of pupils: 7
Special needs catered for: SEBD

West Sussex

Brantridge School
Staplefield Place, Staplefield,
Haywards Heath, West
Sussex RH17 6EQ
Tel: 01444 400228
Headteacher: Gina Wagland
Age range: B6–13
No. of pupils: 27
Special needs catered for:
ADHD, ASD, ASP, BESD, EBD, LD

Farney Close School
Bolney Court, Bolney,
West Sussex RH17 5RD
Tel: 01444 881811
Head: Mr B Robinson MA, BEd(Hons)
Age range: 11–16
No. of pupils: 78
Fees: Day £55,222.10
Special needs catered for: ADHD,
ASP, DYS, EBD, MLD, SP&LD

Hillcrest Slinfold
Stane Street, Slinfold, Horsham,
West Sussex RH13 0QX
Tel: 01403 790939
Principal: Ms Sarah Olliver
Age range: B11–17
Special needs catered for: ADD,
ADHD, ASD, ASP, BESD, DYS, DYSP,
EBD, GLD, MLD, SCD, SEBD

Muntham House School Ltd
Barns Green, Muntham Drive,
Horsham, West Sussex RH13 0NJ
Tel: 01403 730302
Principal: Mr R Boyle
MEd, BEd, AdvDipSE
Age range: B8–18
No. of pupils: 51 VIth12
Special needs catered for:
ADD, ADHD, ASD, BESD, DYS,
EBD, MLD, SP&LD, SPLD

PHILPOTS MANOR SCHOOL
For further details see p. 85
West Hoathly, East Grinstead,
West Sussex RH19 4PR
Tel: 01342 810268
Email: info@
philpotsmanorschool.co.uk
Website: www.philpots
manorschool.co.uk
Education Co-ordinator: Mr
Darin Nobes BA (Hons),
PGCE, NPQH
Age range: 7–19
No. of pupils: 32
Fees: Day £65,000 WB £65,000
Special needs catered for:
ADD, ADHD, ASD, ASP, AUT,
BESD, DEL, DYS, EBD, EPI,
GLD, LD, MLD, SCD, SP&LD

Springboard Education Senior
55 South Street, Lancing,
West Sussex BN15 8HA
Tel: 01903 605980
Head Teacher: Mr Simon
Yorke-Johnson
Age range: 11–18
No. of pupils: 10
Special needs catered for: ADD,
ADHD, ASD, ASP, AUT, BESD, EBD

South-West

Devon

Cambian Devon School
Intek House, 52 Borough Road,
Paignton, Devon TQ4 7DQ
Tel: 0800 138 1184
Head of School: Mr Mike Lee
Age range: 10–18
Special needs catered for:
ASP, AUT, EBD, SEBD

Oakwood Court
7/9 Oak Park Villas, Dawlish,
Devon EX7 0DE
Tel: 01626 864066
Principal: J F Loft BEd,
BPhil(SEN), HNDHIM
Age range: 16–25
Special needs catered for: ADHD,
ASP, DYS, DYSP, EBD, EPI, MLD, SLD

The Libra School
Edgemoor Court, South Radworthy,
South Molton, Devon EX36 3LN
Tel: 01598 740044
Headteacher: Ms J E Wilkes
Age range: 8–18
Special needs catered for: EBD

Dorset

Ivers College
Ivers, Hains Lane, Marnhull,
Sturminster Newton, Dorset DT10 1JU
Tel: 01258 820164
Principal: Linda Matthews
Age range: 18+
No. of pupils: 23
Special needs catered for:
EBD, LD, MLD, SCD

Gloucestershire

Marlowe Education Unit
Hartpury Old School,
Gloucester Road, Hartpury,
Gloucestershire GL19 3BG
Tel: 01452 700855
Head Teacher: Diane McQueen
Age range: 8–16
No. of pupils: 8
Special needs catered for:
EBD, MLD

Somerset

Cambian Somerset School
Creech Court Lane, Creech St.
Michael, Taunton, Somerset TA3 5PX
Tel: 0800 138 1184
Head Teacher: Mr Joshua Fitzgerald
Age range: 10–18
Special needs catered for:
AUT, EBD, HI, SEBD

Inaura School
Moorview House, Burrowbridge,
Bridgwater, Somerset TA7 0RB
Tel: 01823 690211
Headteacher: Dr Adam Abdelnoor
Age range: 8–18
No. of pupils: 24
Fees: Day £45,954
Special needs catered for: ADHD,
ASD, BESD, CLD, EBD, LD, SCD

Newbury Manor School
Newbury, Mells, Nr. Frome,
Somerset BA11 3RG
Tel: 01373 814 980
Head of School: Mr. Andy Holder
Age range: 7–19
Special needs catered for:
ASD, ASP, AUT, SPLD

Phoenix Academy
Newton Road, North Petherton,
Somerset TA6 6NA
Tel: 01271 318 110
Head Teacher: Mr. Jon Lloyd
Age range: 11–16
Special needs catered for: EBD

Somerset Progressive School
Bath House Farm, West Hatch,
Taunton, Somerset TA3 5RH
Tel: 01823 481902
Headteacher: Mr Neil Gage
Age range: 9–19
No. of pupils: 20
Special needs catered for: EBD

The Marchant-Holliday School
North Cheriton, Templecombe, Somerset BA8 0AH
Tel: 01963 33234
Head Teacher: Mr T J Kitts MEd, BEd(Hons), DPSE(SEN)
Age range: B5–13
No. of pupils: 38
Special needs catered for: ADD, ADHD, ASD, ASP, BESD, DYS, DYSP, EBD, SCD
(ⓧ)(ⓧ)(✔)

Wiltshire

The Faringdon Centre
School Lane, Salisbury, Wiltshire SP1 3YA
Tel: 01722 820 970
Head of School: Ms Rebecca Peacock
Age range: 11–16
No. of pupils: 8
Special needs catered for: EBD, MLD

Wessex College
Wessex Lodge, Nunney Road, Frome, Wiltshire BA11 4LA
Tel: 01373 453414
Head of School: Mr Nigel Troop
Age range: 11–16
No. of pupils: 6
Special needs catered for: EBD
(✔)

West Midlands

Cheshire

Aidenswood
48 Parson Street, Congleton, Cheshire CW12 4ED
Tel: 01260 281 353
Head of School: Ms Marion Goodwin
Age range: B13–17
No. of pupils: 6
Special needs catered for: EBD, MLD
(ⓧ)(ⓧ)(✔)

Herefordshire

Cambian Hereford School
Coningsby Road, Leominster, Herefordshire HR6 8LL
Tel: 0800 1381184
Head of School: Ms Kate Reeves
Age range: 11–19
Special needs catered for: EBD
(16+)(✔)

Queenswood School
Callows Hills Farm, Hereford Road, Ledbury, Herefordshire HR8 2PZ
Tel: 01531 670 632
Principal: Mr James Imber
Age range: 11–18
No. of pupils: 15
Special needs catered for: ADD, ADHD, ASD, BESD, DYS, DYSP, MLD, SEBD, SP&LD, SPLD
(ⓧ)(16+)(✔)

Shropshire

Acorn School
Dale Acre Way, Hollinswood, Telford, Shropshire TF3 2EN
Tel: 01952 200410
Head: Ms Sarah Morgan
Age range: 11–16
No. of pupils: 16
Special needs catered for: EBD
(✔)

Care UK Children's Services
46 High Street, Church Stretton, Shropshire SY6 6BX
Tel: 01694 724488
Director: Simon W Rouse BA(Hons), CSS, DipPTh
Age range: 10–18
No. of pupils: 24
Special needs catered for: EBD
(16+)

Ditton Priors School
Station Road, Ditton Priors, Bridgnorth, Shropshire WV16 6SS
Tel: 01746 712985
Headteacher: Mr Stephen Piper
Age range: 11–16
No. of pupils: 10
Special needs catered for: BESD, EBD
(✔)

Smallbrook School
Smallbrook Lodge, Smallbrook Road, Whitchurch, Shropshire SY13 1BX
Tel: 01948 661110
Headteacher: Peter Sinclair
Age range: 11–19
No. of pupils: 15
Special needs catered for: EBD
(16+)(✔)

Young Options College
Lamledge Lane, Shifnal, Shropshire TF11 8SD
Tel: 01952 468220
Head Teacher: Ms Julia Saint
Age range: 7–19
Special needs catered for: ADD, ADHD, ASP, BESD, DEL, EBD, SCD, SEBD
(ⓧ)(✔)

Staffordshire

Bloomfield College
Bloomfield Road, Tipton, Staffordshire DY4 9AH
Tel: 0121 5209408
Headteacher: Mr Andrew Harding
Age range: 11–16
Special needs catered for: EBD
(✔)

Draycott Moor College
Draycott Old Road, Draycott-in-the-Moors, Stoke-on-Trent, Staffordshire ST11 9AH
Tel: 01782 399849
Headteacher: Mr David Rutter
Age range: 11–16
Special needs catered for: EBD
(✔)

Hillcrest Oaklands College
Alrewas Road, Kings Bromley, Staffordshire DE13 7HR
Tel: 03458 727477
Principal: Mr David Biddle MAEd, BA (HONS), CertEd
Age range: G12–19
Special needs catered for: ADD, ADHD, ASD, ASP, BESD, DYS, DYSP, EBD, GLD, MLD, SCD, SEBD
(ⓧ)(ⓧ)(16+)(✔)

Longdon Hall School
Longdon Hall, Rugeley, Staffordshire WS15 4PT
Tel: 01543 491051
Headteacher: Mr Matt Storey
Age range: 7–18
Special needs catered for: BESD, EBD
(16+)(✔)

Young Options Pathway College Stoke
Phoenix House, Marlborough Road, Longton, Stoke-on-Trent, Staffordshire ST3 1EJ
Tel: 01782 320773
Headteacher: Mel Callaghan-Lewis
Age range: 11–19
No. of pupils: 11
Special needs catered for: ADD, ADHD, ASP, AUT, BESD, CLD, DEL, DYS, DYSP, EBD, GLD, HA, LD, MLD, MSI, PMLD, SCD, SEBD, SLD, SPLD
(16+)(✔)

Warwickshire

Arc School – Ansley
Ansley Lane, Ansley, Nuneaton, Warwickshire CV10 9ND
Tel: 01676 543 810
Headteacher: Mr Christian Williams
Age range: 7–16
Special needs catered for: ADHD, ASD, SEBD

Arc School – Old Arley
Old Arley, Ansley, Nuneaton, Warwickshire CV7 8NU
Tel: 01676 543200
Headmistress: Pauline Garret
Age range: 7–11
No. of pupils: 30
Special needs catered for: BESD
(ⓧ)(✔)

Arc School – Napton
Vicarage Road, Napton-on-the-Hill, Warwickshire CV47 8NA
Tel: 01926 817 547
Acting Head Teacher: Cathal Lynch
Age range: 7–16
Special needs catered for: ADHD, ASD

Wathen Grange School
Church Walk, Mancetter, Atherstone, Warwickshire CV9 1PZ
Tel: 01827 714454
Acting Head: Mr Viron Mangat
Age range: 11–16
No. of pupils: 15
Special needs catered for: EBD
(✔)

West Midlands

Blue River Academy
Sara Park, 160 Herbert Road, Small Heath, Birmingham, West Midlands B10 0PR
Tel: 0121 753 1933
Age range: B14–16
Special needs catered for: BESD
(ⓧ)(✔)

The Collegiate Centre for Values Education for Life
51-54 Hockley Hill, Hockley, Birmingham, West Midlands B18 5AQ
Tel: 0121 5230222
Headteacher: Mrs Val Russell
Age range: 11–17
No. of pupils: 25
Special needs catered for: BESD
(✓)

Yorkshire & Humberside

East Riding of Yorkshire

Horton House School
Hilltop Farm, Sutton Road, Wawne, Kingston upon Hull, East Riding of Yorkshire HU7 5YY
Tel: 01482 875191
Head: Mr Matthew Stubbins
Age range: 8–23
Fees: Day £25,000–£50,000 WB £75,000–£150,000 FB £180,000
Special needs catered for: ADD, ADHD, ASD, ASP, AUT, BESD, CLD, DYS, DYSP, EBD, EPI, GLD, LD, MLD, SCD, SCLD, SEBD, SLD, SPLD
(⚐)(✓)

North Yorkshire

Breckenbrough School
Sandhutton, Thirsk, North Yorkshire YO7 4EN
Tel: 01845 587238
Headmaster: Geoffrey Brookes BEd
Age range: B9–19
No. of pupils: 49
Special needs catered for: ADD, ADHD, ASP, BESD, DEL, DYS, EBD, HA
(♿)(⚐)(16+)(✓)

Cambian Scarborough School
Unit 11, Plaxton Park Industrial Estate, Cayton Low Road, Scarborough, North Yorkshire YO11 3BQ
Tel: 0800 138 1184
Head Teacher: Ms Patricia Peake
Age range: 8–18
Special needs catered for: SEBD
(16+)(✓)

Cambian Spring Hill School
Palace Road, Ripon, North Yorkshire HG4 3HN
Tel: 0800 138 1184
Principal: Linda Nelson
Age range: 8–19
No. of pupils: 31
Special needs catered for: ADHD, ASP, AUT, CP, DEL, DYS, DYSP, EBD, EPI, MLD, SLD, SP&LD
(⚐)(16+)(✓)

Clervaux
Clow Beck Centre, Jolby Lane, Croft-on-Tees, North Yorkshire DL2 2TF
Tel: 01325 729860
Strategic Lead: Bonny Etchell-Anderson
Age range: 16–25+
Special needs catered for: ASD, ASP, AUT, BESD, CLD

South Yorkshire

BRANTWOOD SPECIALIST SCHOOL
For further details see p. 88
1 Kenwood Bank, Nether Edge, Sheffield, South Yorkshire S7 1NU
Tel: 0114 258 9062
Email: enquiries@brantwood.rmt.org
Website: www.rmt.org
Headteacher: Christine Haylett
Age range: 7–19
Special needs catered for: ADD, ADHD, ASD, ASP, BESD, CLD, EBD, GLD, LD, MLD, PMLD, SCD, SCLD, SEBD, SPLD
(16+)(✓)

Dove School
194 New Road, Staincross, Barnsley, South Yorkshire S75 6PP
Tel: 01226 381380
Headteacher: Mrs Helen Mangham
Age range: 9–16
Special needs catered for: BESD
(✓)

West Yorkshire

Denby Grange School
Stocksmoor Road, Midgley, Wakefield, West Yorkshire WF4 4JQ
Tel: 01924 830096
Head: Miss Jennie Littleboy
Age range: 11–17
No. of pupils: 36
Special needs catered for: EBD, SCD
(✓)

New Gables School
2 New Close Road, Shipley, West Yorkshire BD18 4AB
Tel: 01274 584705
Teacher-in-charge: Caroline Matson
Age range: 11–16
Special needs catered for: SEBD

The Grange School
2 Milner Way, Ossett, Wakefield, West Yorkshire WF5 9JE
Tel: 01924 378957
Headteacher: Phil Bennett
Age range: 7–14
No. of pupils: 12
Special needs catered for: BESD
(✓)

William Henry Smith School
Boothroyd, Brighouse, West Yorkshire HD6 3JW
Tel: 01484 710123
Principal: B J Heneghan BA, PGCE, DipSpEd
Age range: B8–19
No. of pupils: 64
Fees: Day £57,810 FB £70,435
Special needs catered for: ADD, ADHD, ASD, BESD, CLD, GLD, SCD, SEBD, SPLD
(♿)(⚐)(✎)(16+)(✓)

Northern Ireland

County Down

Camphill Community Glencraig
Craigavad, Holywood, County Down BT18 0DB
Tel: 028 9042 3396
School Co-ordinator: Vincent Reynolds
Age range: 7–19
No. of pupils: 32
Fees: FB £66,500
Special needs catered for: ADHD, ASP, AUT, CP, DYSP, EBD, EPI, HI, MLD, PH, PMLD, SLD, SP&LD, SPLD, VIS
(16+)(⚐)(16+)

Scotland

Edinburgh

Harmeny Education Trust Ltd
Harmeny School, Balerno, Edinburgh EH14 7JY
Tel: 0131 449 3938
Chief Executive: Peter Doran BA(Hons)Econ, CQSW, MA Social Work, AdvCert SW
Age range: 6–13
No. of pupils: 36
Special needs catered for: ADD, ADHD, ASP, DYS, EBD, SPLD

Fife

Falkland House School
Falkland Estate, Cupar, Fife KY15 7AE
Tel: 01337 857268
Head: Mr Stuart Jacob
Age range: B5–18
No. of pupils: 30
Fees: FB £70,000
Special needs catered for: ADD, ADHD, ASP, BESD, DYS, EBD, EPI, SCD, SPLD

Hillside School
Hillside, Aberdour, Fife KY3 0RH
Tel: 01383 860731
Principal: Mrs Anne Smith
Age range: B10–16
No. of pupils: 39
Fees: Day £10,830 FB £26,594–£58,959
Special needs catered for: DYS, EBD, SPLD

Starley Hall School
Aberdour Road, Burntisland, Fife KY3 OAG
Tel: 01383 860314
Head: Philip Barton BA
Age range: 10–16
No. of pupils: 48
Special needs catered for: EBD, MLD

North Lanarkshire

St Philip's School
10 Main Street, Plains, Airdrie, North Lanarkshire ML6 7SF
Tel: 01236 765407
Head: Mr P Hanrahan
Age range: B12–16
No. of pupils: 61
Special needs catered for: EBD

Perth & Kinross

Balnacraig School
Fairmount Terrace, Perth, Perth & Kinross PH2 7AR
Tel: 01738 636456
Head: Charles Kiddie
Age range: 12–16
No. of pupils: 24
Special needs catered for: BESD, EBD

Seamab House School
Rumbling Bridge, Kinross, Perth & Kinross KY13 0PT
Tel: 01577 840307
Chief Executive: Ms Joanna McCreadie
Age range: 5–12
No. of pupils: 15
Special needs catered for: EBD

Renfrewshire

Kibble Education and Care Centre
Goudie Street, Paisley, Renfrewshire PA3 2LG
Tel: 0141 889 0044
CEO Designate: James Gillsepie
Age range: 12–16
No. of pupils: 93
Special needs catered for: EBD, MLD, SCD, SLD, SPLD

Spark of Genius
Trojan House, Phoenix Business Park, Paisley, Renfrewshire PA1 2BH
Tel: 0141 587 2710
Director: Mr Tom McGhee
Age range: 5–18
No. of pupils: 120
Special needs catered for: ADHD, ASD, DYS, DYSP, EBD, SEBD

The Good Shepherd Secure/Close Support Unit
Greenock Road, Bishopton, Renfrewshire PA7 5PW
Tel: 01505 864500
Head: Mr Sand Cunningham
Age range: G12–17
Special needs catered for: EBD, MLD

Stirling

Ballikinrain Residential School
Fintry Road, Balfron, Stirling G63 0LL
Tel: 01360 440244
Manager: Mr Paul Gilroy
Age range: B8–14
No. of pupils: 40
Special needs catered for: BESD

Snowdon School
31 Spittal Street, Stirling FK8 1DU
Tel: 01786 464746
Headteacher: Annette P Davison
Age range: G13–17
Special needs catered for: BESD

West Lothian

Moore House School
21 Edinburgh Road, Bathgate, West Lothian EH48 1EX
Tel: 01506 652312
Age range: 8–16
No. of pupils: 37
Special needs catered for: ADHD, EBD

Wales

Denbighshire

The Branas School
Branas Isaf, Llandrillo, Corwen, Denbighshire LL21 0TA
Tel: 01490 440545
Age range: B12–17
No. of pupils: 12
Special needs catered for: EBD

Monmouthshire

Talocher School
Talocher Farm, Wonastow Road, Monmouth, Monmouthshire NP25 4DN
Tel: 01600 740 777
Principal: Mr Mike Borland
Age range: 9–19
No. of pupils: 25
Special needs catered for: ADD, ADHD, BESD, DYS, DYSP, MLD, SEBD, SPLD

Neath Port Talbot

Blackwood School
Ferryboat House, Ellwood Jersey Marine, Neath, Neath Port Talbot SA10 6NG
Headteacher: Nicky Jones
Age range: B11–18
No. of pupils: 4
Special needs catered for: EBD, SPLD

Pembrokeshire

St David's Education Unit
Pembroke House, Brawdy Business Park, Haverfordwest, Pembrokeshire SA62 6NP
Tel: 01437 721234
Head: Mrs Alison Wilkinson
Age range: 8–17
No. of pupils: 7
Special needs catered for: EBD

Wrexham

Woodlands Children's Development Centre
27 Pentrefelyn Road, Wrexham LL13 7NB
Tel: 01978 262777
Head of School: Ms Baljit Gandhi-Johnson
Age range: B11–18
No. of pupils: 14
Special needs catered for: ADD, ADHD, ASD, ASP, AUT, BESD, DYS, DYSP, EBD, GLD, HA, HI, LD, MLD, SCD, SLD

Schools and colleges specialising in learning difficulties (including dyslexia/SPLD)

Abbreviations

ACLD	Autism, Communication and Associated Learning Difficulties
ADD	Attention Deficit Disorder
ADHD	Attention Deficit and Hyperactive Disorder (Hyperkinetic Disorder)
ASD	Autistic Spectrum Disorder
ASP	Asperger Syndrome
AUT	Autism
BESD	Behavioural, Emotional and Social Difficulties
CCD	Complex Communication Difficulties
CLD	Complex Learning Difficulties
CP	Cerebral Palsy
D	Deaf
DEL	Delicate
DYS	Dyslexia
DYSP	Dyspraxia
EBD	Emotional and Behavioural Difficulties
EBSD	Emotional, Behavioural and/or Social Difficulties
EPI	Epilepsy
GLD	General Learning Difficulties
HA	High Ability
HI	Hearing Impairment
HS	Hospital School
LD	Learning Difficulties
MLD	Moderate Learning Difficulties
MSI	Multi-sensory Impairment
OCD	Obsessive Compulsive Disorder
PD	Physical Difficulties
PH	Physical Impairment
Phe	Partially Hearing
PMLD	Profound and Multiple Learning Difficulties
PNI	Physical Neurological Impairment
PRU	Pupil Referral Unit
SCD	Social and Communication Difficulties
SCLD	Severe and Complex Learning Difficulties
SEBD	Severe Emotional and Behavioural Disorders
SEBN	Social, Emotional and Behavioural Needs
SLD	Severe Learning Difficulties
SLI	Specific Language Impairment
SPLD	Specific Learning Difficulties
SP&LD	Speech and Language Difficulties
SLCN	Speech Language & Communication Needs
VIS	Visually Impaired

Key to Symbols

Type of school:

(♦)	Boys' school
(♣)	Girls' school
(🌐)	International school

School offers:

(A)	A levels
(🏠)	Residential
(16+)	Entrance at 16+
(🧩)	Vocational qualifications
(✎)	Learning support
(✔)	This is a DfE approved independent or non-maintained school under section 41 of the Children and Families Act 2014 or section 342 of the 1996 Education Act

Please note: Unless otherwise indicated, all schools are coeducational day schools. Single-sex and boarding schools will be indicated by the relevant icon.

Central & West

Bristol

Aurora St Christopher's School
Westbury Park, Bristol BS6 7JE
Tel: 0117 974 3133
Head: Ms Louise Tully-Middleton
Age range: 5–19
Special needs catered for: ASD, AUT, CLD, CP, EPI, PhysD, PartH, PMLD, SCLD, SLD, SP&LD
♿

Belgrave School
10 Upper Belgrave Road, Clifton, Bristol BS8 2XH
Tel: 0117 974 3133
Head Teacher: Mr Jonathan Skinner
Age range: 5–13
Fees: Day £6,000
Special needs catered for: ADD, DEL, DYS, DYSP, SP&LD, SLI
✓

Bristol Dyslexia Centre
10 Upper Belgrave Road, Clifton, Bristol BS8 2XH
Tel: 0117 973 9405
Headmistress: Mrs Pat Jones BEd(Hons), SEN, SpLD, CertEd, IrSc, CMBDA
Special needs catered for: DYS, DYSP, SLD

Sheiling School, Thornbury
Thornbury Park, Thornbury, Bristol BS35 1HP
Tel: 01454 412194
Age range: 6–19
No. of pupils: 22
Fees: Day £66,419–£83,428 WB £125,931–£172,096 FB £140,578–£197,157
Special needs catered for: ADD, ADHD, ASD, ASP, AUT, BESD, CLD, CP, DEL, DYS, DYSP, EBD, EPI, GLD, HA, HI, LD, MLD, MSI, PD, Phe, SCD, SCLD, SEBD, SLD, SP&LD, SPLD, SLI
♿ 16+ ✓

Buckinghamshire

MacIntyre Wingrave School
Leighton Road, Wingrave, Buckinghamshire HP22 4PA
Tel: 01296 681274
Principal: Ms Annemari Ottridge
Age range: 10–19
No. of pupils: 38
Fees: FB £182,000
Special needs catered for: ASD, SCD, SLD
♿ 16+ ✓

Gloucestershire

BREDON SCHOOL
For further details see p. 90
Pull Court, Bushley, Tewkesbury, Gloucestershire GL20 6AH
Tel: 01684 293156
Email: enquiries@ bredonschool.co.uk
Website: www.bredonschool.org
Head Teacher: Mr Koen Claeys
Age range: 7–18
Special needs catered for: DYS, DYSP, SPLD
🏃 Ⓐ ♿ £ ✂ 16+

Cambian Southwick Park School
Gloucester Road, Tewkesbury, Gloucestershire GL20 7DG
Tel: 0800 138 1184
Head: Dr Joy Davis
Age range: 7–19
Special needs catered for: ASD, AUT, CLD, DYSP, GLD, LD, MLD, SCD, SCLD, SEBD, SLD, SP&LD, SLI
♿ 16+

RUSKIN MILL COLLEGE
For further details see p. 91
The Fisheries, Horsley, Gloucestershire GL6 0PL
Tel: 01453 837502
Email: enquiries@rmc.rmt.org
Website: www.rmt.org
Principal: Paul Garnault
Age range: 16–25
Special needs catered for: ADHD, ASD, ASP, BESD, CLD, EBD, GLD, LD, MLD, PMLD, SCD, SCLD, SEBD, SPLD
16+ ♿ 16+ ✓

William Morris College
Eastington, Stonehouse, Gloucestershire GL10 3SH
Tel: 01453 824025
Contact: Admissions Group
Age range: 16–25
No. of pupils: 30
Special needs catered for: ASP, AUT, DYSP, EBD, EPI, MLD
♿

Oxfordshire

Bruern Abbey School
Chesterton, Bicester, Oxfordshire OX26 1UY
Tel: 01869 242448
Principal: Mr P Fawkes MBA, CertEd
Age range: B7–13
No. of pupils: 44
Fees: Day £5,703 WB £7,791
Special needs catered for: DYS, DYSP
🏃 🏃 ♿

THE UNICORN SCHOOL
For further details see p. 92
20 Marcham Road, Abingdon, Oxfordshire OX14 1AA
Tel: 01235 530222
Email: info@unicornoxford.co.uk
Website: www.unicornoxford.co.uk
Headteacher: Mr. Andrew Day BEd (Hons)University of Wales (Cardiff)
Age range: 6–16
No. of pupils: 75
Special needs catered for: DYS, DYSP
✂ ✓

Wiltshire

Calder House School
Thickwood Lane, Colerne, Wiltshire SN14 8BN
Tel: 01225 743566
Head: Mrs Karen Parsons
Age range: 6–13
No. of pupils: 48
Fees: Day £16,200
Special needs catered for: DEL, DYS, DYSP, SP&LD, SPLD, SLI
✓

Fairfield Farm College
Dilton Marsh, Westbury, Wiltshire BA13 4DL
Tel: 01373 866066
Principal: Ms Janet Kenward
Age range: 16–25
Special needs catered for: MLD
16+ ♿

Tumblewood Project School
The Laurels, 4 Hawkeridge Road, Heywood, Westbury, Wiltshire BA13 4LF
Tel: 01373 824 466
Head of School: Jennifer Lewis
Age range: G11–18
No. of pupils: 12
Special needs catered for: ADHD, DYS, DYSP, LD
🏃 ♿ 16+ ✓

East

Cambridgeshire

Holme Court School
Abington Woods, Church Lane, Little Abington, Cambridgeshire CB21 6BQ
Tel: 01223 778030
Headteacher: Ms Anita Laws
Age range: 5–16
No. of pupils: 27
Special needs catered for: ADD, ADHD, ASP, CLD, DYS, DYSP, GLD, HA, LD, MLD, SCD, SP&LD, SPLD, VIS
✓

Essex

Doucecroft School
Abbots Lane, Eight Ash Green, Colchester, Essex CO6 3QL
Tel: 01206 771234
Head Teacher: Miss Kathy Cranmer BEd
Age range: 3–19
No. of pupils: 46
Fees: Day £52,779–£54,291 WB £86,211–£88,211
Special needs catered for: ASD, ASP, AUT
♿ 16+ ✓

Woodcroft School
Whitakers Way, Loughton, Essex IG10 1SQ
Tel: 020 8508 1369
Headteacher: Mrs Margaret Newton
Age range: 2–11
No. of pupils: 36
Special needs catered for: ADD, ADHD, ASD, ASP, AUT, CLD, CP, DEL, DYSP, EBD, EPI, LD, MLD, MSI, PH, PMLD, SCLD, SLD, SP&LD, SPLD, SLI, VIS
✓

Hertfordshire

Egerton Rothesay School
Durrants Lane, Berkhamsted, Hertfordshire HP4 3UJ
Tel: 01442 865275
Headteacher: Mr Colin Parker BSc(Hons), Dip.Ed (Oxon), PGCE, C.Math MIMA
Age range: 6–19
No. of pupils: 166
Fees: Day £15,255–£21,711
Special needs catered for:
🏃 ✂

Lincolnshire

Kisimul Upper School
Acacia Hall, Shortwood
Lane, Friesthorpe, Lincoln,
Lincolnshire LN3 5AL
Tel: 01673 880022
Headteacher: Paul Routledge
Age range: 8–19
Special needs catered for: ASD, SLD
⊞

Norfolk

Copperfield School
22 Euston Road, Great
Yarmouth, Norfolk NR30 1DX
Tel: 01493 849 499
Headteacher: Sally Alden
Age range: 11–16
No. of pupils: 12
Special needs catered for:
ADD, ADHD, ASP, BESD, CLD,
DYS, DYSP, EBD, GLD, LD, MLD,
SCD, SCLD, SEBD, SPLD
✔

The Beehive
Stubbs House, Stubbs Green,
Loddon, Norfolk NR14 6EA
Tel: 01508 521190
Headteacher: Mrs Valerie Freear
Age range: 5–14
No. of pupils: 4
Special needs catered for:
ASD, BESD, MLD, SPLD
✔

Suffolk

Centre Academy East Anglia
Church Road, Brettenham,
Ipswich, Suffolk IP7 7QR
Tel: 01449 736404
Principal: Dr. Duncan
Rollo BA, MA, PhD
Age range: 4–19
Fees: Day £18,000–£25,875
WB £24,999–£36,225
Special needs catered for:
ADHD, ASP, CLD, DYS, DYSP,
GLD, HA, LD, SP&LD, SPLD
⊞ £ ✔

East Midlands

Derbyshire

Alderwasley Hall School & Sixth Form Centre
Alderwasley, Belper,
Derbyshire DE56 2SR
Tel: 01629 822586
Headteacher: Miss Sara
Forsyth NPQH
Age range: 5–19
Fees: Day £57,689
WB £83,798 FB £164,446
Special needs catered for:
ADHD, ASD, ASP, AUT, DYSP, GLD,
HA, LD, SCD, SP&LD, SPLD, SLI
⊞ 16+ ✔

Pegasus School
Caldwell Hall, Main Street,
Caldwell, Derbyshire DE12 6RS
Tel: 01283 761352
Head Teacher: Mrs Dawn Coombes
Age range: 8–19
Fees: Day £93,629
WB £216,829 FB £282,172
Special needs catered for: ADHD,
ASD, AUT, CLD, EPI, HI, LD, PMLD,
SCLD, SLD, SP&LD, SPLD, SLI, VIS
⊞ 16+ ✔

Lincolnshire

KISIMUL SCHOOL
For further details see p. 94
The Old Vicarage, 61 High
Street, Swinderby, Lincoln,
Lincolnshire LN6 9LU
Tel: 01522 868279
Email: admissions@kisimul.co.uk
Website: www.kisimul.co.uk
Director of Education: Mr Danny
Carter BA(Hons), MA, MEd
Age range: 8–19
No. of pupils: 60
Special needs catered for:
ASD, AUT, CLD, EPI, LD, MSI,
PMLD, SCLD, SLD, SP&LD, SPLD
⊞ 16+ ✔

Linkage College – Toynton Campus
Toynton All Saints, Spilsby,
Lincolnshire PE23 5AE
Tel: 01790 752499
Age range: 16–25
Special needs catered for:
ADD, ADHD, ASD, ASP, AUT, CLD,
CP, D, DEL, DYS, DYSP, EPI, GLD,
HI, LD, MLD, PD, Phe, PH, SCD,
SCLD, SLD, SP&LD, SPLD, VIS
16+ ⊞

Nottinghamshire

I CAN'S DAWN HOUSE SCHOOL
For further details see p. 93
Helmsley Road, Rainworth,
Mansfield, Nottinghamshire
NG21 0DQ
Tel: 01623 795361
Email: dawnhouse@
ican.notts.sch.uk
Website:
www.dawnhouseschool.org.uk
Principal: Jenny McConnell
Age range: 5–19
No. of pupils: 79
Special needs catered for: CLD,
DYS, DYSP, SCD, SLD, SP&LD, SPLD
⊞ 16+ ✔

Sutherland House – Continuing Education Centre
8 Clinton Avenue, Nottingham,
Nottinghamshire NG5 1AW
Tel: 0115 9693373
Principal: Maria Allen
Age range: 11–19
Special needs catered for: ASD, AUT
16+

Sutherland House School
Bath Street, Sneinton, Nottingham,
Nottinghamshire NG1 1DA
Tel: 0115 960 9263
Head Teacher: Adrian Sugden
Age range: 3–19
No. of pupils: 84
Fees: Day £41,525–£45,473
Special needs catered for:
ASD, ASP, AUT
16+ ✔

Greater London

Essex

St John's RC Special School
Turpins Lane, Woodford
Bridge, Essex IG8 8AX
Tel: 020 8504 1818
Head of School: Wendy Killilea
Age range: 5–19
Special needs catered for:
MLD, SLD
✔

London

Blossom Lower School and Upper House
Station Road, Motspur Park,
New Malden, London KT3 6JJ
Tel: 020 8946 7348
Principal: Joanna Burgess DipCST,
MRCSLT,DipRSA,SpLD,PGCE,HPC
Age range: 3–19
No. of pupils: 214
Special needs catered for:
ADD, ADHD, ASP, DYS,
DYSP, SCD, SP&LD, SPLD
16+ ✔

Middlesex

Hillingdon Manor School
Moorcroft Complex,
Harlington Road, Hillingdon,
Middlesex UB8 3HD
Tel: 01895 813679
Principal: Ms Angela Austin
Age range: 3–19
No. of pupils: 70
Fees: Day £32,646
Special needs catered for:
ASD, CLD
16+ ✔

PIELD HEATH HOUSE SCHOOL
For further details see p. 96
Pield Heath Road, Uxbridge,
Middlesex UB8 3NW
Tel: 01895 258507
Email: admin@
pieldheathschool.org.uk
Website:
pieldheathschool.org.uk
Executive Principal: Sister
Julie Rose
Age range: 7–19
No. of pupils: 96
Special needs catered for:
MLD, SLD, SP&LD
⊞ 16+ ✔

Surrey

Rutherford School
1A Melville Avenue, South
Croydon, Surrey CR2 7HZ
Tel: 020 8688 7560
Interim Head of School: Dr
Carole Nicolson
Age range: 3–19
No. of pupils: 26
Fees: Day £50,400
Special needs catered for:
CP, D, EPI, HI, MSI, PD, Phe, PH,
PMLD, PNI, SLD, SP&LD, VIS
16+ ✓

THE LINK PRIMARY SCHOOL
For further details see p. 97
138 Croydon Road, Beddington,
Croydon, Surrey CR0 4PG
Tel: 020 8688 5239
Email: office@linkprim.co.uk
Website: www.linkprim.co.uk
Head Teacher: Mrs Sandy Turner
Age range: 4–11
No. of pupils: 50
Special needs catered for:
ASD, ASP, DYSP, GLD, LD,
MLD, SCD, SP&LD, SLI
✓

London

East London

Side by Side Kids School
9 Big Hill, London E5 9HH
Tel: 020 8880 8300
Headteacher: Ms R Atkins
Age range: 2–16
No. of pupils: 60
Special needs catered for:
MLD, SLD, SP&LD
✓

North London

Limespring School
Park House, 16 High Road, East
Finchley, London N2 9PJ
Tel: 020 8444 1387
Principal: Denise Drinkwater
Age range: 7–11
Special needs catered for:
DYS, DYSP
✓

North-West London

ABINGDON HOUSE SCHOOL
For further details see p. 98
Broadley Terrace,
London NW1 6LG
Tel: 020 3750 5526
Email: ahs@
abingdonhouseschool.co.uk
Website: www.abingdon
houseschool.co.uk
Head Teacher: Mr Roy English
Age range: 5–16
Special needs catered for:
ADD, ADHD, ASP, DYS,
DYSP, SP&LD, SPLD
✓

Kisharon School
1011 Finchley Road,
London NW11 7HB
Tel: 020 8455 7483
Age range: 4–19
No. of pupils: 35
Fees: Day £27,000–£42,000
Special needs catered for: ADD,
ADHD, ASD, ASP, AUT, BESD, CLD,
CP, D, DEL, DYS, DYSP, EBD, EPI,
GLD, HA, HI, LD, MLD, MSI, PD,
Phe, PH, PMLD, PNI, SCD, SCLD,
SEBD, SLD, SP&LD, SPLD, SLI, VIS
✓

South-East London

Octavia House School, Kennington
214b Kennington Road,
London SE11 6AU
Tel: 020 3651 4396 (Option:3)
Executive Head: Mr James Waite
Special needs catered for: ADD,
ADHD, BESD, EBD, SCD, SEBD

South-West London

Centre Academy London
92 St John's Hill, Battersea,
London SW11 1SH
Tel: 020 7738 2344
Principal: Dr. Duncan
Rollo BA, MA, PhD
Age range: 9–19
Fees: Day £27,600–£40,100
Special needs catered for:
ADD, ADHD, ASD, ASP, AUT,
CLD, DYS, DYSP, HA, SP&LD
£ ✓ 16+ ✓

Fairley House School
30 Causton Street,
London SW1P 4AU
Tel: 020 7976 5456
Headmaster: Mr Michael
Taylor BA (Hons) PGCE FRGS
Age range: 5–16
No. of pupils: 203
Fees: Day £30,300
Special needs catered for:
DYS, DYSP, SPLD
✓

Frederick Hugh House
48 Old Church Street,
London SW3 5BY
Tel: 0207 349 8833
Headteacher: Miss Tanya Jamil
Age range: 10–16
Special needs catered for:
ADHD, ASD, AUT, CLD, CP,
DEL, DYSP, EPI, GLD, LD, MLD,
MSI, PD, SCD, SP&LD, SPLD
✓

Parayhouse School
Hammersmith and Fulham College,
Gliddon Road, London W14 9BL
Tel: 020 8741 1400
Head: Mrs Sarah Jackson
CertEd, DipEd(Complex
Learning Handicap)
Age range: 7–16
No. of pupils: 46
Fees: Day £27,540
Special needs catered for: ADD,
BESD, CLD, CP, DEL, EBD, EPI, MLD,
Phe, SCD, SCLD, SLD, SP&LD
✓

The Dominie
55 Warriner Gardens,
Battersea, London SW11 4DX
Tel: 020 7720 8783
Principal: Miss Anne O'Doherty
Age range: 6–13
No. of pupils: 30
Special needs catered for:
DYS, DYSP, SP&LD
✓

The Moat School
Bishops Avenue, Fulham,
London SW6 6EG
Tel: 020 7610 9018
Head: Ms Clare King
Age range: 9–16
Fees: Day £28,800
Special needs catered for: SPLD
✓

West London

THE INDEPENDENT SCHOOL (TIS)
For further details see p. 99
23-31 Beavor Lane, Ravenscourt
Park, Hammersmith,
London W6 9AR
Tel: 020 3637 7574
Email: admin@tis-london.org
Website: www.tis-london.org
Principal: Ms Tanya Moran
Age range: 11–16
Special needs catered for:
DYS, DYSP, SPLD

North-East

Northumberland

Cambian Dilston College
Dilston Hall, Corbridge,
Northumberland NE45 5RJ
Tel: 0800 138 1184
Vice Principal: Nicola Moxon
Age range: 16–25
Special needs catered for: ADD,
ADHD, ASD, ASP, AUT, BESD, CP,
DEL, EBD, EPI, GLD, LD, MLD,
SCD, SCLD, SLD, SP&LD, SPLD
⊞

Nunnykirk Centre for Dyslexia
Netherwitton, Morpeth,
Northumberland NE61 4PB
Tel: 01670 772685
Headteacher: B Frost NPQH,
MSc, MEd, BA(QTS), PGDip
Age range: 9–18
No. of pupils: 24 VIth7
Fees: Day £12,960–£13,935
WB £21,555–£23,520
Special needs catered for:
DYS, DYSP, SPLD
⊞ (16) ✔

North-West

Cheshire

The David Lewis School
Mill Lane, Warford, Alderley
Edge, Cheshire SK9 7UD
Tel: 01565 640066
Principal: Angie Fisher
Age range: 14–19
No. of pupils: 20
Special needs catered for:
AUT, CP, EPI, HI, PD, PMLD,
SCD, SLD, SP&LD, SPLD, VIS
⊞ (16) ✔

Greater Manchester

Birtenshaw School
Bromley Cross, Bolton, Greater
Manchester BL7 9AB
Tel: 01204 306043
Head Teacher: Mrs Julie Barnes
Age range: 3–19
No. of pupils: 35 VIth25
Fees: Day £49,757–£71,084
Special needs catered for: ADD,
ADHD, ASD, ASP, AUT, CLD, CP,
DEL, EPI, GLD, HI, LD, MLD, MSI,
PD, Phe, PH, PMLD, PNI, SCD,
SCLD, SLD, SP&LD, SLI, VIS
⊞ (16) ✔

Bridge College
Openshaw Campus, Whitworth
Street, Manchester, Greater
Manchester M11 2GR
Tel: 0161 487 4293
Head of School: Lisa Duncalf
Age range: 16–25
No. of pupils: 90
Special needs catered for: ASD,
AUT, CLD, PH, PMLD, SCD

Langdon College
9 Leicester Avenue, Salford,
Greater Manchester M7 4HA
Tel: 0161 740 5900
Principal: Mr Christopher Mayho
Age range: 16–25
Special needs catered for:
ASD, ASP, AUT, BESD, DYS, DYSP,
EBD, GLD, HI, LD, MLD, Phe, PH,
SCD, SP&LD, SPLD, SLI, VIS

Lancashire

Pontville
Black Moss Lane, Ormskirk,
Lancashire L39 4TW
Tel: 01695 578734
Head Teacher: Ms Elaine Riley
Age range: 5–19
No. of pupils: 59
Special needs catered for:
ASD, ASP, CLD, MLD, SCD,
SP&LD, SPLD, SLI
⊞ (16) ✔

Progress School
Gough Lane, Bamber Bridge,
Preston, Lancashire PR26 7TZ
Tel: 01772 334832
Principal: Mrs Lyn Lewis
Age range: 7–19
No. of pupils: 17
Fees: WB £3,269 FB £170,000
Special needs catered for:
AUT, PMLD, SCLD, SLD
⊞ (16) ✔

Merseyside

Liverpool Progressive School
Rice Lane, Liverpool,
Merseyside L9 1NR
Tel: 0151 525 4004
Headteacher: Ms Linda Butcher
Age range: 8–19
No. of pupils: 20
Special needs catered for: AUT, SLD
(16) ✔

Wargrave House School
449 Wargrave Road, Newton-le-
Willows, Merseyside WA12 8RS
Tel: 01925 224899
Principal: Mrs Wendy Mann
BSc, PGCE, DipSpLD, NPQH
Age range: 5–19
No. of pupils: 70
Special needs catered for: ASP, AUT
⊞ (16) ✔

South-East

East Sussex

Frewen College
Brickwall, Rye Road, Northiam,
Rye, East Sussex TN31 6NL
Tel: 01797 252 494
Principal: Mrs Linda Smith
BA(Hons), PGCE
Age range: 7–19
No. of pupils: 103
Fees: Day £13,686–£21,801
WB £21,078–£30,264
FB £21,078–£30,264
Special needs catered for:
DYS, DYSP, SP&LD, SPLD
⊕ ⊞ £ ✎ ✔

Northease Manor School
Rodmell, Lewes, East Sussex BN7 3EY
Tel: 01273 472915
Headteacher: Carmen Harvey-
Browne BA(Hons), PGCE, NPQH
Age range: 10–17
No. of pupils: 95
Special needs catered for:
ADD, ADHD, ASD, ASP, DYS,
DYSP, SCD, SP&LD, SPLD
⊕ ⊞ ✔

Owlswick School
Newhaven Road, Kingston,
Lewes, East Sussex BN7 3NF
Tel: 01273 473078
Headteacher: Michael Mayne
Age range: 10–17
Special needs catered for: ADD,
ADHD, ASD, ASP, BESD, DYS,
DYSP, EBD, GLD, LD, MLD, SCD
⊞ (16) ✔

ST JOHN'S SCHOOL & COLLEGE
For further details see p. 107
Business Centre, 17
Walpole Road, Brighton,
East Sussex BN2 0AF
Tel: 01273 244000
Email: admissions@st-johns.co.uk
Website: www.st-johns.co.uk
Principal & Chief Executive: Mr
Simon Charleton
Age range: 7–25
No. of pupils: 118
Fees: Day £50,000 FB £100,000
Special needs catered for: ADD,
ADHD, ASD, ASP, AUT, BESD, CLD,
CP, D, DEL, DYS, DYSP, EBD, EPI,
GLD, HA, LD, MLD, PD, PNI, SCD,
SCLD, SEBD, SLD, SP&LD, SPLD, SLI
⊞ (16)

Hampshire

Chiltern Tutorial School
Otterbourne New Hall,
Cranbourne Drive, Otterbourne,
Winchester, Hampshire SO21 2ET
Tel: 01962 717696
Headmistress: Mrs Jane
Gaudie BA, CertEd, AMBDA
Age range: 7–12
No. of pupils: 20
Fees: Day £8,850
Special needs catered for:
DYS, DYSP
✓

Clay Hill School
Clay Hill, Lyndhurst,
Hampshire SO43 7DE
Tel: 023 8028 3633
Head of School: Mrs. Helen Sharpe
Age range: 5–19
Special needs catered for: ASD, LD

Minstead Training Project
Minstead Lodge, Minstead,
Lyndhurst, Hampshire SO43 7FT
Tel: 023 80812254
Principal: Mr Martin Lenaerts
Age range: 18+
No. of pupils: 14
Special needs catered for:
GLD, LD, MLD
16+

Sheiling College
Horton Road, Ashley, Ringwood,
Hampshire BH24 2EB
Tel: 01425 477488
Principal: Ms Corine van Barneveld
Age range: 19–25
No. of pupils: 32
Special needs catered for: ASD,
AUT, CLD, EPI, GLD, LD, MLD,
SCD, SCLD, SLD, SP&LD, SPLD
🎓

Sheiling School
Horton Road, Ashley, Ringwood,
Hampshire BH24 2EB
Tel: 01425 477488
Head of School: Ms Corine
van Barneveld
Age range: 6–19
No. of pupils: 31
Fees: Day £39,070
WB £88,260 FB £106,008
Special needs catered for: ASD,
AUT, CLD, EBD, EPI, GLD, LD, MLD,
SCD, SCLD, SLD, SP&LD, SPLD
16+ 🎓 16+ ✓

The Loddon School
Wildmoor Lane, Sherfield-
on-Loddon, Hook,
Hampshire RG27 0JD
Tel: 01256 884600
Principal: Gill Barrett
MEd,BA(Hons),NPQH,PCGE
Age range: 8–19
No. of pupils: 26
Fees: FB £229,000
Special needs catered for:
ADD, ADHD, ASD, AUT, CLD,
EPI, SCLD, SLD, SP&LD
🎓 16+ ✓

Isle of Wight

ST CATHERINE'S SCHOOL
For further details see p. 106
Grove Road, Ventnor,
Isle of Wight PO38 1TT
Tel: 01983 852722
Email: general@
stcatherines.org.uk
Website:
www.stcatherines.org.uk
Principal: Mrs R Weldon
Age range: 7–19
No. of pupils: 53 VIth26
Special needs catered for:
ADD, ADHD, ASD, ASP, AUT,
DYS, DYSP, SCD, SLD, SP&LD, SLI
🎓 16+ ✓

Kent

Great Oaks Small School
Ebbsfleet Farmhouse,
Ebbsfleet Lane, Minster,
Ramsgate, Kent CT12 5DL
Tel: 01843 822 022
Head of School: Mrs Liz Baker
Age range: 10–18
No. of pupils: 18 VIth3
Special needs catered for: SPLD
Ⓐ ✓

Trinity School
13 New Road, Rochester,
Medway, Kent ME1 1BG
Tel: 01634 812233
Principal: Mrs C Dunn BA(Hons),
RSA(Dip), SpLD(NHCSS)
Age range: 6–16
No. of pupils: 43
Fees: Day £9,270–£9,750
Special needs catered for: ASD,
ASP, DYS, DYSP, SLD, SP&LD
✓

Surrey

I CAN'S MEATH SCHOOL
For further details see p. 104
Brox Road, Ottershaw,
Surrey KT16 0LF
Tel: 01932 872302
Email:
meath@meath-ican.org.uk
Website:
www.meathschool.org.uk
Headteacher: Janet Dunn
OBE, MA, AdvDipSpecEduc
No. of pupils: 60
Special needs catered for:
SP&LD
🎓 ✓

KISIMUL SCHOOL –
WOODSTOCK HOUSE
For further details see p. 100
Woodstock Lane North, Long
Ditton, Surbiton, Surrey KT6 5HN
Tel: 020 8335 2570
Email: admissions@kisimul.co.uk
Website: www.kisimul.co.uk
Director of Education: Mr Danny
Carter BA(Hons), MA, MEd
Age range: 8–19
No. of pupils: 40
Special needs catered for:
ASD, AUT, CLD, EPI, LD, MSI,
PMLD, SCLD, SLD, SP&LD, SPLD
🎓 16+ ✓

Moon Hall College
Burys Court, Flanchford Road,
Leigh, Reigate, Surrey RH2 8RE
Tel: 01306 611372
Principal: Mrs Berry Baker
BA(Hons) Hist, PGCE, BSc(Hons)
Psych, BDA Diploma, AMBDA
Age range: 3–16
Fees: Day £6,630–£17,220
Special needs catered for:
DYS, LD, SPLD

Moon Hall School
Pasturewood Road, Holmbury St
Mary, Dorking, Surrey RH5 6LQ
Tel: 01306 731464
Head: Mrs Pamela Lore BA(Hons)
(Psych), MA(Ed), Dip RSA SpLD, PGCE
Age range: 7–13
Fees: Day £14,400–£16,470
WB £16,015–£18,085
Special needs catered for: DYS, SPLD
🌐 🎓 ✓

MOOR HOUSE
SCHOOL & COLLEGE
For further details see p. 102
Mill Lane, Hurst Green,
Oxted, Surrey RH8 9AQ
Tel: 01883 712271
Email: admissionsteam@
moorhouseschool.co.uk;
info@moorhouseschool.co.uk
Website:
www.moorhouseschool.co.uk
Principal: Mrs H A Middleton
Age range: 7–19
No. of pupils: 129
Special needs catered for:
ASP, DYS, DYSP, SLD, SP&LD, SLI
Ⓐ 🎓 ✓

MORE HOUSE SCHOOL
For further details see p. 105
Moons Hill, Frensham,
Farnham, Surrey GU10 3AP
Tel: 01252 792303
Email: schooloffice@
morehouseschool.co.uk
Website:
www.morehouseschool.co.uk
Headmaster: Jonathan
Hetherington BA(Hons),
MSc(ed), QTS
Age range: B8–18
No. of pupils: 470
Fees: Day £12,792–£17,931
WB £19,938–£25,764
FB £22,029–£27,906
Special needs catered for: SPLD
✝ 🌐 🎓 16+ ✓

Orchard Hill College
and Academy Trust
BedZED, 20 Sandmartin Way,
Hackbridge, Surrey SM6 7DF
Tel: 0345 402 0453
Principal: Ms Caroline Allen
OBE, BEd(Hons), MBA(Ed)
Age range: 16+
Special needs catered for: ADD,
ADHD, ASD, ASP, AUT, BESD, CLD,
CP, DEL, DYS, DYSP, EBD, EPI,
GLD, HA, HI, LD, MLD, MSI, PD,
Phe, PH, PMLD, PNI, SCD, SCLD,
SEBD, SLD, SP&LD, SPLD, SLI, VIS

St Dominic's School
Hambledon, Godalming,
Surrey GU8 4DX
Tel: 01428 684693/682741
Principal: Mrs Angela Drayton
Age range: 7–19
No. of pupils: 77 VIth19
Special needs catered for: ADD,
ADHD, ASD, ASP, BESD, CLD, DEL,
DYS, DYSP, EPI, HA, SCD, SP&LD, SPLD
🎓 ✎ ✓

ST JOSEPH'S SPECIALIST
SCHOOL & COLLEGE
For further details see p. 108
Amlets Lane, Cranleigh,
Surrey GU6 7DH
Tel: 01483 272449
Email: admissions@st-
josephscranleigh.surrey.sch.uk
Website: www.st-josephs
cranleigh.surrey.sch.uk
Principal: Mrs Annie Sutton
Age range: 5–19
No. of pupils: 75
Fees: Day £57,905 FB £83,898
Special needs catered for:
ADHD, ASD, CLD, DYS, DYSP,
EPI, MLD, SCLD, SLD, SP&LD
🎓 ✎ 16+ ✓

The Knowl Hill School
School Lane, Pirbright,
Woking, Surrey GU24 0JN
Tel: 01483 797032
Headteacher: Mrs Jan Lusty
Age range: 7–16
No. of pupils: 57
Fees: Day £15,606
Special needs catered for:
DYS, DYSP, SPLD
£ ✎ ✓

Wiltshire

Appleford School
Shrewton, Salisbury,
Wiltshire SP3 4HL
Tel: 01980 621020
Headmaster: Mr. David King
Age range: 7–18
No. of pupils: 126
Fees: Day £16,608 FB £25,491
Special needs catered for:
ADD, ADHD, ASP, DYS, DYSP,
HA, MLD, SP&LD, SPLD
🌐 🎓 16+ ✓

South-West

Devon

Kingsley School
Northdown Road, Bideford,
Devon EX39 3LY
Tel: 01237 426200
Headmaster: Mr Pete Last
Age range: 0–18
No. of pupils: 395
Fees: Day £1,895
WB £5,495 FB £7,070
Special needs catered for:
DYS, DYSP

Somerset

Cambian Lufton College
Lufton, Yeovil, Somerset BA22 8ST
Tel: 0800 138 1184
Principal: Jonathan James
Age range: 16–25
No. of pupils: 72
Special needs catered for:
HI, MLD, PH, PMLD, SLD

Foxes Academy
Selbourne Place, Minehead,
Somerset TA24 5TY
Tel: 01643 708529
Principal: Tracey Clare-Gray
Age range: 16–25
No. of pupils: 80
Special needs catered for:
ADD, ADHD, ASD, ASP, AUT,
BESD, CLD, DEL, DYS, DYSP, EBD,
GLD, HA, HI, LD, MLD, MSI, PD,
Phe, SCD, SCLD, SLD, SPLD

Mark College
Highbridge, Somerset TA9 4NP
Tel: 01278 641 632
Principal: Mr Chris Sweeney
Age range: 10–19
Special needs catered for:
DYS, DYSP, LD, SP&LD, SPLD

SHAPWICK SCHOOL
For further details see p. 110
Shapwick Manor, Station Road,
Shapwick, Somerset TA7 9NJ
Tel: 01458 210384
Email: office@
shapwickschool.com
Website:
www.shapwickschool.com
Principal: Mr A Wylie
B.Ed, PG Dip, NPQH
Age range: 8–19 years
No. of pupils: 84
Fees: Day £18,519–£19,386
WB £24,258 FB £25,560–£27,858
Special needs catered for:
DYS, DYSP

West Midlands

Herefordshire

Rowden House School
Rowden, Bromyard,
Herefordshire HR7 4LS
Tel: 01885 488096
Principal: Mr Martin Carter
NPQH, BEd(Hons), Adv Diploma
(Behaviour Support)
Age range: 8–19
Fees: Day £93,629
WB £216,829 FB £282,172
Special needs catered for: ADD,
ADHD, ASD, AUT, CLD, EPI, GLD, LD,
MLD, PMLD, SCLD, SLD, SP&LD, SPLD

Shropshire

Access School
Holbrook Villa Farm, Harmer
Hill, Broughton, Shrewsbury,
Shropshire SY4 3EW
Tel: 01939 220797
Headteacher: Miss Verity White
Age range: 5–16
No. of pupils: 10
Special needs catered for:
EBD, GLD, MLD

Queensway HLC
Hadley, Telford, Shropshire TF1 6AJ
Tel: 01952 388555
Headteacher: Nigel Griffiths
Age range: 11–16
Special needs catered for:
EBD, SPLD

Staffordshire

Bladon House School
Newton Solney, Burton upon
Trent, Staffordshire DE15 0TA
Tel: 01283 563787
Head Teacher: Mrs Shally Saleri
– Palmer B Ed (Hons), NPQH
Age range: 5–19
Fees: Day £82,223
WB £179,189 FB £215,996
Special needs catered for: ADD,
ADHD, ASD, AUT, CLD, EPI, HI, LD,
MLD, SLD, SP&LD, SPLD, SLI, VIS

Maple Hayes Dyslexia School
Abnalls Lane, Lichfield,
Staffordshire WS13 8BL
Tel: 01543 264387
Principal: Dr E N Brown MSc,
BA, MINS, MSCMe, AFBPsS,
CPsychol, FRSA, CSci
Age range: 7–17
No. of pupils: 118
Fees: Day £14,760–£19,725
Special needs catered for:
DYS, DYSP, SPLD

Regent College
77 Shelton New Road, Shelton,
Stoke-on-Trent, Staffordshire ST4 7AA
Tel: 01782 263326
Principal: Ms Wendy Williams
Age range: 16–25
No. of pupils: 30
Special needs catered for:
CLD, EPI, PD, SLD, SP&LD

West Midlands

ARGENT COLLEGE
For further details see p. 111
New Standard Works, 43-47
Vittoria Street, Birmingham,
West Midlands B1 3PE
Tel: 01453 837502
Email: enquiries@argent.rmt.org
Website: www.rmt.org
Principal: Oliver Cheney
Age range: 16–25
Special needs catered for:
ASD, ASP, AUT, BESD,
CLD, LD, SCLD, SEBD

GLASSHOUSE COLLEGE
For further details see p. 112
Wollaston Road,
Amblecote, Stourbridge,
West Midlands DY8 4HF
Tel: 01453 837502
Email: enquiries@ghc.rmt.org
Website: www.rmt.org
Executive Principal: Oliver
Cheney
Age range: 16–25
Special needs catered for:
ADHD, ASD, ASP, BESD, CLD,
EBD, GLD, LD, PMLD, SCD,
SCLD, SEBD, SLD, SPLD

OVERLEY HALL SCHOOL
For further details see p. 113
Overley, Wellington, Telford,
West Midlands TF6 5HE
Tel: 01952 740262
Email: info@overleyhall.com
Website: www.overleyhall.com
Headteacher: Mrs
Beverley Doran
Age range: 8–19
No. of pupils: 20
Special needs catered for:
ADD, ADHD, ASD, ASP, AUT,
CLD, DYSP, EPI, GLD, LD, PMLD,
SCD, SCLD, SLD, SP&LD

Sunfield School
Clent Grove, Woodman Lane,
Stourbridge, West Midlands DY9 9PB
Tel: 01562 882253
Principal: Caroline Bell
Age range: 6–19
Special needs catered for: ADD,
ADHD, ASD, AUT, BESD, CLD, DYS,
EPI, GLD, LD, MLD, MSI, PMLD,
SCD, SCLD, SEBD, SLD, SP&LD, SLI

Worcestershire

Our Place School
The Orchard, Bransford,
Worcestershire WR6 5JE
Tel: 01886 833378
Head of School: Paula McElearney
Special needs catered for:
ASD, MLD, PMLD, SLD

Yorkshire & Humberside

North-East Lincolnshire

Linkage College – Weelsby Campus
Weelsby Road, Grimsby, North-East Lincolnshire DN32 9RU
Tel: 01472 241044
Director of Education: Hugh Williams
Age range: 16–25
No. of pupils: 220
Special needs catered for:
ADD, ADHD, ASD, ASP, AUT, CLD, CP, D, DEL, DYS, DYSP, EPI, GLD, HI, LD, MLD, Phe, PH, SCD, SCLD, SLD, SP&LD, SPLD, VIS
(16) (£)

South Yorkshire

FREEMAN COLLEGE
For further details see p. 114
Sterling Works, 88 Arundel Street, Sheffield, South Yorkshire S1 2NG
Tel: 01453 837502
Email: enquiries@fmc.rmt.org
Website: www.rmt.org
Principal: Perdita Mousley
Age range: 16–25
Special needs catered for:
ADHD, ASD, ASP, BESD, CLD, EBD, GLD, LD, MLD, PMLD, SCD, SCLD, SEBD, SLD
(16) (£) (✓)

FULLERTON HOUSE COLLEGE
For further details see p. 116
Tickhill Square, Denaby, Doncaster, South Yorkshire DN12 4AR
Tel: 01709 861663
Email: enquiries@hesleygroup.co.uk
Website: www.hesleygroup.co.uk
Head: Richard Webster
Age range: 18–25
Special needs catered for:
ASD, ASP, AUT, CLD, DYS, DYSP, GLD, LD, MLD, SCLD, SLD, SPLD
(£)

FULLERTON HOUSE SCHOOL
For further details see p. 115
Tickill Square, Denaby, Doncaster, South Yorkshire DN12 4AR
Tel: 01709 861663
Email: enquiries@hesleygroup.co.uk
Website: www.fullertonhouseschool.co.uk
General Manager: Michael Cavan
Age range: 8–19
Special needs catered for:
ASD, ASP, AUT, CLD, DYS, DYSP, GLD, LD, MLD, SCLD, SLD, SPLD
(£) (16) (✓)

WILSIC HALL COLLEGE
For further details see p. 116
Wadworth, Doncaster, South Yorkshire DN11 9AG
Tel: 01302 856382
Head: Geoff Turner
Age range: 19–25
No. of pupils: 3
Special needs catered for:
ASD, ASP, AUT, CLD, DYS, DYSP, GLD, LD, MLD, SCLD, SLD, SPLD
(£)

WILSIC HALL SCHOOL
For further details see p. 117
Wadworth, Doncaster, South Yorkshire DN11 9AG
Tel: 01302 856382
Email: enquiries@hesleygroup.co.uk
Website: www.wilsichallschool.co.uk
Head: Geoff Turner
Age range: 11–19
Special needs catered for:
ASD, ASP, AUT, CLD, DYS, DYSP, GLD, LD, MLD, SCLD, SLD, SPLD
(£) (16) (✓)

West Yorkshire

Hall Cliffe School
Dovecote Lane, Horbury, Wakefield, West Yorkshire WF4 6BB
Tel: 01924 663 420
Head of School: Dr. Chris Lingard
Age range: 8–16
Special needs catered for:
ADHD, AUT, BESD, MLD, SLD
(16)

Pennine Camphill Community
Wood Lane, Chapelthorpe, Wakefield, West Yorkshire WF4 3JL
Tel: 01924 255281
Principal: S Hopewell
Age range: 16–25
No. of pupils: 56
Fees: Day £14,000–£45,000
FB £26,000–£69,000
Special needs catered for: ADHD, ASD, ASP, AUT, CLD, DYSP, EBD, EPI, LD, MLD, SCLD, SLD, SPLD
(£) (✐)

Northern Ireland

County Tyrone

Parkanaur College
57 Parkanaur Road, Dungannon, County Tyrone BT70 3AA
Tel: 028 87761272
Principal: Mr Wilfred Mitchell
Age range: 18–65
Special needs catered for: ADD, ADHD, ASP, AUT, BESD, CLD, CP, DYS, DYSP, EBD, EPI, GLD, HA, HI, LD, MLD, PD, Phe, PH, PMLD, PNI, SCD, SCLD, SLD, SPLD, VIS

Scotland

Aberdeen

VSA Linn Moor Campus
Peterculter, Aberdeen AB14 0PJ
Tel: 01224 732246
Head Teacher: Victoria Oumarou
Age range: 5–18
No. of pupils: 25
Fees: Day £38,326
FB £76,650–£239,114
Special needs catered for:
ASD, AUT, CLD, GLD, LD, MLD, SCD, SCLD, SPLD
(£) (16)

Clackmannanshire

New Struan School
Smithfield Loan, Alloa, Clackmannanshire FK10 1NP
Tel: 01259 222000
Principal: Jasmine Miller
Age range: 5–17
Special needs catered for: ASD, AUT
(£)

Glasgow

East Park
1092 Maryhill Road, Glasgow G20 9TD
Tel: 0141 946 2050
Principal: Mrs L Gray
Age range: 0–25
Fees: Day £12,298 FB £22,958
Special needs catered for:
AUT, CP, DEL, EPI, HI, MLD, PH, PMLD, SLD, SP&LD, VIS
(£) (16)

Perth & Kinross

Ochil Tower
140 High Street, Auchterarder, Perth, Perth & Kinross PH3 1AD
Tel: 01764 662416
Co-ordinators: Mr Ueli Ruprecht & Ms Hilary Ruprecht
Age range: 5–18
No. of pupils: 35
Fees: Day £23,500 FB £41,100
Special needs catered for: ADD, ADHD, ASD, BESD, CLD, EBD, EPI, LD, MLD, MSI, PMLD, SCD, SCLD, SP&LD
(£) (16)

THE NEW SCHOOL
For further details see p. 118
Butterstone, Dunkeld,
Perth & Kinross PH8 0HA
Tel: 01350 724216
Email: info@thenewschool.co.uk
Website:
www.thenewschool.co.uk
Head of School: Mr Chris Holmes
Age range: 11–19
No. of pupils: 25
Special needs catered for: ADD,
ADHD, ASD, ASP, AUT, BESD,
CLD, DEL, DYS, DYSP, EBD, GLD,
HA, LD, MLD, SCD, SEBD, SPLD
🏛 £ ✎ 16+

Wales

Denbighshire

Cambian Pengwern College
Sarn Lane, Rhuddlan, Rhyl,
Denbighshire LL18 5UH
Tel: 0800 138 1184
Principal: Tina Ruane
Age range: 16–25
Special needs catered for: ADD,
ADHD, ASD, ASP, AUT, BESD, CLD,
CP, DYSP, EBD, EPI, GLD, HI, LD,
MLD, MSI, PD, Phe, PH, PMLD, SCD,
SCLD, SEBD, SLD, SP&LD, SLI, VIS
🏛 ✎

Gwynedd

Aran Hall School
Rhydymain, Dolgellau,
Gwynedd LL40 2AR
Tel: 01341 450641
Head Teacher: Mr Duncan
Pritchard CertEd, DipAppSS,
BSc(Hons), MSc(psych)
Age range: 11–19
Fees: WB £216,829 FB £282,172
Special needs catered for:
ADHD, ASD, ASP, AUT, CLD,
EPI, GLD, LD, MLD, PMLD, SCD,
SCLD, SLD, SP&LD, SPLD, SLI
🏛 16+

Pembrokeshire

COLEG PLAS DWBL
For further details see p. 119
Mynachlog-ddu, Clunderwen,
Pembrokeshire SA66 7SE
Tel: 01453 837502
Email: enquiries@
plasdwbl.rmt.org
Website: www.rmt.org
Principal: Paul Garnault
Age range: 16–25
Special needs catered for:
ASD, ASP, CLD, EBD

Vale of Glamorgan

Action for Children Headlands School
2 St Augustine's Road, Penarth,
Vale of Glamorgan CF64 1YY
Tel: 02920 709771
Principal: Matthew Burns
Age range: 8–19
Special needs catered for: ADD,
ADHD, ASD, ASP, AUT, BESD,
DYS, EBD, MLD, SP&LD, SPLD
🏛 16+

Wrexham

Prospects for Young People
12 Grosvenor Road,
Wrexham LL11 1BU
Tel: 01978 313777
Headteacher: Mr Neil Dobie
Age range: 11–16
No. of pupils: 21
Special needs catered for:
MLD, SPLD
🏛

Schools and colleges specialising in sensory or physical impairment

Abbreviations

ACLD	Autism, Communication and Associated Learning Difficulties
ADD	Attention Deficit Disorder
ADHD	Attention Deficit and Hyperactive Disorder (Hyperkinetic Disorder)
ASD	Autistic Spectrum Disorder
ASP	Asperger Syndrome
AUT	Autism
BESD	Behavioural, Emotional and Social Difficulties
CCD	Complex Communication Difficulties
CLD	Complex Learning Difficulties
CP	Cerebral Palsy
D	Deaf
DEL	Delicate
DYS	Dyslexia
DYSP	Dyspraxia
EBD	Emotional and Behavioural Difficulties
EBSD	Emotional, Behavioural and/or Social Difficulties
EPI	Epilepsy
GLD	General Learning Difficulties
HA	High Ability
HI	Hearing Impairment
HS	Hospital School
LD	Learning Difficulties
MLD	Moderate Learning Difficulties
MSI	Multi-sensory Impairment
OCD	Obsessive Compulsive Disorder
PD	Physical Difficulties
PH	Physical Impairment
Phe	Partially Hearing
PMLD	Profound and Multiple Learning Difficulties
PNI	Physical Neurological Impairment
PRU	Pupil Referral Unit
SCD	Social and Communication Difficulties
SCLD	Severe and Complex Learning Difficulties
SEBD	Severe Emotional and Behavioural Disorders
SEBN	Social, Emotional and Behavioural Needs
SLD	Severe Learning Difficulties
SLI	Specific Language Impairment
SPLD	Specific Learning Difficulties
SP&LD	Speech and Language Difficulties
SLCN	Speech Language & Communication Needs
VIS	Visually Impaired

Key to Symbols

Type of school:

(symbol)	Boys' school
(symbol)	Girls' school
(symbol)	International school

School offers:

(A)	A levels
(symbol)	Residential
(16+)	Entrance at 16+
(symbol)	Vocational qualifications
(symbol)	Learning support
(✓)	This is a DfE approved independent or non-maintained school under section 41 of the Children and Families Act 2014 or section 342 of the 1996 Education Act

Please note: Unless otherwise indicated, all schools are coeducational day schools. Single-sex and boarding schools will be indicated by the relevant icon.

Central & West

Buckinghamshire

THE PACE CENTRE
For further details see p. 122
Philip Green House,
Coventon Road, Aylesbury,
Buckinghamshire HP19 9JL
Tel: 01296 392739
Email: info@thepacecentre.org
Website:
www.thepacecentre.org
Head Teacher: Mrs Claire Smart
Age range: 0–16
Special needs catered for: CLD,
CP, DYSP, HI, LD, MLD, MSI, PD,
PNI, SCLD, SLD, SP&LD, VIS
(✓)

Gloucestershire

National Star College
Ullenwood, Cheltenham,
Gloucestershire GL53 9QU
Tel: 01242 527631
Acting Assistant Principal: Pauline
Bayliss-Jones
Age range: 16–25
No. of pupils: 178
Special needs catered for:
ASD, ASP, AUT, CLD, CP, DYS,
DYSP, EPI, GLD, HI, LD, MLD, MSI,
PD, Phe, PH, PMLD, PNI, SCD,
SCLD, SLD, SP&LD, SPLD, VIS
(♿)(16)

St Rose's School
Stratford Lawn, Stroud,
Gloucestershire GL5 4AP
Tel: 01453 763793
Headteacher: Mr Jan Daines
Age range: 2–25
No. of pupils: 54
Special needs catered for: CLD,
CP, D, DEL, DYS, DYSP, EPI, GLD, HI,
LD, MLD, MSI, PD, Phe, PH, PMLD,
PNI, SCD, SCLD, SLD, SP&LD, SLI, VIS
(♿)(16)(✓)

West Berkshire

**Mary Hare Primary
School for the Deaf**
Mill Hall, Pigeons Farm Road,
Thatcham, Newbury, West
Berkshire RG19 8XA
Tel: 01635 573800
Head Teacher: Mrs P Robinson
Age range: 5–12
No. of pupils: 27
Fees: Day £25,590 FB £35,844
Special needs catered for:
HI, SP&LD, SLI
(♿)

Mary Hare School
Arlington Manor, Snelsmore
Common, Newbury, West
Berkshire RG14 3BQ
Tel: 01635 244200
Principal: Mr D A J Shaw
BTech, MEd(Aud), NPQH
Age range: 11–19
No. of pupils: 205 VIth68
Fees: Day £28,372 FB £31,676
Special needs catered for: D, HI
(♿)(16)(✓)

East

Hertfordshire

**Aurora Meldreth
Manor School**
Fenny Lane, Meldreth, Royston,
Hertfordshire SG8 6LG
Tel: 01763 268 000
Principal: Ms Debra Eason
Age range: 9–19+
No. of pupils: 30
Special needs catered for: CP,
D, EPI, GLD, HI, LD, MLD, MSI,
PD, Phe, PH, PMLD, SP&LD, VIS
(♿)(16)(✓)

St Elizabeth's School
South End, Much Hadham,
Hertfordshire SG10 6EW
Tel: 01279 844270
Principal: Ms. Sharon Wallin
Age range: 5–19
Special needs catered for:
AUT, CP, DYS, DYSP, EBD, EPI,
MLD, SLD, SP&LD, SPLD
(♿)(16)(✓)

East Midlands

Derbyshire

**ROYAL SCHOOL FOR
THE DEAF DERBY**
For further details see p. 124
Ashbourne Road, Derby,
Derbyshire DE22 3BH
Tel: 01332 362512
Email: enquiries@rsdd.org.uk
Website: www.rsdd.org
Headteacher: Helen Shepherd
Age range: 3–19
Special needs catered for: D, HI
(♿)(16)(✓)

Leicestershire

Homefield College
42 St Mary's Road,
Sileby, Loughborough,
Leicestershire LE12 7TL
Tel: 01509 815696
Principal: Mr Gerry Short
Age range: 16–25
No. of pupils: 54 VIth54
Special needs catered for:
ASD, BESD, LD, SCD
(£)

**RNIB COLLEGE
LOUGHBOROUGH**
For further details see p. 123
Radmoor Road, Loughborough,
Leicestershire LE11 3BS
Tel: 01509 611077
Email: enquiries@
rnibcollege.ac.uk
Website: www.rnibcollege.ac.uk
Principal: June Murray
Age range: 16–65
No. of pupils: 52
Special needs catered for:
ADD, ADHD, ASD, ASP, AUT,
BESD, CLD, CP, DYS, DYSP, EBD,
EPI, GLD, HA, HI, LD, MLD, MSI,
PD, Phe, PH, PNI, SCD, SCLD,
SEBD, SLD, SP&LD, SPLD, SLI, VIS
(16)(♿)

Nottinghamshire

Portland College
Nottingham Road,
Mansfield, Nottingham,
Nottinghamshire NG18 4TJ
Tel: 01623 499111
Principal: Dr Mark Dale
Age range: 16–59
No. of pupils: 230
Special needs catered for:
ASD, ASP, AUT, CP, D, DYS,
DYSP, EBD, EPI, GLD, HI, MLD,
MSI, PD, Phe, PH, PMLD, PNI,
SCLD, SP&LD, SPLD, SLI, VIS
(♿)

Rutland

The Shires School
Shires Lane, Stretton,
Rutland LE15 7GT
Tel: 01780 411944
**Director of Care &
Education:** Gail Pilling
Age range: 11–19
Special needs catered for: AUT, SLD

Greater London

Kent

Nash College
Croydon Road, Bromley,
Kent BR2 7AG
Tel: 020 8315 4844
Principal: Ms Claire Howley-
Mummery BEd (Hons)
Age range: 18–25
Special needs catered for: AUT,
CP, EPI, MLD, PH, PMLD, PNI, SCD,
SCLD, SLD, SP&LD, SPLD, VIS

Middlesex

**RNIB SUNSHINE
HOUSE SCHOOL**
For further details see p. 125
33 Dene Road, Northwood,
Middlesex HA6 2DD
Tel: 01923 822538
Email: sunshinehouse@
rnib.org.uk
Website:
www.rnib.org.uk/sunshinehouse
Head: Jackie Seaman
Age range: 2–14
Special needs catered for: CLD,
CP, D, EPI, GLD, HI, LD, MSI, PD,
Phe, PH, PMLD, SCLD, SPLD, VIS

London

North London

Woodstar School
143 Coppetts Road,
London N10 1JP
Tel: 020 8444 7242
Head of School: Finn Emmerson
Age range: 3–11
Special needs catered for: CP, PD

North-East

Tyne & Wear

Percy Hedley College
Station Road, Forest Hall, Newcastle
upon Tyne, Tyne & Wear NE12 8YY
Tel: 0191 266 5491
Headteacher: Mr N O
Stromsoy MA, DipSE
Age range: 14–19
No. of pupils: 170
Fees: Day £19,944 FB £42,134
Special needs catered for: HI

**Percy Hedley School
– Newcastle**
Great North Road, Newcastle
upon Tyne, Tyne & Wear NE2 3BB
Tel: 0191 281 5821
Headteacher: Mrs Frances Taylor
Age range: 3–19
Fees: Day £13,767–£29,772
FB £19,134–£33,162
Special needs catered for:
AUT, HI, PMLD, SLD, VIS

**Percy Hedley School
– North Tyneside**
Forest Hall, Newcastle upon
Tyne, Tyne & Wear NE12 8YY
Head Teacher: Ms Lynn Watson
Age range: 3–14
Special needs catered for: CP, SCD

North-West

Greater Manchester

Seashell Trust
Stanley Road, Cheadle
Hulme, Cheadle, Greater
Manchester SK8 6RQ
Tel: 0161 610 0
Age range: 2–22
No. of pupils: 83
Fees: Day £37,280–£59,354
FB £61,866–£178,658
Special needs catered for:
ASD, AUT, CLD, CP, D, HI,
MSI, PD, PH, PMLD, PNI, SCD,
SCLD, SLD, SP&LD, VIS
🏛️ 16⁺ ✔

Lancashire

Beaumont College
Slyne Road, Lancaster,
Lancashire LA2 6AP
Tel: 01524 541400
Principal: Mr Graeme Pyle
Age range: 16–25
No. of pupils: 77
Special needs catered for: ASD,
AUT, BESD, CLD, CP, DYS, DYSP, EBD,
EPI, GLD, HI, MSI, PD, PH, PMLD, PNI,
SCD, SCLD, SEBD, SLD, SP&LD, SLI, VIS
16⁺ 🏛️

Merseyside

Royal School for the Blind
Church Road North, Wavertree,
Liverpool, Merseyside L15 6TQ
Tel: 0151 733 1012
Principal: J Byrne
Age range: 2–19
Fees: Day £35,721–£40,418
FB £47,185–£55,649
Special needs catered for:
BESD, CLD, CP, EBD, EPI, HI,
MLD, MSI, PD, PH, PMLD, PNI,
SCLD, SLD, SP&LD, SLI, VIS
🏛️ 16⁺ ✔

St Vincent's School for the Visually Handicapped
Yew Tree Lane, West Derby,
Liverpool, Merseyside L12 9HN
Tel: 0151 228 9968
Headmaster: Mr A Macquarrie
Age range: 3–17
Fees: Day £19,566 FB £27,363
Special needs catered for: MLD, VIS
🏛️ ✔

South-East

East Sussex

CHAILEY HERITAGE SCHOOL
For further details see p. 126
Haywards Heath Road,
North Chailey, Lewes,
East Sussex BN8 4EF
Tel: 01825 724444
Email: office@chf.org.uk
Website: www.chf.org.uk
Charity Chief Executive: Helen Hewitt
Age range: 3–19
No. of pupils: 85
Special needs catered for:
ASD, AUT, CLD, CP, D, EBD, EPI,
HI, MLD, MSI, PD, PH, PMLD,
PNI, SCLD, SLD, SP&LD, VIS
🏛️ 16⁺ ✔

HAMILTON LODGE SCHOOL
For further details see p. 127
9 Walpole Road, Brighton,
East Sussex BN2 0LS
Tel: 01273 682362
Email: admin@hamiltonlsc.co.uk
Website: www.hamiltonls.co.uk
Principal: Mrs A K Duffy MEd
Age range: 5–16
Special needs catered for: D, HI
🏛️ ✔

ST MARY'S SCHOOL & 6TH FORM COLLEGE
For further details see p. 128
Wrestwood Road, Bexhill-on-
Sea, East Sussex TN40 2LU
Tel: 01424 730740
Email: admin@
stmarysbexhill.org
Website: www.stmarysbexhill.org
Principal: Amanda Clugston
Age range: 7–19
No. of pupils: 58
Special needs catered for:
ASD, ASP, AUT, CLD, CP, D,
DEL, DYS, DYSP, EPI, GLD, HI,
LD, MLD, MSI, PD, Phe, PH,
SCD, SP&LD, SPLD, SLI, VIS
🏛️ 16⁺ ✔

Hampshire

TRELOAR SCHOOL
For further details see p. 130
Holybourne, Alton,
Hampshire GU34 4GL
Tel: 01420 547400
Email: admissions@treloar.org.uk
Website: www.treloar.org.uk
Age range: 2–19 yrs
No. of pupils: 87 VIth22
Special needs catered for:
CLD, CP, DEL, DYSP, EPI, HA,
HI, MLD, MSI, PD, Phe, PH, PNI,
SCLD, SP&LD, SPLD, SLI, VIS
🏛️ ✔

Kent

Dorton College of Further Education
Seal Drive, Seal, Sevenoaks,
Kent TN15 0AH
Tel: 01732 592600
Director of Education: Dorothea
Hackman
Age range: 16–19
No. of pupils: 60
Special needs catered for: VIS
16⁺ 🏛️

Surrey

St Piers School and College
St Piers Lane, Lingfield,
Surrey RH7 6PW
Tel: 01342 832243
Chief Executive: Ms Carol
Long BSc(hons),MSc,CQSW
Age range: 5–25
No. of pupils: 181
Special needs catered for: ADD,
ADHD, ASP, AUT, CP, EPI, MLD,
PMLD, PNI, SCD, SCLD, SLD, SP&LD
🏛️ 16⁺ ✔

Stepping Stones School
Tower Road, Hindhead,
Surrey GU26 6SU
Tel: 01428 609083
Headteacher: Melissa Farnham
NPQH,BAQTS(Hon)
Age range: 8–19
No. of pupils: 40
Fees: Day £11,000–£14,800
Special needs catered for: ASD,
ASP, AUT, MLD, PD, SP&LD
✔

THE CHILDREN'S TRUST SCHOOL
For further details see p. 129
Tadworth Court, Tadworth,
Surrey KT20 5RU
Tel: 01737 365810
Email: school@
thechildrenstrust.org.uk
Website: www.thechildrens
trustschool.org.uk
Head Teacher: Samantha
Newton
Age range: 3–19
No. of pupils: 44
Special needs catered for:
CLD, CP, EPI, HI, MSI, PD, PH,
PMLD, PNI, SLD, SP&LD, VIS
🏛️ 16⁺ ✔

West Sussex

Ingfield Manor School
Five Oaks, Billingshurst,
West Sussex RH14 9AX
Tel: 01403 782294/784241
Principal: Hazel Darby
Age range: 3–16
Special needs catered for: CP
🏛️ ✔

South-West

Devon

Dame Hannah Rogers School
Woodland Road, Ivybridge, Devon PL21 9HQ
Tel: 01752 892461
Head Teacher: Mrs Chris Freestone
Age range: 3–18
No. of pupils: 2
Special needs catered for: ASD, MLD, PD, PMLD, SLD

Exeter Royal Academy for Deaf Education
50 Topsham Road, Exeter, Devon EX2 4NF
Tel: 01392 267023
Chief Executive: Jonathan Farnhill
Age range: 5–25
No. of pupils: VIth68
Fees: Day £23,007–£39,195
WB £31,779–£46,800
FB £36,360–£48,990
Special needs catered for: AUT, CP, D, EPI, HI, MLD, MSI, Phe, SP&LD, VIS

On Track Training Centre
Unit 8, Paragon Buildings, Ford Road, Totnes, Devon TQ9 5LQ
Tel: 01803 866462
Head of Centre: Julie Dixon-Higgins
Age range: 11–18
No. of pupils: 24
Special needs catered for: ADD, ADHD, ASD, ASP, AUT, BESD, DEL, DYS, DYSP, EBD, GLD, MLD, MSI, SCD, SPLD

Vranch House
Pinhoe Road, Exeter, Devon EX4 8AD
Tel: 01392 468333
Head Teacher: Miss Viktoria Pavlics MEd(SEN)
Age range: 2–12
Fees: Day £19,425
Special needs catered for: CP, EPI, MLD, PD, PH, PMLD, SP&LD

WESC Foundation – The Specialist College for Visual Impairment
Countess Wear, Exeter, Devon EX2 6HA
Tel: 01392 454200
Principal: Mrs Tracy de Bernhardt-Dunkin
Age range: 16+
Special needs catered for: EPI, PH, PMLD, VIS

WESC Foundation – The Specialist School for Visual Impairment
Countess Wear, Exeter, Devon EX2 6HA
Tel: 01392 454200
Chief Executive: Mrs Tracy de Bernhardt-Dunkin
Age range: 5–16
Special needs catered for: EPI, PH, PMLD, VIS

Dorset

Langside School
Langside Avenue, Parkstone, Poole, Dorset BH12 5BN
Tel: 01202 518635
Principal: J. Seaward BEd (Hons) Oxon NPQH
Age range: 2–19
No. of pupils: 23
Special needs catered for: CLD, CP, EPI, MSI, PD, PMLD, SCD, SCLD, SLD

The Fortune Centre of Riding Therapy
Avon Tyrrell, Bransgore, Christchurch, Dorset BH23 8EE
Tel: 01425 673297
Director: Mrs J Dixon-Clegg SRN
Age range: 16–25
No. of pupils: 47
Special needs catered for: AUT, CP, DEL, DYS, EBD, EPI, HI, MLD, PH, PMLD, SLD, SP&LD, SPLD, VIS

Victoria Education Centre
12 Lindsay Road, Branksome Park, Poole, Dorset BH13 6AS
Tel: 01202 763697
Head: Mrs Christina Davies
Age range: 3–19
No. of pupils: 90
Special needs catered for: DEL, EPI, PH, SP&LD

West Midlands

Herefordshire

The Royal National College for the Blind (RNC)
Venns Lane, Hereford, Herefordshire HR1 1DT
Tel: 01432 376621
Principal: Mr Mark Fisher
Age range: 16–65
Special needs catered for: ASP, AUT, DYS, HA, MLD, PD, Phe, VIS

Shropshire

Derwen College
Oswestry, Shropshire SY11 3JA
Tel: 01691 661234
Director: D J Kendall BEng, FCA, MEd
Age range: 16–25
No. of pupils: 160
Fees: FB £17,928
Special needs catered for: CP, DEL, DYS, EPI, HI, MLD, PH, PMLD, SLD, SP&LD, SPLD, VIS

West Midlands

Hereward College of Further Education
Bramston Crescent, Tile Hill Lane, Coventry, West Midlands CV4 9SW
Tel: 024 7646 1231
Principal: Sheila Fleming
Age range: 16+
No. of pupils: 400
Special needs catered for: ASP, AUT, CP, DEL, DYS, DYSP, EBD, EPI, HA, HI, MLD, PH, SPLD, VIS

National Institute for Conductive Education
Cannon Hill House, Russell Road, Moseley, Birmingham, West Midlands B13 8RD
Tel: 0121 449 1569
Director of Services: Dr Melanie R Brown
Age range: 0–11
No. of pupils: 18
Fees: Day £25,000
Special needs catered for: CP, DYSP, PNI

RNIB PEARS CENTRE FOR SPECIALIST LEARNING
For further details see p. 131
Wheelwright Lane, Ash Green, Coventry, West Midlands CV7 9RA
Tel: 024 7636 9500
Email: pearscentre@rnib.org.uk
Website: www.rnib.org.uk/pearscentre
Headteacher: Angela Farrell
Age range: 2–19
No. of pupils: 30
Special needs catered for: ASD, AUT, BESD, CLD, CP, D, EPI, GLD, HI, LD, MSI, PD, Phe, PH, PMLD, SCLD, SPLD, VIS

Worcestershire

New College Worcester
Whittington Road, Worcester, Worcestershire WR5 2JX
Tel: 01905 763933
Principal: Nic Ross
Age range: usually 11–19
No. of pupils: 88
Fees: Day £30,049–£32,485
WB £40,076–£42,268
FB £44,366–£46,813
Special needs catered for: VIS

Yorkshire & Humberside

North Yorkshire

Henshaws College
Bogs Lane, Harrogate,
North Yorkshire HG1 4ED
Tel: 01423 886451
Head of Education: Mr Robert Jones
Age range: 16–25
Special needs catered for: CLD, CP, D, EPI, HI, LD, MLD, MSI, PD, Phe, SCD, SLD, SP&LD, VIS
16+ ♿

South Yorkshire

Communication Specialist College
Leger Way, Doncaster,
South Yorkshire DN2 6AY
Tel: 01302 386700
Executive Principal: Alan W Robinson
Age range: 16–59
No. of pupils: 185
Special needs catered for: HI
♿

DONCASTER SCHOOL FOR THE DEAF
For further details see p. 134
Leger Way, Doncaster,
South Yorkshire DN2 6AY
Tel: 01302 386733
Email: principal@ddt-deaf.org.uk or secretary@ddt-deaf.org.uk
Website: www.deaf-trust.co.uk
Executive Principal: Mr Alan W Robinson
Age range: 4–19
No. of pupils: 32
Special needs catered for: BESD, CP, D, DYS, GLD, HI, MLD, PH, PMLD, SLD, SP&LD, SPLD, VIS
♿ ✔

Paces High Green School for Conductive Education
Paces High Green Centre, Pack Horse Lane, High Green, Sheffield,
South Yorkshire S35 3HY
Tel: 0114 284 5298
Headteacher: Gabor Fellner
Age range: 0–18
No. of pupils: 30
Fees: Day £27,452
Special needs catered for: CP, PD
16+ ✔

West Yorkshire

Holly Bank School
Roe Head, Far Common Road,
Mirfield, West Yorkshire WF14 0DQ
Tel: 01924 490833
Headteacher: Ms Lyn Pollard
Age range: 5–19
No. of pupils: 20 VIth10
Fees: Day £35,000–£45,000
WB £70,000–£75,000
FB £99,000–£105,000
Special needs catered for: CLD, CP, MSI, PD, PH, PMLD, PNI, SCLD, SLD
♿ 16+

ST JOHN'S CATHOLIC SCHOOL FOR THE DEAF
For further details see p. 132
Church Street, Boston Spa, Wetherby, West Yorkshire LS23 6DF
Tel: 01937 842144
Email: info@stjohns.org.uk
Website: www.stjohns.org.uk
Headteacher: Mrs A Bradbury BA(Hons), MSc, NPQH
Age range: 4–19
No. of pupils: 62
Special needs catered for: ADD, ADHD, ASD, ASP, AUT, BESD, CP, D, DEL, DYS, DYSP, EBD, EPI, HI, LD, MLD, MSI, PD, Phe, PH, PMLD, SCD, SLD, SP&LD, SLI, VIS
♿ 16+ ✔

Northern Ireland

County Antrim

Jordanstown School
85 Jordanstown Road,
Newtownabbey, County Antrim BT37 0QE
Tel: 028 9086 3541
Principal: Adam Smith
Age range: 4–19
No. of pupils: 79
Special needs catered for: ASD, D, EBD, GLD, HI, LD, MSI, PD, SP&LD, VIS
16+

County Tyrone

Buddy Bear Trust Conductive Education School
Killyman Road, Dungannon,
County Tyrone BT71 6DE
Tel: 02887 752 025
Special needs catered for: CP

Scotland

Aberdeen

Camphill School Aberdeen
Murtle House, Bieldside,
Aberdeen AB15 9EP
Tel: 01224 867935
Administrator: Mr Piet Hogenboom
Age range: 3–19
Fees: Day 25,198–50,397
FB 50,397–,794
Special needs catered for:
ADD, ADHD, ASD, ASP, AUT, BESD, CLD, CP, D, DEL, DYS, DYSP, EBD, EPI, GLD, LD, MLD, MSI, PD, PMLD, PNI, SCD, SCLD, SEBD, SLD, SP&LD, SPLD, SLI, VIS
♿ 16+

Edinburgh

THE ROYAL BLIND SCHOOL
For further details see p. 135
43 Canaan Lane,
Edinburgh EH10 4SG
Tel: 0131 446 3120
Email: office@royalblindschool.org.uk
Website: www.royalblind.org/education
Head Teacher: Elaine Brackenridge (BEd)
Age range: 5–19
Special needs catered for: AUT, CP, DEL, EPI, MLD, PH, PMLD, SLD, SP&LD, SPLD, VIS
♿ 16+

Renfrewshire

Corseford School
Milliken Park, Johnstone,
Renfrewshire PA10 2NT
Tel: 01505 702141
Headteacher: Mrs M Boyle
Age range: 3–18
No. of pupils: 50
Special needs catered for: CP, DEL, DYSP, EPI, HI, MLD, PH, SP&LD, SPLD, VIS
♿ 16+

South Lanarkshire

Stanmore House School
Lanark, South Lanarkshire ML11 7RR
Tel: 01555 665041
Head Teacher: Hazel Aitken
Age range: 0–18
No. of pupils: 47
Special needs catered for:
CP, PH, SCLD, SP&LD, VIS
♿ 16+

West Lothian

Donaldson's School
Preston Road, Linlithgow,
West Lothian EH49 6HZ
Tel: 01506 841900
Principal: Ms Laura Battles
Age range: 2–19
No. of pupils: 43
Special needs catered for:
ASP, AUT, D, HI, Phe, PMLD, SCD, SLD, SP&LD, SLI
♿ 16+

Wales

Glamorgan

Craig-y-Parc School
Pentyrch, Cardiff,
Glamorgan CF15 9NB
Tel: 029 2089 0397/2089 0361
Principal: Anthony Mulcamy
Age range: 3–19
Special needs catered for: CP,
EPI, HI, LD, MLD, MSI, PD, Phe, PH,
PMLD, SCLD, SLD, SP&LD, VIS

Special Educational Needs and the independent and non-maintained schools and colleges that cater for them

Attention Deficit Disorder (ADD)

Abingdon House School, London.....................................98, D165
Action for Children Headlands School, Vale of Glamorgan.............D170
Action for Children Parklands Campus, Oxfordshire D151
Appleford School, Wiltshire.....................................D167
Appletree School, Cumbria..................................83, D154
Avon Park School, Warwickshire D146
Belgrave School, Bristol...D163
Belmont School, Lancashire D155
Birtenshaw School, Greater Manchester D166
Bladon House School, Staffordshire D168
Blossom Lower School and Upper House, London...............D164
Bramfield House, Suffolk..D152
Brantwood Specialist School, South Yorkshire...........88, D159
Breckenbrough School, North Yorkshire D159
Brewood School, Kent...D156
Cambian Dilston College, Northumberland D166
Cambian Pengwern College, Denbighshire.................D170
Cambian Potterspury Lodge School, Northamptonshire D142
Camphill School Aberdeen, Aberdeen D177
Cedar House School, Lancashire D155
Centre Academy London, London D165
Chaigeley, Warrington...D155
Chilworth House Upper School, Oxfordshire D151
Coleg Elidyr, Carmarthenshire D147
Copperfield School, Norfolk....................................D164
Cotswold Chine School, Gloucestershire....................D151
Crookhey Hall School, Lancashire D155
Cruckton Hall, Shropshire 70, D146
Demeter House School, North Lincolnshire..................D146
Falkland House School, Fife D160
Farleigh College Mells, Somerset D145
Foxes Academy, Somerset D168
Harmeny Education Trust Ltd, Edinburgh D160
Hillcrest Oaklands College, Staffordshire D158
Hillcrest Park School, Oxfordshire............................D151
Hillcrest Slinfold, West Sussex................................D157
Holme Court School, Cambridgeshire D163
Hope House School, Nottinghamshire D152
Hope View School, Kent D156
Horton House School, East Riding of Yorkshire D159
Insights Independent School, London........................D153
Kisharon School, London..D165
Lakeside School, Merseyside D144
Learn 4 Life, Lancashire D155
Linkage College – Toynton Campus, Lincolnshire D164
Linkage College – Weelsby Campus, North-East Lincolnshire..........D169
Muntham House School Ltd, West Sussex....................D157

North Hill House School, Somerset D145
Northease Manor School, East Sussex D166
Ochil Tower, Perth & Kinross D169
Octavia House School, Kennington, London D165
Octavia House School, Vauxhall, London D153
Octavia House School, Walworth, London D153
On Track Training Centre, Devon D176
Orchard Hill College and Academy Trust, Surrey D167
Overley Hall School, West Midlands 113, D168
Owlswick School, East Sussex D166
Parayhouse School, London....................................D165
Parkanaur College, County Tyrone D169
Philpots Manor School, West Sussex 85, D157
Queen Alexandra College (QAC), West Midlands.......73, D146
Queenswood School, Herefordshire D158
Ripplevale School, Kent..D156
RNIB College Loughborough, Leicestershire 123, D173
Rossendale School, Lancashire D143
Rowden House School, Herefordshire D168
Sheiling School, Thornbury, Bristol...........................D163
Small Haven School, Kent......................................D156
Springboard Education Senior, West Sussex D157
St Catherine's School, Isle of Wight 106, D167
St Dominic's School, Surrey D167
St Edward's School, Hampshire D156
St John's Catholic School for the Deaf, West Yorkshire..............132, D177
St John's School & College, East Sussex................107, D166
St Piers School and College, Surrey D175
Sunfield School, West Midlands D168
Talbot House School, Tyne & Wear D154
Talocher School, Monmouthshire D160
The Linnet Independent Learning Centre, Derbyshire.................D152
The Loddon School, Hampshire D167
The Marchant-Holliday School, Somerset D158
The Mount Camphill Community, East Sussex D156
The New School, Perth & Kinross 118, D170
The Ryes College & Community, Essex D151
Underley Garden School, Cumbria...........................D154
Waterloo Lodge School, Lancashire D155
West Heath School, Kent 86, D157
William Henry Smith School, West Yorkshire D159
Wings School, Cumbria, Cumbria D154
Wings School, Nottinghamshire, Nottinghamshire..............D152
Woodcroft School, Essex D163
Woodlands Children's Development Centre, Wrexham D160
Young Options College, Shropshire..........................D158
Young Options Pathway College Stoke, Staffordshire D158

Attention Deficit and Hyperactive Disorder (ADHD)

3 Dimensions, Somerset D145
Abingdon House School, London.........................98, D165
Action for Children Headlands School, Vale of Glamorgan.............D170
Action for Children Parklands Campus, Oxfordshire D151
Alderwasley Hall School & Sixth Form Centre, Derbyshire D164
Appleford School, Wiltshire.....................................D167
Appletree School, Cumbria..................................83, D154
Aran Hall School, Gwynedd D170
Arc School – Ansley, Warwickshire D158
Arc School – Napton, Warwickshire D158
Avon Park School, Warwickshire D146
Beech Lodge School, Berkshire D155
Belmont School, Lancashire D155
Birtenshaw School, Greater Manchester D166
Bladon House School, Staffordshire D168
Blossom Lower School and Upper House, London...............D164
Bracken School, Lancashire...................................D143
Bramfield House, Suffolk..D152
Brantridge School, West Sussex D157
Brantwood Specialist School, South Yorkshire...........88, D159
Breckenbrough School, North Yorkshire D159
Brewood School, Kent...D156
Cambian Dilston College, Northumberland D166
Cambian Pengwern College, Denbighshire.................D170
Cambian Potterspury Lodge School, Northamptonshire D142

Cambian Spring Hill School, North Yorkshire D159
Camphill Community Glencraig, County Down D159
Camphill School Aberdeen, Aberdeen D177
Cedar House School, Lancashire D155
Centre Academy East Anglia, Suffolk.......................D164
Centre Academy London, London D165
Chaigeley, Warrington...D155
Chilworth House School, Oxfordshire.......................D151
Chilworth House Upper School, Oxfordshire D151
Coleg Elidyr, Carmarthenshire D147
Copperfield School, Norfolk....................................D164
Cotswold Chine School, Gloucestershire....................D151
Crookhey Hall School, Lancashire D155
Cruckton Hall, Shropshire 70, D146
Cumberland School, Lancashire D155
Devon Education and Children's Services, Devon..........D145
Eden Grove School, Cumbria..................................D154
Falkland House School, Fife D160
Farleigh College Mells, Somerset D145
Farney Close School, West Sussex...........................D157
Foxes Academy, Somerset D168
Frederick Hugh House, London D165
Freeman College, South Yorkshire......................114, D169
Glasshouse College, West Midlands 112, D168
Grafham Grange School, Surrey D157

Autistic Spectrum Disorder(s) (ASD)

Asperger Syndrome (ASP)

Autism (AUT)

Behaviour, Emotional and Social Difficulties (BESD) – see also EBSD and SEBD

Complex Learning Difficulties (CLD)

Cerebral Palsy (CP)

Deaf (D) – see also Hearing Impairment (HI)

Delicate (DEL)

Dyslexia (DYSL) – see also SPLD

Dyspraxia (DYSP)

Emotional, Behavioural Difficulties (EBD) – see also BESD and SEBD

Epilepsy (EPI)

General Learning Difficulties (GLD)

High Ability (HA)

Hearing Impairment (HI)

Learning Difficulties (LD)

Moderate Learning Difficulties (MLD)

Multi-sensory Impairment (MSI)

Partially Hearing (Phe)

Physical Difficulties (PD)

Physical Impairment (PH)

Profound and Multiple Learning Difficulties (PMLD)

Physical Neurological Impairment (PNI)

Social and Communication Difficulties (SCD)

Severe and Complex Learning Difficulties (SCLD)

Severe Emotional and Behavioural Difficulties (SEBD) – see also BESD and EBD

Severe Learning Difficulties (SLD)

Speech and Language Difficulties (SP&LD)

Specific Learning Difficulties (SPLD)

Specific Language Impairment (SLI)

Visually Impaired (VIS)

Schools and colleges by category

Maintained special schools and colleges

ENGLAND

BEDFORD BOROUGH COUNCIL

Education Authority

Bedford SEND Team, 5th Floor, Borough Hall, Cauldwell Street, Bedford, MK42 9AP
Tel: 01234 228375 Email: statass@bedford.gov.uk Website: www.bedford.gov.uk

BEDFORD

Ridgeway Special School
Hill Rise, Kempston,
BEDFORD MK42 7EB
Tel: 01234 402402
Acting Head: Mrs H Roy
Category: PD (Coed 2-19)

St Johns Special School & College
Austin Cannons, Kempston,
BEDFORD MK42 8AA
Tel: 01234 345565
Interim Head: Ms A Rizzo
Category: SLD PMLD (Coed 2-19)

CENTRAL BEDFORDSHIRE COUNCIL

Children & Young People Service

Central Bedfordshire SEND Team, Priory House, Monks Walk, Chicksands Shefford, SG17 5TQ
Tel: 0300 300 8088 Email: cbcsendpypps@centralbedfordshire.gov.uk Website: www.centralbedfordshire.gov.uk

BIGGLESWADE

Ivel Valley Primary School
The Baulk, BIGGLESWADE,
Bedfordshire SG18 0PT
Tel: 01767 601010
Head: Miss Julie Mudd
Category: SLD PMLD (Coed 3-10)

Ivel Valley Secondary School
Hitchmead Road, BIGGLESWADE,
Bedfordshire SG18 0NL
Tel: 01767 601010
Head: Miss Julie Mudd
Category: SLD PMLD (Coed 11-19)

DUNSTABLE

The Chiltern Primary School
Beech Road, DUNSTABLE,
Bedfordshire LU6 3LY
Tel: 01582 667106
Head: Mrs Shirley Crosbie
Category: SLD PMLD (Coed 3-10)

HOUGHTON REGIS

The Chiltern Secondary School
Kingsland Campus, Parkside
Drive, HOUGHTON REGIS,
Bedfordshire LU5 5PX
Tel: 01582 667106
Head: Mrs Shirley Crosbie
Category: SLD PMLD (Coed 11-19)

LEIGHTON BUZZARD

Oak Bank School
Sandy Lane, LEIGHTON BUZZARD,
Bedfordshire LU7 3BE
Tel: 01525 374550
Head: Mr Peter Cohen
Category: BESD (Coed 9-16)

WEST BERKSHIRE

Council

West Berkshire FIS, The SEN Team, West Street House, West Street Newbury, Berkshire, RG14 1BZ
Tel: 01635 503100 Email: fis@westberks.gov.uk Website: www.westberks.gov.uk

NEWBURY

The Castle School
Love Lane, Donnington,
NEWBURY, Berkshire RG14 2JG
Tel: 01635 42976
Heads: Mr Jon Hewitt
Category: ASD SLD SPLD
GLD PH (Coed 2-19)

READING

Brookfields Special School
Sage Road, Tilehurst, READING,
Berkshire RG31 6SW
Tel: 01189 421382
Head: Mrs Jane Headland
Category: AUT MSI Complex Needs

BLACKBURN WITH DARWEN
Borough Council

Blackburn SEND Team, 10 Duke Street, Floor 5, Blackburn, Lancashire, BB2 1DH
Tel: 01254 666739 Email: sendss@blackburn.gov.uk Website: www.blackburn.gov.uk

BLACKBURN

Crosshill School
Haslingden Road, BLACKBURN,
Lancashire BB2 3HJ
Tel: 01254 667713
Head: Mr Ian Maddison
Category: MLD (Coed Day 11-16)

Newfield School
Old Bank Lane, Off Shadsworth
Road, BLACKBURN,
Lancashire BB1 2PW
Tel: 01254 588600
Head: Mr Geoff Fitzpatrick
Category: Complex
(Coed Day 2-19)

St. Thomas' Centre
Lambeth Street, BLACKBURN,
Lancashire BB1 1NA
Tel: 01254 680523
Head: Ms Joanne Siddle
Category: Pupil Referral
Unit (Coed Day 5-16)

DARWEN

Sunnyhurst Centre
Salisbury Road, DARWEN,
Lancashire BB3 1HZ
Tel: 01254 702317
Head: Mrs Shazia Sarwar
Category: Pupil Referral
Unit (Coed Day 5-11)

BLACKPOOL
Children and Young People's Department

Blackpool SEN Team, PO Box 4, Town Hall, Municipal Buildings Blackpool, FY1 1NA
Tel: 01253 477100 Email: local.offer@blackpool.gov.uk Website: www.blackpool.gov.uk

BLACKPOOL

Highfurlong School
Blackpool Old Road, BLACKPOOL,
Lancashire FY3 7LR
Tel: 01253 392188
Acting Head: Ms Rosie Sycamore
Category: PH

Woodlands School
Whitegate Drive, BLACKPOOL,
Lancashire FY3 9HF
Tel: 01253 316722
Head: Mr Cole Andrew
Category: SLD PMLD
MSI (Coed 2-19)

BOURNEMOUTH
Children and Families Services

Bournemouth SEN Team, Bournemouth Council, St Stephen's Road, Bournemouth, Dorset, BH2 6DY
Tel: 01202 451451 Email: cs@bournemouth.gov.uk Website: www.bournemouth.gov.uk

BOURNEMOUTH

Linwood School
Alma Road, BOURNEMOUTH,
Dorset BH9 1AJ
Tel: 01202 525107
Acting Head: Mrs Julie Jeanes
Category: ASD MLD SLD
PMLD (Coed 3-19)

Tregonwell Academy
Petersfield Road, BOURNEMOUTH,
Dorset BH7 6QP
Tel: 01202 424361
**Director of Special
Education:** Mrs Nicki Morton
Category: BESD (Coed 7-16)

BRACKNELL FOREST

Information, Advice & Support Service

Bracknell SENDIASS, Time Square, Market Street, Bracknell, Berkshire, RG12 1JD
Tel: 01344 354011 Email: send.support@bracknell-forest.gov.uk Website: www.bracknell-forest.gov.uk

BRACKNELL

Kennel Lane School
Kennel Lane, BRACKNELL,
Berkshire RG42 2EX
Tel: 01344 483872
Head: Ms Andrea de Bunsen
Category: MLD SLD AUT PMLD

BRADFORD

Information, Advice & Support Service

Bradford SENDIASS, Queen's House, Queen's Road, Bradford, West Yorkshire, BD8 7BS
Tel: 01274 481183 Email: bradfordsendiass@barnardos.org.uk

BRADFORD

Chellow Heights School
Thorn Lane, Bingley Road,
BRADFORD, West Yorkshire BD9 6AL
Tel: 01274 484242
Head: Mrs Susan Haithwaite
Category: SLD PMLD ADS (Primary)

Delius School
Barkerend Road, BRADFORD,
West Yorkshire BD3 8QX
Tel: 01274 666472
Head: Miss Sally Joy
Category: SLD PMLD ASD (Primary)

Hazelbeck School
Wagon Lane, Bingley, BRADFORD,
West Yorkshire BD16 1EE
Tel: 01274 777107
Head: Mrs Sue Pierce
Category: SLD PMLD
ASD (Secondary)

High Park School
Thorn lane, BRADFORD,
West Yorkshire BD9 6RY
Tel: 01274 696740
Head: Mrs Ann Andrew
Category: ASD (Primary
& Secondary)

Oastler's School
Flockton Road, BRADFORD,
West Yorkshire BD4 7RH
Tel: 01274 307456
Head: Mrs Lyndsey Brown
Category: (Coed Day 11-19)

Southfield School
Haycliffe Lane, BRADFORD,
West Yorkshire BD5 9ET
Tel: 01274 779662
Head: Mr Dominic Wall
Category: SLD PMLD
ASD (Secondary)

KEIGHLEY

Beechcliffe School
Greenhead Road, KEIGHLEY,
West Yorkshire BD20 6ED
Tel: 01535 603041
Head: Mrs Patricia Pearson
Category: SLD PMLD
ASD (Secondary)

Phoenix School
Braithwaite Avenue, KEIGHLEY,
West Yorkshire BD22 6HZ
Tel: 01535 607038
Head: Mrs Rachel Stirland
Category: SLD PMLD ASD (Primary)

BRIGHTON & HOVE

City Council

Brighton & Hove SEN Team, Kings House, Grand Avenue, Hove, East Sussex, BN3 2LS
Tel: 01273 293552 Fax: 01273 293547 Email: sen.team@brighton-hove.gov.uk Website: www.brighton-hove.gov.uk

BRIGHTON

Cedar Centre
Lynchet Close, Hollingdean,
BRIGHTON, East Sussex BN1 7FP
Tel: 01273 558622
Head: Ms Lalli Howell
Category: MLD

Downs Park School
Foredown Road, Portslade,
BRIGHTON, East Sussex BN41 2FU
Tel: 01273 417448
Head: Ms Jackie Brooks
Category: ASD (Coed 5-16)

Downs View School
Warren Road, BRIGHTON,
East Sussex BN2 6BB
Tel: 01273 601680
Head: Mr Adrian Carver
Category: SLD ASD HI VIS (4-19)

Hillside Special School
Foredown Road, Portslade,
BRIGHTON, East Sussex BN41 2FU
Tel: 01273 416979
Head: Ms Rachel Burstow
Category: SLD

Homewood College
Queensdown Road, BRIGHTON,
East Sussex BN1 7LA
Tel: 01273 604472
Head: Mr Mark Helstrip
Category: SEBD (Coed 5-16)

Patcham House School
7 Old London Road, Patcham,
BRIGHTON, East Sussex BN1 8XR
Tel: 01273 551028
Head: Ms Gayle Adam
Category: PD Del ASP
MLD SPLD (11-16)

BRISTOL

Children and Young People's Services

Bristol SEN Team, Parkview Campus, P.O. Box 3176, Bristol, BS3 9FS
Tel: 0117 922 3700 Email: sen@bristol.gov.uk Website: www.bristol.gov.uk

BRISTOL

Briarwood School
Briar Way, Fishponds,
BRISTOL BS16 4EA
Tel: 01173 532651
Head: Mr David Hussey
Category: SLD PMLD
AUT (Coed 3-19)

Bristol Gateway School
Long Cross, Lawrence
Weston, BRISTOL BS11 0QA
Tel: 01173 772275
Head: Ms Kaye Palmer-Green
Category: SEMH (Coed 10-16)

Claremont School
Henleaze Park, Westbury-
on-Trym, BRISTOL BS9 4LR
Tel: 01173 533622
Head: Ms Alison Ewins
Category: PD SLD PMLD (Coed 3-19)

Elmfield School for Deaf Children
Greystoke Avenue, Westbury-
on-Trym, BRISTOL BS10 6AY
Tel: 01179 030366
Head: Mrs Babs Day
Category: D HI (Coed 5-16)

Kingsweston School
Napier Miles Road, Kingsweston,
BRISTOL BS11 0UT
Tel: 01179 030400
Head: Mr Neil Galloway
Category: MLD SLD AUT (Coed 3-19)

Knowle DGE
Leinster Avenue, Knowle,
BRISTOL BS4 1NN
Tel: 01173 532011
Head: Mr Darren Ewings
Category: CLD SEMH MLD
Complex Needs (Coed 5-16)

New Fosseway School
Teyfant Road, Hartcliffe,
BRISTOL BS13 0RL
Tel: 01179 030220
Head: Mrs Shan Wynne-Jones
Category: SLD PMLD
AUT (Coed 6-19)

Notton House School
28 Notton, Lacock,
BRISTOL SN15 2NF
Tel: 01249 730407
Head: Mr Peter Evans
Category: SEMH (Boys 9-16)

Woodstock School
Rectory Gardens, Henbury,
BRISTOL BS10 7AH
Tel: 01173 772175
Head: Mr Les Haines
Category: SEMH (Primary)

BUCKINGHAMSHIRE

SEND Information, Advice & Support Service

Buckinghamshire SENDIASS, County Hall, Walton Street, Aylesbury, Buckinghamshire, HP20 1UA
Tel: 01296 383754 Email: sendias@buckscc.gov.uk Website: www.buckscc.gov.uk

AMERSHAM

Stony Dean School
Orchard End Avenue, Off
Pineapple Road, AMERSHAM,
Buckinghamshire HP7 9JW
Tel: 01494 762538
Head: Mr Neil Strain
Category: MLD Language &
Communication (Coed 11-18)

AYLESBURY

Booker Park School
Stoke Leys Close, AYLESBURY,
Buckinghamshire HP21 9ET
Tel: 01296 427221
Head: Ms Marianne Murphy
Category: MLD SLD
ASD (Coed 3-11)

Chiltern Way Federation - Wendover House School
Church Lane, Wendover,
AYLESBURY, Buckinghamshire
HP22 6NL
Tel: 01296 622157
Head of Campus: Mr Gary Regan
Category: BESD (Boys
Day/boarding 11-16)

Pebble Brook School
Churchill Avenue, AYLESBURY,
Buckinghamshire HP21 8LZ
Tel: 01296 415761
Head: Mr David Miller
Category: MLD SLC (Coed
Day/boarding 11-19)

Stocklake Park Community School
Stocklake, AYLESBURY,
Buckinghamshire HP20 1DP
Tel: 01296 423507
Head: Ms Gill Mullis
Category: SLD (Coed 11-19)

BEACONSFIELD

Alfriston School
Penn Road, Knotty
Green, BEACONSFIELD,
Buckinghamshire HP9 2TS
Tel: 01494 673740
Head: Mrs Jinna Male
Category: MLD (Girls Day/
boarding 11-19)

CHESHAM

Heritage House School
Cameron Road, CHESHAM,
Buckinghamshire HP5 3BP
Tel: 01494 771445
Head: Mr James Boylan
Category: SLD (Coed 2-19)

GREAT MISSENDEN

Chiltern Way Federation - Prestwood Campus
Nairdwood Lane, Prestwood,
GREAT MISSENDEN,
Buckinghamshire HP16 0QQ
Tel: 01494 863514
Head of Campus: Mr James Sisk
Category: BESD (Boys
Day/boarding 11-16)

HIGH WYCOMBE

Chiltern Gate School
Verney Avenue, HIGH WYCOMBE,
Buckinghamshire HP12 3NE
Tel: 01494 532621
Head: Mr Bradley Taylor
Category: MLD EBD ASD SLD
Communication difficulties
(Coed Day/boarding 4-11)

Maplewood School
Faulkner Way, Downley,
HIGH WYCOMBE,
Buckinghamshire HP13 5HB
Tel: 01494 525728
Head: Mr Bradley Taylor
Category: SLD (Coed 2-19)

Westfield School
Highfield Road, Bourne
End, HIGH WYCOMBE,
Buckinghamshire SL8 5BE
Tel: 01628 533125
Head: Mr Geoff Allen
Category: BESD (Coed 4-11)

WINSLOW

Furze Down School
Verney Road, WINSLOW,
Buckinghamshire MK18 3BL
Tel: 01296 711380
Head: Ms Alison Rooney
Category: A Range Of
Needs (Coed 2-19)

CAMBRIDGESHIRE

SEND Information, Advice & Support Service

Cambridgeshire SEN Team, Box No. CC1101, Castle Court, Cambridge, CB3 0AP
Tel: 01223 699214 Email: local.offer@cambridgeshire.gov.uk Website: www.cambridgeshire.gov.uk

CAMBRIDGE

Castle School
Courtney Way,
CAMBRIDGE CB4 2EE
Tel: 01223 442400
Head: Ms Carol McCarthy
Category: PMLD SLD
MLD (Coed 2-19)

Granta School
Cambridge Road, Linton,
CAMBRIDGE CB21 4NN
Tel: 01223 896890
Head: Mrs Lucie-Claire Calow
Category: ASD PMLD SLD
MLD (Coed 2-19)

Trinity School
8 Station Road, Foxton,
CAMBRIDGE, Cambridgeshire
CB22 6SA
Tel: 01223 712995
Head: Ms Diane Stygal

COTTENHAM

The Centre School
Cottenham Village College,
High Street, COTTENHAM,
Cambridgeshire CB24 8UA
Tel: 01954 288789
Head: Mrs Susan Raven
Category: (Coed 11-16)

ELY

Highfield Special School
Downham Road, ELY,
Cambridgeshire CB6 1BD
Tel: 01353 662085
Head: Mr Simon Bainbridge
Category: PMLD SLD MLD
ASD PD VIS (Coed 2-19)

The Harbour School
Station Road, Wilburton, ELY,
Cambridgeshire CB6 3RR
Tel: 01353 740229
Head: Ms Debra Smith
Category: ADD EBD MLD
SEBN (Coed 5-17)

EYNESBURY

Samuel Pepys School
Cromwell Road, EYNESBURY,
Cambridgeshire PE19 2EZ
Tel: 01480 375012
Head: Ms Joanne Hardwick
Category: ASD PMLD SLD
Complex needs (Coed 2-19)

WISBECH

Meadowgate School
Meadowgate Lane, WISBECH,
Cambridgeshire PE13 2JH
Tel: 01945 461836
Head: Mrs Jackie McPherson
Category: SLD MLD (Coed 2-19)

CHESHIRE EAST

Information, Advice & Support Service

Cheshire East SENDIASS, c/o Municipal Buildings, Earle Street, Crewe, CW1 2BJ
Tel: 0300 123 5166 Email: ceias@cheshireeast.gov.uk Website: www.ceias.cheshireeast.gov.uk

CREWE

Springfield School
Crewe Green Road, CREWE,
Cheshire CW1 5HS
Tel: 01270 685446
Headteacher: Mrs Lisa Hodgkison
Category: SLD (Coed 2-19)

MACCLESFIELD

Park Lane School
Park Lane, MACCLESFIELD,
Cheshire SK11 8JR
Tel: 01625 384040
Headteacher: Mrs Lorraine Warmer
Category: SLD (Coed Day 2-19)

CHESHIRE WEST & CHESTER

Council

Chester SEN Assessment, Monitoring & Support Team, 4 Civic Way, Ellesmere Port, CH65 0BE
Tel: 03001 238123 Email: senteam@cheshirewestandchester.gov.uk Website: www.cheshirewestandchester.gov.uk

CHESTER

Dee Banks School
Dee Banks, Sandy Lane,
CHESTER, Cheshire CH3 5UX
Tel: 01244 981030
Head: Mr Ray Elliott
Category: ASD SLD PMLD
(Coed Day 2-19)

**Dorin Park School &
Specialist SEN College**
Wealstone Lane, Upton,
CHESTER, Cheshire CH2 1HD
Tel: 01244 981191
Head: Ms Jane Hughes
Category: PD Complex
needs (Coed Day 2-19)

ELLESMERE PORT

**Capenhurst
Grange School**
Chester Road, Great
Sutton, ELLESMERE PORT,
Cheshire CH66 2NA
Tel: 01513 382141
Head: Mr Graham Stothard
Category: BESD (Coed 11-16)

Hinderton School
Capenhurst Lane,
Whitby, ELLESMERE PORT,
Cheshire CH65 7AQ
Tel: 01513 382200
Head: Mr Liam Dowling
Category: ASD with complex
learning needs (Coed Day 3-11)

NORTHWICH

Greenbank School
Greenbank Lane, Hartford,
NORTHWICH, Cheshire CW8 1LD
Tel: 01606 288028
Head: Mr Mike McCann
Category: ASD MLD
(Coed Day 6-18)

Rosebank School
Townfield Lane, Barnton,
NORTHWICH, Cheshire CW8 4QP
Tel: 01606 74975
Head: Mrs Judith McGuiness
Category: ASD with complex
learning needs (Coed Day 3-11)

The Russett School
Middlehurst Avenue, Weaverham,
NORTHWICH, Cheshire CW8 3BW
Tel: 01606 853005
Head: Mrs Catherine Lewis
Category: SLD PMLD MSI
(Coed Day 2-19)

WINSFORD

**Hebden Green
Community School**
Woodford Lane West,
WINSFORD, Cheshire CW7 4EJ
Tel: 01606 594221
Head: Ms Alison Ashley
Category: PD Complex needs
(Coed Day/Residential 2-19)

Oaklands School
Montgomery Way, WINSFORD,
Cheshire CW7 1NU
Tel: 01606 551048
Head: Mr Kevin Boyle
Category: HI MLD SP&LD
(Coed Day 11-16)

CORNWALL
Children, Families and Adults

Cornwall SEN Team, 3 West, New County Hall, Truro, Cornwall, TR1 3AY
Tel: 01872 324242 Email: specialeducation@cornwall.gov.uk Website: www.cornwall.gov.uk

PENZANCE

Nancealverne School
Madron Road, PENZANCE,
Cornwall TR20 8TP
Tel: 01736 365039
Head: Miss Sarah Moseley
Category: SLD PMLD (Coed 2-19)

REDRUTH

Curnow School
Drump Road, REDRUTH,
Cornwall TR15 1LU
Tel: 01209 215432
Head: Ms Gina Briggs
Category: PMLD SLD (Coed 2-19)

ST AUSTELL

Doubletrees School
St Blazey Gate, St Blazey, Par, ST
AUSTELL, Cornwall PL24 2DS
Tel: 01726 812757
Interim Head: Ms Jayne Brigg
Category: SLD PMLD (Coed 2-19)

CUMBRIA
Children's Services

Cumbria SEND Team, Cumbria House, 117 Botchergate, Carlisle, Cumbria, CA1 1RD
Tel: 01228 226843 Email: localoffer@cumbria.gov.uk Website: www.cumbria.gov.uk

CARLISLE

James Rennie School
California Road, Kingstown,
CARLISLE, Cumbria CA3 0BX
Tel: 01228 554280
Head: Mrs Kris Williams
Category: SLD PMLD

KENDAL

Sandgate School
Sandylands Road, KENDAL,
Cumbria LA9 6JG
Tel: 01539 792100
Head: Ms Joyce Fletcher
Category: SLD PMLD

ULVERSTON

Sandside Lodge School
Sandside Road, ULVERSTON,
Cumbria LA12 9EF
Tel: 01229 588825
Head: Ms Susan Gill
Category: SLD PMLD

WHITEHAVEN

Mayfield School
Moresby Road, Hensingham,
WHITEHAVEN, Cumbria CA28 8TU
Tel: 01946 691253
Head: Ms Gillian Temple
Category: SLD PMLD

DERBYSHIRE
Children & Younger Adults

Derbyshire Special Needs Section, County Hall, Matlock, Derbyshire, DE4 3AG
Tel: 01629 536539 Email: sen.admin@derbyshire.gov.uk Website: www.derbyshire.gov.uk

ALFRETON

**Alfreton Park Community
Special School**
Alfreton Park, ALFRETON,
Derbyshire DE55 7AL
Tel: 01773 832019
Head: Mrs Cheryl Smart
Category: SLD (2-19)

**Swanwick School and
Sports College**
Hayes Lane, Swanwick,
ALFRETON, Derbyshire DE55 1AR
Tel: 01773 602198
Head: Mr Christopher Greenhough
Category: MLD (5-16)

BELPER

Holbrook School for Autism
Port Way, Holbrook, BELPER,
Derbyshire DE56 0TE
Tel: 01332 880208
Head: Mr Julian Scholefield
Category: AUT (5-19)

BUXTON

Peak School
Buxton Road, Chinley, High Peak,
BUXTON, Derbyshire SK23 6ES
Tel: 01663 750324
Head: Mr John McPherson
Category: SLD (2-19)

CHESTERFIELD

Ashgate Croft School
Ashgate Road, CHESTERFIELD,
Derbyshire S40 4BN
Tel: 01246 275111
Head: Mrs Claire Jones
Category: MLD SLD (2-19)

Holly House School
Church Street North, Old
Whittington, CHESTERFIELD,
Derbyshire S41 9QR
Tel: 01246 450530
Head: Mr Peter Brandt
Category: EBD (7-14)

ILKESTON

**Bennerley Fields
Specialist Speech &
Language College**
Stratford Street, ILKESTON,
Derbyshire DE7 8QZ
Tel: 01159 326374
Acting Head: Ms Anne Harrison
Category: MLD (2-16)

LONG EATON

Brackenfield School
Bracken Road, LONG
EATON NG10 4DA
Tel: 01159 733710
Head: Mrs Sarah Gilraine
Category: MLD (5-16)

**Stanton Vale
Special School**
Thoresby Road, LONG
EATON NG10 3NP
Tel: 01159 72 9769
Head: Mr Christopher White
Category: PMLD SLD (2-19)

SHIREBROOK

Stubbin Wood School
Common Lane, SHIREBROOK,
Derbyshire NG20 8QF
Tel: 01623 742795
Head: Mr Lee Floyd
Category: MLD SLD (2-19)

DERBY CITY

Information & Advice Service

Derby SENDIASS, The Council House, Corporation Street, Derby, Derbyshire, DE1 2FS
Tel: 01332 641414 Email: sendiass@derby.gov.uk Website: www.derby.gov.uk

DERBY

Ivy House School
Moorway Lane, Littleover,
DERBY DE23 2FS
Tel: 01332 777920
Head: Ms Susan Allen
Category: SLD PMLD (Coed 2-19)

Kingsmead School
Bridge Street, DERBY DE1 3LB
Tel: 01332 715970
Head: Mrs Sue Bradley
Category: EBD (Coed 11-16)

St Andrew's School
St Andrew's View, Breadsall
Hilltop, DERBY DE21 4EW
Tel: 01332 832746
Head: Ms Heather Flockton
Category: SLD (Coed 11-19)

St Clare's School
Rough Heanor Road,
Mickleover, DERBY DE3 9AZ
Tel: 01332 511757
Head: Ms Megan Stratton
Category: MLD SP&LD AUT
PD SLD (Coed 11-16)

St Giles' School
Hampshire Road, Chaddesden,
DERBY DE21 6BT
Tel: 01332 343039
Head: Mr Clive Lawrence
Category: SLD AUT (Coed 4-11)

St Martin's School
Bracknell Drive, Alvaston,
DERBY DE24 0BR
Tel: 01332 571151
Head: Ms Debbie Gerring
Category: MLD AUT EBD
SLD (Coed 11-16)

DEVON

Children & Young People's Services

Devon 0-25 SEN Team, County Hall, Topsham Road, Exeter, Devon, EX2 4QD
Tel: 01392 383913 Email: specialeducation0-25-mailbox@devon.gov.uk Website: www.devon.gov.uk

BARNSTAPLE

Pathfield School
Abbey Road, Pilton,
BARNSTAPLE, Devon EX31 1JU
Tel: 01271 342423
Head: Mrs Claire May
Category: SLD PMLD (3-19)

**The Lampard
Community School**
St John's Lane, BARNSTAPLE,
Devon EX32 9DD
Tel: 01271 345416
Head: Mrs Karen Rogers
Category: Complex and
difficulties with communication
and interaction (including
SLCN and/or ASC) (7-16)

BUDLEIGH SALTERTON

**Mill Water Community
School**
Bicton, East Budleigh, BUDLEIGH
SALTERTON, Devon EX9 7BJ
Tel: 01395 568890
Head: Mrs Sarah Pickering
Category: SLD PMLD (3-19)

DAWLISH

Oaklands Park School
John Nash Drive, DAWLISH,
Devon EX7 9SF
Tel: 01626 862363
Head: Mrs Cherie White
Category: SLD ASC PMLD
(Day/boarding 3-19)

Ratcliffe School
John Nash Drive, DAWLISH,
Devon EX7 9RZ
Tel: 01626 862939
Head: Mrs Cherie White
Category: ASC and Associated
Social Development Needs (5-16)

EXETER

Barley Lane School
Barley Lane, St Thomas,
EXETER, Devon EX4 1TA
Tel: 01392 430774
Head: Mr Michael MacCourt
Category: BESD (7-16)

Ellen Tinkham School
Hollow Lane, EXETER,
Devon EX1 3RW
Tel: 01392 467168
Head: Mrs Jacqueline Warne
Category: SLD PMLD (3-19)

Southbrook School
Bishop Westall Road,
EXETER, Devon EX2 6JB
Tel: 01392 258373
Head: Mrs Bronwen Caschere
Category: MLD ASC (11-16)

TORRINGTON

Marland School
Petersmarland, TORRINGTON,
Devon EX38 8QQ
Tel: 01805 601324
Head: Mr Keith Bennett
Category: SEBD (10-16)

TOTNES

Bidwell Brook School
Shinner's Bridge, Dartington,
TOTNES, Devon TQ9 6JU
Tel: 01803 864120
Head: Mrs Jacqueline Warne
Category: SLD PMLD (3-19)

DORSET
County Council

Dorset SEN Team, County Hall, Dorchester, DT1 1XJ
Tel: 01305 224888 Fax: 01305 224547 Email: dorsetdirect@dorsetcc.gov.uk Website: www.dorsetcc.gov.uk

BEAMINSTER

Mountjoy School
Tunnel Road, BEAMINSTER,
Dorset DT8 3HB
Tel: 01308 861155
Head: Ms J Shanks
Category: ASD SLD PMLD
Complex (2-19)

STURMINSTER NEWTON

Yewstock School
Honeymead Lane, STURMINSTER
NEWTON, Dorset DT10 1EW
Tel: 01258 472796
Head: Mr S Kretz
Category: ASD MLD/
Comlex PMLD SLD (2-19)

WEYMOUTH

Westfield Arts College
Littlemoor Road, Preston,
WEYMOUTH, Dorset DT3 6AA
Tel: 01305 833518
Head: Mr A Penman
Category: MLD/Complex ASD (3-16)

Wyvern School
Dorchester Road, WEYMOUTH,
Dorset DT3 5AL
Tel: 01305 817917
Head: Mr B Douglas
Category: ASD PMLD
SLD Complex (2-19)

WIMBORNE

Beaucroft Foundation School
Wimborne Road, Colehill,
WIMBORNE, Dorset BH21 2SS
Tel: 01202 886083
Head: Mr P McGill
Category: MLD/Complex ASD (4-16)

DURHAM
County Council

Durham SEN Team, Children and Adult Services, County Hall, Durham, County Durham, DH1 5UJ
Tel: 03000 265878 Website: www.durham.gov.uk

BISHOP AUCKLAND

Evergreen School
Warwick Road, BISHOP
AUCKLAND, Durham DL14 6LS
Tel: 01388 459721
Head: Mrs Andrea E English
Category: MLD SLD PMLD AUT (2-11)

CONSETT

Villa Real School
Villa Real Road, CONSETT,
Durham DH8 6BH
Tel: 01207 503651
Head: Mrs Jill Bowe
Category: SLD PMLD AUT (2-19)

DURHAM

Durham Trinity School and Sports College
Aykley Heads, DURHAM DH1 5TS
Tel: 01913 864612
Head: Mrs Rachel Grimwood
Category: MLD SLD PMLD AUT (2-19)

FERRYHILL

Windlestone School
Chilton, FERRYHILL,
Durham DL17 0HP
Tel: 01388 720337
Head: Mr Tim Bennett
Category: SEBD (11-16)

NEWTON AYCLIFFE

Walworth School
Bluebell Way, NEWTON
AYCLIFFE, Durham DL5 7LP
Tel: 01325 300194
Head: Mr Peter Wallbanks
Category: SEBD (4-11)

SHERBURN

Elemore Hall School
Littletown, SHERBURN,
Durham DH6 1QD
Tel: 01913 720275
Head: Mr Richard J Royle
Category: SEBD (11-16)

SPENNYMOOR

The Meadows School
Whitworth Lane, SPENNYMOOR,
Durham DL16 7QW
Tel: 01388 811178
Head: Mrs Sarah Took
Category: SEBD (11-16)

The Oaks School
Rock Road, SPENNYMOOR,
Durham DL16 7DB
Tel: 01388 827380
Head: Mrs Andrea E English
Category: MLD SLD
PMLD AUT (11-19)

STANLEY

Croft Community School
Annfield Plain, STANLEY,
Durham DH9 8PR
Tel: 01207 234547
Head: Mr Simon Adams
Category: MLD SLD AUT (5-16)

ESSEX

Essex Parent Partnership Service

Essex SENDIASS, County Hall, Market Road, Chelmsford, Essex, CM1 1QH
Tel: 03330 138913 Email: send.iass@essex.gov.uk Website: www.essex.gov.uk

BASILDON

Castledon School
Bromfords Drive, Wickford,
BASILDON, Essex SS12 0PW
Tel: 01268 761252
Head: Mrs Philippa Holiday
Category: ASD MLD (5-16)

The Pioneer School
Ghyllgrove, BASILDON,
Essex SS14 2LA
Tel: 01268 243300
Head: Ms Jackie Brathwaite
Category: CLD (3-19)

BENFLEET

Cedar Hall School
Hart Road, Thundersley,
BENFLEET, Essex SS7 3UQ
Tel: 01268 774723
Head: Mr Nic Maxwell
Category: MLD (4-16)

Glenwood School
Rushbottom Lane, New
Thundersley, BENFLEET,
Essex SS7 4LW
Tel: 01268 792575
Head: Mrs Judith Salter
Category: SLD (3-19)

BILLERICAY

Ramsden Hall School
Heath Road, Ramsden Heath,
BILLERICAY, Essex CM11 1HN
Tel: 01277 624580
Head: Mr Garry Walker
Category: BESD (Boys 11-16)

BRAINTREE

The Edith Borthwick School
Springwood Drive, BRAINTREE,
Essex CM7 2YN
Tel: 01376 529300
Head: Mr Dan Woodman
Category: ASD MLD SLD (3-19)

BRENTWOOD

Grove House School
Sawyers Hall Lane, BRENTWOOD,
Essex CM15 9DA
Tel: 01277 361498
Head: Ms Lisa Christodoulides
Category: SP&LD Communication
Difficulties (9-19)

The Endeavour School
Hogarth Avenue, BRENTWOOD,
Essex CM15 8BE
Tel: 01277 217330
Head: Mr John Chadwick
Category: MLD (5-16)

CHELMSFORD

**The Columbus
School & College**
Oliver Way, CHELMSFORD,
Essex CM1 4ZB
Tel: 01245 491492
Head: Mrs Ginny Bellard

Thriftwood School
Slades Lane, Galleywood,
CHELMSFORD, Essex CM2 8RW
Tel: 01245 266880
Head: Mrs Georgina Pryke
Category: LD (5-13)

CHIGWELL

Wells Park School
School Lane, Lambourne Road,
CHIGWELL, Essex IG7 6NN
Tel: 02085 026442
Head: Mr Matthew Surman
Category: BESD (5-12)

CLACTON ON SEA

Shorefields School
114 Holland Road, CLACTON
ON SEA, Essex CO15 6HF
Tel: 01255 424412
Head: Mrs Jennifer Grotier
Category: ASD MLD SLD (3-19)

COLCHESTER

Kingswode Hoe School
Sussex Road, COLCHESTER,
Essex CO3 3QJ
Tel: 01206 576408
Head: Mrs Elizabeth Drake
Category: MLD (5-16)

Langham Oaks School
School Road, Langham,
COLCHESTER, Essex CO4 5PA
Tel: 01206 271571
Head: Ms Emma Paramor
Category: SEMH (Boys 10-16)

Lexden Springs School
Halstead Road, Lexden,
COLCHESTER, Essex CO3 9AB
Tel: 01206 563321
Head: Mr Simon Wall
Category: SLD (3-19)

Market Field School
School Road, Elmstead Market,
COLCHESTER, Essex CO7 7ET
Tel: 01206 825195
Head: Mr Gary Smith
Category: ASD MLD SLD (4-16)

HARLOW

**Harlow Fields School
& College**
Tendring Road, HARLOW,
Essex CM18 6RN
Tel: 01279 423670
Head: Mrs Kathleen Wall
Category: ASD MLD SLD (3-19)

LOUGHTON

Oak View School
Whitehills Road, LOUGHTON,
Essex IG10 1TS
Tel: 02085 084293
Head: Ms Dianne Ryan
Category: MLD SLD (3-19)

WITHAM

Southview School
Conrad Road, WITHAM,
Essex CM8 2TA
Tel: 01376 503505
Head: Mr Julian Cochrane
Category: PD (3-19)

GLOUCESTERSHIRE

Information Advice & Support Service

Gloucestershire SENDIASS, Messenger House (2nd Floor), 35 St. Michael's Square, Gloucester, GL1 1HX
Tel: 0800 158 3603 Email: sendiass@carersgloucestershire.org.uk Website: www.gloucestershire.gov.uk/learning

CHELTENHAM

**Battledown Centre for
Children and Families**
Harp Hill, Battledown,
CHELTENHAM,
Gloucestershire GL52 6PZ
Tel: 01242 525472
Head: Ms Jane Cummins
Category: VI SLCN ASD
SEMH PD MLD SLD (2-7)

Belmont School
Warden Hill Road, CHELTENHAM,
Gloucestershire GL51 3AT
Tel: 01242 216180
Head: Mr Kevin Day
Category: MLD (Coed 4-16)

Bettridge School
Warden Hill Road, CHELTENHAM,
Gloucestershire GL51 3AT
Tel: 01242 514934
Head: Ms Mandy Roberts
Category: VI SLCN ASD SLD (2-19)

CIRENCESTER

Paternoster School
Watermoor Road, CIRENCESTER,
Gloucestershire GL7 1JR
Tel: 01285 652480
Head: Ms Julie Mantell
Category: SLD (2-17)

COLEFORD

**Heart of the Forest
Community School**
Speech House, Coalway,
COLEFORD, Gloucestershire
GL16 7EJ
Tel: 01594 822175
Head: Mrs Melissa Bradshaw
Category: SLD PMLD (Coed 3-19)

GLOUCESTER

The Milestone School
Longford Lane, GLOUCESTER,
Gloucestershire GL2 9EU
Tel: 01452 874000
Head: Mrs Lyn Dance
Category: VI SLCN ASD SEMH
PD MLD SLD (Coed 2-16)

STONEHOUSE

The Shrubberies School
Oldends Lane, STONEHOUSE,
Gloucestershire GL10 2DG
Tel: 01453 822155
Head: Ms Jane Jones
Category: SLD (Coed 2-19)

TEWKESBURY

Alderman Knight School
Ashchurch Road, TEWKESBURY,
Gloucestershire GL20 8JJ
Tel: 01684 295639
Head: Mrs Clare Steel
Category: MLD (4-16)

SOUTH GLOUCESTERSHIRE

Council

0-25 Service, Department for Children, Adults & Health, PO Box 298, Civic
Centre, High Street Bristol, South Gloucestershire, BS15 0DQ
Tel: 01454 863301 or 01454 863173 Website: www.southglos.gov.uk

DOWNEND

Pathways Learning Centre
Overndale Road, DOWNEND,
South Gloucestershire BS16 2RQ
Tel: 01454 862630
Head: Ms Louise Leader
Category: (Day 4-16)

KINGSWOOD

**New Horizons
Learning Centre**
Mulberry Drive, KINGSWOOD,
South Gloucestershire BS15 4EA
Tel: 01454 865340
Head: Mrs Tania Craig
Category: BESD

THORNBURY

New Siblands School
Easton Hill Road, THORNBURY,
South Gloucestershire BS35 2JU
Tel: 01454 862888
Head: Mr Andrew Buckton
Category: SLD

Sheiling School
Thornbury Park, Park
Road, THORNBURY, South
Gloucestershire BS35 1HP
Tel: 01454 412 194
Head: Ms Rikke Julin
Category: (Day & Boarding)

WARMLEY

Warmley Park School
Tower Road North, WARMLEY,
South Gloucestershire BS30 8XL
Tel: 01454 867272
Head: Ms Lisa Parker
Category: SLD (Day 3-19)

YATE

Culverhill School
Kelston Close, YATE, South
Gloucestershire BS37 8SZ
Tel: 01454 866930
Head: Ms Nicki Jones
Category: CLD (Day 7-16)

HALTON

Borough Council

Halton SEND Partnership, Rutland House, Halton Lea, Runcorn, Cheshire, WA7 2GW
Tel: 01515 117733 Email: sendpartnership@halton.gov.uk Website: www3.halton.gov.uk

WIDNES

Ashley School
Cawfield Avenue, WIDNES,
Cheshire WA8 7HG
Tel: 01514 244892
Head: Mrs Linda King
Category: MLD Complex
emotional needs (11-16)

Brookfields School
Moorfield Road, WIDNES,
Cheshire WA8 0JA
Tel: 01514 244329
Head: Mrs Sara Ainsworth
Category: SLD (2-11)

**Chesnut Lodge School &
Specialist SEN College**
Green Lane, WIDNES,
Cheshire WA8 7HF
Tel: 01514 240679
Head: Mrs Heather Austin
Category: PH (2-16)

HAMPSHIRE
County Council

Children's Services Department, Elizabeth II Court, The Castle, Winchester, Hampshire, SO23 8UG
Tel: 03005 551384 Email: childrens.services@hants.gov.uk Website: www.hants.gov.uk

ANDOVER

Icknield School
River Way, ANDOVER,
Hampshire SP11 6LT
Tel: 01264 365297
Head: Ms Sharon Salmon
Category: SLD (Coed 2-19)

Norman Gate School
Vigo Road, ANDOVER,
Hampshire SP10 1JZ
Tel: 01264 323423
Head: Ms Christine Gayler
Category: MLD ASD (Coed 2-11)

The Mark Way School
Batchelors Barn Road, ANDOVER,
Hampshire SP10 1HR
Tel: 01264 351835
Head: Ms Sonia Longstaff-Bishop
Category: MLD ASD (Coed 11-16)

Wolverdene Special School
22 Love Lane, ANDOVER,
Hampshire SP10 2AF
Tel: 01264 362350
Head: Mr Paul Van Walwyk
Category: BESD (Coed 5-11)

BASINGSTOKE

Coppice Spring School
Pack Lane, BASINGSTOKE,
Hampshire RG22 5TH
Tel: 01256 336601
Head: Mr Matthew McLoughlin-Parker
Category: BESD (Coed 11-16)

Dove House School
Sutton Road, BASINGSTOKE,
Hampshire RG21 5SU
Tel: 01256 351555
Head: Mr Tom Pegler
Category: MLD ASD (Coed 11-16)

Limington House School
St Andrews Road, BASINGSTOKE,
Hampshire RG22 6PS
Tel: 01256 322148
Head: Mr Justin Innes
Category: SLD (Coed 2-19)

Maple Ridge School
Maple Crescent, BASINGSTOKE,
Hampshire RG21 5SX
Tel: 01256 323639
Head: Mrs Debby Gooderham
Category: MLD ASD (Coed 4-11)

Saxon Wood School
Rooksdown, Barron Place, BASINGSTOKE,
Hampshire RG24 9NH
Tel: 01256 356635
Head: Mr Richard Parratt
Category: PD (Coed 2-11)

BORDON

Hollywater School
Mill Chase Road, BORDON,
Hampshire GU35 0HA
Tel: 01420 474396
Head: Ms Steph Clancy
Category: LD (Coed 2-19)

CHANDLERS FORD

Lakeside School
Winchester Road, CHANDLERS FORD, Hampshire SO53 2DW
Tel: 02380 266633
Head: Mr Gareth Evans
Category: BESD (Boys 11-16)

FAREHAM

Baycroft School
Gosport Road, Stubbington,
FAREHAM, Hampshire PO14 2AE
Tel: 01329 664151
Head: Mr Chris Toner
Category: MLD ASD (Coed 11-16)

Heathfield School
Oldbury Way, FAREHAM,
Hampshire PO14 3BN
Tel: 01329 845150
Head: Mrs Nicola Cunningham
Category: MLD ASD PD (Coed 2-11)

St Francis Special School
Patchway Drive, Oldbury Way,
FAREHAM, Hampshire PO14 3BN
Tel: 01329 845730
Head: Mr Steve Hollinghurst
Category: SLD (Coed 2-19)

FARNBOROUGH

Henry Tyndale School
Ship Lane, FARNBOROUGH,
Hampshire GU14 8BX
Tel: 01252 544577
Head: Mr Rob Thompson
Category: LD ASD (Coed 2-19)

Samuel Cody Specialist Sports College
Ballantyne Road,
Cove, FARNBOROUGH,
Hampshire GU14 6SS
Tel: 01252 514194
Head: Mrs Anna Dawson
Category: MLD ASD (Coed 11-16)

HAVANT

Prospect School
Freeley Road, HAVANT,
Hampshire PO9 4AQ
Tel: 02392 485150
Head: Ms Marijke Miles
Category: BESD (Boys 11-16)

PORTSMOUTH

Glenwood School
Washington Road,
Emsworth, PORTSMOUTH,
Hampshire PO10 7NN
Tel: 01243 373120
Head: Ms Ruth Witton
Category: MLD ASD (Coed 11-16)

SOUTHAMPTON

Forest Park Primary School
Ringwood Road,
Totton, SOUTHAMPTON,
Hampshire SO40 8EB
Tel: 02380 864949
Head: Mr Robert Hatherley
Category: LD (Coed 2-11)

Forest Park Secondary School
Commercial Road,
Totton, SOUTHAMPTON,
Hampshire SO40 3AF
Tel: 02380 864211
Head: Mr Robert Hatherley
Category: LD (Coed 11-19)

Lord Wilson School
Montiefiore Drive, Sarisbury
Green, SOUTHAMPTON,
Hampshire SO31 7NL
Tel: 01489 582684
Head: Mr Stuart Parker-Tyreman
Category: BESD (Male 11-16)

Oak Lodge School
Roman Road, Dibden
Purlieu, SOUTHAMPTON,
Hampshire SO45 4RQ
Tel: 02380 847213
Head: Ms Tessa Care
Category: MLD ASD (Coed 11-16)

WATERLOOVILLE

Rachel Madocks School
Eagle Avenue, Cowplain,
WATERLOOVILLE,
Hampshire PO8 9XP
Tel: 02392 241818
Head: Ms Jacqueline Sumner
Category: SLD (Coed 2-19)

Riverside Community Special School
Scratchface Lane,
Purbrook, WATERLOOVILLE,
Hampshire PO7 5QD
Tel: 02392 250138
Head: Ms Catherine Marsh
Category: MLD ASD (Coed 3-11)

The Waterloo School
Warfield Avenue, WATERLOOVILLE,
Hampshire PO7 7JJ
Tel: 02392 255956
Head: Ms Kirsty Roman
Category: BESD (Boys 4-11)

WINCHESTER

Osborne School
Athelstan Road, WINCHESTER,
Hampshire SO23 7GA
Tel: 01962 854537
Head: Ms Sonia O'Donnell
Category: LD ASD (Coed 11-19)

Shepherds Down Special School
Shepherds Lane, Compton,
WINCHESTER, Hampshire SO21 2AJ
Tel: 01962 713445
Head: Ms Jane Sansome
Category: LD ASD (Coed 4-11)

HARTLEPOOL

Information, Advice & Support Service

Hartlepool SEN Team, IASS, Civic Centre, Victoria Road, Hartlepool, TS24 8AY
Tel: 01429 284866 Email: hartlepooliass@hartlepool.gov.uk Website: www.hartlepool.gov.uk

HARTLEPOOL

Springwell School
Wiltshire Way, HARTLEPOOL TS26 0TB
Tel: 01429 280600
Head: Ms Zoe Westley
Category: MLD SLD PMLD
ASD BESD (Coed 3-11)

HEREFORDSHIRE

The Children, Young People and Families Directorate

Herefordshire SEN Team, Herefordshire Council, Plough Lane, Hereford, Herefordshire, HR4 0LE
Tel: 01432 260088 or 01432 260089 Email: senteam@herefordshire.gov.uk Website: www.herefordshire.gov.uk

HEREFORD

Barrs Court School
Barrs Court Road,
HEREFORD HR1 1EQ
Tel: 01432 265035
Head: Ms Lisa Appleton
Category: CLD PMLD MSI PD ADHD
ASD OCD SP&LD SLD (Coed 11-19)

Blackmarston School
Honddu Close, HEREFORD HR2 7NX
Tel: 01432 272376
Head: Mrs Sian Bailey
Category: SLD ASD
PMLD(Coed 3-11)

LEOMINSTER

Westfield School
Rylands Road, LEOMINSTER HR6 8NZ
Tel: 01568 613147
Head: Mrs Nicki Gilbert
Category: SLD ASD
PMLD (Coed 2-19)

HERTFORDSHIRE

Children's Services

Hertfordshire SEN Team, County Hall, Pegs Lane, Hertford, SG13 8DQ
Tel: 03001 234043 Email: hertsdirect@hertscc.gov.uk Website: www.hertsdirect.org

BALDOCK

Brandles School
Weston Way, BALDOCK,
Hertfordshire SG7 6EY
Tel: 01462 892189
Head: Mr David Vickery
Category: EBD (Boys 11-16)

BUSHEY

Meadow Wood School
Cold Harbour Lane, BUSHEY,
Hertfordshire WD23 4NN
Tel: 02084 204720
Head: Mr Nathan Taylor
Category: PI (Coed Day 3-12)

HATFIELD

Southfield School
Woods Avenue, HATFIELD,
Hertfordshire AL10 8NN
Tel: 01707 276504
Head: Ms Libby Duggan
Category: MLD (Coed Day 3-11)

HEMEL HEMPSTEAD

Haywood Grove School
St Agnells Lane, HEMEL HEMPSTEAD,
Hertfordshire HP2 7BG
Tel: 01442 250077
Head Teacher: C Smith
Category: EBD (Coed Day 5-11)

The Collett School
Lockers Park Lane, HEMEL
HEMPSTEAD, Hertfordshire HP1 1TQ
Tel: 01442 398988
Head: Mr Stephen Hoult-Allen
Category: MLD AUT (Coed 4-16)

Woodfield School
Malmes Croft, Leverstock
Green, HEMEL HEMPSTEAD,
Hertfordshire HP3 8RL
Tel: 01442 253476
Head: Mrs Gill Waceba
Category: SLD AUT (Coed Day 3-19)

HERTFORD

Hailey Hall School
Hailey Lane, HERTFORD,
Hertfordshire SG13 7PB
Tel: 01992 465208
Head: Ms Heather Boardman
Category: EBD (Boys 11-16)

LETCHWORTH GARDEN CITY

Woolgrove School Special Needs Academy
Pryor Way, LETCHWORTH GARDEN
CITY, Hertfordshire SG6 2PT
Tel: 01462 622422
Head: Mrs Susan Selley
Category: MLD AUT
(Coed Day 5-11)

REDBOURN

St Luke's School
Crouch Hall Lane, REDBOURN,
Hertfordshire AL3 7ET
Tel: 01582 626727
Head: Mr P Johnson
Category: MLD (Coed Day 9-16)

ST ALBANS

Batchwood School
Townsend Drive, ST ALBANS,
Hertfordshire AL3 5RP
Tel: 01727 868021
Acting Head: Mrs Anne Spencer
Category: EBD (Coed 11-16)

Heathlands School
Heathlands Drive, ST ALBANS,
Hertfordshire AL3 5AY
Tel: 01727 807807
Head: Ms Deborah Jones-Stevens
Category: HI (Coed Day
& boarding 3-16)

Watling View School
Watling View, ST ALBANS,
Hertfordshire AL1 2NU
Tel: 01727 850560
Head: Ms Pauline Atkins
Category: SLD (Coed Day 2-19)

STEVENAGE

Greenside School
Shephall Green, STEVENAGE,
Hertfordshire SG2 9XS
Tel: 01438 315356
Head: Mr David Victor
Category: SLD AUT (Coed Day 2-19)

Larwood School
Webb Rise, STEVENAGE,
Hertfordshire SG1 5QU
Tel: 01438 236333
Head: Mr Sean Trimble
Category: EBD (Coed
Day & boarding 5-11)

Lonsdale School
Brittain Way, STEVENAGE,
Hertfordshire SG2 8BL
Tel: 01438 726999
Head Teacher: Ms
Annemarie Ottridge
Category: PH (Coed Day
& boarding 5-19)

The Valley School
Valley Way, STEVENAGE,
Hertfordshire SG2 9AB
Tel: 01438 747274
Head: Mrs Corina Foster
Category: MLD (Coed Day 11-19)

WARE

**Amwell View School &
Specialist Sports College**
Stanstead Abbotts, WARE,
Hertfordshire SG12 8EH
Tel: 01920 870027
Head: Mrs Janet Liversage
Category: SLD AUT (Coed Day 2-19)

Middleton School
Walnut Tree Walk, WARE,
Hertfordshire SG12 9PD
Tel: 01920 485152
Head: Ms Donna Jolly
Category: MLD AUT
(Coed Day 5-11)

Pinewood School
Hoe Lane, WARE,
Hertfordshire SG12 9PB
Tel: 01920 412211
Acting Head: Mr Dave McGachen
Category: MLD (Coed
Residential 11-16)

WATFORD

Breakspeare School
Gallows Hill Lane, Abbots Langley,
WATFORD, Hertfordshire WD5 0BU
Tel: 01923 263645
Head Teacher: M Paakkonen
Category: SLD (Coed Day 3-19)

Colnbrook School
Hayling Road, WATFORD,
Hertfordshire WD19 7UY
Tel: 0208 428 1281
Head: Ms Kerry Harris
Category: MLD AUT
(Coed Day 4-11)

Falconer School
Falconer Road, Bushey, WATFORD,
Hertfordshire WD23 3AT
Tel: 0208 950 2505
Head Teacher: Mr Jonathan Kemp
Category: EBD (Boys Day/
boarding 10-19)

Garston Manor School
Horseshoe Lane, Garston,
WATFORD, Hertfordshire WD25 7HR
Tel: 01923 673757
Head: Miss Christine
deGraft-Hanson
Category: MLD (Coed Day 11-16)

WELWYN GARDEN CITY

Knightsfield School
Knightsfield, WELWYN GARDEN
CITY, Hertfordshire AL8 7LW
Tel: 01707 376874
Head: Mrs Lucy Leith
Category: HI (Coed Day
& boarding 10-19)

Lakeside School
Stanfield, Lemsford Lane,
WELWYN GARDEN CITY,
Hertfordshire AL8 6YN
Tel: 01707 327410
Head: Mrs Judith Chamberlain
Category: SLD PD (Coed Day 2-19)

FORTROSE

**Black Isle Education
Centre**
Raddery, FORTROSE IV10 8SN
Tel: 01381 621600
Head: Mr Ross Waldie
Category: BESD (Boys Day 9-16)

ISLE OF WIGHT

Children's Services Directorate

Isle of Wight SEN Service, Thompson House, Sandy Lane, Newport, Isle of Wight, PO30 3NA
Tel: 01983 821000 (Ext: 8421) Website: www.iwight.com; www.iwight.com/localoffer

NEWPORT

**Medina House
Special School**
School Lane, NEWPORT,
Isle of Wight PO30 2HS
Tel: 01983 522917
Head: Ms Julie Stewart
Category: Severe & complex
needs (Coed 2-11)

St George's School
Watergate Road, NEWPORT,
Isle of Wight PO30 1XW
Tel: 01983 524634
Head: Mrs Sue Holman
Category: Severe complex
needs (Coed 11-19)

KENT

Information, Advice & Support Service

Kent SENDIASS, Shepway Centre, Oxford Road, Maidstone, Kent, ME15 8AW
Tel: **03000 412412** Fax: **01622 671198** Email: **iask@kent.gov.uk** Website: **www.kent.gov.uk**

ASHFORD

Goldwyn Community Special School
Godinton Lane, Great Chart, ASHFORD, Kent TN23 3BT
Tel: 01233 622958
Head: Mr Robert Law
Category: BESD (Coed 11-16)

The Wyvern School
Great Chart Bypass, ASHFORD, Kent TN23 4ER
Tel: 01233 621468
Head: Mr David Spencer
Category: PMLD SLD CLD PD (Coed 3-19)

BROADSTAIRS

Stone Bay School
70 Stone Road, BROADSTAIRS, Kent CT10 1EB
Tel: 01843 863421
Head: Mr Billy McInally
Category: SLD AUT SLCN MLD C&I (Coed Day & residential 11-19)

The Foreland School
Lanthorne Road, BROADSTAIRS, Kent CT10 3NX
Tel: 01843 863891
Head Teacher: Mr Adrian Mount
Category: ASD PMLD SLD PSCN (Coed 2-19)

CANTERBURY

St Nicholas' School
Holme Oak Close, Nunnery Fields, CANTERBURY, Kent CT1 3JJ
Tel: 01227 464316
Headteacher: Mr Daniel Lewis
Category: PMLD SLD CLD PSCN (Coed 3-19)

The Orchard School
Cambridge Road, CANTERBURY, Kent CT1 3QQ
Tel: 01227 769220
Headteacher: Ms Annabel Lilley
Category: MLD CLD B&L (Coed 11-16)

DARTFORD

Rowhill School
Main Road, Longfield, DARTFORD, Kent DA3 7PW
Tel: 01474 705377
Head: Mr Timothy South
Category: B&L AUT LD Complex needs Behavioural difficulties (Coed Day 4-16)

DOVER

Harbour School
Elms Vale Road, DOVER, Kent CT17 9PS
Tel: 01304 201964
Head Teacher: Mr Warren Deane
Category: BESD ASD MLD B&L (Coed 4-16)

Portal House School
Sea Street, St Margarets-at-Cliffe, DOVER, Kent CT15 6SS
Tel: 01304 853033
Head: Mrs Rose Bradley
Category: BESD (Coed 11-16)

FOLKESTONE

Highview School
Moat Farm Road, FOLKESTONE, Kent CT19 5DJ
Tel: 01303 258755
Executive Headteacher: Mr Neil Birch
Category: MLD CLD Complex needs (Coed 4-17)

GRAVESEND

The Ifield School
Cedar Avenue, GRAVESEND, Kent DA12 5JT
Tel: 01474 365485
Headteacher: Mrs Pamela Jones
Category: CLD PMLD SLD MLD PSCN (Coed 4-18)

HYTHE

Foxwood School
Seabrook Road, HYTHE, Kent CT21 5QJ
Tel: 01303 261155
Executive Headteacher: Mr Neil Birch
Category: AUT SLD (Coed 2-19)

MAIDSTONE

Bower Grove School
Fant Lane, MAIDSTONE, Kent ME16 8NL
Tel: 01622 726773
Headteacher: Mrs Lynn Salter
Category: BESD MLD ASD B&L (Coed Day 5-16)

Five Acre Wood School
Boughton Lane, Loose Valley, MAIDSTONE, Kent ME15 9QF
Tel: 01622 743925
Head: Ms Peggy Murphy
Category: ASD PMLD SLD PD CLD PSCN (Coed 4-19)

MARGATE

St Anthony's School
St Anthony's Way, MARGATE, Kent CT9 3RA
Tel: 01843 292015
Headteacher: Mr Robert Page
Category: MLD ASD LD SEBD SLCN B&L (Coed 3-11)

RAMSGATE

Laleham Gap School
Ozengell Place, RAMSGATE, Kent CT12 6FH
Tel: 01843 570598
Deputy Head: Ms Katie Reeves
Category: AUT ABD PD SLCN C&I (Coed 3-16)

SEVENOAKS

Grange Park School
Borough Green Road, Wrotham, SEVENOAKS, Kent TN15 7RD
Tel: 01732 882111
Head Teacher: Mr Robert Wyatt
Category: AUT C&I (Coed 11-19)

SITTINGBOURNE

Meadowfield School
Swanstree Avenue, SITTINGBOURNE, Kent ME10 4NL
Tel: 01795 477788
Head: Ms Jill Palmer
Category: CLD PMLD SLD ASD SP&LD PSCN (Coed 4-19)

SWANLEY

Broomhill Bank School (North)
Rowhill Road, Hextable, SWANLEY, Kent BR8 7RP
Tel: 01322 662937
Acting Head: Mrs R Cottage

TONBRIDGE

Ridge View School
Cage Green Road, TONBRIDGE, Kent TN10 4PT
Tel: 01732 771384
Head Teacher: Ms Jacqui Tovey
Category: PMLD SLD CLD PSCN (Coed 2-19)

TUNBRIDGE WELLS

Broomhill Bank School (West)
Broomhill Road, Rusthall, TUNBRIDGE WELLS, Kent TN3 0TB
Tel: 01892 510440
Executive Headteacher: Ms Emma Leitch
Category: MLD SP&LD CLD AUT C&I (Girls Boarding & day 8-19)

Oakley School
Pembury Road, TUNBRIDGE WELLS, Kent TN2 4NE
Tel: 01892 823096
Headteacher: Mr Gordon Tillman
Category: PMLD ASD MLD PSCN (Coed 3-19)

WESTERHAM

Valence School
Westerham Road, WESTERHAM, Kent TN16 1QN
Tel: 01959 562156
Head: Mr Roland Gooding
Category: PD Sensory Medical (Coed Day/boarding 4-19)

KINGSTON UPON HULL

City Council

0-25 Integrated SEN Team, Hull City Council, Children & Young People's Services, Brunswick House, Strand Close Hull, HU2 9DB
Tel: 01482 300300 Email: send@hullcc.gov.uk Website: www.hullcc.gov.uk

KINGSTON UPON HULL

Bridgeview School
262a Pickering Road, KINGSTON UPON HULL HU4 7AB
Tel: 01482 303300
Head: Mrs C Patton
Category: BESD

Frederick Holmes School
Inglemire Lane, KINGSTON UPON HULL HU6 8JJ
Tel: 01482 804766
Head: Mrs B Ribey
Category: PH

Ganton Primary School
The Compass, 1 Burnham Road, KINGSTON UPON HULL HU4 7EB
Tel: 01482 564 646
Head: Mrs S Jones
Category: SLD

Ganton Secondary School
294 Anlaby Park Road South, KINGSTON UPON HULL HU4 7JB
Tel: 01482 564646
Head: Mrs S Jones
Category: SLD

Northcott School
Dulverton Close, Bransholme, KINGSTON UPON HULL HU7 4EL
Tel: 01482 825311
Head: Mrs K Coxall
Category: Vulnerable ASD

Oakfield School
Hopewell Road, KINGSTON UPON HULL HU9 4HD
Tel: 01482 854588
Head: Mrs R Davies
Category: BESD

Tweendykes School
Midmere Avenue, Leads Road, KINGSTON UPON HULL HU7 4PW
Tel: 01482 826508
Head: Mrs B Moorcroft
Category: SLD

LANCASHIRE

Information, Advice & Support Service

Lancashire SENDIASS, PO Box 78, County Hall, Fishergate Preston, Lancashire, PR1 8XJ
Tel: 03001 236706 Email: information.lineteam@lancashire.gov.uk Website: www.lancashire.gov.uk

ACCRINGTON

Broadfield Specialist School for SEN
Fielding Lane, Oswaldtwistle, ACCRINGTON, Lancashire BB5 3BE
Tel: 01254 381782
Head: Mrs Angela Wilson
Category: MLD SLD ASD (Coed 4-16)

White Ash School
Thwaites Road, Oswaldtwistle, ACCRINGTON, Lancashire BB5 4QG
Tel: 01254 235772
Head: Mr Mark Montgomery
Category: SLD ASD PMLD (Coed 3-19)

BURNLEY

Holly Grove School
Burnley Campus, Barden Lane, BURNLEY, Lancashire BB10 1JD
Tel: 01282 682278
Head: Ms Sue Kitto
Category: SLD MLD PMLD ASD Medical needs (Coed 2-11)

Ridgewood Community High School
Eastern Avenue, BURNLEY, Lancashire BB10 2AT
Tel: 01282 682316
Head: Mrs Frances Entwhistle
Category: MSI PD LD (Coed 11-16)

The Rose School
Greenock Street, BURNLEY, Lancashire BB11 4DT
Tel: 01282 683050
Head: Mr Russell Bridge
Category: BESD (Coed 11-16)

CARNFORTH

Bleasdale House School
27 Emesgate Lane, Silverdale, CARNFORTH, Lancashire LA5 0RG
Tel: 01524 701217
Head: Ms Kairen Dexter
Category: PMLD PH (Coed 2-19)

CHORLEY

Astley Park School
Harrington Road, CHORLEY, Lancashire PR7 1JZ
Tel: 01257 262227
Head: Mr Kieran Welsh
Category: MLD SLD ASD EBD(Coed 4-17)

Mayfield Specialist School
Gloucester Road, CHORLEY, Lancashire PR7 3HN
Tel: 01257 263063
Head: Ms Rachel Kay
Category: CLD ASD EBD (Coed 2-19)

COLNE

Pendle View Primary School
Gibfield Road, COLNE, Lancashire BB8 8JT
Tel: 01282 865011
Head: Ms Debbie Morris
Category: LD PD SLD PMLD ASD MSI (Coed 2-11)

HASLINGDEN

Tor View Community Special School
Clod Lane, HASLINGDEN, Lancashire BB4 6LR
Tel: 01706 214640
Head: Mr Andrew Squire
Category: AUT MLD SLD PMLD MSI (Coed 4-19)

KIRKHAM

Pear Tree School
29 Station Road, KIRKHAM, Lancashire PR4 2HA
Tel: 01772 683609
Head: Ms Lesley Sullivan
Category: SLD PMLD ASD (Coed 2-19)

LANCASTER

The Loyne Specialist School
Sefton Drive, LANCASTER, Lancashire LA1 2PZ
Tel: 01524 64543
Head: Ms Susan Campbell
Category: MSI LD CLD PD AUT EPI (2-19)

Wennington Hall School
Lodge Lane, Wennington, LANCASTER, Lancashire LA2 8NS
Tel: 01524 221333
Head: Mr Joseph Prendergast
Category: SEBD (Boys Day or resident 11-16)

MORECAMBE

Morecambe Road School
Morecambe Road, MORECAMBE, Lancashire LA3 3AB
Tel: 01524 414384
Head: Mr Paul Edmondson
Category: LD ASD BESD (Coed 3-16)

NELSON

Pendle Community High School and College
Oxford Road, NELSON, Lancashire BB9 8LF
Tel: 01282 682240
Head: Mr Paul Wright
Category: MLD BESD ASD (Coed 11-19)

POULTON-LE-FYLDE

Brookfield School
Fouldrey Avenue, POULTON-LE-FYLDE, Lancashire FY6 7HE
Tel: 01253 886895
Head: Mrs Jane Fallon
Category: SEBD ADHD ASD SPLD (Coed 11-16)

PRESTON

Acorns Primary School
Blackpool Road, Moor Park,
PRESTON, Lancashire PR1 6AU
Tel: 01772 792681
Head: Ms Gail Beaton
Category: AUT SLD
PMLD (Coed 2-19)

**Hillside Specialist
School and College**
Ribchester Road, Longridge,
PRESTON, Lancashire PR3 3XB
Tel: 01772 782205
Head: Mrs Alison Foster
Category: ASD (Coed 2-16)

Moor Hey School
Far Croft, off Leyland Road, Lostock
Hall, PRESTON, Lancashire PR5 5SS
Tel: 01772 336976
Head: Mrs Helen-Ruth McLenahan
Category: MLD CLD EBD (4-16)

Moorbrook School
Ainslie Road, Fulwood, PRESTON,
Lancashire PR2 3DB
Tel: 01772 774752
Head: Mrs Claire Thompson
Category: SEBN (11-16)

Royal Cross Primary School
Elswick Road, Ashton-on-Ribble,
PRESTON, Lancashire PR2 1NT
Tel: 01772 729705
Head: Ms Ruth Bonney
Category: SLCN D ASD (Coed 4-11)

**Sir Tom Finney Community
High School**
Ribbleton Hall Drive, PRESTON,
Lancashire PR2 6EE
Tel: 01772 795749
Head: Mr Shaun Jukes
Category: PD PMLD BESD
MLD (Coed 2-19)

The Coppice School
Ash Grove, Bamber Bridge,
PRESTON, Lancashire PR5 6GY
Tel: 01772 336342
Head: Mrs Liz Davies
Category: SLD PMLD CLD
Medical needs (Coed 2-19)

RAWTENSTALL

**Cribden House
Community Special School**
Haslingden Road, RAWTENSTALL,
Lancashire BB4 6RX
Tel: 01706 213048
Head: Ms Siobhan Halligan
Category: SEBD (Coed 5-11)

SKELMERSDALE

**Elm Tree Community
Primary School**
Elmers Wood Road, SKELMERSDALE,
Lancashire WN8 6SA
Tel: 01695 50924
Head: Mr David Lamb
Category: BESD (Coed)

Hope High School
Clay Brow, SKELMERSDALE,
Lancashire WN8 9DP
Tel: 01695 721066
Head: Ms Helen Dunbavin
Category: EBD (Coed 11-16)

Kingsbury Primary School
School Lane, Chapel
House, SKELMERSDALE,
Lancashire WN8 8EH
Tel: 01695 722991
Head: Ms Fiona Grieveson
Category: SLD PMLD LD
ASD MLD (Coed 2-11)

**West Lancashire
Community High School**
School Lane, Chapel
House, SKELMERSDALE,
Lancashire WN8 8EH
Tel: 01695 721487
Head: Mrs Austin
Category: MLD SLD PMLD
AUT (Coed 11-19)

THORNTON-CLEVELEYS

Great Arley School
Holly Road, THORNTON-
CLEVELEYS, Lancashire FY5 4HH
Tel: 01253 821072
Head: Mrs Anne Marshfield
Category: MLD ASD SLD
BESD (Coed Day 4-16)

Red Marsh School
Holly Road, THORNTON-
CLEVELEYS, Lancashire FY5 4HH
Tel: 01253 868451
Head: Ms Catherine Dellow
Category: SLD PMLD
CLD (Coed 2-19)

LEICESTER CITY COUNCIL

Education Authority

Leicester SEN Team, City Hall, 115 Charles Street, Leicester, LE1 1FZ
Tel: 01164 541000 Website: www.leicester.gov.uk

LEICESTER

**Carisbrooke Specialist
Learning Centre (PRU)**
126 Wigston Lane, Aylestone,
LEICESTER LE2 8TN
Tel: 0116 3033281 (Option 2)
Head: Mr Shaun Whittingham
Category: Children Centre, PRU

Children's Hospital School
University Hospitals of Leicester
NHS Trust, Infirmary Square,
LEICESTER LE1 5WW
Tel: 01162 585330
Head: Mr Stephen
Corsie-Deadman
Category: HS

Ellesmere College
40 Braunstone Lane East,
LEICESTER LE3 2FD
Tel: 01162 894224
Heads: Ms Lisa Pittwood &
Ms Linda Richardson

Keyham Lodge School
Keyham Lane, LEICESTER LE5 1FG
Tel: 01162 41 6852
Head: Mr Chris Bruce
Category: EBD (Boys Secondary)

**Millgate Lodge Specialist
Learning Centre**
495 Welford Road,
LEICESTER LE2 6BN
Tel: 0116 3033281 (Option 1)
Head: Mr Shaun Whittingham
Category: PRU

Millgate School
18A Scott Street, LEICESTER LE2 6DW
Tel: 01162 704922
Head: Mr Chris Bruce

Nether Hall School
Keyham Lane West,
LEICESTER LE5 1RT
Tel: 01162 417258
Head: Ms Erica Dennies

Oaklands School
Whitehall Road, LEICESTER LE5 6GJ
Tel: 01162 415921
Head: Mrs E Shaw
Category: MLD (Primary)

Phoenix (PRU)
c/o Thurnby Lodge Primary School,
Dudley Avenue, LEICESTER LE5 2EG
Tel: 01162 419538
Team Leader: Ms Allison Benson
Category: Primary PRU

The ARC (PRU)
c/o Holy Cross Primary School,
Stonesby Avenue, LEICESTER LE2 6TY
Tel: 01162 832185
Team Leader: Mrs C H Pay
Category: Primary PRU

West Gate School
Glenfield Road, LEICESTER LE3 6DN
Tel: 01162 856181
Head: Ms Virginia Ursell
Category: SLD MLD

LEICESTERSHIRE

Information Advice & Support Service

Leicestershire SENDIASS, Abington House, 85 Station Road, Wigston, Leicestershire, LE18 2DP
Tel: 0116 305 6545 Email: sendqueries@leics.gov.uk Website: www.leics.gov.uk

HINCKLEY

Sketchley Hill Menphys Nursery
Sketchley Road, Burbage,
HINCKLEY, Leicestershire LE10 2DY
Tel: 01455 890684
Head: Miss Laura Jeffs

LOUGHBOROUGH

Ashmount School
Thorpe Hill, LOUGHBOROUGH,
Leicestershire LE11 4SQ
Tel: 01509 268506
Head: Mr Dave Thomas
Category: SLD PMLD (2-18)

Maplewell Hall School
Maplewell Road, Woodhouse
Eaves, LOUGHBOROUGH,
Leicestershire LE12 8QY
Tel: 01509 890237
Head: Mr Jason Brooks
Category: MLD AUT (10-15)

MELTON MOWBRAY

Birch Wood (Melton Area Special School)
Grange Drive, MELTON MOWBRAY,
Leicestershire LE13 1HA
Tel: 01664 483340
Head: Ms Nina Watts
Category: MLD SLD AUT (5-19)

WIGSTON

Wigston Birkett House Community Special School
Launceston Road, WIGSTON,
Leicestershire LE18 2FZ
Tel: 01162 885802
Head: Mrs Susan Horn
Category: SLD PMLD (2-18)

Wigston Menphys Centre
Launceston Road, WIGSTON,
Leicestershire LE18 2FZ
Tel: 01162 889977
Head: Mrs Helen Johnston

LINCOLNSHIRE

Information, Advice & Support Service

Lincolnshire SENDIASS, County Offices, Newland, Lincoln, Lincolnshire, LN1 1YL
Tel: 0800 195 1635 Email: iass@lincolnshire.gov.uk Website: www.lincolnshire.gov.uk

BOSTON

John Fielding School
Ashlawn Drive, BOSTON,
Lincolnshire PE21 9PX
Tel: 01205 363395
Executive Head Teacher: Mr
Daran Bland
Category: SLD (2-19)

BOURNE

Willoughby School
South Road, BOURNE,
Lincolnshire PE10 9JD
Tel: 01778 425203
Head: Mr James Husbands
Category: SLD (2-19)

GOSBERTON

Gosberton House School
11 Westhorpe Road, GOSBERTON,
Lincolnshire PE11 4EW
Tel: 01775 840250
Head: Ms Louise Stanton
Category: MLD (3-11)

GRANTHAM

Sandon School
Sandon Close, GRANTHAM,
Lincolnshire NG31 9AX
Tel: 01476 564994
Principal: Ms Sara Ellis
Category: SLD (2-19)

The Ambergate Sports College Specialist Education Centre
Dysart Road, GRANTHAM,
Lincolnshire NG31 7LP
Tel: 01476 564957
Principal: Mr James Ellis
Category: MLD (5-16)

HORNCASTLE

St Lawrence School
Bowl Alley Lane, HORNCASTLE,
Lincolnshire LN9 5EJ
Tel: 01507 522563
Head: Ms Michelle Hockham
Category: MLD (5-16)

LINCOLN

St Christopher's School
Hykeham Road, LINCOLN,
Lincolnshire LN6 8AR
Tel: 01522 528378
Head: Mr Allan Lacey
Category: MLD (3-16)

St Francis School
Wickenby Crescent, Ermine Estate,
LINCOLN, Lincolnshire LN1 3TJ
Tel: 01522 526498
Head: Mrs Ann Hoffmann
Category: PD Sensory (2-19)

The Fortuna Primary School
Kingsdown Road, Doddington
Park, LINCOLN, Lincolnshire LN6 0FB
Tel: 01522 705561
Head: Ms Hanna Jones
Category: EBD (4-11)

The Pilgrim School
Carrington Drive, LINCOLN,
Lincolnshire LN6 0DE
Tel: 01522 682319
Head: Mr Steve Barnes
Category: HS (4-16)

The Sincil Sports College
South Park Avenue, LINCOLN,
Lincolnshire LN5 8EL
Tel: 01522 534559
Interim Head: Ms Bridget Robson
Category: EBD (11-16)

LOUTH

St Bernard's School
Wood Lane, LOUTH,
Lincolnshire LN11 8RS
Tel: 01507 603776
Head: Ms Ann Stebbings
Category: SLD (2-19)

SLEAFORD

The Ash Villa School
Willoughby Road, Greylees,
SLEAFORD, Lincolnshire NG34 8QA
Tel: 01529 488066
Head: Mr Leigh Bentley
Category: HS (8-16)

SPALDING

The Garth School
Pinchbeck Road, SPALDING,
Lincolnshire PE11 1QF
Tel: 01775 725566
Head of Site: Dr Richard Gamman
Category: SLD (2-19)

The Priory School
Neville Avenue, SPALDING,
Lincolnshire PE11 2EH
Tel: 01775 724080
Head of Site: Mr Barrie Taylor
Category: MLD (11-16)

SPILSBY

The Eresby School
Eresby Avenue, SPILSBY,
Lincolnshire PE23 5HU
Tel: 01790 752441
Head: Ms Michele Holiday
Category: SLD (2-19)

The Lady Jane Franklin School
Partney Road, SPILSBY,
Lincolnshire PE23 5EJ
Tel: 01790 753902
Head: Mr Chris Armond
Category: EBD (11-16)

NORTH LINCOLNSHIRE
People Directorate

North Lincolnshire SEND Team, Hewson House, PO Box 35, Station Road Brigg, North Lincolnshire, DN20 8XJ
Tel: 01724 297148 Email: special.needssection@northlincs.gov.uk Website: www.northlincs.gov.uk

SCUNTHORPE

St Hugh's Communication & Interaction Specialist College
Bushfield Road, SCUNTHORPE,
North Lincolnshire DN16 1NB
Tel: 01724 842960
Head: Mrs Tracy Millard
Category: MLD SLD
PMLD (Coed 11-19)

St Luke's Primary School
Grange Lane North, SCUNTHORPE,
North Lincolnshire DN16 1BN
Tel: 01724 844560
Head: Mr Alastair Sutherland
Category: PMLD SLD
MLD (Coed 3-11)

NORTH EAST LINCOLNSHIRE
Family Information Service

NE Lincolnshire SEN Team, Riverside Children's Centre, Central Parade, Grimsby, DN34 4HE
Tel: 01472 323250 Email: fis@nelincs.gov.uk Website: www.nelincs.gov.uk

London

BARKING & DAGENHAM
Education, Health and Care Team

Barking & Dagenham Education Inclusion Team, 5th Floor, Roycraft House, 15 Linton Road, Barking, Essex, IG11 8HE
Tel: 020 8227 2636 Email: joseph.wilson@lbbd.gov.uk

BARKING

Riverside Bridge school
Renwick Road, BARKING,
Essex IG11 0FU
Tel: 02087 248033
Head: Ms Anna Hope

DAGENHAM

Hopewell School
Baden Powell Close,
DAGENHAM, Essex RM9 6XN
Tel: 02030 024287
Head: Ms Susan Mayo

Trinity School
Heathway, DAGENHAM,
Essex RM10 7SJ
Tel: 02082 701601
Head: Mr Peter McPartland
Category: SLD ASD
PMLD (Coed 3-19)

London

BARNET
Information, Advice & Support Service

Barnet SENDIASS, North London Business Park, Oakleigh Road South, London, N11 1NP
Tel: 020 8359 7637 Fax: 020 8359 2480 Email: sendiass@barnet.gov.uk Website: www.barnet.gov.uk

LONDON

Mapledown School
Claremont Road, Golders
Green, LONDON NW2 1TR
Tel: 02084 554111
Head: Mr S Caroll
Category: SLD CLD (Mixed 11-19)

Northway School
The Fairway, Mill Hill,
LONDON NW7 3HS
Tel: 02083 595450
Head: Ms L Burgess
Category: CLD AUT (Mixed 5-11)

Oak Lodge School
Heath View, Off East End
Road, LONDON N2 0QY
Tel: 02084 446711
Head: Mrs L Walker
Category: MLD ASD SCLN
EBD (Mixed 11-19)

Oakleigh School
Oakleigh Road North,
Whetstone, LONDON N20 0DH
Tel: 02083 685336
Head: Ms J Gridley
Category: SLD AUT
PMLD (Mixed 3-11)

London

LONDON BOROUGH OF BEXLEY

Directorate of Education and Social Care

Bexley SEN Team, Civic Offices, 2 Watling Street, Bexleyheath, Kent, DA6 7AT
Tel: 02083 037777 Email: specialneeds.els@bexley.gov.uk Website: www.bexley.gov.uk

BELVEDERE

Woodside School
Halt Robin Road, BELVEDERE,
Kent DA17 6DW
Tel: 01322 433494
Executive Head Teacher: Ms
Madelaine Caplin
Category: MLD (Primary/
Secondary)

BEXLEYHEATH

Oakwood School
Woodside Road, BEXLEYHEATH,
Kent DA7 6LB
Tel: 01322 553787
Head: Mrs Beverley Evans
Category: BESD (Coed 11-16)

CRAYFORD

Shenstone School
94 Old Road, CRAYFORD,
Kent DA1 4DZ
Tel: 01322 524145
Head Teacher: Ms Lori Mackey
Category: SLD (2-11)

SIDCUP

Marlborough School
Marlborough Park Avenue,
SIDCUP, Kent DA15 9DP
Tel: 02083 006896
Headteacher: Ms Linda Lee
Category: SLD (11-19)

WELLING

Westbrooke School
Gypsy Road South,
WELLING, Kent DA16 1JB
Tel: 02083 041320
Head: Mr Phill Collins
Category: BESD (5-11)

London

BRENT

Information, Advice & Support Service

Brent SENDIASS, Brent Civic Centre, Engineers Way, Wembley, Middlesex, HA9 0FJ
Tel: 020 8937 3434 Email: sendias@brent.gov.uk Website: www.brent.gov.uk

KENSALE RISE

Manor School
Chamberlayne Road, KENSALE
RISE, London NW10 3NT
Tel: 02089 683160
Head: Ms Jayne Jardine
Category: MLD SLD CLD
ASD (Coed 4-11)

KINGSBURY

The Village School
Grove Park, KINGSBURY,
London NW9 0JY
Tel: 02082 045396
Head: Ms Kay Charles
Category: LD DD VIS Medical
needs (Coed 2-19)

Woodfield School
Glenwood Avenue, KINGSBURY,
London NW9 7LY
Tel: 02082 051977
Head: Ms Desi Lodge-Patch
Category: MLD BESD
ASD (Coed 11-16)

NEASDEN

Phoenix Arch School
Drury Way, NEASDEN,
London NW10 0NQ
Tel: 02084 516961
Head: Ms Jude Towell
Category: BESD LD ADHD
ASD (Coed 5-11)

Maintained special schools and colleges

London

BROMLEY

Information, Advice & Support Service

Bromley SENDIASS, Blenheim Children & Family Centre, Blenheim Road, Orpington, Kent, BR6 9BH
Tel: 01689 881024 Email: iass@bromley.gov.uk Website: www.bromley.gov.uk

BECKENHAM

Riverside School Beckenham (ASD Centre)
Hayne Road, BECKENHAM,
Kent BR3 4HY
Tel: 020 8639 0079
Head: Mr Steve Solomons
Category: ASD (Coed 4-19)

CHISLEHURST

Marjorie McClure School
Hawkwood Lane,
CHISLEHURST, Kent BR7 5PS
Tel: 02084 670174
Head: Mrs Denise James-Mason
Category: PD SLD Medical
needs (Coed 4-19)

ORPINGTON

Riverside School
Main Road, St Paul's Cray,
ORPINGTON, Kent BR5 3HS
Tel: 01689 870519
Head: Mr Steve Solomons
Category: ASD (Coed 4-19)

WEST WICKHAM

Glebe School
Hawes Lane, WEST
WICKHAM, Kent BR4 9AE
Tel: 02087 774540
Head: Mr Keith Seed
Category: Complex needs
SCD ASD SLD (Coed 11-19)

London Borough

CAMDEN

Information, Advice and Support Service

Camden SENDIASS, 10th Floor, 5 Pancras Square, c/o Town Hall, Judd Street London, WC1H 9JE
Tel: 020 7974 6500 Email: sendiass@camden.gov.uk Website: www.camden.gov.uk

LONDON

Frank Barnes Primary School for Deaf Children
4 Wollstonecraft Street,
LONDON N1C 4BT
Tel: 02073 917040
Acting Head: Mr Dani Sive
Category: HI (Coed 2-11)

SEBD Special School
Harmood Street, LONDON NW1 8DP
Tel: 02079 748906
Head: Ms Jeanette Lowe
Category: BESD (Coed 11-16)

Swiss Cottage School
80 Avenue Road,
LONDON NW8 6HX
Tel: 02076 818080
Head: Ms Vijita Patel
Category: LD (2-16)

The Children's Hospital School
Great Ormond Street,
LONDON WC1N 3JH
Tel: 02078 138269
Head: Ms Jayne Franklin
Category: HS (Coed 0-19)

The Royal Free Hospital Children's School
Royal Free Hospital, Pond
Street, LONDON NW3 2QG
Tel: 02074 726298
Head: Mr Alex Yates
Category: HS (5-16)

London

CROYDON

Children, Young People & Learners

Croydon SEN Team, 4th Floor, Zone A, Weatherill House, 8 Mint Walk Croydon, Surrey, CR0 1EA
Tel: 0208 604 7263 Email: senenquiries@croydon.gov.uk Website: www.croydon.gov.uk

BECKENHAM

Beckmead School
Monks Orchard Road,
BECKENHAM, Kent BR3 3BZ
Tel: 020 8777 9311
Executive Head Teacher: Mr
Jonty Clark
Category: BESD (Boys 7-16)

CROYDON

Bramley Bank Short Stay School
170 Sanderstead Road,
CROYDON, Surrey CR2 0LY
Tel: 020 8686 0393
Head: Ms Alison Page
Category: Behaviour
Support (Coed 5-11)

Chaffinch Brook School
32 Moorland Road, CROYDON,
Surrey CR0 6NA
Tel: 020 8325 4612
Head: Ms Judith Azzopardi
Category: AUT (Coed 5-11)

Red Gates
Farnborough Avenue,
CROYDON, Surrey CR2 8HD
Tel: 020 8651 6540
Head Teacher: Mrs Susan Beaman
Category: SLD AUT (Coed 4-12)

St Giles School
207 Pampisford Road,
CROYDON, Surrey CR2 6DF
Tel: 020 8680 2141
Head Teacher: Ms Virginia Marshall
Category: PD PMLD
MLD (Coed 4-19)

PURLEY

St Nicholas School
Old Lodge Lane, PURLEY,
Surrey CR8 4DN
Tel: 020 8660 4861
Headteacher: Mr Nick Dry
Category: MLD AUT (Coed 4-11)

THORNTON HEATH

Bensham Manor School
Ecclesbourne Road, THORNTON
HEATH, Surrey CR7 7BN
Tel: 020 8684 0116
Head Teacher: Mr Philip Poulton
Category: MLD AUT (Coed 11-16)

UPPER NORWOOD

Priory School
Hermitage Road, UPPER
NORWOOD, Surrey SE19 3QN
Tel: 020 8653 7879
Headteacher: Mr Simon Vines
Category: SLD AUT (Coed 11-19)

London

EALING

Education Department

Ealing SEN Team, 2nd Floor NE, Perceval House, 14-16 Uxbridge Road London, W5 2HL
Tel: 02088 255533 Email: education@ealing.gov.uk Website: www.ealing.gov.uk

EALING

Castlebar School
Hathaway Gardens, EALING,
London W13 0DH
Tel: 02089 983135
Head: Mr Paul Adair
Category: MLD SLD ASD
(Coed Day 4-11)

Springhallow School
Compton Close, Cavendish
Ave, EALING, London W13 0JG
Tel: 02088 328979
Acting Head: Mr Cathal Owens
Category: ASD (Coed Day 4-16/17)

GREENFORD

Mandeville School
Horsenden Lane North,
GREENFORD, Middlesex UB6 0PA
Tel: 02088 644921/0911
Head: Ms Denise Feasey
Category: SLD ASD PMLD
(Coed Day 2-12)

HANWELL

St Ann's School
Springfield Road, HANWELL,
London W7 3JP
Tel: 02085 676291
Head: Ms Gillian Carver
Category: SLD MSI PNLD
SLCN Complex medical
conditions (Coed Day 11-19)

NORTHOLT

Belvue School
Rowdell Road, NORTHOLT,
London UB5 6AG
Tel: 02088 455766
Head: Mrs Shelagh O'Shea
Category: MLD SLD ASD
(Coed Day 11-18)

John Chilton School
Compton Crescent, NORTHOLT,
London UB5 5LD
Tel: 02088 421329
Head: Mr Simon Rosenberg
Category: PH/Medical
(Coed Day 2-18)

London

ENFIELD

Education & Learning

Enfield SEN Team, Civic Centre, Silver Street, Enfield, Middlesex, EN1 3XY
Tel: 020 8379 5667 Email: sen@enfield.gov.uk Website: www.enfield.gov.uk

EDMONTON

West Lea School
Haselbury Road, EDMONTON,
London N9 9TU
Tel: 02088 072656
Head: Mrs Susan Tripp
Category: HA ASD PD
LD (Coed 4-18)

ENFIELD

Aylands School
Keswick Drive, ENFIELD,
London EN3 6NY
Tel: 01992 761229
Head: Ms Sashikala Sivaloganathan
Category: EBD (Coed 7-16)

Durants School
4 Pitfield Way, ENFIELD,
London EN3 5BY
Tel: 02088 041980
Head: Mr Peter De Rosa
Category: CLD ASD (Coed 4-19)

Russet House School
11 Autumn Close, ENFIELD,
London EN1 4JA
Tel: 02083 500650
Head: Mrs Julie Foster
Category: AUT (Coed 3-11)

Waverley School
105 The Ride, ENFIELD,
London EN2 7DL
Tel: 02088 051858
Head: Ms Gail Weir
Category: PMLD SLD (Coed 3-19)

SOUTHGATE

Oaktree School
Chase Side, SOUTHGATE,
London N14 4HN
Tel: 02084 403100
Head: Mr Richard Yarwood
Category: Complex
needs (Coed 7-19)

London

ROYAL BOROUGH OF GREENWICH
Children's Services

Greenwich SEN Team, The Woolwich Centre, 35 Wellington Street, Woolwich London, SE18 6HQ
Tel: 020 8921 8044 Email: special-needs@royalgreenwich.gov.uk Website: www.royalgreenwich.gov.uk

LONDON

Moatbridge School
Eltham Palace Road,
LONDON SE9 5LX
Tel: 02088 508081
Head: Mr Rich Buerckner
Category: BESD (Boys 11-19)

Waterside School
Robert Street, Plumstead,
LONDON SE18 7NB
Tel: 02083 177659
Head: Meic Griffiths
Category: BESD (Coed 5-11)

Willow Dene School
Swingate Lane, Plumstead,
LONDON SE18 2JD
Tel: 02088 549841
Executive Head: Mr John Camp
Category: SCLD CLD PMLD
PD ASD (Coed 3-11)

London

HACKNEY
Hackney Learning Trust

Hackney SEN Team, Hackney Family Information Service, 1 Reading Lane, London, E8 1GQ
Tel: 02088 207000 Fax: 02088 207001 Email: localoffer@learningtrust.co.uk Website: www.hackneylocaloffer.co.uk

LONDON

Ickburgh School
Kenworthy Road, LONDON E9 5RB
Tel: 02088 064638
Head: Ms Sue Davis
Category: SLD PMLD (2-19)

New Regents College (PRU)
Ickburgh Road, LONDON E5 8AD
Tel: 02089 856833
Head of Lower School: Ms
Sue Parillon

Stormont House School
Downs Park Road, LONDON E5 8NP
Tel: 02089 854245
Head: Mr Kevin McDonnell
Category: Complex
needs (Secondary)

The Garden School
Wordsworth Road,
LONDON N16 8BZ
Tel: 02072 548096
Head: Ms Pat Quigley
Category: MLD ASD (Secondary)

London

HAMMERSMITH & FULHAM
Council

Hammersmith & Fulham SEN Team, Kensington Town Hall, 2nd Floor, Green Zone, Hammersmith London, W8 7NX
Tel: 020 7361 3311 Email: sen@rbkc.gov.uk Website: www.lbhf.gov.uk

LONDON

Cambridge School
61 Bryony Road, Hammersmith,
LONDON W12 0SP
Tel: 02087 350980
Head: Mr Anthony Rawdin
Category: MLD (11-16)

Jack Tizard School
South Africa Road,
LONDON W12 7PA
Tel: 02087 353590
Head: Ms Cathy Welsh
Category: SLD PMLD
(Coed Day 3-19)

Queensmill School
1 Askham Road, Shepherds
Bush, LONDON W12 0NW
Tel: 02073 842330
Head: Ms Jude Ragan
Category: ASD (Coed 3-19)

**The Courtyard at
Langford Primary**
The Courtyard, Langford Primary,
Gilstead Road, LONDON SW6 2LG
Tel: 02076 108075
Head: Ms Janet Packer
Category: BESD (5-11)

Woodlane High School
Du Cane Road, LONDON W12 0TN
Tel: 02087 435668
Head: Mr Peter Harwood
Category: SCLN SPLD SEBD MSI
Medical difficulties (Coed 11-16)

Maintained special schools and colleges

London

HARINGEY
Council

Haringey Additional Needs & Disabilities, 40 Cumberland Road, London, N22 7SG
Tel: 020 8489 1913 Email: sen@haringey.gov.uk Website: www.haringey.gov.uk

MUSWELL HILL

Blanche Nevile Secondary School
Burlington Road, MUSWELL HILL, London N10 1NJ
Tel: 02084 422750
Head: Ms Veronica Held
Category: HI (Coed Day 11-18)

NORTH HILL

Blanche Nevile Primary School
Storey Road, NORTH HILL, London N6 4ED
Tel: 02083 473760
Head: Ms Veronica Held
Category: HI (Coed Day 3-10)

TOTTENHAM

Riverside School
Wood Green Inclusive Learning Campus, White Hart Lane, TOTTENHAM, London N22 5QJ
Tel: 02088 897814
Head: Mr Martin Doyle

The Brook on Broadwaters
Adams Road, TOTTENHAM, London N17 6HW
Tel: 02088 087120
Head: Ms Margaret Sumner
Category: CP EPI (Coed Day 4-11)

WEST GREEN

The Vale School
Northumberland Park Community School, Trulock Road, WEST GREEN, London N17 0PG
Tel: 02088 016111
Head: Ms Sarah McLay
Category: PD (Coed Day 2-16)

London

BOROUGH OF HARROW
Childrens Service

Harrow SEN Team, Alexandra Avenue Health & Social Care Centre, 275 Alexandra Avenue, South Harrow, Middlesex, HA2 9DX
Tel: 020 8966 6483 Fax: 020 8966 6489 Email: senassessment.reviewservice@ harrow.gov.uk Website: www.harrow.gov.uk

EDGWARE

Woodlands School
Bransgrove Road, EDGWARE, Middlesex HA8 6JP
Tel: 02083 812188
Head: Ms Anna Smakowska
Category: SLD PMLD ASD (Coed 3-11)

HARROW

Alexandra School
Alexandra Avenue, HARROW, Middlesex HA2 9DX
Tel: 02088 642739
Head: Ms Perdy Buchanan-Barrow
Category: MLD EBD ASD (Coed 4-11)

Kingsley High School
Whittlesea Road, HARROW, Middlesex HA3 6ND
Tel: 02084 213676
Head: Mrs Hazel Paterson
Category: SLD PMLD (Coed 11-19)

Shaftesbury High School
Headstone Lane, HARROW, Middlesex HA3 6LE
Tel: 02084 282482
Head: Mr Paul Williams
Category: MLD EBD ASD (Coed 11-19)

London Borough of

HAVERING
Education Authority

Havering Early Education Inclusion Team, 9th Floor, Mercury House, Mercury Gardens, Romford, Essex, RM1 3DW
Tel: 01708 431783 Email: localoffer@havering.gov.uk Website: www.havering.gov.uk

ROMFORD

Dycorts School
Settle Road, Harold Hill, ROMFORD, Essex RM3 9YA
Tel: 01708 343649
Executive Head: Mr Gary Pocock
Category: MLD

Ravensbourne School
Neave Cres, Faringdon Ave, Harold Hill, ROMFORD, Essex RM3 8HN
Tel: 01708 341800
Head: Ms Joanna Cliffe
Category: SLD PMLD

UPMINSTER

Corbets Tey School
Harwood Hall Lane, Corbets Tey,
UPMINSTER, Essex RM14 2YQ
Tel: 01708 225888
Head: Mrs Emma Allen
Category: MLD/SLD/
Complex Needs

London
HILLINGDON
Education

Hillingdon SEN Team, 4E/05, Civic Centre, High Street, Uxbridge, Middlesex, UB8 1UW
Tel: 01895 250244 Fax: 01895 250878 Email: cmoses@hillingdon.gov.uk Website: www.hillingdon.gov.uk

HAYES
Hedgewood Special School
Weymouth Road, HAYES,
Middlesex UB4 8NF
Tel: 02088 456756
Head: Mr John Goddard
Category: MLD ASD
Complex moderate learning
needs (Coed 5-11)

ICKENHAM
Pentland Field School
Pentland Way, ICKENHAM,
Middlesex UB10 8TS
Tel: 01895 609120
Head: Audrey Pantelis
Category: MLD SLD (Coed 4-19)

PINNER
Grangewood School
Fore Street, Eastcote, PINNER,
Middlesex HA5 2JQ
Tel: 01895 676401
Head: Ms Karen Clark
Category: SLD PMLD
AUT (Coed 3-11)

UXBRIDGE
Meadow High School
Royal Lane, Hillingdon,
UXBRIDGE, Middlesex UB8 3QU
Tel: 01895 443310
Head: Mr Ross McDonald
Category: CLD ASD
Complex moderate learning
needs (Coed 11-19)

London
HOUNSLOW
Information, Advice & Support Service

Hounslow SENDIASS, Civic Centre, Lampton Road, Hounslow, TW3 4DN
Tel: 02085 832672 Email: sendiass@hounslow.gov.uk Website: www.hounslow.gov.uk

BEDFONT
Marjory Kinnon School
Hatton Road, BEDFONT,
London TW14 9QZ
Tel: 02088 908890
Head: Ms Denise Morton
Category: MLD AUT (5-16)

FELTHAM
The Rise School
Browells Lane, FELTHAM,
London TW13 7EF
Tel: 02080 990640
Head: Ms Sarah Roscoe
Category: AUT (4-18)

ISLEWORTH
Oaklands School
Woodlands Road, ISLEWORTH,
London TW7 6JZ
Tel: 02085 603569
Head: Ms Anne Clinton
Category: SLD (Secondary)

CRANFORD
The Cedars Primary School
High Street, CRANFORD,
London TW5 9RU
Tel: 02082 300015
Head: Mrs Lesley Julian
Category: EBD (Primary)

HANWORTH
The Lindon Bennett School
Main Street, HANWORTH,
London TW13 6ST
Tel: 02088 980479
Head: Ms Clare Longhurst
Category: SLD (3-11)

London

ISLINGTON

Special Educational Needs team

Islington SEN Team, First Floor, 222 Upper Street, London, N1 1XR
Tel: 0-13: 020 7527 5518; 14-25: 020 7527 4860 Email: sen@islington.gov.uk Website: www.islington.gov.uk

LONDON

Richard Cloudesley Primary School
Golden Lane Campus,
101 Whitecross Street,
LONDON EC1Y 8JA
Tel: 020 7786 4800
Head: Mr Sean McDonald
Category: PD (Coed 2-11)

Richard Cloudesley Secondary School
Tudor Rose Building, 1 Prebend Street, LONDON N1 8RE
Tel: 020 7704 8127
Head: Mr Sean McDonald
Category: PD (Coed 11-19)

Samuel Rhodes Primary School
Montem Community Campus,
Hornsey Road, LONDON N7 7QT
Tel: 020 7281 5114
Head: Ms Julie Keylock
Category: MLD ASD
BESD (Coed 5-11)

Samuel Rhodes Secondary School
11 Highbury New Park,
LONDON N5 2EG
Tel: 020 7704 7490
Head: Ms Julie Keylock
Category: MLD ASD
BESD (Coed 11-18)

The Bridge Primary School
251 Hungerford Road,
LONDON N7 9LD
Tel: 020 7619 1000
Head: Ms Penny Barratt
Category: ASD SLD
PMLD (Coed 2-11)

The Bridge Secondary School
28 Carleton Road, LONDON N7 0EQ
Tel: 020 7715 0320
Head: Ms Penny Barratt
Category: ASD SLD
PMLD (Coed 11-19)

London

ROYAL BOROUGH OF KINGSTON UPON THAMES

Education Authority

Richmond & Kingston SENDIASS, Moor Lane Centre, Chessington Kingston upon Thames, Surrey, KT9 2AA
Tel: 020 8831 6179 Email: richmondkingston@kids.org.uk Website: www.kingston.gov.uk

CHESSINGTON

St Philip's School & Post 16
Harrow Close, Leatherhead Road,
CHESSINGTON, Surrey KT9 2HR
Tel: 02083 972672
Head: Mrs Jude Bowen
Category: MLD SLD ASD (11-19)

KINGSTON UPON THAMES

Bedelsford School
Grange Road, KINGSTON UPON THAMES, Surrey KT1 2QZ
Tel: 02085 469838
Head: Ms Julia James
Category: PD PMLD MSI CLD (2-19)

SURBITON

Dysart School
190 Ewell Road, SURBITON,
Surrey KT6 6HL
Tel: 02084 122600
Head: Ms Leigh Edser
Category: SLD ASD PMLD (5-19)

London

LAMBETH

Children & Young People's Service

Lambeth SEN Team, 10th Floor, International House, Canterbury Crescent, Brixton London, SW9 7QE
Email: sendsupport@lambeth.gov.uk Website: www.lambeth.gov.uk

RUSKIN PARK

The Michael Tippet School
Heron Road, RUSKIN PARK,
London SE24 0HZ
Tel: 02073 265898
Head: Ms Marilyn Ross
Category: CLD AUT PD
SLD PMLD (Coed 11-18)

STOCKWELL

Lansdowne School
Argyll Close, Dalyell Road,
STOCKWELL, London SW9 9QL
Tel: 02077 373713
Head: Ms Linda Adams
Category: MLD SEBD ASD
CLD SLD (Coed 11-15)

STREATHAM

The Livity School
Adare walk, STREATHAM,
London SW16 2PW
Tel: 02087 691009
Acting Head: Ms Carol Argent
Category: SLD PMLD
ASD (Coed 2-11)

WEST DULWICH

Turney School
Turney Road, WEST DULWICH,
London SE21 8LX
Tel: 02086 707220
Head: Ms Linda Adams
Category: MLD SLD CLD
ASD (Coed 5-10)

WEST NORWOOD

Elm Court School
96 Elm Park, WEST NORWOOD,
London SW2 2EF
Tel: 02086 743412
Head: Ms Joanna Tarrant
Category: SEBN SLCN (Coed 6-16)

London

LEWISHAM

Children & Young People

Lewisham SEN Team, Kaleidoscope Child Development Centre, 32 Rushey Green, London, SE6 4JF
Tel: 02030 491475 Email: sen@lewisham.gov.uk Website: www.lewisham.gov.uk

BROMLEY

Drumbeat School
Roundtable Road, Downham,
BROMLEY, Kent BR1 5LE
Tel: 02086 989738
Head: Dr Vivan Hinchcliffe
Category: ASD (5-19)

DOWNHAM

New Woodlands School
49 Shroffold Road,
DOWNHAM, Kent BR1 5PD
Tel: 02086 952380
Head: Mr Duncan Harper
Category: BESD (Coed 5-14)

LONDON

Abbey Manor College
40 Falmouth Close, Lee,
LONDON SE12 8PJ
Tel: 02082 977060
Head: Dr Liz Jones
Category: BESD (Coed 11-19)

Brent Knoll School
Mayow Road, Forest Hill,
LONDON SE23 2XH
Tel: 02086 991047
Head: Mr Jonathan Sharpe
Category: AUT ASP SLCN
Emotionally Vulnerable (Coed 4-16)

Greenvale School
Waters Road, LONDON SE6 1UF
Tel: 02084 650740
Head: Ms Lynne Haines
Category: SLD PMLD (Coed 11-19)

Watergate School
Lushington Road, Bellingham,
LONDON SE6 3WG
Tel: 02086 956555
Head: ¡ine Nì Ruairc
Category: SLD PMLD (Coed 3-11)

London

MERTON

Department of Children, Schools and Families

Merton SENDIS, 1st Floor, Civic Centre, London Road, Morden, Surrey, SM4 5DX
Tel: 02085 454810 Email: sen@merton.gov.uk Website: www.merton.gov.uk

MITCHAM

Cricket Green School
Lower Green West, MITCHAM,
Surrey CR4 3AF
Tel: 02086 401177
Head: Mrs Celia Dawson
Category: CLD (Coed 5-19)

Melrose School
Church Road, MITCHAM,
Surrey CR4 3BE
Tel: 02086 462620
Head: Mr Steve Childs
Category: SEBD (Coed 11-16)

MORDEN

Perseid School
Bordesley Road, MORDEN,
Surrey SM4 5LT
Tel: 02086 489737
Head: Mrs Tina Harvey
Category: PMLD (Coed 3-19)

London

NEWHAM

Council

Newham SEN Team, Newham Dockside, 1000 Dockside Road, London, E16 2QU
Tel: 02084 302000 Website: www.newham.gov.uk

BECKTON

**Eleanor Smith KS3
Annexe (Secondary)**
90a Lawson Close, BECKTON,
London E16 3LU
Tel: 020 7511 3222
Head Teacher: Mr Graham Smith
Category: SEBD (11-16)

PLAISTOW

**Eleanor Smith
School (Primary)**
North Street, PLAISTOW,
London E13 9HN
Tel: 020 8471 0018
Head Teacher: Mr Graham Smith
Category: SEBD (5-10)

STRATFORD

John F Kennedy School
Pitchford Street, STRATFORD,
London E15 4RZ
Tel: 020 8534 8544
Executive Head Teacher: Ms
Diane Rochford
Category: SLD PMLD ASD Complex
medical needs (Coed 2-19)

London

REDBRIDGE

Education Authority

Redbridge SEN Team, Lynton House, 255-259 High Road, Ilford, Essex, IG1 1NN
Tel: 02085 545000 Email: customer.cc@redbridge.gov.uk Website: www.redbridge.gov.uk

GOODMAYES

**Newbridge School -
Barley Lane Campus**
258 Barley Lane, GOODMAYES,
Essex IG3 8XS
Tel: 02085 991768
Head: Mrs L Parr
Category: SLD PMLD ASD
Complex medical needs (11-19)

HAINAULT

New Rush Hall School
Fencepiece Road,
HAINAULT, Essex IG6 2LB
Tel: 02085 013951
Head: Mr J V d'Abbro OBE
Category: SEMH (5-15)

ROMFORD

**Little Heath
Foundation School**
Hainault Road, Little Heath,
ROMFORD, Essex RM6 5RX
Tel: 02085 994864
Head: Mr J Brownlie
Category: MLD Learning difficulties
& complex needs (11-19)

**Newbridge School -
Gresham Drive Campus**
161 Gresham Drive, Chadwell
Heath, ROMFORD, Essex RM6 4TR
Tel: 02085 907272
Head: Mrs L Parr
Category: SLD PMLD ASD
Complex medical needs (2-11)

WOODFORD GREEN

Hatton School
Roding Lane South, WOODFORD
GREEN, Essex IG8 8EU
Tel: 02085 514131
Head: Mrs Sue Blows
Category: AUT SP&LD (3-11)

London

RICHMOND UPON THAMES

Parent Partnership Service

Richmond SEN Team, Parent Partnership Service, Croft Centre, Windham Road, Richmond, Middlesex, TW9 2HP
Tel: 020 8891 7541 Website: www.richmond.gov.uk

HAMPTON

Clarendon School
Hanworth Road, HAMPTON,
Surrey TW12 3DH
Tel: 02089 791165
Head: Mr John Kipps
Category: MLD (7-16)
(offsite EBD 7-11)

RICHMOND

Strathmore School
Meadlands Drive, Petersham,
RICHMOND, Surrey TW10 7ED
Tel: 02089 480047
Head: Mr Ivan Pryce
Category: SLD PMLD (7-19)

London

SOUTHWARK

Council

Southwark SEN Team, PO Box 64529, London, SE1P 5LX
Tel: 02075 254278 Email: sen@southwark.gov.uk Website: www.southwark.gov.uk

BERMONDSEY

Beormund Primary School
Crosby Row, Long Lane,
BERMONDSEY SE1 3PS
Tel: 02075 259027
Head: Mr Andrew Henderson
Category: EBD (Boys 5-11)

Cherry Garden School
Macks Road, BERMONDSEY
SE16 3XU
Tel: 02072 374050
Head: Ms Teresa Neary
Category: SCLD (Coed 2-11)

Spa School
Monnow Road,
BERMONDSEY SE1 5RN
Tel: 02072 373714
Head: Mr Simon Eccles
Category: MLD AUT ASP
SLD SCD (Coed 11-19)

PECKHAM

Highshore Secondary School
Bellenden Road,
PECKHAM SE15 5BB
Tel: 02076 397211
Head: Ms Christine Wood
Category: DYS PD SLCN EBD
Complex needs (Coed 11-16)

Newlands School
Stuart Road, PECKHAM SE15 3AZ
Tel: 02076 392541
Head: Ms Debbie Lipkin
Category: SEBD (Boys 11-16)

Tuke Secondary School
Daniels Gardens,
PECKHAM SE15 6ER
Tel: 02076 395584
Head: Ms Heidi Tully
Category: SLD PMLD
ASD (Coed 11-19)

London

SUTTON

Local Offer

Sutton SEN Team, Civic Offices, St Nicholas Way, Sutton, Surrey, SM5 3AL
Tel: 02087 706000 Email: familyinfo@sutton.gov.uk Website: www.sutton.gov.uk

WALLINGTON

Sherwood Park School
Streeters Lane, WALLINGTON,
Surrey SM6 7NP
Tel: 02087 739930
Head: Mrs Ann Nanasi
Category: SLD PMLD (Coed 2-19)

London

TOWER HAMLETS

Family Information Service (FIS)

Tower Hamlets SEN Team, 30 Greatorex Street, London, E1 5NP
Tel: 020 7364 6486 Email: fis@towerhamlets.gov.uk Website: www.towerhamlets.gov.uk

BOW

Cherry Trees School
68 Campbell Road, BOW,
London E3 4EA
Tel: 02089 834344
Head: Mr Stuart Walker
Category: SEBD (Boys Day 5-11)

Phoenix School
49 Bow Road, BOW, London E3 2AD
Tel: 02089 804740
Head: Mr Stewart Harris
Category: ASD (Coed Day 3-19)

BROMLEY-BY-BOW

Ian Mikardo High School
60 William Guy Gardens,
Talwin Street, BROMLEY-BY-
BOW, London E3 3LF
Tel: 02089 812413
Head: Ms Claire Lillis
Category: SEBD (Boys Day 11-16)

LIMEHOUSE

Stephen Hawking School
2 Brunton Place, LIMEHOUSE,
London E14 7LL
Tel: 02074 239848
Head: Dr Matthew Rayner
Category: PMLD (Coed Day 2-11)

MILE END

Beatrice Tate School
Poplar Day Centre, 40 Southern
Grove, MILE END, London E3 4PX
Tel: 02089 833760
Acting Head: Mr Michael Whaley
Category: PMLD SLD
(Coed Day 11-19)

London

WALTHAM FOREST

Special Educational Needs Disability Information, Advice & Support Service

Waltham Forest SENDIASS, 220 Hoe Street, Walthamstow London, E17 3AY
Tel: 020 3233 0251 Email: wfsendiass@walthamforestcab.org.uk Website: www.walthamforest.gov.uk

HALE END

Joseph Clarke School
Vincent Road, Highams Park,
HALE END, London E4 9PP
Tel: 02085 234833
Head: Ms Isobel Cox
Category: VIS Complex
needs (Coed 2-18)

LEYTON

Belmont Park School
101 Leyton Green Road,
LEYTON, London E10 6DB
Tel: 02085 560006
Head: Mr Bruce Roberts
Category: Challenging
behaviour (Coed 11-16)

WALTHAMSTOW

Whitefield Schools
Macdonald Road, WALTHAMSTOW,
London E17 4AZ
Tel: 02085 313426
Executive Principal: Ms Laura Pease
Category: LD MSI SP&LD (Coed 2-19)

London

WANDSWORTH

Family Information Service (FIS)

Wandsworth SEN Team, The Town Hall, High Street, Wandsworth London, SW18 3LL
Tel: 020 8871 7899 Email: fis@wandsworth.gov.uk Website: fis.wandsworth.gov.uk

BALHAM

Oak Lodge School
101 Nightingale Lane,
BALHAM, London SW12 8NA
Tel: 02086 733453
Head: Ms Shanee Buxton
Category: D (Coed, Day/
boarding 11-19)

BROADSTAIRS

Bradstow School
34 Dumpton Park Drive,
BROADSTAIRS, Kent CT10 1BY
Tel: 01843 862123
Head: Ms Sarah Dunn
Category: PD AUT Challenging
behaviour (Coed 5-19)

EARLSFIELD

Garratt Park School
Waldron Road, EARLSFIELD,
London SW18 3BT
Tel: 02089 465769
Head: Mrs Irene Parks
Category: MLD SP&LD (Coed 11-18)

PUTNEY

Paddock Primary School
St Margaret's Crescent,
PUTNEY, London SW15 6HL
Tel: 02087 885648
Head: Mrs Sarah Santos
Category: ASD MLD SLD (Coed 3-11)

ROEHAMPTON

Greenmead School
St Margaret's Crescent,
ROEHAMPTON, London SW15 6HL
Tel: 02087 891466
Head: Ms Toni Edmonds-Smith
Category: PD PMLD (Coed 3-11)

Paddock Secondary School
Priory Lane, ROEHAMPTON,
London SW15 5RT
Tel: 02088 781521
Head: Mrs Sarah Santos
Category: SCLD ASD with
SLD (Coed 11-19)

SOUTHFIELDS

Linden Lodge School
61 Princes Way, SOUTHFIELDS,
London SW19 6JB
Tel: 02087 880107
Head: Mr Roger Legate
Category: VIS PMLD MSI (Coed 3-11)

TOOTING

Nightingale School
Beechcroft Road, TOOTING,
London SW17 7DF
Tel: 02088 749096
Head: Ms Alina Page
Category: BESD (Boys 11-19)

London

CITY OF WESTMINSTER

Children's Service Authority

Westminster SEN Team, The Town Hall, 2nd Floor, Green Zone, Hornton Street London, W8 7NX
Tel: 02073 613311 Website: www.westminster.gov.uk

LONDON

College Park School
Garway Road, LONDON W2 4PH
Tel: 020 7221 3454
Head: Mr Andy Balmer
Category: MLD (Coed 4-19)

Queen Elizabeth II Jubilee School
Kennet Road, LONDON W9 3LG
Tel: 020 7641 5825
Head: Mr Andy Balmer
Category: SLD (Coed 5-19)

LUTON

Information, Advice & Support Service

Luton SENDIAS, Futures House, The Moakes, Luton, LU3 3QB
Tel: 01525 719754 Email: parentpartnership@luton.gov.uk Website: www.luton.gov.uk

LUTON

Lady Zia Werner School
Ashcroft Road, LUTON,
Bedfordshire LU2 9AY
Tel: 01582 728705
Head: Mrs Diane May
Category: SLD PMLD (Yr
1-6 & Early Years)

Richmond Hill School
Sunridge Avenue, LUTON,
Bedfordshire LU2 7JL
Tel: 01582 721019
Head: Mrs Jill Miller
Category: SLD PMLD (Primary Yr 1-6)

Woodlands Secondary School
Northwell Drive, LUTON,
Bedfordshire LU3 3SP
Tel: 01582 572880
Head: Mrs Debbie Foolkes
Category: SLD PMLD (11-19)

Greater Manchester

BOLTON

Children's Services Offices

Bolton Inclusion & Statutory Assessment, Paderborn House, 16 Howell Croft North, Bolton, BL1 1AU
Tel: 01204 338612 Email: ea.sen@bolton.gov.uk Website: www.bolton.gov.uk

BOLTON

Firwood School
Stitch Mi Lane, BOLTON BL2 4HU
Tel: 01204 333044
Head: Mrs Sally McFarlane
Category: SLD PMLD
ASD (Coed 11-19)

Ladywood School
Masefield Road, Little
Lever, BOLTON BL3 1NG
Tel: 01204 333400
Head: Mrs Sally McFarlane
Category: MLD with Complex
needs incl ASD PD MSI (Coed 4-11)

Rumworth School
Armadale Road, Ladybridge,
BOLTON BL3 4TP
Tel: 01204 333600
Head: Mr Gary Johnson
Category: MLD with Complex
needs incl ASD PD MSI (Coed 11-19)

**Thomasson
Memorial School**
Devonshire Road, BOLTON BL1 4PJ
Tel: 01204 333118
Head: Mr Bill Wilson
Category: D HI (Coed 4-11)

FARNWORTH

Green Fold School
Highfield Road,
FARNWORTH BL4 0RA
Tel: 01204 335883
Head: Mr Andrew Feeley
Category: SLD ASD
PMLD (Coed 4-11)

HORWICH

Lever Park School
Stocks Park Drive, HORWICH BL6 6DE
Tel: 01204 332666
Head: Mr Colin Roscoe
Category: SEBD (Coed 11-16)

Greater Manchester

BURY

Information, Advice & Support Service

Bury SENDIAS, Town Hall, Knowsley Street, Bury, Lancashire, BL9 0SW
Tel: 0161 705 4366 Email: iass@pointoldham.co.uk Website: www.iassbury.co.uk

BURY

**Elms Bank Specialist
Arts College**
Ripon Avenue, Whitefield,
BURY M45 8PJ
Tel: 01617 661597
Head: Mrs Elaine Parkinson
Category: LD (Coed 11-19)

Millwood School
School Street, Radcliffe,
BURY M26 3BW
Tel: 01617 242266
Head: Ms Helen Chadwick
Category: SLD PMLD ASD AUT
Complex needs (Coed 2-11)

Primary PRU - The Ark
The Pupil Learning Centre,
Whitefield, BURY M45 8NH
Tel: 01617 963259
Head: Ms Julie Hart
Category: (Coed 5-11)

PRESTWICH

**Cloughside College
(Hospital Special School)**
Bury New Road,
PRESTWICH M25 3BL
Tel: 01617 724625
Interim Head: Ms Janice Cahill
Category: HS (Coed 11-19)

RAMSBOTTOM

**Secondary PRU - New
Summerseat House**
Summerseat Lane,
RAMSBOTTOM BL0 9UD
Tel: 01204 885275
Head: Mr Thomas Gledhill
Category: (Coed 9-16)

Greater Manchester

MANCHESTER
City Council

Manchester SEN Team, Children's Services, 1st Floor, Universal Square,
Devonshire Street North Manchester, Lancashire, M12 6JH
Tel: 01612 457459 Fax: 01612 747084 Email: sen@manchester.gov.uk Website: www.manchester.gov.uk

CONGLETON

Buglawton Hall
Buxton Road, CONGLETON,
Cheshire CW12 3PQ
Tel: 01260 274492
Head of Centre: Mr Jonathan Gillie
Category: SEBD
(Residential Boys 8-16)

MANCHESTER

Ashgate School
Crossacres Road, Peel
Hall, Wythenshawe,
MANCHESTER M22 5DR
Tel: 01612 196642
Headteacher: Ms Dianne
Wolstenholme
Category: SLD (5-11)

Camberwell Park
Bank House Road, Blackley,
MANCHESTER M9 8LT
Tel: 01617 401897
Headteacher: Mrs Mary Isherwood
Category: SLD (5-11)

Grange School
Matthews Lane, Longsight,
MANCHESTER M12 4GR
Tel: 01612 312590
Headteacher: Mr Keith Cox
Category: ASD CLD (4-19)

Lancasterian School
Elizabeth Springer Road, West
Didsbury, MANCHESTER M20 2XA
Tel: 01614 450123
Headteacher: Mrs Katie Cass
Category: PD (2-16)

**Manchester Hospital
Schools & Home
Teaching Service**
Third Floor School, Royal
Manchester Children's
Hospital, Oxford Road,
MANCHESTER M13 9WL
Tel: 01617 010684
Head of Centre: Mrs Sandra Hibbert
Category: HS

Meade Hill School
Chain Road, Higher Blackley,
MANCHESTER M9 6GN
Tel: 01612 343925
Head of Centre: Mr
George Campbell
Category: SEBD (11-16)

Melland High School
Gorton Education Village,
50 Wembley Road, Gorton,
MANCHESTER M18 7DT
Tel: 01612 239915
Headteacher: Ms Sue Warner
Category: SLD (11-19)

North Ridge High School
Higher Blackley Education
Village, Alworth Road,
MANCHESTER M9 0RP
Tel: 01612 343588
Headteacher: Mrs Bernice Kostick
Category: MLD (11-19)

Piper Hill High School
Firbank Road, Newall Green,
MANCHESTER M23 2YS
Tel: 01614 363009
Headteacher: Ms Linda Jones
Category: SLD (11-19)

Rodney House School
Albert Grove, Longsight,
MANCHESTER M12 4WF
Tel: 0161 230 6854
Headteacher: Ms Nuala Finegan
Category: ASD (2-7)

Southern Cross School
Barlow Hall Road, Chorlton,
MANCHESTER M21 7JJ
Tel: 01618 812695
Head of Centre: Ms Kate Scott
Category: SEBD (11-16)

The Birches
Newholme Road, West Didsbury,
MANCHESTER M20 2XZ
Tel: 01614 488895
Headteacher: Mr Rob O'Hara
Category: SLD (5-11)

Greater Manchester

OLDHAM
Parent Partnership Service

Oldham SENDIASS, Italia House, Pass Street, Oldham, Greater Manchester, OL9 6HZ
Tel: 01616 672055 Email: iass@pointoldham.co.uk Website: www.oldham.gov.uk

CHADDERTON

**The Kingfisher Community
Special School**
Foxdenton Lane,
CHADDERTON OL9 9QR
Tel: 01617 705910
Head: Mrs Anne Redmond
Category: PMLD SLD
ASD (Coed 4-11)

OLDHAM

**New Bridge
Learning Centre**
St Martin's Road, Fitton
Hill, OLDHAM OL8 2PZ
Tel: 01618 832402
Head: Mrs Jean Warner
Category: (Coed 16-19)

New Bridge School
Roman Road, Hollinwood,
OLDHAM, Greater
Manchester OL8 3PH
Tel: 01618 832401
Head: Mrs Jane Hilldrup
Category: PMLD SLD MLD
ASD PD (Coed 11-19)

Spring Brook School
Heron Street, OLDHAM, Greater
Manchester OL8 4JD
Tel: 01617 705007
Head: Ms Rebeckah Hollingsworth
Category: BESD (Coed 4-16)

Greater Manchester

ROCHDALE
Metropolitan Borough Council

Rochdale SEN Assessment Team, Number One Riverside, Smith Street, Rochdale, OL16 1XU
Tel: 01706 925981 Email: sen@rochdale.gov.uk Website: www.rochdale.gov.uk

MIDDLETON

Newlands School
Waverley Road,
MIDDLETON M24 6JG
Tel: 01616 550220
Head: Mrs Deborah Rogers
Category: Generic Primary
Special School (Coed 3-11)

ROCHDALE

Brownhill School
Heights Lane, ROCHDALE OL12 0PZ
Tel: 03003 038384
Head: Mrs Kate Connolly
Category: EBD (Coed 7-16)

Redwood School
Hudson's Walk, ROCHDALE OL11 5EF
Tel: 01706 750815
Head: Mr Stuart Pidgeon
Category: Generic Secondary
Special School (Coed 11-19)

Springside School
Albert Royds Street,
ROCHDALE OL16 2SU
Tel: 01706 764451
Head: Ms Clare John
Category: Generic Primary
Special School (Coed 3-11)

Greater Manchester

SALFORD
Information, Advice & Support Services

Salford SENDIASS, Salford Civic Centre, Chorley Road, Swinton Salford, M27 5AW
Tel: 0161 778 0335 Email: siass@salford.gov.uk Website: www.salford.gov.uk

ECCLES

Chatsworth High School
Chatsworth Road, Ellesmere
Park, ECCLES M30 9DY
Tel: 01619 211405
Head: Mr Martin Hanbury
Category: SLD PMLD
ASD (Coed 11-19)

New Park High School
Green Lane, ECCLES M30 0RW
Tel: 01619 212000
Head: Ms Almut Bever-Warren
Category: SEBD LD (Coed 8-16)

SWINTON

Springwood Primary School
Barton Road, SWINTON M27 5LP
Tel: 01617 780022
Head: Ms Jacqui Wennington
Category: ASD MLD SLD
PMLD (Coed 2-11)

Greater Manchester

STOCKPORT
Metropolitan Borough Council

Stockport SEN Team, Town Hall, Edward Street, Stockport, SK1 3XE
Tel: 0161 474 2525 Email: sen@stockport.gov.uk Website: www.stockport.gov.uk

STOCKPORT

Castle Hill High School
The Fairway, Offerton,
STOCKPORT SK2 5DS
Tel: 01612 853925
Head: Mr John Law
Category: EBD GLD
CLD (Coed 11-16)

Heaton School
St James Road, Heaton Moor,
STOCKPORT SK4 4RE
Tel: 01614 321931
Head: Ms Jo Chambers-Shirley
Category: SLD PMLD (Coed 10-19)

Lisburne School
Half Moon Lane, Offerton,
STOCKPORT SK2 5LB
Tel: 01614 835045
Head: Ms Samantha Benson
Category: CLD (Coed 4-11)

Oakgrove School
Matlock Road, Heald Green,
STOCKPORT SK8 3BU
Tel: 01614 374956
Head: Mr Rob Metcalfe
Category: SEBD (Coed 5-11)

Valley School
Whitehaven Road, Bramhall,
STOCKPORT SK7 1EN
Tel: 01614 397343
Head: Ms Debbie Thompson
Category: PMLD ASD
SLD (Coed 2-11)

Windlehurst School
Windlehurst Road, Hawk Green,
Marple, STOCKPORT SK6 7HZ
Tel: 01614 274788
Head: Ms Lesley Abercromby
Category: EBD (Coed 11-16)

Greater Manchester

TAMESIDE

Services for Children and Young People

Tameside SENDIASS, Jubilee Gardens, Gardenfold Way, Droylsden, Tameside, M43 7XU
Tel: 0161 342 3383 Website: www.tameside.gov.uk

ASHTON-UNDER LYNE

Samuel Laycock School
Broadoak Road, ASHTON-UNDER LYNE, Tameside OL6 8RF
Tel: 01613 441992
Head: Mr Alistair Macdonald
Category: MLD (Secondary)

AUDENSHAW

Hawthorns School
Sunnyside Moss Campus, Lumb Lane, AUDENSHAW, Tameside M34 5SF
Tel: 01613 701312
Head: Mrs Moira Thompson
Category: MLD (Primary)

DUKINFIELD

Cromwell School
Yew Tree Lane, DUKINFIELD, Tameside SK16 5BJ
Tel: 01613 389730
Head: Mr Andrew Foord
Category: SLD PMLD MLD (Secondary)

Oakdale School
Cheetham Hill Road, DUKINFIELD, Tameside SK16 5LD
Tel: 01613 679299
Head: Ms Linda Lester
Category: SLD PMLD (Primary)

White Bridge College
Globe Lane, DUKINFIELD, Tameside SK16 4UJ
Tel: 0161 214 8484
Head: Mr Michael Wain
Category: (Secondary)

HYDE

Thomas Ashton School
Bennett Street, HYDE, Tameside SK14 4SS
Tel: 01613 686208
Head: Mr Robin Elms
Category: BESD (Primary)

Greater Manchester

TRAFFORD

Family Information Service

Trafford FIS, 2nd Floor, Waterside House, Sale, Manchester, M33 72F
Tel: 01619 121053 Email: fis@trafford.gov.uk Website: www.trafford.gov.uk/localoffer

ALTRINCHAM

Pictor School
Grove Lane, Timperley, ALTRINCHAM, Cheshire WA15 6PH
Tel: 01619 123082
Head: Ms Jacqui Wheble
Category: SLCN SPLD ASD PD MLD (Coed 2-11)

FLIXTON

Delamere School
Irlam Road, FLIXTON, Greater Manchester M41 6AP
Tel: 01617 475893
Head: Mrs Sally Burston
Category: ASD SLD (Coed 2-11)

Nexus Education Centre (Pupil Referral Unit)
Lydney Road, FLIXTON, Manchester M41 8RN
Tel: 01619 121479
Category: (Coed 5-16)

Trafford Medical Education Service (Pupil Referral Unit)
The Flixton Centre, 350 Flixton Road, FLIXTON, Manchester M41 5GW
Tel: 01619 124766

SALE

Brentwood High School & Community College
Cherry Lane, SALE, Cheshire M33 4GY
Tel: 01619 052371
Head: Mrs Hilary Moon
Category: ASD SLD (Coed 11-19)

STRETFORD

Longford Park School
74 Cromwell Road, STRETFORD, Greater Manchester M32 8QJ
Tel: 01619 121895
Head: Mr Andrew Taylor
Category: SEMH MLD ASD (Coed 5-11)

URMSTON

Egerton High School
Kingsway Park, URMSTON, Greater Manchestereof, SEMH (Coed 5-16)
Tel: 01617 497094
Head: Mr Burgess, SEMH (Coed 5-16)

Greater Manchester

WIGAN

Information, Advice & Support Service

Wigan SENDIASS, Wigan Council, PO Box 100, Wigan, Greater Manchester, WN1 3DS
Tel: 01942 486131 Website: www.wigan.gov.uk

ATHERTON

Rowan Tree Primary School
Green Hall Close, ATHERTON,
Greater Manchester M46 9HP
Tel: 01942 883928
Head: Ms Elizabeth Loftus
Category: PD CLD AUT (Coed 2-11)

WIGAN

Hope School and College
Kelvin Grove, Marus Bridge,
WIGAN WN3 6SP
Tel: 01942 824150
Head: Ms Sue Lucas
Category: ASD SLD
PMLD (Coed 2-19)

Landgate School
Landgate Lane, Bryn,
WIGAN WN4 0EP
Tel: 01942 776688
Head: Ms Kathy Claxton
Category: AUT SP&LD (Coed 4-19)

**Newbridge Learning
Community School**
Moss Lane, Platt Bridge,
WIGAN WN2 3TL
Tel: 01942 776020
Head: Mrs Elaine Kucharski

Oakfield High School
Long Lane, Hindley Green,
WIGAN WN2 4XA
Tel: 01942 776142
Head: Ms Sue Allen
Category: MLD SLD PD
SEBD (Coed 11-19)

**Willow Grove
Primary School**
Willow Grove, Ashton-in-
Makerfield, WIGAN WN4 8XF
Tel: 01942 727717
Head: Mrs Joanna Murphy
Category: SEBD (Coed 5-11)

MEDWAY

Local Offer

Medway SEN Team, Family Information Service, Gun Wharf, Dock Road Chatham, ME4 4TR
Tel: 01634 332195 Email: familyinfo@medway.gov.uk Website: www.medway.gov.uk

CHATHAM

Inspire Free School
Silverbank, Churchill Avenue,
CHATHAM, Kent ME5 0LB
Tel: 01634 827372
Head: Ms Sharon McDermott
Category: SEMH (Coed 11-19)

GILLINGHAM

Danecourt School
Hotel Road, Watling Street,
GILLINGHAM, Kent ME8 6AA
Tel: 01634 232589
Head: Ms Deanne Daburn
Category: ASD SLD (Coed 4-11)

Rivermead School
Forge Lane, GILLINGHAM,
Kent ME7 1UG
Tel: 01634 338348
Head: Mrs Tina Lovey
Category: ASD Complex
emotional needs (Coed 11-19)

STROOD

Abbey Court
Rede Court Road, STROOD,
Kent ME2 3SP
Tel: 01634 338220
Head: Ms Karen Joy
Category: SLD PMLD (Coed 4-19)

Merseyside

KNOWSLEY

Children & Family Services

Knowsley SEN Team, The Cordingley Building, Scotchbarn Lane, Prescot, Merseyside, L35 7JD
Tel: 01514 435145 Email: sen@knowsley.gov.uk Website: www.knowsley.gov.uk

HALEWOOD

Finch Woods Academy
Baileys Lane, HALEWOOD,
Merseyside L26 0TY
Tel: 01512 888930
Head: Ms Pam Kilham
Category: SEBD (Coed 6-16)

HUYTON

**Alt Bridge Secondary
Support Centre**
Wellcroft Road, HUYTON,
Merseyside L36 7TA
Tel: 01514 778310
Head: Mr Barry Kerwin
Category: MLD SPLD CLD
ASD SLD PD (Coed 11-16)

**Knowsley Central Primary
Support Centre**
Mossbrow Road, HUYTON,
Merseyside L36 7SY
Tel: 01514 778450
Head: Mrs Patricia Thomas
Category: CLD SEBD (Coed 2-11)

KIRKBY

Bluebell Park School
Cawthorne Walk, Southdene,
KIRKBY, Merseyside L32 3XP
Tel: 01514 778350
Head: Mr John Parkes
Category: PD PMLD SLD
MLD (Coed 2-19)

STOCKBRIDGE VILLAGE

Meadow Park School
Haswell Drive, STOCKBRIDGE
VILLAGE, Merseyside L28 1RX
Tel: 01514 778100
Head: Mr Mike Marshall

Merseyside

LIVERPOOL
City Council

Liverpool Children's Services (Education), Municipal Buildings, Dale Street, Liverpool, L2 2DH
Tel: 01512 333000 Email: liverpool.direct@liverpool.gov.uk Website: www.liverpool.gov.uk

LIVERPOOL

Abbot's Lea School
Beaconsfield Road, Woolton,
LIVERPOOL, Merseyside L25 6EE
Tel: 01514 281161
Head: Mrs Ania Hildrey
Category: AUT (Coed 5-19)

Bank View High School
177 Long Ln, LIVERPOOL,
Merseyside L9 6AD
Tel: 01512 336120
Head: Ms Juliette Gelling
Category: CLD (Coed 11-18)

Childwall Abbey School
Childwall Abbey Rd, LIVERPOOL,
Merseyside L16 5EY
Tel: 01517 221995
Head: Mrs C Piercy
Category: CLD ASD

Clifford Holroyde School
Thingwall Lane, LIVERPOOL,
Merseyside L14 7NX
Tel: 01512 289500
Head: Mr Neil Oxley
Category: EBD (Coed 7-16)

Ernest Cookson School
54 Bankfield Road, West Derby,
LIVERPOOL, Merseyside L13 0BQ
Tel: 01512 201874
Head: Mr Ian Moxham
Category: EBD (Boys 5-16)

Hope School
Naylorsfield Drive, LIVERPOOL,
Merseyside L27 0YD
Tel: 01514 984055
Head: Mr Rohit Naik
Category: EBD (Boys 5-16)

Millstead Special Needs Primary
Iliad St, Everton, LIVERPOOL,
Merseyside L5 3LU
Tel: 01512 074656
Head: Ms Michelle Beard
Category: SLD (Coed 2-11)

Palmerston School
Beaconsfield Road, Woolton,
LIVERPOOL, Merseyside L25 6EE
Tel: 01514 282128
Head: Mrs Alison Burbage
Category: SLD (Coed 11-19)

Princes Primary School
Selborne Street, LIVERPOOL,
Merseyside L8 1YQ
Tel: 01517 092602
Head: Mrs Kathy Brent
Category: SLD (Coed 2-11)

Redbridge High School
Long Ln, LIVERPOOL,
Merseyside L9 6AD
Tel: 01512 336170
Head: Mr Paul Cronin
Category: SLD (Coed 11-19)

Sandfield Park School
Sandfield Walk, West Derby,
LIVERPOOL, Merseyside L12 1LH
Tel: 01512 280324
Head: Mr Mark Hilton
Category: PD HS (Coed 11-19)

Woolton High School
Woolton Hill Road, Woolton,
LIVERPOOL, Merseyside L25 6JA
Tel: 01514 284071
Head: Mr M Christian
Category: (Coed 11-16)

Merseyside

SEFTON
Children, Schools & Families

Sefton SEN Team, Town Hall, Bootle, Merseyside, L20 7AE
Tel: 01519 343250 Email: special.needs@sefton.gov.uk Website: www.sefton.gov.uk

BOOTLE

Rowan Park School
Sterrix Lane, BOOTLE,
Merseyside L21 0DB
Tel: 01512 224894
Head: Ms K Lynskey
Category: SLD (Coed 3-18)

CROSBY

Crosby High School
De Villiers Avenue, CROSBY,
Merseyside L23 2TH
Tel: 01519 243671
Head: Ms T Oxton-Grant
Category: MLD (Coed 11-16)

Newfield School
Edge Lane, CROSBY,
Merseyside L23 4TG
Tel: 01519 342991
Head: Mrs J Starkey
Category: BESD (Coed 5-17)

SOUTHPORT

Merefield School
Westminster Drive, SOUTHPORT,
Merseyside PR8 2QZ
Tel: 01704 577163
Head: Mrs S Clare
Category: SLD (Coed 3-16)

Presfield High School and Specialist College
Preston New Road, SOUTHPORT,
Merseyside PR9 8PA
Tel: 01704 227831
Head: Ms N Zielonka
Category: ASD (Coed 11-16)

Merseyside

ST HELENS

Community, Education & Leisure Services Department

St Helens Additional Needs Team, Atlas House, Corporation Street, St Helens, Merseyside, WA9 1LD
Tel: 01744 671104 Website: www.sthelens.gov.uk

NEWTON-LE-WILLOWS

Penkford School
Wharf Road, Earlestown, NEWTON-LE-WILLOWS, Merseyside WA12 9XZ
Tel: 01744 678745
Head: Ms Julie Johnson
Category: SEBD (9-16)

ST HELENS

Lansbury Bridge School
Lansbury Avenue, Parr, ST HELENS, Merseyside WA9 1TB
Tel: 01744 678579
Head: Mrs Jane Grecic
Category: CLD PD MLD ASD (Coed 3-16)

Mill Green School
Lansbury Avenue, Parr, ST HELENS, Merseyside WA9 1BU
Tel: 01744 678760
Head: Mr Warren Brooks
Category: SLD CLD PMLD ASD (Coed 14-19)

Merseyside

WIRRAL

Local Offer

Wirral SEN Team, St James Centre, 344 Laird Street, Birkenhead Wirral, CH41 7AL
Tel: 0151 666 4488 Email: sallytittle@wirral.gov.uk Website: www.wirral.gov.uk

BIRKENHEAD

Kilgarth School
Cavendish Street, BIRKENHEAD, Merseyside CH41 8BA
Tel: 01516 528071
Acting Head: Mr Steven Baker
Category: EBD ADHD (Boys 11-16)

PRENTON

The Observatory School
Bidston Village Road, Bidston, PRENTON, Merseyside CH43 7QT
Tel: 01516 527093
Head: Mr Greg Chiswell
Category: SEBD LD (Coed 11-16)

WALLASEY

Elleray Park School
Elleray Park Road, WALLASEY, Merseyside CH45 0LH
Tel: 01516 393594
Acting Head: Mr Col Hughes
Category: CLD SLD PD AUT PMLD (Coed 2-11)

Orrets Meadow School
Chapelhill Road, Moreton, WALLASEY, Merseyside CH46 9QQ
Tel: 01516 788070
Head: Mrs Carolyn Duncan
Category: SPLD SP&LD LD AUT ASD EBD (Coed 7-11)

WIRRAL

Clare Mount Specialist Sports College
Fender Lane, Moreton, WIRRAL, Merseyside CH46 9PA
Tel: 01516 069440
Head: Mrs Kim Webster
Category: MLD (Coed 11-19)

Gilbrook School
Glebe Hey Road, Woodchurch, WIRRAL, Merseyside CH49 8HE
Tel: 01515 223900
Head: Mrs Kirsten Brown
Category: EBD DYS (Coed 4-12)

Hayfield School
Manor Drive, Upton, WIRRAL, Merseyside CH49 4LN
Tel: 01516 779303
Head: Mr Lee Comber
Category: MLD CLD ASD (Coed 4-11)

Meadowside School
Pool Lane, Woodchurch, WIRRAL, Merseyside CH49 5LA
Tel: 01516 787711
Head: Ms Paula Wareing
Category: CLD SLD (Coed 11-19)

Wirral Hospitals School
Joseph Paxton Campus, 157 Park Road North, Claughton, WIRRAL, Merseyside CH41 0EZ
Tel: 01514 887680
Head: Mr Derek Kitchin
Category: HS (Coed 2-19)

WOODCHURCH

Foxfield School
New Hey Road, Moreton, WOODCHURCH, Merseyside CH49 5LF
Tel: 01516 418810
Head: Mr Andre Baird
Category: ADHD SLD ASD PD (Coed 11-19)

MIDDLESBROUGH
Education and Learning

Middlesbrough SEN Team, Civic Centre, P.O. Box 505, Middlesbrough, TS1 9FZ
Tel: 01642 728677 Email: sen@middlesbrough.gov.uk Website: www.middlesbrough.gov.uk

MIDDLESBROUGH

Beverley School
Saltersgill Avenue,
MIDDLESBROUGH,
Cleveland TS4 3JS
Tel: 01642 811350
Head: Ms Joanne Smith
Category: AUT (Coed 3-19)

Holmwood School
Saltersgill Avenue, Easterside,
MIDDLESBROUGH,
Cleveland TS4 3PT
Tel: 01642 819157
Head: Mrs Jan Mather
Category: EBD (Coed 4-11)

Priory Woods School
Tothill Avenue, Netherfields,
MIDDLESBROUGH,
Cleveland TS3 0RH
Tel: 01642 770540
Head: Ms Janis French
Category: SLD PMLD (Coed 4-19)

MILTON KEYNES
Children and Families Service

Milton Keynes SEND Team, Saxon Court, 502 Avebury Boulevard, Milton Keynes, MK9 3HS
Tel: 01908 253414 Email: sen@milton-keynes.gov.uk Website: www.milton-keynes.gov.uk

MILTON KEYNES

Romans Field School
Shenley Road, Bletchley, MILTON
KEYNES, Buckinghamshire MK3 7AW
Tel: 01908 376011
Head: Dr Diane Elleman
Category: SEBD (Coed
Day/boarding 5-12)

Slated Row School
Old Wolverton Road,
Wolverton, MILTON KEYNES,
Buckinghamshire MK12 5NJ
Tel: 01908 316017
Head: Mr Jonathan Budd
Category: MLD Complex
needs (Coed Day 4-19)

The Redway School
Farmborough, Netherfield, MILTON
KEYNES, Buckinghamshire MK6 4HG
Tel: 01908 206400
Head: Ms Ruth Sylvester
Category: PMLD CLD
SCD (Coed Day 2-19)

The Walnuts School
Admiral Drive, Hazeley, MILTON
KEYNES, Buckinghamshire MK8 0PU
Tel: 01908 563885
Head: Ms Jo Yates
Category: ASD SCD (Coed
Day/boarding 4-19)

White Spire School
Rickley Lane, Bletchley, MILTON
KEYNES, Buckinghamshire MK3 6EW
Tel: 01908 373266
Head: Mr Finlay Douglas
Category: MLD (Coed
Day & boarding 5-19)

NORFOLK
Children's Services

Norfolk SEN Team, County Hall, Martineau Lane, Norwich, Norfolk, NR1 2DH
Tel: 03448 008020 Email: send@norfolk.gov.uk Website: www.norfolk.gov.uk

ATTLEBOROUGH

Chapel Road School
Chapel Road, ATTLEBOROUGH,
Norfolk NR17 2DS
Tel: 01953 453116
Head: Mrs Karin Heap
Category: Complex
needs (Coed 3-19)

CROMER

Sidestrand Hall School
Cromer Road, Sidestrand,
CROMER, Norfolk NR27 0NH
Tel: 01263 578144
Head: Mrs Sarah Young
Category: Complex
Needs (Coed 7-19)

DEREHAM

Fred Nicholson School
Westfield Road, DEREHAM,
Norfolk NR19 1JB
Tel: 01362 693915
Head: Ms Jane Hayman
Category: Complex
Needs (Coed 7-16)

GREAT YARMOUTH

John Grant School
St George's Drive, Caister-
on-Sea, GREAT YARMOUTH,
Norfolk NR30 5QW
Tel: 01493 720158
Head: Mrs Pamela Ashworth
Category: Complex
Needs (Coed 3-19)

KING'S LYNN

Churchill Park School
Winston Churchill Drive, KING'S LYNN, Norfolk PE30 4RP
Tel: 01553 763679
Head: Mr Paul Donkersloot
Category: Complex Needs (Day 2-19)

NORWICH

Hall School
St Faith's Road, Old Catton, NORWICH, Norfolk NR6 7AD
Tel: 01603 466467
Head: Mr Keith McKenzie
Category: Complex Needs (Coed 3-19)

Harford Manor School
43 Ipswich Road, NORWICH, Norfolk NR2 2LN
Tel: 01603 451809
Head: Mr Paul Eteson
Category: Complex Needs (Coed 3-19)

The Clare School
South Park Avenue, NORWICH, Norfolk NR4 7AU
Tel: 01603 454199
Head: Mr Fyfe Johnston
Category: iPhysical & Sensoryî Complex Needs (Coed 3-19)

The Parkside School
College Road, NORWICH, Norfolk NR2 3JA
Tel: 01603 441126
Head: Mr Robert Holderness
Category: Complex Needs (Coed 3-19)

SHERINGHAM

Sheringham Woodfields School
Holt Road, SHERINGHAM, Norfolk NR26 8ND
Tel: 01263 820520
Head: Mr James Stanbrook
Category: Complex Needs (Coed 3-19)

NORTHAMPTONSHIRE
County Council

Northamptonshire CYPS, John Dryden House, 8-10 The Lakes, Northampton, NN4 7YD
Tel: 01001 261000 Email: education@northamptonshire.gov.uk Website: www.northamptonshire.gov.uk

KETTERING

Isebrook SEN Cognition & Learning College
Eastleigh Road, KETTERING, Northamptonshire NN15 6PT
Tel: 01536 500030
Head: Mrs Denise Williams
Category: MLD ASD SLD SP&LD PH (11-19)

Wren Spinney Community Special School
Westover Road, KETTERING, Northamptonshire NN15 7LB
Tel: 01536 481939
Head: Mr Simon Bishop
Category: SLD PMLD ASD MSI (11-19)

NORTHAMPTON

Fairfields School
Trinity Avenue, NORTHAMPTON, Northamptonshire NN2 6JN
Tel: 01604 714777
Head: Ms Karen Lewis
Category: PMLD PH MSI SLD ASD (3-11)

Greenfields School and Sports College
Prentice Court, Lings Way, Goldings, NORTHAMPTON, Northamptonshire NN3 8XS
Tel: 01604 741960
Head: Mrs Lisa-Marie Atack
Category: PMLD SLD ASD MSI (11-19)

Kings Meadow School
Manning Road, Moulton Leys, NORTHAMPTON, Northamptonshire NN3 7AR
Tel: 01604 673730
Head: Ms Helen McCormack
Category: BESD (4-11)

Northgate School Arts College
Queens Park Parade, NORTHAMPTON, Northamptonshire NN2 6LR
Tel: 01604 714098
Head: Miss Sheralee Webb & Mike Trundley
Category: MLD SLD ASD (11-19)

TIFFIELD

The Gateway School
St Johns Road, TIFFIELD, Northamptonshire NN12 8AA
Tel: 01604 878977
Head: Mr Conor Renihan
Category: BESD (11-19)

WELLINGBOROUGH

Rowan Gate Primary School
Finedon Road, WELLINGBOROUGH, Northamptonshire NN8 4NS
Tel: 01933 304970
Head: Mrs Laura Clarke
Category: PMLD ASD (3-11)

NORTHUMBERLAND
County Council

Northumberland SENDIASS, County Hall, Morpeth, Northumberland, NE61 2EF
Tel: 01670 623555 Email: sen@northumberland.gov.uk Website: www.northumberland.gov.uk

ALNWICK

Barndale House School
Howling Lane, ALNWICK, Northumberland NE66 1DQ
Tel: 01665 602541
Head: Mr Colin Bradshaw
Category: SLD

BERWICK UPON TWEED

The Grove Special School
Grove Gardens, Tweedmouth, BERWICK UPON TWEED, Northumberland TD15 2EN
Tel: 01289 306390
Head: Ms Penelope Derries
Category: SLD

BLYTH

The Dales School
Cowpen Road, BLYTH, Northumberland NE24 4RE
Tel: 01670 352556
Head: Mr Hugh Steele
Category: MLD CLD PH EBD

CHOPPINGTON

Cleaswell Hill School
School Avenue, Guide Post, CHOPPINGTON, Northumberland NE62 5DJ
Tel: 01670 823182
Head: Mr Kevin Burdis
Category: MLD

CRAMLINGTON

Atkinson House School
North Terrace, Seghill,
CRAMLINGTON,
Northumberland NE23 7EB
Tel: 0191 2980838
Head: Mr Derek Cogle
Category: EBD

Cramlington Hillcrest School
East View Avenue, CRAMLINGTON,
Northumberland NE23 1DY
Tel: 01670 713632
Head: Mrs Andrea Mead
Category: MLD

HEXHAM

Hexham Priory School
Corbridge Road, HEXHAM,
Northumberland NE46 1UY
Tel: 01434 605021
Head: Mr Michael Thompson
Category: SLD

MORPETH

Collingwood School & Media Arts College
Stobhillgate, MORPETH,
Northumberland NE61 2HA
Tel: 01670 516374
Head: Mr Richard Jones
Category: MLD CLD AUT
SP&LD PH Emotionally fragile
Specific medical conditions

NOTTINGHAM

Children, Families and Cultural Services

Nottingham SEN Team, Glenbrook Management Centre, Wigman Road, Bilborough Nottingham, NG8 4PD
Tel: 01158 764300 Email: special.needs@nottinghamcity.gov.uk Website: www.nottinghamcity.gov.uk

NOTTINGHAM

Oak Field School and Specialist Sports College
Wigman Road, Bilborough,
NOTTINGHAM NG8 3HW
Tel: 01159 153265
Head: Mr David Stewart
Category: SCD ASD SPLI
(Coed Day 3-19)

Rosehill Special School
St Matthias Road, St Ann's,
NOTTINGHAM NG3 2FE
Tel: 01159 155815
Head: Mr Andy Sloane
Category: AUT (Coed Day 4-19)

Westbury School
Chingford Road, Bilborough,
NOTTINGHAM NG8 3BT
Tel: 01159 155858
Executive Head: Mr John Dyson
Category: EBD (Coed Day 7-16)

Woodlands Special School
Beechdale Road, Aspley,
NOTTINGHAM NG8 3EZ
Tel: 01159 155734
Executive Head: Mr John Dyson
Category: MLD (Coed Day 3-16)

NOTTINGHAMSHIRE

Children, Families and Cultural Services

Integrated Children's Disability Service (ICDS), Meadow House, Littleworth, Mansfield, Nottinghamshire, NG18 2TB
Tel: 0115 8041275 Email: icds.duty@nottscc.gov.uk Website: www.nottinghamshire.sendlocaloffer.org.uk

ASHFIELD

Bracken Hill School
Chartwell Road, ASHFIELD,
Nottinghamshire NG17 7HZ
Tel: 01623 477268
Head: Mrs Catherine Askham
Category: (Coed Day 3-19)

GEDLING

Carlton Digby School
Digby Avenue, Mapperley,
GEDLING, Nottingham NG3 6DS
Tel: 01159 568289
Head: Ms Janet Spratt-Burch
Category: (Coed 3-19)

Derrymount School (Lower)
Churchmoor Lane, Arnold,
GEDLING, Nottingham NG5 8HN
Tel: 01159 534015
Head: Ms Catherine Clay
Category: (Coed 3-13)

Derrymount School (Upper)
Sherbrook Road, Daybrook,
GEDLING, Nottingham NG5 6AT
Head: Mrs Kathy McIntyre
Category: (Coed 14-19)

MANSFIELD

Fountaindale School
Nottingham Road, MANSFIELD,
Nottinghamshire NG18 5BA
Tel: 01623 792671
Head: Mr Mark Dengel
Category: PD (Coed 3-19)

Redgate School
Somersall Street, MANSFIELD,
Nottinghamshire NG19 6EL
Tel: 01623 455944
Acting Executive Head: Pauline Corfield
Category: (Coed Day 3-11)

Yeoman Park School
Park Hall Road, Mansfield
Woodhouse, MANSFIELD,
Nottinghamshire NG19 8PS
Tel: 01623 459540
Acting Executive Head: Jane Cooper
Category: (Coed Day 3-19)

NEWARK

**The Newark Orchard
School (Lower)**
Appleton Gate, NEWARK,
Nottinghamshire NG24 1JR
Tel: 01636 682255
Head: Ms Margot Tyers
Category: (Coed 3-14)

**The Newark Orchard
School (Upper)**
London Road, New
Balderton, NEWARK,
Nottinghamshire NG24 3AL
Tel: 01636 682256
Head: Ms Margot Tyers
Category: (Coed 14-19)

RETFORD

St Giles School
North Road, RETFORD,
Nottinghamshire DN22 7XN
Tel: 01777 703683
Head: Ms Kathy McIntyre
Category: (Coed 3-19)

RUSHCLIFFE

Ash Lea School
Owthorpe Road, RUSHCLIFFE,
Nottinghamshire NG12 3PA
Tel: 01159 892744
Head: Mrs Dawn Wigley
Category: (Coed Day 3-19)

OXFORDSHIRE
County Council

**CSEN Business Support Team, Children with Special Educational Needs Service,
Children's Services Directorate, County Hall, New Road Oxford, OX1 1ND**
Tel: **01865 815275** Email: **senbusinesssupport@oxfordshire.gov.uk** Website: **www.oxfordshire.gov.uk/localoffer**

BANBURY

Frank Wise School
Hornbeam Close, BANBURY,
Oxfordshire OX16 9RL
Tel: 01295 263520
Head: Mr Sean O'Sullivan
Category: SLD PMLD (Coed 2-19)

BICESTER

Bardwell School
Hendon Place, Sunderland Drive,
BICESTER, Oxfordshire OX26 4RZ
Tel: 01869 242182
Head: Mr John Riches
Category: SLD PMLD (Coed 2-19)

OXFORD

John Watson School
Littleworth Road, Wheatley,
OXFORD OX33 1NN
Tel: 01865 452725
Head: Mr Stephen Passey
Category: SLD PMLD (Coed 2-19)

Mabel Prichard School
Cuddesdon Way, OXFORD OX4 6SB
Tel: 01865 777878
Head: Mrs Jane Wallington
Category: SLD PMLD (Coed 2-19)

Northfield School
Knights Road, Blackbird
Leys, OXFORD OX4 6DQ
Tel: 01865 771703
Head: Mr Peter Marshall
Category: BESD (Boys 11-18)

Oxfordshire Hospital School
The Harlow Centre, Raymund Road,
Old Marston, OXFORD OX3 0SW
Tel: 01865 253177
Headteacher: Ms Angela Ransby
Category: HS (Coed 3-18)

Woodeaton Manor School
Woodeaton, OXFORD OX3 9TS
Tel: 01865 558722
Head: Mrs Anne Pearce
Category: SEMH (Coed 7-18 Day/
residential weekday boarding)

SONNING COMMON

**Bishopswood
Special School**
Grove Road, SONNING COMMON,
Oxfordshire RG4 9RH
Tel: 01189 724311
Head: Mrs Janet Kellett
Category: SLD PMLD (Coed 2-16)

WITNEY

Springfield School
The Bronze Barrow, Cedar
Drive, Madley Park, WITNEY,
Oxfordshire OX28 1AR
Tel: 01993 703963
Head: Mrs Emma Lawley
Category: SLD (Coed 2-16)

PETERBOROUGH
SEND Partnership Service

Peterborough SEN Team, Town Hall, Bridge Street, Peterborough, PE1 1HF
Tel: **01733 863979** Email: **pps@peterborough.gov.uk** Website: **www.peterborough.gov.uk**

PETERBOROUGH

Heltwate School
North Bretton, PETERBOROUGH,
Cambridgeshire PE3 8RL
Tel: 01733 262878
Head: Mr Adam Brewster
Category: MLD SLD AUT
PD SCD (Coed 4-16)

Marshfields School
Eastern Close, Dogsthorpe,
PETERBOROUGH,
Cambridgeshire PE1 4PP
Tel: 01733 568058
Head: Mrs Janet James
Category: MLD SCD SEBD
SLD (Coed 11-19)

NeneGate School
Park Lane, Eastfield,
PETERBOROUGH,
Cambridgeshire PE1 5GZ
Tel: 01733 349438
Head: Ms Ruth O'Sullivan
Category: EBD (Coed 11-16)

Phoenix School
Clayton, Orton Goldhay,
PETERBOROUGH,
Cambridgeshire PE2 5SD
Tel: 01733 391666
Head: Mr Phil Pike
Category: SLD PMLD PD SCN
ASD MSI (Coed 2-19)

PLYMOUTH
City Council

Plymouth SEN Team, Ballard House, West Hoe Road, Plymouth, Devon, PL1 3BJ
Tel: 01752 307409 Email: senadmin@plymouth.gov.uk Website: www.plymouth.gov.uk

PLYMOUTH

Brook Green Centre for Learning
Bodmin Road, Whitleigh,
PLYMOUTH, Devon PL5 4DZ
Tel: 01752 773875
Head: Ms Sara Jordan
Category: MLD BESD (11-16)

Cann Bridge School
Miller Way, Estover, PLYMOUTH,
Devon PL6 8UN
Tel: 01752 207909
Head: Mr Michael Loveman
Category: SLD (3-19)

Courtlands School
Widey Lane, Crownhill,
PLYMOUTH, Devon PL6 5JS
Tel: 01752 776848
Head: Mr Lee Earnshaw
Category: MLD BESD (4-11)

Longcause Community Special School
Longcause, Plympton,
PLYMOUTH, Devon PL7 1JB
Tel: 01752 336881
Head: Mrs Anne Thorne
Category: MLD (5-17)

Mill Ford Community Special School
Rochford Crescent, Ernesettle,
PLYMOUTH, Devon PL5 2PY
Tel: 01752 300270
Head: Mrs Claire Wills
Category: SLD PMLD (3-19)

Mount Tamar School
Row Lane, Higher St Budeaux,
PLYMOUTH, Devon PL5 2EF
Tel: 01752 365128
Head: Mr Brett Storry
Category: BESD (5-16)

Woodlands School
Picklecombe Drive, Off
Tamerton Foliot Road, Whitleigh,
PLYMOUTH, Devon PL6 5ES
Tel: 01752 300101
Head: Mrs Andrea Hemmens
Category: PD PMLD MSI (2-19)

BOROUGH OF POOLE
Information, Advice & Support Service

Poole SENDIASS, Quay Advice Centre, 18 Hill Street, Poole, Dorset, BH15 1NR
Tel: 01202 261933 Email: sendiass@poole.gov.uk Website: www.poole.gov.uk

POOLE

Winchelsea School
Guernsey Road, Parkstone,
POOLE, Dorset BH12 4LL
Tel: 01202 746240
Head: Mr Geoff Cherrill
Category: ADHD ASD
ASP MLD (3-16)

PORTSMOUTH
Directorate of Children, Families and Learning

Portsmouth SEN Team, Floor 2 Core 1, Civic Offices, Guildhall Square Portsmouth, Hampshire, PO1 2EA
Tel: 02392 841238 Email: sen.education@portsmouthcc.gov.uk Website: www.portsmouthlocaloffer.org

PORTSMOUTH

Mary Rose School
Gisors Road, Southsea,
PORTSMOUTH, Hampshire PO4 8GT
Tel: 02392 852330
Executive Head: Ms Alison Beane
Category: SCN ASD
PMLD (Coed 2-19)

Redwood Park School
Wembley Grove, Cosham,
PORTSMOUTH, Hampshire PO6 2RY
Tel: 02392 377500
Executive Head: Ms Alison Beane
Category: CLD ASD (Coed 11-16)

The Harbour School
Tipner Lane, PORTSMOUTH,
Hampshire PO2 8RA
Tel: 02392 665664
Head: Mr Ian Hunkin
Category: BESD

READING

Directorate of Education, Adult & Children's Services

Reading SEN Team, Civic Offices, Bridge Street, Reading, RG1 2LU
Tel: 01189 372674 Email: sen@reading.gov.uk Website: www.reading.gov.uk/servicesguide

READING

Phoenix College
40 Christchurch Road,
READING, Berkshire RG2 7AY
Tel: 01189 375524
Head: Mrs Ekie Lansdown-Bridge
Category: BESD ADHD (Coed 11-16)

**The Holy Brook
Special School**
145 Ashampstead Road, Southcote,
READING, Berkshire RG30 3LJ
Tel: 01189 375489
Head: Mr Lee Smith

REDCAR & CLEVELAND

Information, Advice & Support Service

Redcar & Cleveland SENDIASS, Redcar Children's Centre, Kielder Close, Redcar, Middlesborough, TS10 4HS
Tel: 01642 759073 Email: sendiass@redcar-cleveland.gov.uk Website: www.redcar-cleveland.gov.uk

MIDDLESBROUGH

Pathways School
Tennyson Avenue, Grangetown,
MIDDLESBROUGH TS6 7NP
Tel: 01642 779292
Head: Mr Steve O'Gara
Category: SEBD (Coed Day 7-15)

REDCAR

Kirkleatham Hall School
Kirkleatham Village, REDCAR,
Cleveland TS10 4QR
Tel: 01642 483009
Head: Mrs Karen Robson
Category: SLD PMLD SLCN ASC
PD CLDD (Coed Day 4-19)

RUTLAND

Information Advice & Support Service

Rutland SENDIASS, Rutland Citizens Advice Bureau, 56 High Street, Oakham, Rutland, LE15 6AL
Tel: 01572 757420 Email: office@rutlandcab.org.uk Website: www.rutland.gov.uk

OAKHAM

The Parks School
Burley Road, OAKHAM,
Rutland LE15 6GY
Tel: 01572 722404
Head: Mr Steven Cox
Category: AUT MLD PMLD
SP&LD VIS SEBD (Coed 2-5)

SHROPSHIRE
Shropshire Council

Shropshire SEN Team, The Shirehall, Abbey Foregate, Shrewsbury, Shropshire, SY2 6ND
Tel: 01743 254366 Email: senteam@shropshire.gov.uk Website: www.shropshire.gov.uk

OSWESTRY

Acorns Centre
Middleton Road, OSWESTRY,
Shropshire SY11 2LF
Head: Mr Robin Wilson
Category: SEMH (Coed 9-11)

SHREWSBURY

Woodlands School
Tilley Green, Wem, SHREWSBURY,
Shropshire SY4 5PJ
Tel: 01939 232372
Head: Mr Robin Wilson
Category: SEMH (Coed 11-16)

SLOUGH
Slough Borough Council

Slough SEN Team, Slough Family Information Service (FIS), St Martins Place, 51 Bath Road Slough, Berkshire, SL1 3UF
Tel: 01753 476589 Email: fis@slough.gov.uk Website: www.slough.gov.uk

SLOUGH

Arbour Vale School
Farnham Road, SLOUGH,
Berkshire SL2 3AE
Tel: 01753 515560
Head: Mrs Debbie Richards
Category: SLD ASD MLD (Coed 2-19)

**Haybrook College/
Millside School**
112 Burnham Lane, SLOUGH,
Berkshire SL1 6LZ
Tel: 01628 696077/696079
Executive Head: Ms Helen Huntley
Category: BESD (Coed 11-16)

Littledown School
Queen's Road, SLOUGH,
Berkshire SL1 3QW
Tel: 01753 521734
Head: Jo Matthews
Category: BESD (Coed 5-11)

SOMERSET
Children and Young People's Services

Somerset SEN Team, County Hall, Taunton, Somerset, TA1 4DY
Tel: 0300 123 2224 Email: somersetdirect@somerset.gov.uk Website: www.somerset.gov.uk

BRIDGWATER

Elmwood School
Hamp Avenue, BRIDGWATER,
Somerset TA6 6AW
Tel: 01278 456243
Head: Ms Elizabeth Hayward
Category: SLD MLD ASD
EBD (Coed Day 11-16)

Penrose School
Albert Street, Willow Brook,
BRIDGWATER, Somerset TA6 7ET
Tel: 01278 423660
Head: Mrs E Hayward
Category: CLD ASD SLD
(4-10 and Post-16)

FROME

Critchill School
Nunney Road, FROME,
Somerset BA11 4LB
Tel: 01373 464148
Head: Mr Mark Armstrong
Category: SLD MLD CLD
(Coed Day 4-16)

STREET

Avalon Special School
Brooks Road, STREET,
Somerset BA16 0PS
Tel: 01458 443081
Head: Mrs Alison Murkin
Category: SLD MLD PMLD
ASD (Coed Day 3-16)

TAUNTON

Selworthy School
Selworthy Road, TAUNTON,
Somerset TA2 8HD
Tel: 01823 284970
Head: Mr Mark Ruffett
Category: SLD PMLD MLD
ASD BESD (Coed Day 4-19)

**Sky College (formerly
The Priory School)**
Pickeridge Close, TAUNTON,
Somerset TA2 7HW
Tel: 01823 275569
Executive Head: Mr Richard Berry
Category: EBD (Boys Boarding 11-16)

YEOVIL

Fairmead School
Mudford Road, YEOVIL,
Somerset BA21 4NZ
Tel: 01935 421295
Head: Miss Diana Denman
Category: MLD SEBD AUT
SLD (Coed 4-16)

Fiveways Special School
Victoria Road, YEOVIL,
Somerset BA21 5AZ
Tel: 01935 476227
Head: Mr M Collis
Category: SLD PMLD ASD
(Coed Day 4-19)

NORTH SOMERSET
Children and Young People's Services

North Somerset SEN Team, Town Hall, Room 119, Weston-Super-Mare, North Somerset, BS23 1UJ
Tel: 01275 888297 Website: www.n-somerset.gov.uk

NAILSEA

Ravenswood School
Pound Lane, NAILSEA, North
Somerset BS48 2NN
Tel: 01275 854134
Head: Mrs Philippa Clark
Category: CLD SLD (3-19)

WESTON-SUPER-MARE

Baytree School
The Campus, Highlands
Lane, WESTON-SUPER-MARE,
North Somerset BS24 7DX
Tel: 01934 427555
Acting Head: Mr Ed Bowen-Roberts
Category: SLD (3-19)

Westhaven School
Ellesmere Road, Uphill,
WESTON-SUPER-MARE,
North Somerset BS23 4UT
Tel: 01934 632171
Head: Mrs Tracy Towler
Category: CLD (7-16)

SOUTHAMPTON
City Council

Southampton SEN Team, Civic Centre (North Block), Southampton, Hampshire, SO14 7LY
Tel: 02380 832248 Email: sen.team@southampton.gov.uk Website: www.southampton.gov.uk

SOUTHAMPTON

Great Oaks School
Vermont Close, SOUTHAMPTON,
Hampshire SO16 7LT
Tel: 02380 767660
Head: Mr Andy Evans
Category: MLD AUT ASP SLD (11-18)

Springwell School
Hinkler Road, Thornhill,
SOUTHAMPTON,
Hampshire SO19 6DH
Tel: 02380 445981
Head: Ms Jackie Partridge
Category: CLD SP&LD AUT SLD
Challenging behaviour (4-11)

The Cedar School
Redbridge Lane,
Nursling, SOUTHAMPTON,
Hampshire SO16 0NX
Tel: 02380 734205
Head: Mr Jonathan Howells
Category: PD (3-16)

The Polygon School
Handel Terrace, SOUTHAMPTON,
Hampshire SO15 2FH
Tel: 02380 636776
Head: Mrs Anne Hendon-John
Category: EBD (Boys 11-16)

Vermont School
Vermont Close, Off Winchester
Rd, SOUTHAMPTON,
Hampshire SO16 7LT
Tel: 02380 767988
Head: Ms Maria Smyth
Category: EBD (Boys 5-11)

SOUTHEND-ON-SEA
Borough Council

Southend-on-Sea SEN Team, Civic Centre, Victoria Avenue, Southend-on-Sea, Essex, SS2 6ER
Tel: 01702 215007 Email: council@southend.gov.uk Website: www.southend.gov.uk

SOUTHEND-ON-SEA

Kingsdown School
Snakes Lane, SOUTHEND-
ON-SEA, Essex SS2 6XT
Tel: 01702 527486
Executive Head: Mr Dave Cook
Category: SLD PMLD PNI
PD (Coed Day 5-14)

Seabrook College
Burr Hill Chase, SOUTHEND-
ON-SEA, Essex SS2 6PE
Tel: 01702 347490
Interim Principal: Ms Linda Burrage
Category: SEBD (Coed Day 11-16)

St Nicholas School
Philpott Avenue, SOUTHEND-
ON-SEA, Essex SS2 4RL
Tel: 01702 462322
Head: Mrs June Mitchell
Category: MLD AUT SEMH
(Coed Day 11-16)

WESTCLIFF-ON-SEA

Lancaster School
Prittlewell Chase, WESTCLIFF-
ON-SEA, Essex SS0 0RT
Tel: 01702 342543
Head: Ms Melanie Hall
Category: SLD PMLD PNI
PD (Coed Day 14-19)

STAFFORDSHIRE

Children & Lifelong Learning Directorate

The SEN Team, Tipping Street, Stafford, Staffordshire, ST16 2DH
Tel: 03001 118000 Email: education@staffordshire.gov.uk Website: www.staffordshire.gov.uk

BURNTWOOD

Chasetown Community School
Church Street, Chasetown, BURNTWOOD, Staffordshire WS7 3QL
Tel: 01543 686315
Head: Dr Linda James
Category: SEBD (Coed Day 4-11)

BURTON UPON TRENT

The Fountains High School
Bitham Lane, Stretton, BURTON UPON TRENT, Staffordshire DE13 0HB
Tel: 01283 239161
Head: Mrs Sarah Gilraine
Category: Generic (Coed Day 11-19)

The Fountains Primary School
Bitham Lane, Stretton, BURTON UPON TRENT, Staffordshire DE13 0HB
Tel: 01283 239700
Head: Mrs Sarah Gilraine
Category: Generic (Coed Day 2-11)

CANNOCK

Hednesford Valley High School
Stanley Road, Hednesford, CANNOCK, Staffordshire WS12 4JS
Tel: 01543 423714
Head: Mrs Anita Rattan
Category: Generic (Coed Day 11-19)

Sherbrook Primary School
Brunswick Road, CANNOCK, Staffordshire WS11 5SF
Tel: 01543 510216
Head: Ms Carol Shaw
Category: Generic (Coed Day 2-11)

LEEK

Horton Lodge Community Special School & Key Learning Centre
Reacliffe Road, Rudyard, LEEK, Staffordshire ST13 8RB
Tel: 01538 306214
Head: Ms Jane Dambach
Category: PD MSI SP&LD (Coed Day/Boarding 2-11)

Meadows Special School
Springfield Road, LEEK, Staffordshire ST13 6EU
Tel: 01538 225050
Head: Mr Christopher Best
Category: Generic (Coed Day 11-19)

Springfield Community Special School
Springfield Road, LEEK, Staffordshire ST13 6LQ
Tel: 01538 383558
Head: Ms Diane Finney
Category: Generic (Coed Day 2-11)

LICHFIELD

Queen's Croft High School
Birmingham Road, LICHFIELD, Staffordshire WS13 6PJ
Tel: 01543 510669
Head: Mr Peter Hawksworth
Category: Generic (Coed Day11-19)

Rocklands School
Purcell Avenue, LICHFIELD, Staffordshire WS13 7PH
Tel: 01543 510760
Head: Ms Sandra Swift
Category: ASD MLD PMLD SLD (Coed Day 2-11)

NEWCASTLE UNDER LYME

Merryfields School
Hoon Avenue, NEWCASTLE UNDER LYME, Staffordshire ST5 9NY
Tel: 01782 296076
Head: Mrs Sarah Poyner
Category: Generic (Coed Day 2-11)

STAFFORD

Greenhall Nursery
Second Avenue, Holmcroft, STAFFORD, Staffordshire ST16 1PS
Tel: 01785 246159
Head: Ms Joanne di Castiglione
Category: PD (Coed Day 2-5)

Marshlands Special School
Second Avenue, STAFFORD, Staffordshire ST16 1PS
Tel: 01785 356385
Head: Mrs Kim Ellis
Category: Generic (Coed Day 2-11)

TAMWORTH

Two Rivers High School
Deltic, off Silver Link Road, Glascote, TAMWORTH, Staffordshire B77 2HJ
Tel: 01827 475690
Head: Mr Anthony Dooley
Category: Generic (Coed Day 11-19)

Two Rivers Primary School
Quince, Amington Heath, TAMWORTH, Staffordshire B77 4EN
Tel: 01827 475740
Head: Mr Anthony Dooley
Category: Generic (Coed Day 2-11)

WOLVERHAMPTON

Cherry Trees School
Giggetty Lane, Wombourne, WOLVERHAMPTON, West Midlands WV5 0AX
Tel: 01902 894484
Head: Mr Paul Elliot
Category: Generic (Coed Day 2-11)

Wightwick Hall School
Tinacre Hill, Wightwick, WOLVERHAMPTON, West Midlands WV6 8DA
Tel: 01902 761889
Head: Mr Paul Elliot
Category: Generic (Coed Day 11-19)

STOCKTON-ON-TEES
Borough Council

Stockton-on-Tees FIS, The SEN Team, 16 Church Road, Stockton-on-Tees, TS18 1XE
Tel: 01642 527225 Email: fis@stockton.gov.uk Website: www.stockton.gov.uk

STOCKTON-ON-TEES

Horizons Specialist Academy Trust, Abbey Hill Academy & Sixth Form
Ketton Road, Hardwick Green, STOCKTON-ON-TEES TS19 8BU
Tel: 01642 677113
Principal: Ms Rebecca Whelan
Category: SLD PMLD AUT (Coed 11-19)

Horizons Specialist Academy Trust, Westlands at Green Gates
Melton Road, STOCKTON-ON-TEES TS19 0JD
Tel: 01642 570104
Principal: Mrs Anita Amos
Category: BESD (Coed Residential 5-11)

STOKE-ON-TRENT
Local Offer

Stoke-on-Trent SEND Services, The Mount Education Centre, Mount Avenue, Penkhull Stoke-on-Trent, Staffordshire, ST4 7JU
Tel: 01782 232538 Email: localoffer@stoke.gov.uk Website: www.stoke.gov.uk

BLURTON

Kemball Special School
Beconsfield Drive, BLURTON, Stoke-on-Trent ST4 3NR
Tel: 01782 883120
Acting Head: Ms Lisa Hughes
Category: PMLD SLD ASD CLD (Coed Day 2-19)

BLYTHE BRIDGE

Portland School and Specialist College
Uttoxeter Road, BLYTHE BRIDGE, Staffordshire ST11 9JG
Tel: 01782 392071
Head: Mr Rob Faulkner
Category: MLD SEBD (Coed Day 3-16)

STOKE-ON-TRENT

Abbey Hill School and Performing Arts College
Box Lane, Meir, STOKE-ON-TRENT, Staffordshire ST3 5PR
Tel: 01782 882882
Head: Mr Philip Kidman
Category: MLD AUT (Coed Day 2-18)

TUNSTALL

Watermill Special School
Turnhurst Road, Packmoor, TUNSTALL, Stoke-on-Trent ST6 6JZ
Tel: 01782 883737
Head: Mr Jonathon May
Category: MLD (Coed Day 5-16)

SUFFOLK
County Council

Suffolk SENDIASS, Endeavour House, 8 Russell Road, Ipswich, Suffolk, IP1 2BX
Tel: 01473 264702 Email: sendiass@suffolk.gov.uk Website: www.suffolk.gov.uk

BURY ST EDMUNDS

Riverwalk School
South Close, BURY ST EDMUNDS, Suffolk IP33 3JZ
Tel: 01284 764280
Head: Mrs Jan Hatchell
Category: SLD (Coed Day 3-19)

IPSWICH

The Bridge School (Primary Campus)
Sprites Lane, IPSWICH, Suffolk IP8 3ND
Tel: 01473 556200
Head: Mr Odran Doran
Category: SLD PMLD (Coed Day 3-11)

The Bridge School (Secondary Campus)
Sprites Lane, Belstead, IPSWICH, Suffolk IP8 3ND
Tel: 01473 556200
Head: Mr Odran Doran
Category: SLD PMLD (Coed Day 11-16)

LOWESTOFT

Warren School
Clarkes Lane, LOWESTOFT, Suffolk NR33 8HT
Tel: 01502 561893
Head: Mrs Janet Bird
Category: SLD PMLD (Coed Day 3-19)

SUDBURY

Hillside School
Hitchcock Place, SUDBURY,
Suffolk CO10 1NN
Tel: 01787 372808
Head: Mrs Sue Upson
Category: SLD PMLD
(Coed day 3-19)

SURREY

City Council

The SEN Team, County Hall, Penrhyn Road, Kingston upon Thames, Surrey, KT1 2DN
Tel: 03456 009009 Email: localoffer@surreycc.gov.uk **Website:** www.surreycc.gov.uk

ADDLESTONE

Philip Southcote School
Addlestone Moor, ADDLESTONE,
Surrey KT15 2QH
Tel: 01932 562326
Head: Mr R W Horton
Category: HI LD (11-19)

CAMBERLEY

Carwarden House Community School
118 Upper Chobham Road,
CAMBERLEY, Surrey GU15 1EJ
Tel: 01276 709080
Head: Mr Jarlath O'Brien
Category: LD (11-19)

Portesbery School
Newfoundland Road,
CAMBERLEY, Surrey GU15 3SZ
Tel: 01276 63078
Head: Mr M Sartin
Category: SLD (2-19)

CATERHAM

Clifton Hill School
Chaldon Road, CATERHAM,
Surrey CR3 5PH
Tel: 01883 347740
Executive Head: Mrs
Sharon Lawrence
Category: SLD (11-19)

Sunnydown School
Portley House, 152 Whyteleafe
Road, CATERHAM, Surrey CR3 5ED
Tel: 01883 342281
Head: Mr Paul Jensen
Category: ASD SLCN
(Boarding & day 11-16)

DORKING

Starhurst School
Chart Lane South, DORKING,
Surrey RH5 4DB
Tel: 01306 883763
Executive Head: Mr Craig Anderson
Category: BESD (Boarding
& day 11-16)

FARNHAM

The Abbey School
Menin Way, FARNHAM,
Surrey GU9 8DY
Tel: 01252 725059
Head: Mr Nathan Aspinall
Category: LD (11-16)

The Ridgeway Community School
Frensham Road, FARNHAM,
Surrey GU9 8HB
Tel: 01252 724562
Head: Mr D Morgan
Category: SLD (2-19)

GUILDFORD

Gosden House School
Horsham Road, Bramley,
GUILDFORD, Surrey GU5 0AH
Tel: 01483 892008
Interim Head: Mr Darryl Morgan
Category: LD (Day 5-16)

Pond Meadow School
Larch Avenue, GUILDFORD,
Surrey GU1 1DR
Tel: 01483 532239
Head: Mr D J Monk
Category: SLD (2-19)

Wey House School
Horsham Road, Bramley,
GUILDFORD, Surrey GU5 0BJ
Tel: 01483 898130
Interim Head: Mr Simon Dawson
Category: BESD (Day only 7-11)

LEATHERHEAD

West Hill School
Kingston Road, LEATHERHEAD,
Surrey KT22 7PW
Tel: 01372 814714
Head: Mrs J V Nettleton
Category: LD (11-16)

Woodlands School
Fortyfoot Road, LEATHERHEAD,
Surrey KT22 8RY
Tel: 01372 273427
Head: Mrs Adrienne Knight
Category: SLD (Day 12-19)

OXTED

Limpsfield Grange School
89 Bluehouse Lane, Limpsfield,
OXTED, Surrey RH8 0RZ
Tel: 01883 713928
Head: Ms Sarah Wild
Category: ELD (Boarding
& day 11-16)

REDHILL

St Nicholas School
Taynton Drive, Merstham,
REDHILL, Surrey RH1 3PU
Tel: 01737 215488
Head: Mr Craig Anderson
Category: BESD (Boarding
& day 11-16)

Woodfield School
Sunstone Grove, Merstham,
REDHILL, Surrey RH1 3PR
Tel: 01737 642623
Head: Mrs S Lawrence
Category: LD (11-19)

REIGATE

Brooklands School
27 Wray Park Road,
REIGATE, Surrey RH2 0DF
Tel: 01737 249941
Head: Mr Mark Bryant
Category: SLD (2-11)

SHEPPERTON

Manor Mead School
Laleham Road, SHEPPERTON,
Middlesex TW17 8EL
Tel: 01932 241834
Executive Head: Ms Linda Mardell
Category: SLD (2-11)

WALTON-ON-THAMES

Walton Leigh School
Queens Road, WALTON-ON-
THAMES, Surrey KT12 5AB
Tel: 01932 223243
Executive Head: Ms Linda Mardell
Category: SLD (11-19)

WOKING

Freemantles School
Smarts Heath Road, Mayford
Green, WOKING, Surrey GU22 0AN
Tel: 01483 545680
Head: Mr Justin Price
Category: ASD (4-19)

The Park School
Onslow Crescent, WOKING,
Surrey GU22 7AT
Tel: 01483 772057
Co-Heads: Mrs K Eastwood
& Mr Paul Walsh
Category: LD (11-16)

WORCESTER PARK

Linden Bridge School
Grafton Road, WORCESTER
PARK, Surrey KT4 7JW
Tel: 02083 303009
Head: Ms Rachel Watt
Category: ASD (Residential
& day 4-19)

EAST SUSSEX

Children's Services Authority

East Sussex ISEND Assessment & Planning Team, PO Box 4, County Hall, St Anne's Crescent Lewes, East Sussex, BN7 1UE
Tel: 01273 336740 Fax: 01273 481599 Email: sen.caseworkassistants@eastsussex.gov.uk
Website: www.eastsussex.gov.uk

CROWBOROUGH

Grove Park School
Church Road, CROWBOROUGH,
East Sussex TN6 1BN
Tel: 01892 663018
Head: Ms Angela Wellman
Category: CLD/ASD (Coed 2-19)

EASTBOURNE

Hazel Court Special School
Larkspur Drive, EASTBOURNE,
East Sussex BN23 8EJ
Tel: 01323 465720
Head: Ms Sophie Gurney
Category: CLD/ASD (Coed 11-19)

WEST SUSSEX

Local Offer

West Sussex SEN Team, County Hall, West Street, Chichester, West Sussex, PO19 1RQ
Tel: 0330 222 8555 Email: localoffer@westsussex.gov.uk Website: www.westsussex.gov.uk

BURGESS HILL

Woodlands Meed
Chanctonbury Road, BURGESS
HILL, West Sussex RH15 9EY
Tel: 01444 244133
Head: Mr Adam Rowland
Category: LD (Coed 2-19)

CHICHESTER

Fordwater School
Summersdale Road, CHICHESTER,
West Sussex PO19 6PP
Tel: 01243 782475
Head: Mrs Sue Meekings
Category: SLD (Coed 2-19)

Littlegreen School
Compton, CHICHESTER,
West Sussex PO18 9NW
Tel: 02392 631259
Head: Ms Lynda Butt
Category: SEBD (Boys 7-16)

St Anthony's School
Woodlands Lane, CHICHESTER,
West Sussex PO19 5PA
Tel: 01243 785965
Head: Ms Helen Ball
Category: MLD (Coed 4-16)

CRAWLEY

Manor Green College
Lady Margaret Road, Ifield,
CRAWLEY, West Sussex RH11 0DX
Tel: 01293 520351
Head: Mr Grahame Robson
Category: LD (Coed 11-19)

Manor Green Primary School
Lady Margaret Road, Ifield,
CRAWLEY, West Sussex RH11 0DU
Tel: 01293 526873
Head: Mr David Reid
Category: LD (Coed 2-11)

HORSHAM

Queen Elizabeth II Silver Jubilee School
Compton's Lane, HORSHAM,
West Sussex RH13 5NW
Tel: 01403 266215
Head: Mrs Lesley Dyer
Category: SLD AUT
PMLD (Coed 2-19)

LITTLEHAMPTON

Cornfield School
Cornfield Close, Wick,
LITTLEHAMPTON, West
Sussex BN17 6HY
Tel: 01903 731277
Head: Mrs Maria Davis
Category: SEBD (Coed 7-16)

SHOREHAM-BY-SEA

Herons Dale Primary School
Hawkins Crescent, SHOREHAM-
BY-SEA, West Sussex BN43 6TN
Tel: 01273 596904
Head: Ms Isabel Robson
Category: LD (Coed 4-11)

WORTHING

Oak Grove College
The Boulevard, WORTHING,
West Sussex BN13 1JX
Tel: 01903 708870
Head: Mr Phillip Potter
Category: LD (Coed 11-19)

Palatine Primary School
Palatine Road, Goring-By-Sea,
WORTHING, West Sussex BN12 6JP
Tel: 01903 242835
Head: Mrs Catriona Goldsmith
Category: LD (Coed 3-11)

SWINDON
Borough Council

Swindon SEN Team, Civic Offices, Euclid Street, Swindon, Wiltshire, SN1 2JH
Email: sendproject@swindon.gov.uk Website: www.swindon.gov.uk

SWINDON

Brimble Hill School
Tadpole Lane, Redhouse,
SWINDON, Wiltshire SN25 2NB
Tel: 01793 493900
Head: Mrs Alison Paul
Category: SLD (2-11)

Chalet School
Liden Drive, Liden, SWINDON,
Wiltshire SN3 6EX
Tel: 01793 534537
Head: Ms Katherine Bryan
Category: CLD including ASD (2-11)

Crowdys Hill School
Jefferies Avenue, Cricklade Road,
SWINDON, Wiltshire SN2 7HJ
Tel: 01793 332400
Head: Mrs Mags Clarke
Category: CLD & other
difficulties (11-16)

Nyland Campus
Nyland Road, Nythe,
SWINDON, Wiltshire SN3 3RD
Tel: 01793 535023
Head: Ms Becky O'Brien
Category: BESD (5-11)

St Luke's School
Cricklade Road, SWINDON,
Wiltshire SN2 7AS
Tel: 01793 705566
Head: Mr Geoff Cherrill
Category: BESD (11-16)

Uplands School
The Learning Campus, Tadpole
Lane, Redhouse, SWINDON,
Wiltshire SN25 2NB
Tel: 01793 493910
Head: Mrs Jackie Smith
Category: SLD (11-19)

TELFORD & WREKIN
Information, Advice & Support Service

Telford & Wrekin SENDIASS, The Glebe Centre, Glebe Street, Wellington Telford, TF1 1JP
Tel: 01952 457176 Email: info@iass.org.uk Website: www.telford.gov.uk

TELFORD

Haughton School
Queen Street, Madeley,
TELFORD, Shropshire TF7 4BW
Tel: 01952 387540
Head: Mrs Gill Knox
Category: MLD ASD SLD
SP&LD BESD (Coed 5-11)

Mount Gilbert School
Hinkshay Road, Dawley,
TELFORD, Shropshire TF4 3PP
Tel: 01952 387670
Head: Mrs Lisa Lyon
Category: SEBD SPLD
AUT (Coed 11-16)

Queensway HLC
Hadley, TELFORD, Shropshire TF1 6AJ
Tel: 01952 388555
Head: Mr Nigel Griffiths
Category: ASD (11-18)

Southall School
Off Rowan Avenue, Dawley,
TELFORD, Shropshire TF4 3PN
Tel: 01952 387600
Acting Head: Ms Abi Martin
Category: MLD ASD
SEBD (Coed 11-16)

The Bridge
HLC, Waterloo Road, Hadley,
TELFORD, Shropshire TF1 5NQ
Tel: 01952 387108
Head: Ms Heather Davies
Category: (3-16)

THURROCK
Information, Advice & Support Service

Thurrock SEN Team, Parent Advisory Team Thurrock (PATT), The Beehive, West Street Grays, Essex, RM17 6XP
Tel: 01375 389 894 Email: info@patt.org.uk Website: www.thurrock.gov.uk

GRAYS

**Beacon Hill Academy
(Post 16 Provision)**
Buxton Road, GRAYS,
Essex RM16 2WU
Tel: 01375 898656
Head: Mrs Sue Hewitt
Category: SLD PNI PMLD
(Coed 16-19)

Treetops School
Buxton Road, GRAYS,
Essex RM16 2WU
Tel: 01375 372723
Head: Mr Paul Smith
Category: MLD ASD (Coed 3-16)

Treetops School (6th Form)
Buxton Road, GRAYS,
Essex RM16 2WU
Tel: 01375 372723
Head: Mr Paul Smith

TORBAY
Council

Torbay SEN Team, Tor Hill House, c/o Torquay Town Hall, Torquay, Devon, TQ1 3DR
Tel: 01803 208274 Email: sensection@torbay.gov.uk Website: www.torbay.gov.uk

PAIGNTON

Torbay School
170b Torquay Road, Preston,
PAIGNTON, Devon TQ3 2AL
Tel: 01803 665522
Executive Head: Mr James Evans
Category: BESD (11-16)

TORQUAY

Mayfield School
Moor Lane, Watcombe,
TORQUAY, Devon TQ2 8NH
Tel: 01803 328375
Head: Mrs June Palmer
Category: SLD PMLD PH
AUT (3-19) BESD (5-11)

Tyne & Wear
GATESHEAD
Council

Gateshead SEND Team, Civic Centre, Regent Street, Gateshead, Tyne & Wear, NE8 1HH
Tel: 0191 433 3626 Email: senteam@gateshead.gov.uk Website: www.gateshead.gov.uk

GATESHEAD

Dryden School Business & Enterprise College
Shotley Gardens, Low Fell,
GATESHEAD, Tyne & Wear NE9 5UR
Tel: 01914 203811
Executive Head: Ms Jayne Bryant
Category: SLD (Coed 11-19)

Eslington Primary School
Hazel Road, GATESHEAD,
Tyne & Wear NE8 2EP
Tel: 01914 334131
Head: Ms Michelle Richards
Category: EBD (Coed 5-11)

Furrowfield School
Whitehills Drive, Felling,
GATESHEAD, Tyne & Wear NE10 9RZ
Tel: 01914 954700
Head: Ms Michelle Richards
Category: EBD (Boys 11-16)

Hill Top Specialist Arts College
Wealcroft, Leam Lane Estate,
GATESHEAD, Tyne & Wear NE10 8LT
Tel: 01914 692462
Executive Head: Ms Jayne Bryant
Category: MLD AUT (Coed 11-16)

NEWCASTLE UPON TYNE

Gibside School
Burnthouse Lane, Whickham,
NEWCASTLE UPON TYNE,
Tyne & Wear NE16 5AT
Tel: 01914 410123
Head: Ms Judith Donovan
Category: SLD MLD AUT (Coed 4-11)

Tyne & Wear
NEWCASTLE UPON TYNE
City Council

Newcastle SEN Assessment Service, Room 213, Civic Centre, Newcastle upon Tyne, Tyne & Wear, NE1 8QH
Tel: 01912 774650 Email: localoffer@newcastle.gov.uk Website: www.newcastlechildrenservices.org.uk

NEWCASTLE UPON TYNE

Hadrian School
Bertram Crescent, Pendower,
NEWCASTLE UPON TYNE,
Tyne & Wear NE15 6PY
Tel: 01912 734440
Head: Mr Christopher Rollings
Category: PMLD SLD
(Coed Day 2-11)

Linhope Pupil Referral Unit
Linhope Centre, Linhope
Road, NEWCASTLE UPON TYNE,
Tyne & Wear NE5 2NW
Tel: 01912 674447
Head: Mr Jeff Lough
Category: (Coed Day 5-16)

Newcastle Bridges School
c/o Kenton College, Drayton
Road, Kenton, NEWCASTLE UPON
TYNE, Tyne & Wear NE3 3RU
Tel: 01918 267086
Head: Mrs Margaret Dover
Category: HS (Coed 2-19)

Sir Charles Parson School
Westbourne Avenue, NEWCASTLE
UPON TYNE, Tyne & Wear NE6 4ED
Tel: 01912 952280
Head: Mr Nick Sharing
Category: SLD PD PMLD
(Coed Day 11-19)

Thomas Bewick School
Linhope Road, West Denton,
NEWCASTLE UPON TYNE,
Tyne & Wear NE5 2LW
Tel: 01912 296020
Head: Ms Diane Scott
Category: AUT (Coed
Day/boarding 3-19)

Trinity School
Condercum Road, NEWCASTLE
UPON TYNE, Tyne & Wear NE4 8XJ
Tel: 01912 986950
Head: Mr Bill Curley
Category: SEBD (Coed Day 7-16)

Tyne & Wear

SUNDERLAND

Children's Services

**Sunderland SEN and Accessibility Team, Sunderland Customer Service Centre,
Bunny Hill, Hylton Lane Sunderland, Tyne & Wear, SR5 4BW**

Tel: 01915 205553 Email: sen@sunderland.gov.uk Website: www.sunderland.gov.uk

SUNDERLAND

Sunningdale School
Shaftoe Road, Springwell,
SUNDERLAND, Tyne & Wear SR3 4HA
Tel: 01915 535880
Head: Mrs C Wright
Category: PMLD SLD
(Coed Day 2-11)

WASHINGTON

Columbia Grange School
Oxclose Road, WASHINGTON,
Tyne & Wear NE38 7NY
Tel: 01912 193860
Head: Mrs L Mavin
Category: SLD ASD (Coed Day 3-11)

Tyne & Wear

NORTH TYNESIDE

Information, Advice & Support Service

**North Tyneside SENDIASS, Floor 2, Quadrant West, Cobalt Business Park,
Silverlink North North Tyneside, Tyne & Wear, NE27 0BY**

Tel: 0191 643 8313/0191 643 8317 Email: sendiass@northtyneside.gov.uk Website: www.northtyneside.gov.uk

LONGBENTON

Benton Dene School
Hailsham Avenue, LONGBENTON,
Tyne & Wear NE12 8FD
Tel: 01916 432730
Head: Mrs Alison McAllister-Williams
Category: MLD ASD (Coed 5-11+)

NORTH SHIELDS

Southlands School
Beach Road, Tynemouth, NORTH
SHIELDS, Tyne & Wear NE30 2QR
Tel: 01912 006348
Head: Mr Dave Erskine
Category: MLD BESD (Coed 11-16+)

WALLSEND

Beacon Hill School
Rising Sun Cottages, High Farm,
WALLSEND, Tyne & Wear NE28 9JW
Tel: 01916 433000
Head: Mrs Justina Terretta
Category: ASD SLD
PMLD (Coed 2-16)

Silverdale School
Langdale Gardens, WALLSEND,
Tyne & Wear NE28 0HG
Tel: 01916 053230
Head: Mr Peter Gannon
Category: BESD (Coed 7-16)

WHITLEY BAY

Woodlawn School
Drumoyne Gardens, Monkseaton,
WHITLEY BAY, Tyne & Wear NE25 9DL
Tel: 01916 432590
Head: Mrs Gill Wilson
Category: PD MSI Medical
needs (Coed 2-16)

Tyne & Wear

SOUTH TYNESIDE

Pupil Services

South Tynesdie SEN Team, Children, Adults & Families, Level 0, Town Hall & Civic Offices, Westoe Road South Shields, Tyne & Wear, NE33 2RL

Tel: 01914 247808 Email: tracey.wilson@southtyneside.gov.uk Website: www.southtyneside.info

HEBBURN

Hebburn Lakes Primary School
Campbell Park Road, HEBBURN, Tyne & Wear NE31 1QY
Tel: 01914 839122
Head: Mr A S Watson
Category: BESD LD Complex medical needs

Keelman's Way School
Campbell Park Road, HEBBURN, Tyne & Wear NE31 1QY
Tel: 01914 897480
Head: Mrs Paula Selby
Category: PMLD SLD (Coed Day 2-19)

JARROW

Epinay Business & Enterprise School
Clervaux Terrace, JARROW, Tyne & Wear NE32 5UP
Tel: 01914 898949
Head: Mrs Hilary Harrison
Category: MLD EBD (Coed 5-17)

Fellgate Autistic Unit
Oxford Way, Fellgate Estate, JARROW, Tyne & Wear NE32 4XA
Tel: 01914 894801
Head: Miss C Wilson
Category: AUT (Coed 3-11)

Hedworthfield Language Development Unit
Linkway, Hedworth Estate, JARROW, Tyne & Wear NE32 4QF
Tel: 01915 373373
Head: Ms G Jeynes
Category: SP&LD (Coed)

Jarrow School
Field Terrace, JARROW, Tyne & Wear NE32 5PR
Tel: 01914 283200
Head: Miss J Gillies
Category: HI ASD

Simonside Primary School
Glasgow Road, JARROW, Tyne & Wear NE32 4AU
Tel: 01914 898315
Head: Ms Bland
Category: HI

SOUTH SHIELDS

Ashley Child Development Centre
Temple Park Road, SOUTH SHIELDS, Tyne & Wear NE34 0QA
Tel: 01914 564977
Head: Mrs D Todd
Category: Other Early Years

Bamburgh School
Horsley Hill Community Campus, SOUTH SHIELDS, Tyne & Wear NE34 7TD
Tel: 01914 274330
Head: Mr Peter Nord
Category: PD MED VIS HI MLD (Coed Day 2-17)

Harton Speech and Language and ASD Resource Bases
c/o Harton Technology College, Lisle Road, SOUTH SHIELDS, Tyne & Wear NE34 6DL
Tel: 01914 274050
Head: Mr K A Gibson
Category: Speech and language ASD

Park View School
Temple Park Road, SOUTH SHIELDS, Tyne & Wear NE34 0QA
Tel: 01914 541568
Head: Mr Chris Rue
Category: BESD (Coed Day 11-16)

WARRINGTON

Children & Young People

Warrington Pupil Assessment Support Team, New Town House, Buttermarket Street, Warrington, WA1 2NH

Tel: 01925 443322 Email: contact@warrington.gov.uk Website: www.warrington.gov.uk

WARRINGTON

Fox Wood School
Holes Lane, Woolston, WARRINGTON, Cheshire WA1 4LS
Tel: 01925 818534
Headteacher: Mrs Lucinda Duffy
Category: SLD (Coed Day 4-19)

Green Lane Community Special School
Holes Lane, Woolston, WARRINGTON, Cheshire WA1 4LS
Tel: 01925 811617
Headteacher: Mr Paul King
Category: MLD CLD (Coed Day 4-19)

Woolston Brook School
Green Lane, Padgate, WARRINGTON, Cheshire WA1 4JL
Tel: 01925 818549
Headteacher: Mr Michael Frost
Category: BESD (Coed Day 7-16)

WARWICKSHIRE

Information, Advice & Support Service

Warwickshire SENDIASS, Canterbury House, Exhall Grange Campus, Easter Way, Ash Green Coventry, Warwickshire, CV7 9HP
Tel: 024 7636 6054 Email: jo.gordon@family-action.org.uk Website: www.warwickshire.gov.uk

ASH GREEN

Exhall Grange School & Science College
Easter Way, ASH GREEN, Warwickshire CV7 9HP
Tel: 02476 364200
Head: Mrs Christine Marshall
Category: VIS PD Med (Coed Day 2-19)

COLESHILL

Woodlands School
Packington Lane, COLESHILL, West Midlands B46 3JE
Tel: 01675 463590
Head: Mr Iain Paterson
Category: Generic SLD VIS HI AUT MSI PD MLD PMLD (Coed Day 2-19)

HENLEY-IN-ARDEN

River House School
Stratford Road, HENLEY-IN-ARDEN, West Midlands B95 6AD
Tel: 01564 792514
Head: Ms Francesca Cannarella
Category: SEBD (Boys Day 11-16)

NUNEATON

Oak Wood Primary School
Morris Drive, NUNEATON, Warwickshire CV11 4QH
Tel: 02476 740907
Head: Mr George Smith
Category: Generic SLD MLD VIS HI AUT MSI PD PMLD (Coed Day 2-11)

Oak Wood Secondary School
Morris Drive, NUNEATON, Warwickshire CV11 4QH
Tel: 02476 740901
Head: Mr George Smith
Category: Generic SLD MLD VIS HI AUT MSI PD PMLD (Coed Day 11-16)

RUGBY

Brooke School
Overslade Lane, RUGBY, Warwickshire CV22 6DY
Tel: 01788 812324
Head: Mr Christopher Pollitt
Category: Generic SLD VIS HI AUT MSI PD MLD PMLD (Coed Day 2-19)

STRATFORD-UPON-AVON

Welcombe Hills School
Blue Cap Road, STRATFORD-UPON-AVON, Warwickshire CV37 6TQ
Tel: 01789 266845
Head: Mrs Judith Humphry
Category: Generic SLD VIS HI AUT MSI PD MLD PMLD (Coed Day 2-19)

WARWICK

Ridgeway School
Deansway, WARWICK, Warwickshire CV34 5DF
Tel: 01926 491987
Head: Ms Debra Hewitt
Category: Generic SLD VIS HI AUT MSI PD MLD PMLD (Coed Day 2-11)

Round Oak School, Support Service & Sports College
Brittain Lane, off Myton Road, WARWICK, Warwickshire CV34 6DX
Tel: 01926 423311
Head: Mrs Jayne Naylor
Category: Generic SLD VIS HI AUT MSI PD MLD PMLD (Coed Day 11-19)

West Midlands

BIRMINGHAM

City Council

Birmingham SENDIASS Team, Council House, Victoria Square, Birmingham, B1 1BB
Tel: 0121 303 5004 Email: sendiass@birmingham.gov.uk Website: www.birmingham.gov.uk

EDGBASTON

Baskerville School
Fellows Lane, Harborne, EDGBASTON, Birmingham B17 9TS
Tel: 01214 273191
Head: Mrs Rosemary Adams
Category: ASD (Coed boarding 11-19)

ERDINGTON

Queensbury School
Wood End Road, ERDINGTON, Birmingham B24 8BL
Tel: 01213 735731
Head: Mrs Sherree Watkins-McGirl
Category: MLD AUT SLD (Coed Day 11-19)

The Pines Special School
Marsh Hill, ERDINGTON, Birmingham B23 7EY
Tel: 0121 4646136
Head: Miss Emma Pearce
Category: SP&LD ASD (Coed Day 2-11)

HALL GREEN

Fox Hollies School
Highbury Community Campus, Queensbridge Road, Moseley, HALL GREEN, Birmingham B13 8QB
Tel: 01214 646566
Head: Mr Keith Youngson
Category: SLD PD CLD MSI (Coed Day 11-19)

Uffculme School
Queensbridge Road, Moseley, HALL GREEN, Birmingham B13 8QB
Tel: 01214 645250
Head: Mr Alex MacDonald
Category: ASD (Coed day 3-19)

HODGE HILL

Beaufort School
Stechford Road, HODGE HILL, Birmingham B34 6BJ
Tel: 01216 758500
Head: Ms Fiona Woolford
Category: SLD AUT PMLD (Coed Day 2-11)

Braidwood School
Bromford Road, HODGE HILL, Birmingham B36 8AF
Tel: 01214 645558
Head: Mrs Karen Saywood
Category: D HI ASD MLD (Coed Day 11-19)

KITTS GREEN

Hallmoor School
Scholars Gate, KITTS GREEN, Birmingham B33 0DL
Tel: 01217 833972
Head: Mr Stuart Cameron
Category: MLD MSI SP&LD (Coed Day 4-19)

NORTHFIELD

Longwill Primary School for Deaf Children
Bell Hill, NORTHFIELD,
Birmingham B31 1LD
Tel: 01214 753923
Head: Mrs Alison Carter
Category: HI D (Coed Day 2-12)

Victoria School
Bell Hill, NORTHFIELD,
Birmingham B31 1LD
Tel: 01214 769478
Head: Mrs Caroline Lane
Category: PD (Coed Day 2-19)

PERRY BARR

Hamilton School
Hamilton Road, Handsworth,
PERRY BARR, Birmingham B21 8AH
Tel: 01214 641676
Head: Mr Jonathan Harris
Category: ASD SP&LD
(Coed Day 4-11)

Mayfield School
Heathfield Road, Handsworth,
PERRY BARR, Birmingham B19 1HJ
Tel: 0121 5237321
Head: Ms Susan Bainbridge
Category: SLD PMLD
(Coed Day 3-19)

Oscott Manor School
Old Oscott Hill, Kingstanding,
PERRY BARR, Birmingham B44 9SP
Tel: 01213 608222
Head: Ms Joy Hardwick
Category: PMLD ASD MLD
(Coed Day 11-19)

Priestley Smith School
Beeches Road, Great Barr, PERRY
BARR, Birmingham B42 2PY
Tel: 01213 253900
Head: Mrs Helen Porter
Category: VIS (Coed Day 2-19)

REDDITCH

Skilts School
Gorcott Hill, REDDITCH,
West Midlands B98 9ET
Tel: 01527 853851
Head: Mr Dominic Crompton
Category: EBD (Coed
Boarding 5-12)

SELLY OAK

Cherry Oak School
60 Frederick Road, SELLY
OAK, Birmingham B29 6PB
Tel: 01214 642037
Head: Ms Julie Fardell
Category: SLD PMLD
(Coed Day 3-11)

Lindsworth School
Monyhull Hall Road, Kings Norton,
SELLY OAK, Birmingham B30 3QA
Tel: 01216 935363
Head: Mrs Janet Collins
Category: SEBD (Coed
Boarding 11-16)

Selly Oak Trust School
Oak Tree Lane, SELLY OAK,
Birmingham B29 6HZ
Tel: 01214 720876
Head: Mr Chris Field
Category: MLD (Coed Day 11-19)

The Dame Ellen Pinsent School
Ardencote Road, SELLY OAK,
Birmingham B13 0RW
Tel: 01216 752487
Head: Miss Denise Fountain
Category: ASD EBD SP&LD
HI (Coed day 5-11)

SOLIHULL

Springfield House Community Special School
Kenilworth Road, Knowle,
SOLIHULL, West Midlands B93 0AJ
Tel: 01564 772772
Head: Mrs Janet Collins
Category: SEBD (Coed
Boarding 5-12)

SUTTON COLDFIELD

Langley School
Trinity Road, SUTTON COLDFIELD,
West Midlands B75 6TJ
Tel: 01216 752929
Head: Mrs Fiona Woolford
Category: MLD ASD
(Coed Day 3-11)

The Bridge School
Coppice View Road, SUTTON
COLDFIELD, Birmingham B73 6UE
Tel: 01214 648265
Head: Mrs Jane Edgerton
Category: PMLD AUT
ASD (Coed 2-11)

YARDLEY

Brays School
Brays Road, Sheldon, YARDLEY,
Birmingham B26 1NS
Tel: 01217 435730
Head: Ms Ann Whitehouse
Category: PD SLD EBD
CLD MSI (Coed 2-11)

West Midlands

COVENTRY
Education Authority

Coventry SEN & Inclusion, Civic Centre 2.3, Earl Street, Coventry, West Midlands, CV1 5RS
Tel: 02476 831624 Website: www.coventry.gov.uk

COVENTRY

Baginton Fields Secondary School
Sedgemoor Road, COVENTRY,
West Midlands CV3 4EA
Tel: 02476 303854
Head: Mr Simon Grant
Category: SLD (Coed Day 11-19)

Castle Wood
Deedmore Road, COVENTRY,
West Midlands CV2 1EQ
Tel: 02476 709060
Head: Mrs Yvonne McCall
Category: (Coed Day 3-11)

Corley Centre
Church Lane, Fillongley, COVENTRY,
West Midlands CV7 8AZ
Tel: 01676 540218
Head: Ms Lisa Batch
Category: Complex
SCD (Coed 11-19)

River Bank Academy
Ashington Grove, COVENTRY,
West Midlands CV3 4DE
Tel: 02476 303776
Head: Mr David Lisowski/
Mrs Jackie Smith
Category: (Coed Day 11-19)

Sherbourne Fields Primary & Secondary School
Rowington Close, Off
Kingsbury Road, COVENTRY,
West Midlands CV6 1PS
Tel: 02476 591501
Head: Ms Shivaun Moriaty
Category: PD (Coed Day 2-19)

Tiverton Primary
Rowington Close, Off
Kingsbury Road, COVENTRY,
West Midlands CV6 1PS
Tel: 02476 594954
Head: Mrs Carolyn Claridge
Category: SLD (Coed Day 3-11)

Woodfield School
Stoneleigh Road Primary Site,
COVENTRY, West Midlands CV4 7AB
Tel: 02476 418755
Head: Mr Steve Poole
Category: ESBD (Coed Day 5-11)

Woodfield School
Hawthorn Lane Secondary Site,
COVENTRY, West Midlands CV4 9PB
Tel: 02476 462335
Head: Mr Steve Poole
Category: EBD (Boys Day 11-16)

West Midlands

DUDLEY

Information, Advice & Support Service

Dudley SENDIASS, Saltwells Education Centre, Bowling Green Road, Netherton Dudley, West Midlands, DY2 9LY
Tel: 01384 817373 Website: www.dudley.gov.uk

DUDLEY

Old Park School
Thorns Road, Quarry Bank,
DUDLEY, West Midlands DY5 2JY
Tel: 01384 818905
Head: Mrs G Cartwright
Category: SLD (4-19)

Rosewood School
Bell Street, Coseley, DUDLEY,
West Midlands WV14 8XJ
Tel: 01384 816800
Head: Mr D Kirk
Category: EBD (11-16)

The Brier School
Bromley Lane, Kingswinford,
DUDLEY, West Midlands DY6 8QN
Tel: 01384 816000
Head: Mr R Hinton
Category: MLD (4-16)

The Sutton School & Specialist College
Scotts Green Close, Russells
Hall Estate, DUDLEY, West
Midlands DY1 2DU
Tel: 01384 818670
Head: Mr D Charles
Category: MLD (11-16)

The Woodsetton School
Tipton Road, Woodsetton,
DUDLEY, West Midlands DY3 1BY
Tel: 01384 818265
Head: Mr P A Rhind-Tutt
Category: MLD (4-11)

HALESOWEN

Halesbury School
Feldon Lane, HALESOWEN,
West Midlands B62 9DR
Tel: 01384 818630
Acting Head: Mr J Kulyk
Category: MLD (4-16)

STOURBRIDGE

Pens Meadow School
Ridge Hill, Brierley Hill Road,
Wordsley, STOURBRIDGE,
West Midlands DY8 5ST
Tel: 01384 818945
Head: Mrs M Hunter
Category: SLD (3-19)

West Midlands

SANDWELL

Children & Families Services

Sandwell SEN Service, PO Box 16230, Sandwell Council House, Freeth Street Oldbury, West Midlands, B69 9EX
Tel: 01215 698240 Email: children_families@sandwell.gov.uk Website: www.sandwell.gov.uk

LICHFIELD

Shenstone Lodge School
Birmingham Road, Shenstone,
LICHFIELD, Staffordshire WS14 0LB
Tel: 01543 480369
Head: Mr N C Toplass
Category: EBD (Coed Day 4-16)

OLDBURY

The Meadows Sports College
Dudley Road East, OLDBURY,
West Midlands B69 3BU
Tel: 01215 697080
Head: Miss J Cliffe
Category: PMLD (Coed Day 11-19)

The Orchard School
Causeway Green Road, OLDBURY,
West Midlands B68 8LD
Tel: 01215 697040
Head: Mrs D Ellingham
Category: PMLD(Coed Day 2-11)

ROWLEY REGIS

The Westminster School
Curral Road, ROWLEY REGIS,
West Midlands B65 9AN
Tel: 01215 616884
Head: Mrs C Hill
Category: MLD (Coed Day 11-19)

West Midlands

SOLIHULL
Metropolitan Borough Council

Solihull SEN Team, Council House, Manor Square, Solihull, West Midlands, B91 3QB
Tel: 0121 704 6690 Email: edsen@solihull.gov.uk Website: www.solihull.gov.uk

BIRMINGHAM

Forest Oak School
Windward Way, Smith's
Wood, BIRMINGHAM, West
Midlands B36 0UE
Tel: 01217 170088
Principal: Mrs A R Mordey
Category: MLD (Coed Day 4-18)

Merstone School
Windward Way, Smith's
Wood, BIRMINGHAM, West
Midlands B36 0UE
Tel: 01217 171040
Principal: Mrs A R Mordey
Category: SLD (Coed Day 2-19)

Northern House School
Lanchester Way, Castle
Bromwich, BIRMINGHAM,
West Midlands B36 9LF
Tel: 01217 489760
Head: Mr Trevor Scott
Category: SEMH (Coed Day 11-16)

SOLIHULL

Hazel Oak School
Hazel Oak Road, Shirley, SOLIHULL,
West Midlands B90 2AZ
Tel: 01217 444162
Head: Mr Andy Simms
Category: MLD (Coed Day 4-18)

Reynalds Cross School
Kineton Green Road, SOLIHULL,
West Midlands B92 7ER
Tel: 01217 073012
Head: Mrs Jane Davenport
Category: SLD (Coed Day 2-19)

West Midlands

WALSALL
Walsall Information, Advice & Support Service

Walsall SEN Team, Blakenhall Village Centre, Thames Road, Blakenhall Walsall, West Midlands, WS3 1LZ
Tel: 01922 650330 Email: iasssend@walsall.gov.uk Website: www.walsall.gov.uk

WALSALL

**Castle Business &
Enterprise College**
Odell Road, Leamore, WALSALL,
West Midlands WS3 2ED
Tel: 01922 710129
Head: Mrs Christine Fraser
Category: MLD, Additional
Needs (Coed Day 7-19)

Elmwood School
King George Crescent, Rushall,
WALSALL, West Midlands WS4 1EG
Tel: 01922 721081
Head: Mr Lee Cross
Category: EBD (Coed Day 11-16)

Mary Elliot Special School
Leamore Lane, WALSALL,
West Midlands WS2 7NR
Tel: 01922 490190
Head: Mr Adrian Coleman
Category: SLD PMLD AUT
(Coed day 11-19)

Oakwood School
Druids Walk, Walsall Wood,
WALSALL, West Midlands WS9 9JS
Tel: 01543 452040
Head: Mrs Kay Mills
Category: SLD CLD PMLD
ASD Challenging behaviour
(Coed Day 3-11)

Old Hall School
Bentley Lane, WALSALL,
West Midlands WS2 7LU
Tel: 01902 368045
Head: Mrs Jenny Thompson
Category: SLD PMLD AUT
(Coed day 3-11)

Phoenix Primary School
Odell Road, Leamore, WALSALL,
West Midlands WS3 2ED
Tel: 01922 712834
Acting Head: Mrs Jeanette Ashwin
Category: EBD (Coed Day 4-11)

**The Jane Lane School - A
College for Cognition
and Learning**
Churchill Road, Bentley, WALSALL,
West Midlands WS2 0JH
Tel: 01922 721161
Head: Mr Tony Milovsorov
Category: MLD, Additional
Needs (Coed Day 7-19)

West Midlands

WOLVERHAMPTON
Information, Advice & Support Service

Wolverhampton SENDIASS, Civic Centre, St Peter's Square, Wolverhampton, West Midlands, WV1 1RT
Tel: 01902 556945 Email: ppservice@wolverhampton.gov.uk Website: www.wolverhampton.gov.uk

WOLVERHAMPTON

Green Park School
The Willows, Green Park Avenue,
Bilston, WOLVERHAMPTON,
West Midlands WV14 6EH
Tel: 01902 556429
Head: Mrs L Dawney
Category: PMLD SLD
(Coed Day 4-19)

Penn Fields Special School
Boundary Way, Penn,
WOLVERHAMPTON, West
Midlands WV4 4NT
Tel: 01902 558640
Head: Miss E Stanley
Category: MLD SLD ASD
(Coed Day 4-19)

Penn Hall School
Vicarage Road, Penn,
WOLVERHAMPTON, West
Midlands WV4 5HP
Tel: 01902 558355
Head: Mr D Parry
Category: PD SLD MLD
(Coed Day 3-19)

Tettenhall Wood School
Regis Road, Tettenhall,
WOLVERHAMPTON, West
Midlands WV6 8XF
Tel: 01902 556519
Head: Ms S Llewellyn
Category: ASD (Coed Day 5-19)

Wolverhampton Vocational Training Centre (WVTC)
Upper Villiers Street,
WOLVERHAMPTON, West
Midlands WV2 4NP
Tel: 01902 552285
Head: Ms H Andrioli
Category: MLD SLD ASD
ADHD (Coed Day 16-18)

WILTSHIRE
Children & Education Department

Wiltshire SEN/Disability 0-25 Service, County Hall, Bythesea Road, Trowbridge, Wiltshire, BA14 8JN
Tel: 01225 757985 Email: Statutorysen.service@wiltshire.gov.uk Website: www.wiltshirelocaloffer.org.uk

CHIPPENHAM

St Nicholas School
Malmesbury Road, CHIPPENHAM,
Wiltshire SN15 1QF
Tel: 01249 650435
Head: Mrs Ros Way
Category: SLD PMLD
(Coed Day 3-19)

DEVIZES

Downland School
Downlands Road, DEVIZES,
Wiltshire SN10 5EF
Tel: 01380 724193
Head: Mrs George Keily-Theobald
Category: BESD SPLD
(Boys Boarding 11-16)

Rowdeford School
Rowde, DEVIZES, Wiltshire SN10 2QQ
Tel: 01380 850309
Head: Mrs Ingrid Sidmouth
Category: MLD (Coed
Boarding 11-16)

TROWBRIDGE

Larkrise School
Ashton Street, TROWBRIDGE,
Wiltshire BA14 7EB
Tel: 01225 761434
Head: Mr Phil Cook
Category: SLD MLD
(Coed Day 3-19)

WINDSOR & MAIDENHEAD
Adult, Children and Health Services

Windsor & Maidenhead CYPDS, Town Hall, St Ives Road, Maidenhead, Berkshire, SL6 1RF
Tel: 01628 685878 Email: CYPDS@rbwm.gov.uk Website: www.rbwm.gov.uk

MAIDENHEAD

Manor Green School
Cannon Road, MAIDENHEAD,
Berkshire SL6 3LE
Tel: 01628 513800
Head: Joolz Scarlett
Category: SLD PMLD ASD
MLD (Coed 2-19)

WOKINGHAM

Children's Services

Wokingham SEN Team, Highwood Annexe, Fairwater Drive, Woodley Wokingham, Berkshire, RG5 3RU
Tel: 01189 746216 Email: sen@wokingham.gov.uk Website: www.wokingham.gov.uk

WOKINGHAM

Addington School
Woodlands Avenue, Woodley,
WOKINGHAM, Berkshire RG5 3EU
Tel: 01189 669073
Head: Mrs Liz Meek
Category: SLD PMLD ASD
MLD (Coed 4-18)

Northern House School
Gipsy Lane, WOKINGHAM,
Berkshire RG40 2HR
Tel: 01189 771293
Head: Mr Dominic Geraghty
Category: BESD (Coed 7-16)

WORCESTERSHIRE

Children's Services Directorate

Worcestershire SENDIASS, WCC Young People's Support Services, Tolladine Road, Worcester, WR4 9NB
Tel: 01905 768153 Email: sendiass@worcestershire.gov.uk Website: www.worcestershire.gov.uk

BROMSGROVE

Chadsgrove School & Specialist Sports College
Meadow Road,
Catshill, BROMSGROVE,
Worcestershire B61 0JL
Tel: 01527 871511
Head: Mrs Debbie Rattley
Category: PD PMLD MSI LD (2-19)

Rigby Hall School
19 Rigby Lane, Astonfields,
BROMSGROVE,
Worcestershire B60 2EP
Tel: 01527 875475
Head: Mrs Tracey Smith
Category: SLD MLD ASD (3-19)

EVESHAM

Vale of Evesham School
Four Pools Lane, EVESHAM,
Worcestershire WR11 1BN
Tel: 01386 443367
Head: Mr Stephen Garside
Category: SLD MLD PMLD ASD (4-19)

KIDDERMINSTER

Wyre Forest School
Habberley Road, KIDDERMINSTER,
Worcestershire DY11 6FA
Tel: 01562 827785
Head: Mrs Rebecca Garratt
Category: MLD SLD ASD
BESD (Coed 7-16)

REDDITCH

Kingfisher School
Clifton Close, Matchborough,
REDDITCH, Worcestershire B98 0HF
Tel: 01527 502486
Head: Mr Ian Taylor
Category: BESD (Coed 7-16)

Pitcheroak School
Willow Way, Brockhill, REDDITCH,
Worcestershire B97 6PQ
Tel: 01527 65576
Head: Ms Sheila Holden
Category: SLD MLD AUT (2-19)

WORCESTER

Fort Royal Community Primary School
Wylds Lane, WORCESTER WR5 1DR
Tel: 01905 355525
Head: Mr Edward Francis
Category: MLD PD SLD (2-11)

Regency High School
Carnforth Drive,
WORCESTER WR4 9JL
Tel: 01905 454828
Head: Mrs Sara Harding
Category: PD MLD SLD (11-19)

Riversides School
Thorneloe Road,
WORCESTER WR1 3HZ
Tel: 01905 21261
Head: Mr Paul Yeomans
Category: BESD (Coed 7-16)

CITY OF YORK

Information, Advice & Support Service

York SENDIASS, West Offices, Station Rise, York, YO1 6GA
Tel: 01904 554319 Email: yorksendiass@york.gov.uk Website: www.yorksendiass.org.uk

YORK

Applefields School
Bad Bargain Lane, YORK YO31 0LW
Tel: 01904 553900
Head: Mr Adam Booker
Category: MLD AUT SLD PMLD

Hob Moor Oaks School
Green Lane, Acomb,
YORK YO24 4PS
Tel: 01904 555000
Principal: Ms Vicki Ward
Category: MLD AUT SLD PMLD

EAST RIDING OF YORKSHIRE
Information, Advice & Support Service

E Riding of Yorkshire SENDIASS, Families Information Service Hub (FISH),
County Hall, Beverley, East Riding of Yorkshire, HU17 9BA
Tel: 01482 396469 Email: sendiass@eastriding.gov.uk Website: www.eastriding.gov.uk

BROUGH

**St Anne's School &
Sixth Form College**
St Helen's Drive, Welton, BROUGH,
East Riding of Yorkshire HU15 1NR
Tel: 01482 667379
Headteacher: Mrs Lesley Davis
Category: SLD

DRIFFIELD

Kings Mill School & Nursery
Victoria Road, DRIFFIELD, East
Riding of Yorkshire YO25 6UG
Tel: 01377 253375
Headteacher: Mrs Gail Lawton
Category: SLD

GOOLE

Riverside Special School
Ainsty Street, GOOLE, East
Riding of Yorkshire DN14 5JS
Tel: 01405 763925
Acting Headteacher: Mr
Andrew Hall
Category: MLD and other
complex needs

NORTH YORKSHIRE
Education Authority

North Yorkshire SEN Team, County Hall, Northallerton, North Yorkshire, DL7 8AD
Email: send@northyorks.gov.uk Website: www.northyorks.gov.uk

BEDALE

Mowbray School
Masham Road, BEDALE,
North Yorkshire DL8 2SD
Tel: 01677 422446
Head: Mr Jonathan Tearle
Category: MLD SP&LD (2-16)

HARROGATE

Forest Moor School
Menwith Hill Road, HARROGATE,
North Yorkshire HG3 2RA
Tel: 01423 779232
Head: Mr Marc Peart
Category: BESD (Boys 11-16)

Springwater School
High Street, Starbeck, HARROGATE,
North Yorkshire HG2 7LW
Tel: 01423 883214
Head: Mrs Sarah Edwards
Category: SLD PMLD (2-19)

KIRKBYMOORSIDE

Welburn Hall School
KIRKBYMOORSIDE, York YO62 7HQ
Tel: 01751 431218
Head: Mrs Marianne Best
Category: PHLD (8-18)

KNARESBOROUGH

The Forest School
Park Lane, KNARESBOROUGH,
North Yorkshire HG5 0DG
Tel: 01423 864583
Head: Mr Peter Hewitt
Category: MLD (2-16)

NORTHALLERTON

The Dales School
Morton-on-Swale,
NORTHALLERTON, North
Yorkshire DL7 9QW
Tel: 01609 772932
Head: Mrs Hanne Barton
Category: SLD PMLD (2-19)

SCARBOROUGH

Brompton Hall School
Brompton-by-Sawdon,
SCARBOROUGH, North
Yorkshire YO13 9DB
Tel: 01723 859121
Head: Mr Mark Mihkelson
Category: BESD (Boys 8-16)

Springhead School
Barry's Lane, Seamer Road,
SCARBOROUGH, North
Yorkshire YO12 4HA
Tel: 01723 367829
Head: Mrs Debbie Wilson
Category: SLD PMLD (2-19)

SKIPTON

Brooklands School
Burnside Avenue, SKIPTON,
North Yorkshire BD23 2DB
Tel: 01756 794028
Head: Mrs Denise Sansom
Category: MLD SLD PMLD (2-19)

South Yorkshire

BARNSLEY

Families Information Service

Barnsley SEN Team, Families Information Service, Gateway Plaza, Sackville Street Barnsley, South Yorkshire, S70 2RD
Tel: 0800 0345 340 Email: infofis@barnsley.go.uk Website: www.barnsley.gov.uk

BARNSLEY

Greenacre School
Keresforth Hill Road, BARNSLEY,
South Yorkshire S70 6RG
Tel: 01226 287165
Acting Head: Ms Diane Greaves
Category: SLD CLD PMLD
MSI AUT (Coed Day 2-19)

Springwell Learning Community
St Helen's Boulevard, Carlton Road,
BARNSLEY, South Yorkshire S71 2AY
Tel: 01226 291133
Head: Mr David Whitaker

South Yorkshire

DONCASTER

Council

Doncaster SEN Team, Civic Office, Waterdale, Doncaster, DN1 3BU
Tel: 01302 737209 Email: sen@doncaster.gov.uk Website: www.doncaster.gov.uk

DONCASTER

Coppice School
Ash Hill Road, Hatfield,
DONCASTER, South
Yorkshire DN7 6JH
Tel: 01302 844883
Head: Mr Karl O'Reilly
Category: SLD ASD BESD
(Coed Day 3-19)

Heatherwood School
Leger Way, DONCASTER,
South Yorkshire DN2 6HQ
Tel: 01302 322044
Head: Mrs Lisa Suter
Category: SLD PD (Coed Day 3-19)

North Ridge Community School
Tenter Balk Lane, Adwick
le Street, DONCASTER,
South Yorkshire DN6 7EF
Tel: 01302 720790
Head: Mrs Christine Djezzar
Category: SLD (Coed Day 3-19)

Stone Hill School
Barnsley Road, Scawsby,
DONCASTER, South
Yorkshire DN5 7UB
Tel: 01302 800090
Head: Mr Steve Leone
Category: MLD (Coed 6-16)

South Yorkshire

ROTHERHAM

Education, Health & Care Assessment Team

Rotherham SENDIASS, Riverside House, 1st Floor, Wing C, Main Street Rotherham, South Yorkshire, S65 1AE
Tel: 01709823627 Website: www.rotherhamsendiass.org.uk

MEXBOROUGH

Milton School
Storey Street, Swinton,
MEXBOROUGH, South
Yorkshire S64 8QG
Tel: 01709 570246
Head: Ms Rebecca Hughes
Category: MLD (5-16) ASD (5-11)

ROTHERHAM

Abbey School
Little Common Lane,
Kimberworth, ROTHERHAM,
South Yorkshire S61 2RA
Tel: 01709 740074
Head: Ms Lucy Windle
Category: MLD

Hilltop School
Larch Road, Maltby, ROTHERHAM,
South Yorkshire S66 8AZ
Tel: 01709 813386
Heads: Mr David Burdett
Category: SLD

Kelford School
Oakdale Road, Kimberworth,
ROTHERHAM, South
Yorkshire S61 2NU
Tel: 01709 512088
Head: Ms Jackie Tattershall
Category: SLD

Newman School
East Bawtry Road, Whiston,
ROTHERHAM, South
Yorkshire S60 3LX
Tel: 01709 828262
Head: Ms Julie Mott
Category: PH Medical needs

The Willows School
Locksley Drive, Thurcroft,
ROTHERHAM, South
Yorkshire S66 9NT
Tel: 01709 542539
Head: Mrs Anne Sanderson
Category: MLD

South Yorkshire

SHEFFIELD

Information, Advice & Support Service

Sheffield SENDIASS, Floor 6, North Wing, Moorfoot Building, Sheffield, S1 4PL
Tel: 0114 273 6009 Email: ed-parent.partnership@sheffield.gov.uk Website: www.sheffield.gov.uk

SHEFFIELD

Becton School
Beighton Community Hospital,
Sevenairs Road, SHEFFIELD,
South Yorkshire S20 1NZ
Tel: 01143 053121
Head: Mrs Sacha Schofield
Category: LD EBD SCD ADHD
Speech&LangD (Coed 5-18)

Bents Green School
Ringinglow Road, SHEFFIELD,
South Yorkshire S11 7TB
Tel: 01142 363545
Category: AUT ASD
SCD (Coed 11-19)

**Heritage Park
Foundation School**
Norfolk Park Road, SHEFFIELD,
South Yorkshire S2 2RU
Tel: 01142 796850
Executive Head: Mr Tony Middleton
Category: BESD (KS 2/3/4)

**Holgate Meadows
Foundation School**
Lindsay Road, SHEFFIELD,
South Yorkshire S5 7WE
Tel: 01142 456305
Head: Mr Tony Middleton
Category: BESD (KS 2/3/4)

Mossbrook Special School
Bochum Parkway, SHEFFIELD,
South Yorkshire S8 8JR
Tel: 01142 372768
Head: Mr Dean Linkhorn
Category: AUT SCD LD (Coed 4-11)

Norfolk Park School
Park Grange Road, SHEFFIELD,
South Yorkshire S2 3QF
Tel: 01142 726165
Interim Head: Ms Jan Kartawick
Category: PMLD LD (Coed 3-11)

Rowan School
4 Durvale Court, Furniss Avenue,
SHEFFIELD, South Yorkshire S17 3PT
Tel: 01142 350479
Category: AUT (Primary)

Seven Hills School
Granville Road, SHEFFIELD,
South Yorkshire S2 2RJ
Tel: 01142 743560
Heads: Ms Elaine Everett
& Mr Clive Rockliff
Category: SLD PMLD

Talbot Specialist School
Lees Hall Road, SHEFFIELD,
South Yorkshire S8 9JP
Tel: 01142 507394
Executive Head: Ms Judith Smith
Category: LD (Coed 11-19)

**Woolley Wood Community
Primary School**
Chaucer Road, SHEFFIELD,
South Yorkshire S5 9QN
Tel: 01142 327160
Head: Mr David Whitehead
Category: SLD PMLD

West Yorkshire

CALDERDALE

Children & Young People's Services

Calderdale SEN Team, Town Hall, PO Box 51, Halifax, West Yorkshire, HX1 1TP
Tel: 01422 394141 Email: sen.team@calderdale.gov.uk Website: www.calderdale.gov.uk

BRIGHOUSE

Highbury School
Lower Edge Road, Rastrick,
BRIGHOUSE, West Yorkshire HD6 3LD
Tel: 01484 716319
Head: Ms Debbie Sweet
Category: All (3-11)

HALIFAX

Ravenscliffe High School
Skircoat Green, HALIFAX,
West Yorkshire HX3 0RZ
Tel: 01422 358621
Head: Mr Martin Moorman
Category: All (11-18)

Wood Bank School
Dene View, Luddendenfoot,
HALIFAX, West Yorkshire HX2 6PB
Tel: 01422 884170
Head: Mr Richard Pawson
Category: All (4-11)

West Yorkshire

KIRKLEES

Directorate for Children & Young People

Kirklees SEN Team, Kirkgate Building, Byram Street, Huddersfield, West Yorkshire, HD1 1BY
Tel: **01484 456888** Email: **senact@kirklees.gov.uk** Website: **www.kirklees.gov.uk**

BATLEY

Fairfield School
White Lee Road, BATLEY,
West Yorkshire WF17 8AS
Tel: 01924 326103
Head: Mr John Page
Category: SLD (Coed Day 3-19)

DEWSBURY

Ravenshall School
Ravensthorpe Road, Thornhill Lees,
DEWSBURY, West Yorkshire WF12 9EE
Tel: 01924 456811
Head: Mrs Jeanette Tate
Category: MLD (Coed Day 5-16)

HOLMFIRTH

Lydgate School
Kirkroyds Lane, New Mill,
HOLMFIRTH, West Yorkshire HD9 1LS
Tel: 01484 222484
Head: Mrs Nicola Rogers
Category: MLD (Coed Day 5-16)

HUDDERSFIELD

Castle Hill School
Newsome Road South,
Newsome, HUDDERSFIELD,
West Yorkshire HD4 6JL
Tel: 01484 226659
Head: Mrs Gill Robinson
Category: SLD AUT PMLD
(Coed Day 3-19)

Woodley School & College
Dog Kennel Bank, HUDDERSFIELD,
West Yorkshire HD5 8JE
Tel: 01484 223937
Head: Ms Anne Lawton
Category: MLD AUT SEMH
(Coed Day 5-16)

West Yorkshire

LEEDS

SEND Information Advice & Support Service

Leeds SENDIASS, Adams Court, Kildare Terrace, Leeds, West Yorkshire, LS12 1DB
Tel: **01133 951200** Email: **sendiass@leeds.gov.uk** Website: **www.educationleeds.co.uk**

LEEDS

East SILC - John Jamieson (main site)
Hollin Hill Drive, Oakwood,
LEEDS, West Yorkshire LS8 2PW
Tel: 01132 930236
Head: Ms Diane Reynard
Category: Complex
physical, learning and care
needs (Coed 2-19)

North West SILC - Penny Field (main site)
Tongue Lane, Meanwood,
LEEDS, West Yorkshire LS6 4QD
Tel: 01133 368270
Head: Mr Michael Purches
Category: Complex
physical, learning and care
needs (Coed 2-19)

South SILC - Broomfield (main site)
Broom Place, Belle Isle, LEEDS,
West Yorkshire LS10 3JP
Tel: 01132 771603
Head: Mr John Fryer
Category: Complex
physical, learning and care
needs (Coed 2-19)

West Oaks SEN Specialist School & College
Westwood Way, Boston
Spa, Wetherby, LEEDS, West
Yorkshire LS23 6DX
Tel: 01937 844772
Head: Mr Andrew Hodkinson
Category: Complex
physical, learning and care
needs (Coed 2-19)

West Yorkshire

WAKEFIELD

Early Support Advice, Information & Liaison

Wakefield SEN Team, Wakefield One, PO Box 700, Burton Street Wakefield, WF1 2EB
Tel: 01924 379015 Email: wesail@kids.org.uk Website: www.wakefield.gov.uk

CASTLEFORD

Kingsland School Castleford
Poplar Avenue, Townville, CASTLEFORD, West Yorkshire WF10 3QJ
Tel: 01977 723085
Head: Miss Paula Trow
Category: SLD MLD (Coed 4-11)

OSSETT

Highfield School
Gawthorpe Lane, Gawthorpe, OSSETT, West Yorkshire WF5 9BS
Tel: 01924 302980
Head: Mrs Pat Marshall
Category: MLD (Coed 11-16)

PONTEFRACT

High Well School
Rookhill Road, PONTEFRACT, West Yorkshire WF8 2DD
Tel: 01924 572100
Head: Ms Louise Quinn
Category: EBD (Coed 11-16)

Oakfield Park School
Barnsley Road, Ackworth, PONTEFRACT, West Yorkshire WF7 7DT
Tel: 01977 613423
Head: Mr Stephen Copley
Category: SLD PMLD (Coed 11-19)

WAKEFIELD

Kingsland School Stanley
Aberford Road, Stanley, WAKEFIELD, West Yorkshire WF3 4BA
Tel: 01924 303100
Head: Miss Paula Trow
Category: SLD PMLD (Coed 2-11)

CHELTENHAM

The Ridge Primary Academy
Clyde Crescent, CHELTENHAM, Gloucestershire GL52 5QH
Tel: 01242 512680
Head: Mr Peter Hales
Category: SEBD (Coed 5-11)

DURSLEY

Greenfield Academy
Drake Lane, DURSLEY, Gloucestershire GL11 5HD
Tel: 01453 542130
Head: Mr Richard Lewis
Category: SEBD (Coed Day 11-16)

Peak Academy
Drake Lane, DURSLEY, Gloucestershire GL11 5HD
Tel: 01453 542130
Head: Mr Richard Lewis
Category: SEBD (Boys Day 11-16)

GUERNSEY

The Education Department

Guernsey SEN Team, PO Box 32, Grange Road, St Peter Port, Guernsey, GY1 3AU
Tel: 01481 733000 Email: office@education.gov.gg Website: www.education.gg

FOREST

Le Rondin School and Centre
Rue des Landes, FOREST, Guernsey GY8 0DP
Tel: 01481 268300
Head: Mrs P Sullivan
Category: MLD SLD PMLD (3-11)

ST SAMPSON'S

Le Murier School
Rue de Dol, ST SAMPSON'S, Guernsey GY2 4DA
Tel: 01481 246660
Head: Mr J Teehan
Category: MLD PMLD SLD (Coed 11-16)

ST. PETER PORT

Les Voies School
Collings Road, ST. PETER PORT, Guernsey GY1 1FW
Tel: 01481 710721
Head: Mr J Furley
Category: SEBD (Coed 4-16)

JERSEY

Education Support Team

Jersey SEN Team, PO Box 142, Highlands Campus, St. Saviour, Jersey, JE4 8QJ
Tel: 01534 449424 Email: education@gov.je Website: www.gov.je/esc

ST HELIER

Mont a l'Abbe School
La Grande Route de St Jean, La Pouquelaye, ST HELIER, Jersey JE2 3FN
Tel: 01534 875801
Head: Ms Sharon Eddie
Category: LD (3-19)

ST SAVIOUR

D'Hautree House
St Saviour's Hill, ST SAVIOUR, Jersey JE2 7LF
Tel: 01534 618042
Head: Mr Robert Mathews
Category: SEBD (Coed 11-16)

The Alternative Curriculum
Oakside House, La Grande Route de St Martin, Five Oaks, ST SAVIOUR, Jersey JE2 7GS
Tel: 01534 872840
Head: Mr Kevin Mansell
Category: EBD

NORTHERN IRELAND

BELFAST

The Education Authority

Education Authority, SEN Team, 40 Academy Street, Belfast, Northern Ireland, BT1 2NQ
Tel: +44 (0)28 9056 4000 Email: info@eani.org.uk Website: www.eani.org.uk

BELFAST

Belfast Hospital School
Royal Belfast Hospital School
for Sick Children, Falls Road,
BELFAST, Co Antrim BT12 6BE
Tel: 02890 633498
Head: Mrs Michele Godfrey
Category: HS (Coed 4-19)

Cedar Lodge School
24 Lansdowne Park North,
BELFAST, Co Antrim BT15 4AE
Tel: 02890 777292
Head: Mrs Lois Little
Category: EPI ASD ADHD
Medical needs (Coed 4-16)

Clarawood School
Clarawood Park, BELFAST,
Co Antrim BT5 6FR
Tel: 02890 472736
Head: Ms Joanne White
Category: SEBD (Coed 8-12)

Fleming Fulton School
35 Upper Malone Road,
BELFAST, Co Antrim BT9 6TY
Tel: 02890 613877
Head: Ms Karen Hancock
Category: PH MLD (Coed 3-19)

Glenveagh School
Harberton Park, BELFAST,
Co Antrim BT9 6TX
Tel: 02890 669907
Head: Ms Anne Moore
Category: SLD (Coed 8-19)

Greenwood House Assessment Centre
Greenwood Avenue, Upper
Newtownards Road, BELFAST,
Co Antrim BT4 3JJ
Tel: 02890 471000
Head: Mrs Katherine Calvert
Category: SP&LD MLD EBD SLD
Medical needs (Coed 4-7)

Harberton Special School
Haberton Park, BELFAST,
Co Antrim BT9 6TX
Tel: 02890 381525
Head: Mr Martin McGlade
Category: AUT ASP SP&LD EBD
Medical needs (Coed 4-11)

Loughshore Educational Resource Centre
889 Shore Road, BELFAST,
Co Antrim BT36 7DH
Tel: 02890 773062
Head: Mrs G Cameron

Mitchell House School
Marmont Park, Holywood Road,
BELFAST, Co Antrim BT4 2GT
Tel: 02890 768407
Head: Miss Laura Matchett
Category: PD MSI (Coed 3-18)

Oakwood Assessment Centre
Harberton Park, BELFAST,
Co Antrim BT9 6TX
Tel: 02890 605116
Head: Mrs P McCann
Category: SLD PMLD
ASD (Coed 3-8)

Park Education Resource Centre
145 Ravenhill Road, BELFAST,
Co Antrim BT6 8GH
Tel: 02890 450513
Head: Ms R McCausland
Category: MLD (Coed 11-16)

St Gerard's School & Support Services
Blacks Road, BELFAST,
Co Antrim BT10 0NB
Tel: 02890 600330
Head: Mrs Siobh·n McIntaggart
Category: MLD (Coed 4-16)

St Teresa's Speech, Language & Communication Centre
Glen Road, BELFAST, Co
Antrim BT11 8BL
Tel: 02890 611943
Co-ordinator: Miss N Campbell

St Vincent's Centre
6 Willowfield Drive, BELFAST,
Co Antrim BT6 8HN
Tel: 02890 461444
Teacher in Charge: Mr J McAuley

NORTH EASTERN

The Education Authority

Education Authority, SEN Team, 182 Galgorm Road, Ballymena, Northern Ireland, BT42 1HN
Tel: +44 (0)28 2565 3333 Email: info@eani.org.uk Website: www.eani.org.uk

ANTRIM

Riverside School
Fennel Road, ANTRIM,
Co Antrim BT41 4PB
Tel: 02894 428946
Head: Mr Colin Ward
Category: SLD

BALLYMENA

Castle Tower School
91 Fry's Road, BALLYMENA,
Co Antrim BT43 7EN
Tel: 02825 648264
Head: Mr Raymond McFeeters
Category: MLD SLD PD SEBD

COLERAINE

Sandelford Special School
4 Rugby Avenue, COLERAINE,
Co Londonderry BT52 1JL
Tel: 02870 343062
Category: SLD

MAGHERAFELT

Kilronan School
46 Ballyronan Road, MAGHERAFELT,
Co Londonderry BT45 6EN
Tel: 02879 632168
Head: Mrs Alison Millar
Category: SLD

NEWTOWNABBEY

Hill Croft School
3 Manse Way, NEWTOWNABBEY,
Co Antrim BT36 5UW
Tel: 02890 837488
Category: SLD

Jordanstown Special School
85 Jordanstown Road,
NEWTOWNABBEY, Co
Antrim BT37 0QE
Tel: 02890 863541
Head: Mr Adam Smith
Category: HI VIS (Coed 4-19)

Rosstulla Special School
2 Jordanstown Road,
NEWTOWNABBEY, Co
Antrim BT37 0QS
Tel: 02890 862743
Head: Mrs Fiona Burke
Category: MLD (Coed 5-16)

SOUTH EASTERN

The Education Authority

Education Authority, SEN Team, Grahamsbridge Road, Dundonald, Northern Ireland, BT16 2HS
Tel: +44 (0)28 9056 6200 Email: info@eani.org.uk Website: www.eani.org.uk

BANGOR

Clifton Special School
292A Old Belfast Road,
BANGOR, Co Down BT19 1RH
Tel: 02891 270210
Head: Mrs Stephanie Anderson
Category: SLD

Lakewood Special School
96 Newtownards Road,
BANGOR, Co Down BT19 1GZ
Tel: 02891 456227
Head: Mr Jon Bleakney

BELFAST

Longstone Special School
Millar's Lane, Dundonald,
BELFAST, Co Down BT16 2DA
Tel: 02890 480071
Head: Mr Ioannis Skarmoutsos
Category: MLD

Tor Bank School
5 Dunlady Road, Dundonald,
BELFAST, Co Down BT16 1TT
Tel: 02890 484147
Head: Mr Colm Davis
Category: SLD

CRAIGAVON

Brookfield School
65 Halfpenny Gate Road, Moira,
CRAIGAVON, Co Armagh BT67 0HP
Tel: 02892 622978
Head: Mrs Barbara Spence
Category: MLD (Coed 5-11)

DONAGHADEE

Killard House
Cannyreagh Road, DONAGHADEE,
Co Down BT21 0AU
Tel: 02891 882361
Head: Mr Colin Millar
Category: MLD

DOWNPATRICK

Ardmore House
95A Saul Street, DOWNPATRICK,
Co Down BT30 6NJ
Tel: 02844 614881
Head: Mr Barry Fettes
Category: EBD

Knockevin Special School
33 Racecourse Hill, DOWNPATRICK,
Co Down BT30 6PU
Tel: 02844 612167
Head: Mrs Anne Cooper
Category: SLD

HILLSBOROUGH

Beechlawn Special School
3 Dromore Road, HILLSBOROUGH,
Co Down BT26 6PA
Tel: 02892 682302
Head: Mrs Barbara Green
Category: MLD

LISBURN

Parkview Special School
2 Brokerstown Road, LISBURN,
Co Antrim BT28 2EE
Tel: 02892 601197
Head: Mr James Curran
Category: SLD

SOUTHERN

The Education Authority

Education Authority, SEN Team, 3 Charlemont Place, The Mall, Armagh, Northern Ireland, BT61 9AX
Tel: +44 (0)28 3751 2200 Email: info@eani.org.uk Website: www.eani.org.uk

ARMAGH

Lisanally School
85 Lisanally Lane, ARMAGH,
Co Armagh BT61 7HF
Tel: 02837 523563
Head: Ms Sandra Flynn
Category: SLD (Coed)

BANBRIDGE

Donard School
22A Castlewellan Road,
BANBRIDGE, Co Down BT32 4XY
Tel: 02840 662357
Head: Mrs Edel Lavery
Category: SLD (Coed)

CRAIGAVON

Ceara School
Sloan Street, Lurgan, CRAIGAVON,
Co Armagh BT66 8NY
Tel: 02838 323312
Head: Dr Peter Cunningham
Category: SLD (Coed)

NEWRY

Rathore School
23 Martin's Lane, Carnagat,
NEWRY, Co Down BT35 8PJ
Tel: 02830 261617
Head: Mr Raymond Cassidy
Category: SLD (Coed)

WESTERN

The Education Authority

Education Authority, SEN Team, 1 Hospital Road, Omagh, Northern Ireland, BT79 0AW
Tel: +44 (0)28 8241 1411 Email: info@eani.org.uk Website: www.eani.org.uk

ENNISKILLEN

Willowbridge School
8 Lough Shore Road,
Drumlyon, ENNISKILLEN, Co
Fermanagh BT74 7EY
Tel: 02866 329947
Principal: Mrs Julie Murphy
Category: SLD MLD (Coed)

LIMAVADY

Rossmar School
2 Ballyquin Road, LIMAVADY,
Co Londonderry BT49 9ET
Tel: 02877 762351
Head: Mr Brian McLaughlin
Category: MLD (Coed)

LONDONDERRY

**Ardnashee School and
College (Lower Campus)**
15-17 Racecourse Road,
LONDONDERRY, Co
Londonderry BT48 7RE
Tel: 02871 263270
Acting Principal: Mr
Raymond McFeeters
Category: SLD (Coed)

OMAGH

**Arvalee School &
Resource Centre**
Strule Campus, Gortin Road,
OMAGH, Co Tyrone BT79 7DH
Tel: 02882 255710
Principal: Mr Jonathan Gray
Category: MLD SLD (Coed)

STRABANE

**Knockavoe School and
Resource Centre**
10A Melmount Gardens,
STRABANE, Co Tyrone BT82 9EB
Tel: 02871 883319
Head: Ms Martina McComish
Category: SLD MLD (Coed)

SCOTLAND

ABERDEEN
Education, Culture & Sport

Aberdeen ASN Team, Business Hub 13, Second Floor North, Marischal College, Broad Street Aberdeen, AB10 1AB
Tel: 03000 200293 Email: fis@aberdeencity.gov.uk Website: www.aberdeencity.gov.uk

ABERDEEN

**Aberdeen School
for the Deaf**
c/o Sunnybank School, Sunnybank
Road, ABERDEEN AB24 3NJ
Tel: 01224 261722
Head: Ms Alison Buchan
Category: HI

Cordyce School
Riverview Drive, Dyce,
ABERDEEN AB21 7NF
Tel: 01224 724215
Head: Ms Maureen Simmers
Category: EBD

Hazlewood School
Fernielea Road,
ABERDEEN AB15 6GU
Tel: 01224 321363
Head: Ms Jill Barry
Category: SLD MLD PMLD

**Hospital and Home
Tuition Service**
Royal Aberdeen Children's
Hospital, Lowit Unit, Westburn
Road, ABERDEEN AB25 2ZG
Tel: 01224 550317
Head: Ms Maureen Simmers
Category: HS

Woodlands School
Regent Walk, ABERDEEN AB24 1SX
Tel: 01224 524393
Head: Ms Caroline Stirton
Category: PMLD

ABERDEENSHIRE
Education & Children's Services

Aberdeenshire ASN Team, St Leonards, Sandyhill Road, Banff, AB45 1BH
Tel: 01261 813340 Email: education.development@aberdeenshire.gov.uk Website: www.aberdeenshire.gov.uk

FRASERBURGH

Westfield School
Argyll Road, FRASERBURGH,
Aberdeenshire AB43 9BL
Tel: 01346 518699
Head: Ms Kerri Dalton
Category: PMLD SCLD
(Coed 5-18, 0-3 Nursery)

INVERURIE

St Andrew's School
St Andrew's Garden, INVERURIE,
Aberdeenshire AB51 3XT
Tel: 01467 621215
Head: Ms Gina Drummond
Category: PMLD SCLD (Coed 3-18)

PETERHEAD

Anna Ritchie School
Grange Gardens, PETERHEAD,
Aberdeenshire AB42 2AP
Tel: 01779 473293
Head: Ms Sharon Ferguson
Category: PMLD SCLD (Coed 3-18)

STONEHAVEN

Carronhill School
Mill of Forest Road, STONEHAVEN,
Kincardineshire AB39 2GZ
Tel: 01569 763886
Head: Ms Katie Timney
Category: PMLD SCLD (Coed 3-18)

EAST AYRSHIRE
Education & Social Services

East Ayrshire ASN Team, Council Headquarters, London Road, Kilmarnock, KA3 7BU
Tel: 01563 576000 Website: www.east-ayrshire.gov.uk

CUMNOCK

Hillside School
Dalgleish Avenue, CUMNOCK,
East Ayrshire KA18 1QQ
Tel: 01290 423239
Head: Ms Debbie Skeoch
Category: SLD PMLD (Coed 6-17)

KILMARNOCK

Park School
Beech Avenue, KILMARNOCK,
East Ayrshire KA1 2EW
Tel: 01563 549988
Acting Head: Ms Carol Anne Burns
Category: LD PD (Coed 5-18)

Willowbank School
Grassyards Road, KILMARNOCK,
East Ayrshire KA3 7BB
Tel: 01563 526115
Head: Ms Tracy Smallwood
Category: SLD PMLD

SOUTH AYRSHIRE
Council

South Ayrshire ASN Team, County Buildings, Wellington Square, Ayr, KA7 1DR
Tel: 03001 230900 Website: www.south-ayrshire.gov.uk

AYR

Southcraig Campus
Belmont Avenue, AYR,
South Ayrshire KA7 2ND
Tel: 01292 612146
Head: Mrs Jane Gordon
Category: SLD CLD (Coed 1-5)

GIRVAN

Invergarven School
15 Henrietta Street, GIRVAN,
South Ayrshire KA26 9EB
Tel: 01465 716808
Head: Ms Kimberley Keenan
Category: SLD CLD PD
MSI (Coed 3-16)

CLACKMANNANSHIRE
Council

Clackmannanshire Educational Service, Kilncraigs, Greenside Street, Alloa, Clackmannanshire, FK10 1EB
Tel: 01259 450000 Fax: 01259 452440 Email: education@clacks.gov.uk Website: www.clacksweb.org.uk

ALLOA

**Extended Additional
Support Needs Provision
within Alloa Academy**
Bowhouse Road, ALLOA,
Clackmannanshire FK10 1DN
Tel: 01259 214979
Headteacher: Jackie Ebsworth
Category: CLD MSI PD PH PMLD SLD

**Primary School Support
Service located in
Park Primary School**
East Castle Street, ALLOA,
Clackmannanshire FK10 1BB
Tel: 01259 724064
Acting Headteacher: Hayley
Cleland
Category: SEBD EBSD BESD

ALVA

**Primary ASD Provision
within Alva Primary**
Brook Street, ALVA,
Clackmannanshire FK12 5AN
Tel: 01259 760987
Headteacher: Rosemary McAuly
Category: ASD AUT ADHD ADD

**Secondary ASD Provision
within Alva Academy**
Academy Avenue, ALVA,
Clackmannanshire FK12 5FE
Tel: 01259 760342
Headteacher: Sharee MacKerron
Category: ASD AUT ADHD ADD

SAUCHIE

Lochies School
Gartmorn Road, SAUCHIE,
Clackmannanshire FK10 3PB
Tel: 01259 452312
Headteacher: Rhoda MacDougall
Category: CLD SLD (Coed 5-11)

TILLICOULTRY

**Inclusion Support Service
located in Tillicoultry
Primary School**
Fir Park, TILLICOULTRY,
Clackmannanshire FK13 6PL
Tel: 01259 750228
Headteacher: Linda Coutts
Category: Supports all children
with ASN in mainstream schools

COMHAIRLE NAN EILEAN SIAR
Department of Education & Children's Services

Comhairle Nan Eilean Siar ASN Team, Sandwick Road, Stornoway, Isle of Lewis, HS1 2BW
Tel: 08456 007090 Email: enquiries@cne-siar.gov.uk Website: www.cne-siar.gov.uk

SANDWICK

**Sandwickhill
Learning Centre**
East Street, SANDWICK,
Isle of Lewis HS2 0AG
Tel: 01851 822680
Principal Teacher: Mrs A Campbell
Category: SLD PMLD (Coed 3-11)

EAST DUNBARTONSHIRE
Council

East Dunbartonshire ASN Team, 12 Strathkelvin Place, Kirkintilloch, Glasgow, Lanarkshire, G66 1TJ
Tel: 0300 123 4510 Email: education@eastdunbarton.gov.uk Website: www.eastdunbarton.gov.uk

KIRKINTILLOCH
Merkland School
Langmuir Road, KIRKINTILLOCH,
East Dunbartonshire G66 2QF
Tel: 01419 552336
Head: Ms Anne Mulvenna
Category: MLD PH

LENZIE
Campsie View School
Boghead Road, LENZIE, East
Dunbartonshire G66 4DP
Tel: 01419 552339
Head: Mrs Carole Bowie
Category: SCLD

WEST DUNBARTONSHIRE
Council

West Dunbartonshire ASN Team, Educational Services, Council Offices, Garshake Road Dunbarton, G82 3PU
Tel: 01389 737374 Email: contact.centre@west-dunbarton.gov.uk Website: www.west-dunbarton.gov.uk

CLYDEBANK

Cunard School
Cochno Street, Whitecrook,
CLYDEBANK, West
Dunbartonshire G81 1RQ
Tel: 01419 521621
Head: Jenni Curson
Category: SEBD (Primary)

Kilpatrick School
Mountblow Road,
Dalmuir, CLYDEBANK, West
Dunbartonshire G81 4SW
Tel: 01389 872171
Head: Debbie Queen
Category: SCLD (Primary/
Secondary)

CITY OF EDINBURGH
Council

Edinburgh ASN Team, Waverley Court, 4 East Market Street, Edinburgh, Midlothian, EH8 8BG
Tel: 0131 200 2000 Website: www.edingburgh.gov.uk

EDINBURGH

Braidburn Special School
107 Oxgangs Road North,
EDINBURGH EH14 1ED
Tel: 01313 122320
Head: Ms Morna Phillips
Category: EPI PH (Coed 2-18)

Kaimes School
140 Lasswade Road,
EDINBURGH EH16 6RT
Tel: 01316 648241
Head: Mrs Ros Miller
Category: SP&LD ASD (Coed 5-18)

Oaklands School
750 Ferry Road,
EDINBURGH EH4 4PQ
Tel: 01313 158100
Category: SLD CLD PD MSI

Panmure St Ann's
6 South Grays Close,
EDINBURGH EH1 1TQ
Tel: 01315 568833

Pilrig Park Special School
12 Balfour Place,
EDINBURGH EH6 5DW
Tel: 01314 677960
Head: Ms Rebecca Chad
Category: MLD SLD (Coed 11-16)

**Prospect Bank
Special School**
81 Restalrig Road,
EDINBURGH EH6 8BQ
Tel: 01315 532239
Head: Ms Susan McLaren
Category: LD SP&LD (Coed 5-12)

Redhall Special School
3c Redhall Grove,
EDINBURGH EH14 2DU
Tel: 01314 431256
Head: Ms Susan Shipway
Category: LD (Coed 4-11)

Rowanfield Special School
67c Groathill Road North,
EDINBURGH EH4 2SA
Tel: 01313 436116
Category: EBD

St Crispin's Special School
19 Watertoun Road,
EDINBURGH EH9 3HZ
Tel: 01316 674831
Head: Ms Ruth Hendery
Category: SLD AUT (Coed 5-16)

Woodlands Special School
36 Dolphin Avenue,
EDINBURGH EH14 5RD
Tel: 01314 493447

FALKIRK
Council

Falkirk Additional Support for Learning, Sealock House, 2 Inchyra Road, Grangemouth, FK3 9XB
Tel: 01324 506649 Email: additionalsupport@falkirk.gov.uk Website: www.falkirk.gov.uk

FALKIRK

Mariner Support Service
Weedingshall, Edinburgh Road,
Polmont, FALKIRK FK2 0XS
Tel: 01324 506770
Acting Head: Ms Gillian Macadam
Category: SEBD (Secondary)

Windsor Park School
Bantaskine Road, FALKIRK FK1 5HT
Tel: 01324 508640
Head: Mrs Catherine Finestone
Category: D (Coed 3-16)

GRANGEMOUTH

Oxgang School
c/o Moray Primary School, Moray
Place, GRANGEMOUTH FK3 9DL
Tel: 01324 501311
Acting Head: Mr David MacKay
Category: BESD (5-11)

LARBET

Carrongrange School
Carrongrange Avenue,
LARBET, Falkirk FK5 3BH
Tel: 01324 555266
Head: Ms Gillian Robertson
Category: CLD MLD (Secondary)

FIFE
Education Service

Fife ASN Team, Rothesay House, Rothesay Place, Glenrothes, Fife, KY7 5PQ
Tel: 03451 555555 (Ext 442126) Email: jennifer.allan@fife.gov.uk Website: www.fifedirect.org.uk/fifecouncil

CUPAR

Kilmaron School
Balgarvie Road, CUPAR,
Fife KY15 4PE
Tel: 01334 659480
Head: Ms Isla Lumsden
Category: CLD PD (Coed 3-18)

DUNFERMLINE

Calaiswood School
Nightingale Place,
DUNFERMLINE, Fife KY11 8LW
Tel: 01383 602481
Head: Ms Deborah Davidson
Category: CLD (Coed 3-18)

Woodmill High School ASN
Shields Road, DUNFERMLINE,
Fife KY11 4ER
Tel: 01383 602406
Category: SEBD

GLENROTHES

John Fergus School
Erskine Place, GLENROTHES,
Fife KY7 4JB
Tel: 01592 583489
Head: Ms Pamela Kirkum
Category: CD PD (Coed Day 3-18)

KIRKCALDY

Rosslyn School
Windmill Community
Campus, Windmill Road,
KIRKCALDY, Fife KY1 3AL
Tel: 01592 583482
Head: Mr Paul Meijer
Category: SLD PMLD PD (Coed 3-19)

LEVEN

Hyndhead School
Barncraig Street, Buckhaven,
LEVEN, Fife KY8 1JE
Tel: 01592 583480
Head: Ms Marion Reid
Category: SLD (Coed 5-18)

GLASGOW
Education Services

Glasgow ASN Team, 40 John Street, Glasgow, G1 1JL
Tel: 01412 872000 Website: www.glasgow.gov.uk

GLASGOW

Abercorn Secondary School
195 Garscube Road,
GLASGOW G4 9QH
Tel: 01413 326212
Head: Ms Patricia McGowan
Category: MLD

Ashton Secondary School
100 Avenue End Road,
GLASGOW G33 3SW
Tel: 01417 743428
Head: Mr Danny McGrorry
Category: PH VIS CLD

Broomlea Primary School
Keppoch Campus, 65 Stonyhurst
Street, GLASGOW G22 5AX
Tel: 01413 368428
Head: Ms Fiona Shields
Category: CLD

Cardinal Winning Secondary School
30 Fullarton Avenue,
GLASGOW G32 8NJ
Tel: 01417 783714
Head: Mr Gerard McDonald
Category: MLD

Cartvale Secondary School
3 Burndyke Court,
GLASGOW G51 2BG
Tel: 01414 451767
Head: Ms Pauline Harte
Category: SEBN

Croftcroighn Primary School
290 Mossvale Road,
GLASGOW G33 5NY
Tel: 01417 743760
Head: Mrs Margaret McFadden
Category: CLD

Drummore Primary School
129 Drummore Road,
GLASGOW G15 7NH
Tel: 01419 441323
Head: Ms Fiona McLean
Category: MLD

Eastmuir Primary School
211 Hallhill Road,
GLASGOW G33 4QL
Tel: 01417 713464
Head: Mrs Lorraine Campbell
Category: MLD

Greenview Learning Centre
384 Drakemire Drive,
GLASGOW G45 9SR
Tel: 01416 341551
Head: Mrs Aisling Boyle
Category: SEBN

Hampden Primary School
18 Logan Gardens,
GLASGOW G5 0LJ
Tel: 01414 296095
Head: Ms Seana Moore
Category: CLD

Hazelwood School
50 Dumbreck Court,
GLASGOW G41 5DQ
Tel: 01442 79334
Head: Ms Julia Haugh-Reid
Category: HI VIS CLD (2-19)

Howford Primary School
487 Crookston Road,
GLASGOW G53 7TX
Tel: 01418 822605
Head: Ms Karen Keith
Category: MLD

**Kelbourne Park
Primary School**
109 Hotspur Street,
GLASGOW G20 8LH
Tel: 01419 461405
Head: Ms Andrea MacBeath
Category: PH CLD

Kirkriggs Primary School
500 Croftfoot Road,
GLASGOW G45 0NJ
Tel: 01416 347158
Acting Head: Ms Denise Laverty
Category: MLD

Langlands Primary School
Glenside Avenue,
GLASGOW G53 5FD
Tel: 01418 920952
Head: Mr Mark Beattie
Category: CLD

Middlefield School
80 Ardnahoe Avenue,
GLASGOW G42 0DL
Tel: 01413 340159
Head: Ms Catherine Gilius
Category: ASD (Day)

Newhills Secondary School
42 Newhills Road,
GLASGOW G33 4HJ
Tel: 01417 731296
Head: Ms Alison Lochrie
Category: CLD

Parkhill Secondary School
375 Cumbernauld Road,
GLASGOW G31 3LP
Tel: 01415 542765
Head: Ms Evelyn Hill
Category: MLD

St Kevin's Primary School
25 Fountainwell Road,
GLASGOW G21 1TN
Tel: 01415 573722
Head: Ms Lorna Ferguson
Category: MLD

**St Oswald's
Secondary School**
9 Birgidale Road,
GLASGOW G45 9NJ
Tel: 01416 373952
Head: Ms Margaret MacLeay
Category: MLD

Westmuir High School
255 Rigby Street,
GLASGOW G32 6DJ
Tel: 01415 566276
Head: Ms Pauline Harte
Category: SEBN

HIGHLAND

Education, Culture & Sport Service

Highland ASN Team, Glenurquhart Road, Inverness, IV3 5NX
Tel: 01463 702801 Website: www.highland.gov.uk

INVERNESS

Drummond School
Drummond Road, Inverness,
INVERNESS, Highland IV2 4NZ
Tel: 01463 701050
Head: Mr Mark Elvines
Category: SLD PMLD
CLD (Coed 3-16)

The Bridge
12-14 Seafield Road, INVERNESS,
Highland IV1 1SG
Tel: 01463 256606
Head: Mr Raymond Hall

ROSS-SHIRE

St Clement's School
Tulloch Street, Dingwall, ROSS-
SHIRE, Highland IV15 9JZ
Tel: 01349 863284
Head: Ms Toni Macartney
Category: SP&LD VIS
HI PD (Coed 5-11)

St Duthus School
Academy Street, Tain, ROSS-
SHIRE, Highland IV19 1ED
Tel: 01862 894407
Head: Ms Clare Whiteford
Category: SLD PLD CLD (Coed 3-18)

INVERCLYDE

Council

Inverclyde ASN Team, Wallace Place, Greenock, PA15 1JB
Tel: 01475 717171 Email: admin.educationhq@inverclyde.gov.uk Website: www.inverclyde.gov.uk

GOUROCK

Garvel Deaf Centre
c/o Moorfoot Primary School,
GOUROCK, Inverclyde PA19 1ES
Tel: 01475 715642
Head: Ms Sylvia Gillen
Category: D

PORT GLASGOW

Craigmarloch School
New Port Glasgow Community
Campus, Kilmacolm Road, PORT
GLASGOW, Inverclyde PA14 6PP
Tel: 01475 715345
Head: Mr George Walker

NORTH LANARKSHIRE
Council

North Lanarkshire ASN Team, Learning and Leisure Services, Municipal Buildings, Kildonan Street Coatbridge, ML5 3BT
Tel: 01236 812790 Website: www.northlan.gov.uk

AIRDRIE

Mavisbank School and Nursery
Mitchell Street, AIRDRIE, North Lanarkshire ML6 0EB
Tel: 01236 632108
Head: Mr John Lochrie
Category: PMLD (Coed 3-18)

COATBRIDGE

Buchanan High School
67 Townhead Road, COATBRIDGE, North Lanarkshire ML5 2HT
Tel: 01236 632052
Head: Mrs M Fannan
Category: (Coed Day 12-18)

Drumpark School
Albert Street, COATBRIDGE, North Lanarkshire ML5 3ET
Tel: 01236 794884
Category: MLD PH SP&LD (3-18)

Pentland School
Tay Street, COATBRIDGE, North Lanarkshire ML5 2NA
Tel: 01236 794833
Head: Ms Kathleen Cassidy
Category: SEBD (Coed 5-11)

Portland High School
31-33 Kildonan Street, COATBRIDGE, North Lanarkshire ML5 3LG
Tel: 01236 632060
Head: Mr McGovern
Category: SEBD (Coed 11-16)

Willowbank School
299 Bank Street, COATBRIDGE, North Lanarkshire ML5 1EG
Tel: 01236 632078
Category: SEBD (Coed 11-18)

CUMBERNAULD

Glencryan School
Greenfaulds Road, CUMBERNAULD, North Lanarkshire G67 2XJ
Tel: 01236 794866
Category: MLD PH ASD (Coed 5-18)

Redburn School and Nursery
Kildrum Ring Road, CUMBERNAULD, North Lanarkshire G67 2EL
Tel: 01236 736904
Category: SLD CLD PH (Coed 2-18)

MOTHERWELL

Bothwellpark High School
Annan Street, MOTHERWELL, North Lanarkshire ML1 2DL
Tel: 01698 274939
Category: SLD (Coed 11-18)

Clydeview School and Nursery
Magna Street, MOTHERWELL, North Lanarkshire ML1 3QZ
Tel: 01698 264843
Head: Ms Marie Jo McGurl
Category: SLD (Coed 5-11)

Firpark Primary School
177 Milton Street, MOTHERWELL, North Lanarkshire ML1 1DL
Tel: 01698 274933
Category: (Coed Day 3-10)

Firpark Secondary School
Firpark Street, MOTHERWELL, North Lanarkshire ML1 2PR
Tel: 01698 251313
Category: MLD PH (Coed 11-18)

UDDINGSTON

Fallside Secondary School
Sanderson Avenue, Viewpark, UDDINGSTON, North Lanarkshire G71 6JZ
Tel: 01698 274986
Category: EBD (Coed 11-16)

SOUTH LANARKSHIRE
Council

South Lanarkshire ASN Team, Council Offices, Almada Street, Hamilton, ML3 0AA
Tel: 03031 231015 Email: customer.services@southlanarkshire.gov.uk Website: www.southlanarkshire.gov.uk

CAMBUSLANG

Rutherglen High School
Langlea Road, CAMBUSLANG, South Lanarkshire G72 8ES
Tel: 01416 433480
Head: Mrs Jan Allen

CARLUKE

Victoria Park School
Market Road, CARLUKE, South Lanarkshire ML8 4BE
Tel: 01555 750591
Head: Miss Anne Fisher
Category: PMLD SLD

EAST KILBRIDE

Greenburn School
Maxwellton Avenue, EAST KILBRIDE, South Lanarkshire G74 3DU
Tel: 01355 237278
Head: Mrs Helen Nicol
Category: PMLD

Sanderson High School
High Common Road, St Leonard's, EAST KILBRIDE, South Lanarkshire G74 2LP
Tel: 01355 588625
Head: Mrs Aisling Boyle

West Mains School
Logie Park, EAST KILBRIDE, South Lanarkshire G74 4BU
Tel: 01355 249938
Head: Mrs Rosemary Payne
Category: SLD

HAMILTON

Hamilton School for the Deaf
Anderson Street, HAMILTON, South Lanarkshire ML3 0QL
Tel: 01698 823377
Head: Ms Eileen Burns
Category: D

MIDLOTHIAN
Education, Communities & Economy

Midlothian ASN Team, Fairfield House, 8 Lothian Road, Dalkeith, Midlothian, EH22 3ZG
Tel: 01312 713689 Email: asn.officer@midlothian.gov.uk Website: www.midlothian.gov.uk

DALKEITH

Saltersgate School
3 Cousland Road, DALKEITH,
Midlothian EH22 2PS
Tel: 01316 544703
Head: Ms Fiona Hume
Category: GLD (Coed Secondary)

WEST LOTHIAN
Education & Learning

West Lothian Inclusion & Wellbeing Service, West Lothian Civic Centre,
Howden South Road, Livingston, West Lothian, EH54 6FF

Tel: 01506 280000 Email: customer.services@westlothian.gov.uk Website: www.westlothian.gov.uk

BATHGATE

Pinewood Special School
Elm Grove, Blackburn, BATHGATE,
West Lothian EH47 7QX
Tel: 01506 656374
Head: Ms Pamela Greig
Category: SCLD (Primary/
Secondary)

BLACKBURN

Connolly School Campus
Hopefield Road, BLACKBURN,
West Lothian EH47 7HZ
Tel: 01506 283888
Head: Mrs Catriona Grant
Category: SEBN (Primary)

LIVINGSTON

Beatlie School Campus
The Mall, Craigshill, LIVINGSTON,
West Lothian EH54 5EJ
Tel: 01506 777598
Head: Mrs Carol Robbie
Category: SCLD MSI PD
(Nursery - Secondary)

Cedarbank School
Cedarbank, Ladywell East,
LIVINGSTON, West Lothian EH54 6DR
Tel: 01506 442172
Acting Head: Mrs Catriona Grant
Category: ASD LD (Secondary)

Ogilvie School Campus
Ogilvie Way, Knightsridge,
LIVINGSTON, West Lothian EH54 8HL
Tel: 01506 777489
Head: Ms Liz Speirs
Category: SCLD (Primary)

WHITBURN

**Inclusion and
Wellbeing Centre**
The Avenue, WHITBURN,
West Lothian EH47 0BX
Tel: 01501 678100
Head: Mrs Catriona Grant
Category: SEBN (Secondary)

PERTH & KINROSS
Education & Children's Services

Perth & Kinross SEN Team, Pullar House, 35 Kinnoull Street, Perth, PH1 5GD
Tel: 01738 476200 Email: enquiries@pkc.gov.uk Website: www.pkc.gov.uk

PERTH

Fairview School
Oakbank Crescent, PERTH,
Perthshire & Kinross PH1 1DF
Tel: 01738 473050
Head: Ms Fiona Gillespie
Category: SLD CLD (Coed 2-18)

RENFREWSHIRE
Education & Learning

Renfrewshire ASN Team, Renfrewshire House, Cotton Street, Paisley, PA1 1UJ
Tel: 03003 000170 Email: asn.els@renfrewshire.gov.uk Website: www.renfrewshire.gov.uk

LINWOOD

Clippens School
Brediland Road, LINWOOD,
Renfrewshire PA3 3RX
Tel: 01505 325333
Acting Head: Ms Teresa Brown
Category: ASD CLD PI
MSI (Coed 5-19)

PAISLEY

Kersland School
Ben Nevis Road, PAISLEY,
Renfrewshire PA2 7BU
Tel: 01418 898251
Head: Ms Michelle Welsh
Category: SLD (Coed 5-18)

Mary Russell School
Hawkhead Road, PAISLEY,
Renfrewshire PA2 7BE
Tel: 01418 897628
Head: Mrs Julie McCallum
Category: MLD (Coed 5-18)

EAST RENFREWSHIRE
Education Department

East Renfrewshire ASN Team, Council Offices, 211 Main Street, Barrhead, East Renfrewshire, G78 1SY
Tel: 0141 577 3001 Email: customerservices@eastrenfrewshire.gov.uk Website: www.eastrenfrewshire.gov.uk

NEWTON MEARNS

The Isobel Mair School
58 Stewarton Road, NEWTON
MEARNS, East Renfrewshire G77 6NB
Tel: 0141 577 7600
Head: Mrs Sarah Clark
Category: CLD (Coed 5-18)

STIRLING
Council

Stirling ASN Team, Teith House, Kerse Road, Stirling, FK7 7QA
Tel: 01786 233212 Email: additionalsupportneeds@stirling.gov.uk Website: www.stirling.gov.uk

CALLANDER

Callander ASD Provision (at Callander Primary School)
Bridgend, CALLANDER FK17 8AG
Tel: 01877 331576
Acting Headteacher: Tanya Starkey
Category: ASD

STIRLING

ASN Outreach Service
Raploch Community Campus,
Drip Road, STIRLING FK8 1SD
Tel: 01786 272333
Co-ordinator: Christine Stones

Castleview School
Raploch Community Campus,
Drip Road, STIRLING FK8 1SD
Tel: 01786 272326
Acting Head: Donna Wheater
Category: PD PMLD

Ochil House (at Wallace High School)
Airthrey Road, STIRLING FK9 5HW
Tel: 01786 462166
Headteacher: Scott Pennock
Category: CLD SLD PD PH PMLD

Riverside ASD Provision (at Riverside Primary)
Forrest Road, STIRLING FK8 1UJ
Tel: 01786 474128
Headteacher: Kay Robertson
Category: ASD

SEBN Support Service (S1-S3)
Riverside, 18 Forrest Road,
STIRLING FK8 1UG
Tel: 01786 448929
Category: SEBD EBSD BESD

SEBN Support Service (S3-S5)
Chartershall, Fairhill Road, Whins
of Milton, STIRLING FK7 0LL
Tel: 01786 812667
Category: SEBD EBSD BESD

St Modan's ASD Provision (at St Modan's High School)
Royal Stuart Way, STIRLING FK7 7WS
Tel: 01786 470962
Headteacher: Raymond O'Neill
Category: ASD

WALES

BLAENAU GWENT

County Borough Council

Blaenau Gwent SEN Team, Anvil Court, Church Street, Abertillery, NP13 1DB
Tel: 01495 311556 Email: education.department@blaenau-gwent.gov.uk Website: www.blaenau-gwent.gov.uk

EBBW VALE

Pen-y-Cwm Special School
Ebbw Fawr Learning Community,
Strand Annealing Lane, EBBW
VALE, Blaenau Gwent NP23 6AN
Tel: 01495 357755
Head: Ms Darya Brill-Williams
Category: SLD PMLD

BRIDGEND

County Borough Council

Bridgend Access & Inclusion Service, The SEN Team, Civic Offices, Angel Street Bridgend, CF31 4WB
Tel: 01656 815230 Email: inclusionservice@bridgend.gov.uk Website: www.bridgend.gov.uk

BRIDGEND

Heronsbridge School
Ewenny Road, BRIDGEND CF31 3HT
Tel: 01656 815725
Head: Mr J Evans
Category: PMLD VIS AUT (Coed
Day & boarding 3-18)

Ysgol Bryn Castell
Bryncethin Campus,
Abergarw Road, Brynmenyn,
BRIDGEND CF32 9NZ
Tel: 01656 815595
Head: Mrs H Ridout
Category: EBD LD HI ASD MLD
SLD SP&LD (Coed 3-19)

CAERPHILLY

Family Information Service

Caerphilly FIS, The SEN Team, Penallta House, Tredomen Park Ystrad Mynach, Hengoed, CF82 7PG
Tel: 01443 863232 Email: fis@caerphilly.gov.uk Website: your.caerphilly.gov.uk/fis

CAERPHILLY

Trinity Fields Special School
Caerphilly Road, Ystrad Mynach,
CAERPHILLY CF82 7XW
Tel: 01443 866000
Head: Mr Ian Elliott
Category: SLD VIS HI CLD
SP&LD (Coed 3-19)

CARDIFF
Education Service

SNAP Cymru, County Hall, Atlantic Wharf, Cardiff, CF10 4UW
Tel: 08451 203730 Email: helpline@snapcymru.org Website: www.cardiff.gov.uk

CARDIFF

Greenhill School
Heol Brynglas, Rhiwbina,
CARDIFF CF14 6UJ
Tel: 02920 693786
Head: Mrs Jane Counsell
Category: SEBD (Coed 11-16)

Meadowbank School
Colwill Road, Llandaff North,
CARDIFF CF14 2QQ
Tel: 02920 616018
Head: Mrs Lorraine Felstead
Category: SLCD (Coed 4-11)

Riverbank School
Vincent Road, Caerau,
CARDIFF CF5 5AQ
Tel: 02920 563860
Head: Mrs Amanda Gibson-Evans
Category: MLD SLD (Coed 4-11)

The Court School
Station Road, Llanishen,
CARDIFF CF14 5UX
Tel: 02920 752713
Head: Mrs Beverley Smith
Category: SEBD (Coed 4-11)

The Hollies School
Brynheulog, CARDIFF CF23 7XG
Tel: 02920 734411
Head: Miss Kath Keely
Category: ASD PMED (Coed 4-11)

Ty Gwyn School
Vincent Road, Caerau,
CARDIFF CF5 5AQ
Tel: 02920 838560
Head: Mr Kevin Tansley
Category: PMLD ASD (Coed 4-19)

Woodlands High School
Vincent Road, Caerau,
CARDIFF CF5 5AQ
Tel: 02920 561279
Head: Mr Russell Webb
Category: MLD SLD (Coed 11-19)

CARMARTHENSHIRE
County Council

The Department for Education & Children, Building 2, St David's Park, Job's
Well Road, Carmarthen, Carmarthenshire, SA31 3HB
Tel: 01267 246500 Email: ecs@carmarthenshire.gov.uk Website: www.carmarthenshire.gov.wales

CARMARTHEN

**Rhydygors School &
Support Services**
Rhyd-y-gors, Johnstown,
CARMARTHEN,
Carmarthenshire SA31 3QU
Tel: 01267 231171
Head: Mr. Ian Berryman
Category: EBD

LLANELLI

Ysgol Heol Goffa
Heol Goffa, LLANELLI,
Carmarthenshire SA15 3LS
Tel: 01554 759465
Head: Mrs N Symmons
Category: SLD PMLD

CONWY
Education Services

Conwy SEN Team, Government Buildings, Dinerth Road, Colwyn Bay, LL28 4UL
Tel: 01492 575038 Email: education@conwy.gov.uk Website: www.conwy.gov.uk

LLANDUDNO

Ysgol Y Gogarth
Ffordd Nant y Gamar, Craig y Don,
LLANDUDNO, Conwy LL30 1YE
Tel: 01492 860077
Head: Mr Jonathan Morgan
Category: General SEN (2-19)

DENBIGHSHIRE
County Council

Denbighshire ALN Team, PO Box 62, Ruthin, Denbighshire, LL15 9AZ
Tel: 0845 120 3730 Email: helpline@snapcymru.org Website: www.denbighshire.gov.uk

DENBIGH

Ysgol Plas Brondyffryn
Park Street, DENBIGH,
Denbighshire LL16 3DR
Tel: 01745 813914
Head: Mr David Price
Category: AUT SLD (Coed 4-19)

RHYL

Ysgol Tir Morfa
Derwen Road, RHYL,
Denbighshire LL18 2RN
Tel: 01745 350388
Interim Head: Mr John Cannon
Category: MLD SLD (Coed 4-19)

FLINTSHIRE
County Council

Flintshire Education Department, County Hall, Mold, Flintshire, CH7 6ND
Website: www.flintshire.gov.uk

FLINT

Ysgol Maes Hyfryd
Fifth Avenue, FLINT,
Flintshire CH6 5QL
Tel: 01352 792720
Head: Mrs Helen Millard
Category: (Coed 11-16)

Ysgol Pen Coch
Prince of Wales Avenue,
FLINT, Flintshire CH6 5DL
Tel: 01352 792730
Head: Ms Ange Anderson
Category: (Coed 5-11)

GWYNEDD
Council

Gwynedd SEN Team, Council Offices, Penrallt, Caernarfon, Gwynedd, LL55 1BN
Tel: 01766 771000 Email: education@gwynedd.gov.uk Website: www.gwynedd.gov.uk

CAERNARFON

Ysgol Pendalar
Ffordd Bethel, CAERNARFON,
Gwynedd LL55 1DU
Tel: 01248 672141
Head: Ms Bethan Morris-Jones
Category: SLD (3-18)

PENRHYNDEUDRAETH

Ysgol Hafod Lon
Parc Busnes Eryri,
PENRHYNDEUDRAETH,
Gwynedd LL48 6LD
Tel: 01766 772140
Head: Mrs Donna Rees-Roberts
Category: SLD (3-18)

MERTHYR TYDFIL
Integrated Children's Services

Merthyr Tydfil Additional Learning Needs Service, Unit 5, Triangle Business Park, Pentrebach, Merthyr Tydfil, CF48 4TQ
Tel: 01685 724616 Email: sen@merthyr.gov.uk Website: www.merthyr.gov.uk

MERTHYR TYDFIL

Greenfield Special School
Duffryn Road, Pentrebach,
MERTHYR TYDFIL CF48 4BJ
Tel: 01443 690468
Head: Mr Wayne Murphy
Category: SLD MLD PMLD ASD
EBD MSI SP&LD (Coed 3-19)

MONMOUTHSHIRE
County Council

Monmouthshire SEN Department, @Innovation House, Wales 1 Business Park, Magor, Monmouthshire, NP26 3DG
Tel: 01633 644528 Email: sen@monmouthshire.gov.uk Website: www.monmouthshire.gov.uk

CHEPSTOW

Mounton House School
Pwyllmeyric, CHEPSTOW,
Monmouthshire NP16 6LA
Tel: 01291 635050
Head: Mr P Absolom
Category: EBD (Boys Day/
Boarding 11-16)

NEATH PORT TALBOT
The Child Care (Disability) Team

Neath Port Talbot SEN Team, 2nd Floor, Neath Port Talbot CBC, Civic Centre, Neath, SA11 3QZ
Tel: 01639 685862 Email: education@npt.gov.uk Website: www.neath-porttalbot.gov.uk

NEATH

Ysgol Hendrefelin
Heol Hendre, Bryncoch,
NEATH SA10 7TY
Tel: 01639 642786
Head: Mr Jonathan Roberts
Category: GLD (Coed 3-16)

Ysgol Maes Y Coed
Heol Hendre, Bryncoch,
NEATH SA10 7TY
Tel: 01639 643648
Head: Mrs Helen Glover
Category: GLD (Coed 2-19)

NEWPORT
City Council

Newport Education Inclusion Department, Civic Centre, Newport, NP20 4UR
Tel: 01633 656656 Email: education@newport.gov.uk Website: www.newport.gov.uk

NEWPORT

Brynglas ASD Centre
St Johns Road, Maindee,
NEWPORT, Newport NP20 3DG
Tel: 01633 815480
Head: Ms Julie Nichols
Category: ASD AUT ASP

Maes Ebbw Bach
St Johns Road, Maindee,
NEWPORT, Newport NP19 8GR
Tel: 01633 815480
Head: Ms Julie Nichols

Maes Ebbw School
Maesglas Road, Maesglas,
NEWPORT, Newport NP20 3DG
Tel: 01633 815480
Head: Ms Julie Nichols
Category: SLD PMLD AUT PH

PEMBROKESHIRE
Education Department

Pembrokeshire Inclusion and SEN Service, County Hall, Haverfordwest, Pembrokeshire, SA61 1TP
Tel: 01437 775094 Email: nichola.jones@pembrokeshire.gov.uk Website: www.pembrokeshire.gov.uk/inclusion

HAVERFORDWEST

Portfield School
off Portfield, HAVERFORDWEST,
Pembrokeshire SA61 1BS
Tel: 01437 762701
Head: Mrs S Painter
Category: SLD PMLD CLD
ASC (Coed 4-18+)

POWYS
County Council

Powys SEN Team, Powys County Hall, Spa Road East, Llandrindod Wells, Powys, LD1 5LG
Tel: 01597 826437 Email: alndepartment@powys.gov.uk Website: www.powys.gov.uk

BRECON

Ysgol Penmaes
Canal Road, BRECON,
Powys LD3 7HL
Tel: 01874 623508
Head: Mrs Julie Kay
Category: SLD ASD PMLD
(Coed Day/Residential 3-19)

NEWTOWN

Brynllywarch Hall School
Kerry, NEWTOWN, Powys SY16 4PB
Tel: 01686 670276
Head: Mr Gavin Randell
Category: MLD EBD

Ysgol Cedewain
Maesyrhandir, NEWTOWN,
Powys SY16 1LH
Tel: 01686 627454
Head: Mrs Pippa Sillitoe
Category: SLD ASD PMLD
(Coed Day 3-19)

RHONDDA CYNON TAFF
County Borough Council

Rhondda Cynon Taff SEN Team, Ty Trevithick, Abercynon, Mountain Ash, CF45 4UQ
Tel: 01443 744000 Email: customerservices@rctcbc.gov.uk Website: www.rctcbc.gov.uk

ABERDARE

Maesgwyn Special School
Cwmdare Road, Cwmdare,
ABERDARE, Rhondda
Cynon Taf CF44 8RE
Tel: 01685 873933
Head: Mr S K Morgan
Category: MLD (Coed 11-18)

Park Lane Special School
Park Lane, Trecynon, ABERDARE,
Rhondda Cynon Taf CF44 8HN
Tel: 01685 874489
Head: Miss M C Hopkin
Category: SLD (3-19)

PENTRE

Ysgol Hen Felin
Gelligaled Park, Ystrad, PENTRE,
Rhondda Cynon Taf CF41 7SZ
Tel: 01443 431571
Head: Mr A Henderson
Category: SLD (3-19)

PONTYPRIDD

Ysgol Ty Coch
Lansdale Drive, Tonteg,
PONTYPRIDD, Rhondda
Cynon Taf CF38 1PG
Tel: 01443 203471
Head: Mr D Jenkins
Category: SLD (3-19)

Ysgol Ty Coch - Buarth y Capel
Ynysybwl, PONTYPRIDD,
Rhondda Cynon Taf CF38 1PG

SWANSEA
City and County of

Education Directorate

Swansea SEN Team, Civic Centre, Oystermouth Road, Swansea, SA1 3SN
Tel: 01792 636000 Email: education.department@swansea.gov.uk Website: www.swansea.gov.uk

SWANSEA

Ysgol Crug Glas
Croft Street, SWANSEA SA1 1QA
Tel: 01792 652388
Head: Mrs Lisa Marshall
Category: SLD PMLD

Ysgol Pen-y-Bryn
Glasbury Road, Morriston,
SWANSEA SA6 7PA
Tel: 01792 799064
Head: Mr Gethin Sutton
Category: MLD SLD AUT

TORFAEN
County Borough Council

Torfaen Inclusion Service, Civic Centre, Pontypool, Torfaen, NP4 6YB
Tel: 01495 766929 Website: www.torfaen.gov.uk

CWMBRAN

Crownbridge School
Turnpike Road, Croesyceiliog,
CWMBRAN, Torfaen NP44 2BJ
Tel: 01633 624201
Head: Mrs Lesley Bush
Category: SLD (2-19)

VALE OF GLAMORGAN
Family Information Service
Vale of Glamorgan FIS, Dock Offices, Subway Road, Barry, CF63 4RT
Tel: 01446 704704 Email: fis@valeofglamorgan.gov.uk Website: www.valeofglamorgan.gov.uk

PENARTH

Ysgol Y Deri
Sully Road, PENARTH, Vale
of Glamorgan CF64 2TP
Tel: 02920 352280
Head: Mr Chris Britten
Category: AUT PMLD MLD SLD
(Coed 5 Day/Residential 3-19)

WREXHAM
County Borough Council
Wrexham SEN Team, 16 Lord Street, Wrexham, LL11 1LG
Tel: 01978 292000 Email: education@wrexham.gov.uk Website: www.wrexham.gov.uk

WREXHAM

St Christopher's School
Brynycabanau Road,
WREXHAM LL13 7BW
Tel: 01978 346910
Head: Mrs Maxine Pittaway
Category: MLD SLD
PMLD (Coed 6-19)

ACADEMIES (in local authority area)

ENGLAND

BATH & NORTH-EAST SOMERSET

Bath

Aspire Academy
Frome Road, Odd Down,
BATH BA2 5RF
Tel: 01225 832212
Head: Mr Colin Cattanach
Category: EBD (Coed 4-16)

Fosse Way School
Longfellow Road, Midsomer
Norton, BATH BA3 3AL
Tel: 01761 412198
Head: Mr Justin Philcox
Category: PH SLD SPLD ASD
MLD MSI CLD (Coed 3-19)

Three Ways School
180 Frome Road, Odd
Down, BATH BA2 5RF
Tel: 01225 838070
Head: Mrs Julie Dyer
Category: PH SLD SPLD ASD
MLD MSI CLD (Coed 2-19)

BEDFORD

Grange Academy
Halsey Road, Kempston, BEDFORD,
Bedfordshire MK42 8AU
Tel: 01234 407100
Head: Mr B Geen
Category: MLD with provision
for ASD (Coed 5-16)

CENTRAL BEDFORDSHIRE

Dunstable

Weatherfield Academy
Brewers Hill Road, DUNSTABLE,
Bedfordshire LU6 1AF
Tel: 01582 605632
Head: Mr Joe Selmes
Category: MLD (7-18)

BLACKPOOL

Park Community Academy
158 Whitegate Drive, BLACKPOOL,
Lancashire FY3 9HF
Tel: 01253 764130
Head: Mr Keith Berry
Category: MLD CLD
SEBD (Coed 4-16)

BRISTOL

Venturers' Academy
Withywood Road, BRISTOL BS13 9AX
Tel: 0117 3010819
Head: Mr Trystan Williams
Category: ASC (4-16)

CAMBRIDGESHIRE

Huntingdon

Spring Common Academy
American Lane, HUNTINGDON,
Cambridgeshire PE29 1TQ
Tel: 01480 377403
Head: Mrs Kim Taylor
Category: PMLD SLD MLD
ASD EBD (Coed 2-19)

CHESHIRE EAST

Crewe

Adelaide School
Adelaide Street, CREWE,
Cheshire CW1 3DT
Tel: 01270 685151
Executive Head: Mr Lloyd Willday
Category: BESD (Coed 11-16)

Knutsford

St John's Wood Academy
Longridge, KNUTSFORD,
Cheshire WA16 8PA
Tel: 01625 383045
Headteacher: Mr Robert James
Category: BESD (Coed Day 11-16)

CORNWALL

Truro

Pencalenick School
St Clement, TRURO, Cornwall TR1 1TE
Tel: 01872 520385
Head: Mr Andrew Barnett
Category: SCLD (Coed 11-16)

CUMBRIA

Barrow In Furness

George Hastwell School
Moor Tarn Lane, Walney, BARROW
IN FURNESS, Cumbria LA14 3LW
Tel: 01229 475253
Head: Mrs Karen Baxter
Category: SLD PMLD

DURHAM

Peterlee

Hopewood Academy (Ascent Trust)
Crawlaw Road, Easington Colliery,
PETERLEE, Durham SR8 3LP
Tel: 01915 691420
Head: Mrs Carolyn Barker
Category: MLD SLD PMLD AUT (2-19)

HALTON

Runcorn

Cavendish Academy
Lincoln Close, RUNCORN,
Cheshire WA7 4YX
Tel: 01928 561706
Head: Mrs Elaine Haver
Category: SLD (11-19)

HARTLEPOOL

Catcote Academy
Catcote Road,
HARTLEPOOL TS25 4EZ
Tel: 01429 264036
Head: Mr Alan Chapman
Category: MLD SLD PMLD
ASD BESD (Coed 11-25)

HEREFORDSHIRE

Hereford

The Brookfield School & Specialist College
Grandstand Road,
HEREFORD HR4 9NG
Tel: 01432 265153
Head: Dame Oremi Evans
Category: BESD MLD ASD
ADHD (Coed 7-16)

KENT

Dartford

Milestone Academy
Ash Road, New Ash Green,
DARTFORD, Kent DA3 8JZ
Tel: 01474 709420
Head: Mr Nigel Jones
Category: PMLD SLD AUT
MLD PSCN (Coed 2-19)

LEICESTERSHIRE

Coalville

Forest Way School
Warren Hills Road, COALVILLE,
Leicestershire LE67 4UU
Tel: 01530 831899
Head: Mrs Lynn Slinger
Category: SLD PMLD (2-18)

Hinckley

Dorothy Goodman School Hinckley
Stoke Road, HINCKLEY,
Leicestershire LE10 0EA
Tel: 01455 634582
Head: Ms Janet Thompson
Category: (2-18)

Grantham

The Phoenix Academy Trust
Great North Road, GRANTHAM,
Lincolnshire NG31 7US
Tel: 01476 574112
Head: Mrs Diana Bush
Category: EBD (11-16)

NORTH-EAST LINCOLNSHIRE

Grimsby

Humberston Park Special School
Church Lane, Humberston, GRIMSBY, N E Lincolnshire DN36 4HZ
Tel: 01472 813474
Head: Mrs Jo Everitt
Category: SLD PMLD PD CLD MSI (Coed 3-19)

The Cambridge Park Academy
Cambridge Road, GRIMSBY, N E Lincolnshire DN34 5EB
Tel: 01472 230110
Head: Mr Mark Eames
Category: ASD SLCN MLD SLD (Coed 3-19)

LONDON – BROMLEY

Bromley

Bromley Beacon Academy (Bromley Campus)
Old Homesdale Road, BROMLEY, Kent BR2 9LJ
Tel: 020 3319 0503
Executive Head Teacher: Mr Neil Miller
Category: SEMH (Coed 7-18)

Orpington

Bromley Beacon Academy (Orpington Campus)
Avalon Road, ORPINGTON, Kent BR6 9BD
Tel: 01689 821205
Executive Head Teacher: Mr Neil Miller
Category: SEMH (Coed 7-18)

LONDON – ROYAL BOROUGH OF GREENWICH

Charlton Park Academy
Charlton Park Road, LONDON SE7 8HX
Tel: 02082 496844
Head: Mr Mark Dale-Emberton
Category: SCLD SCD PMLD PD ASD (Coed 11-19)

LONDON – HILLINGDON

HAYES

The Willows School Academy Trust
Stipularis Drive, HAYES, Middlesex UB4 9QB
Tel: 02088 417176
Head: Mr Malcolm Shaw
Category: SEBD ASD ADHD Challenging behaviour (Coed 3-11)

Uxbridge

Moorcroft (Eden Academy)
Bramble Close, Hillingdon, UXBRIDGE, Middlesex UB8 3BF
Tel: 01895 437799
Head: Mr Andrew Sanders
Category: SLD PMLD AUT (Coed 11-19)

West Drayton

Young People's Academy
Falling Lane, Yiewsley, WEST DRAYTON, Middlesex UB7 8AB
Tel: 01895 446747
Head: Ms Laurie Cornwell
Category: BESD AUT ADHD (Coed 11-16)

LONDON – SUTTON

Carshalton

Wandle Valley School
Welbeck Road, CARSHALTON, Surrey SM5 1LW
Tel: 02086 481365
Head: Mr Mal Fjord-Roberts
Category: SEBD (Coed 5-16)

Wallington

Carew Academy
Church Road, WALLINGTON, Surrey SM6 7NH
Tel: 02086 478349
Head: Mr John Prior
Category: MLD ASD (Coed 7-16)

LONDON – WALTHAM FOREST

Walthamstow

Hornbeam Academy - William Morris Site
Folly Lane, WALTHAMSTOW, London E17 5NT
Tel: 02085 032225
Executive Principal: Mr Gary Pocock
Category: MLD SLD PMLD (Coed 11-16)

Woodford green

Hornbeam Academy - Brookfield House Site
Alders Avenue, WOODFORD GREEN, Essex IG8 9PY
Tel: 02085 272464
Executive Principal: Mr Gary Pocock
Category: HI PD Complex medical needs (Coed 2-16)

GREATER MANCHESTER – SALFORD

Eccles

Oakwood Academy
Chatsworth Road, Ellesmere Park, ECCLES M30 9DY
Tel: 01619 212880
Executive Principal: Ms Amanda Nicolson
Category: MLD HI VIS SEBD Complex needs (Coed 10-19)

GREATER MANCHESTER – TRAFFORD

Sale

Manor Academy
Manor Avenue, SALE, Cheshire M33 5JX
Tel: 01619 761553
Head: Mrs Helen Wilson
Category: ASD SEMH MLD (Coed 11-18)

MEDWAY

Chatham

Bradfields Academy
Churchill Avenue, CHATHAM, Kent ME5 0LB
Tel: 01634 683990
Head: Mr Kim Johnson
Category: MLD SLD ASD (Coed 11-19)

MILTON KEYNES

Stephenson Academy
Crosslands, Stantonbury, MILTON KEYNES, Buckinghamshire MK14 6AX
Tel: 01908 889400
Head: Dr Neil Barrett
Category: EBD (Boys Day/boarding 12-16)

NORFOLK

Norwich

Eaton Hall Specialist Academy
Pettus Road, NORWICH, Norfolk NR4 7BU
Tel: 01603 457480
Head: Mr Keith Bates
Category: SEBD (Boys 7-16)

NORTHANTS

Corby

Maplefields School
Tower Hill Road, CORBY, Northamptonshire NN18 0TH
Tel: 01536 424090
Head: Ms Beverley Wright
Category: BESD (5-19)

Kettering

Kingsley Special Academy Trust
Churchill Way, KETTERING, Northamptonshire NN15 5DP
Tel: 01536 316880
Head: Mr Tom O'Dwyer
Category: PMLD SLD ASD (3-11)

Northampton

Billing Brook Special Academy Trust School
Penistone Road, NORTHAMPTON, Northamptonshire NN3 8EZ
Tel: 01604 773910
Head: Mrs Caroline Grant
Category: MLD ASD SLD SPLD PH (3-19)

Wellingborough

Friars Academy
Friar's Close, WELLINGBOROUGH, Northamptonshire NN8 2LA
Tel: 01933 304950
Head: Mrs Suzzanne Ijewsky
Category: MLD SLD ASD (11-19)

NOTTINGHAMSHIRE

Nottingham

Nethergate School
Swansdowne Drive, Clifton, NOTTINGHAM NG11 8HX
Tel: 01159 152959
Head: Mrs Tracey Ydlibi

Broxtowe

Foxwood Academy
Off Derby Road, Bramcote Hills, Beeston, BROXTOWE, Nottingham NG9 3GF
Tel: 01159 177202
Head: Mr Chris Humphreys
Category: (Coed 3-19)

Mansfield

The Beech Academy
Fairholme Drive, MANSFIELD, Nottinghamshire NG19 6DX
Tel: 01623 626008
Head: Mr Adrian O'Malley
Category: (Coed 11-19)

PETERBOROUGH

City of Peterborough Special School
Reeves Way, PETERBOROUGH, Cambridgeshire PE1 5LQ
Tel: 01733 821403
Head: Mrs Sue Bailey
Category: (Coed 4-18)

POOLE

Longspee Academy
Learoyd Road, Canford Heath, POOLE, Dorset BH17 8PJ
Tel: 01202 380266
Head: Ms Nicky Morton
Category: BESD (5-14)

Montacute School
3 Canford Heath Road, POOLE, Dorset BH17 9NG
Tel: 01202 693239
Head: Ms Jill Owen
Category: PMLD SLD CLD PH Medical needs (3-19)

PORTSMOUTH

Cliffdale Primary Academy
Battenburg Avenue, PORTSMOUTH, Hampshire PO2 0SN
Tel: 02392 662601
Executive Head: Ms Alison Beane
Category: CLD ASD (Coed 4-11)

READING

The Avenue Special School
Conwy Close, Tilehurst, READING, Berkshire RG30 4BZ
Tel: 01189 375554
Head: Mrs Sue Bourne
Category: CLD (Coed 2-19)

REDCAR & CLEVELAND

Saltburn-By-Sea

KTS Academy
Marshall Drive, Brotton, SALTBURN-BY-SEA, Cleveland TS12 2UW
Tel: 01287 677265
Head: Mr Kevin Thompson
Category: SLD PMLD SLCN ASC PD CLDD (Coed day 2-19)

SHROPSHIRE

Shrewsbury

Severndale Specialist Academy
Monkmoor Campus, Woodcote Way, Monkmoor, SHREWSBURY, Shropshire SY2 5SL
Tel: 01743 281600
Principal: Ms Sabrina Hobbs
Category: PMLD SLD MLD CLDD (Coed Day 2-19)

SOUTHEND-ON-SEA

Leigh-On-Sea

The St Christopher School
Mountdale Gardens, LEIGH-ON-SEA, Essex SS9 4AW
Tel: 01702 524193
Head: Mrs Jackie Mullan
Category: AUT ADHD SEBD (Coed Day 3-11) ADHD AUT (Coed 11-16)

STAFFORDSHIRE

Lichfield

Saxon Hill Special School
Kings Hill Road, LICHFIELD, Staffordshire WS14 9DE
Tel: 01543 414892
Head: Mr Ronald Thickett
Category: Generic (Coed Day/Boarding 2-19)

Newcastle Under Lyme

Blackfriars Academy
Priory Road, NEWCASTLE UNDER LYME, Staffordshire ST5 2TF
Tel: 01782 297780
Head: Ms Alison Parr
Category: Generic (Coed Day 11-19)

The Coppice Academy
Abbots Way, NEWCASTLE UNDER LYME, Staffordshire ST5 2EY
Tel: 01782 297490
Head: Ms Aileen Jones
Category: Generic (Coed Day 11-16)

Stafford

Walton Hall Academy
Stafford Road, Eccleshall, STAFFORD, Staffordshire ST21 6JR
Tel: 01785 850420
Head: Mrs Pauline Carmichael
Category: Generic (Coed Day/Boarding 11-19)

Stoke On Trent

Cicely Haughton Community Special School
Westwood Manor, Wetley Rocks, STOKE ON TRENT, Staffordshire ST9 0BX
Tel: 01782 297780
Head: Mr Richard Redgate
Category: SEBD (Coed Boarding 4-11)

Uttoxeter

Loxley Hall School
Stafford Road, Loxley, UTTOXETER, Staffordshire ST14 8RS
Tel: 01889 256390
Head: Mr Richard Redgate
Category: SEBD (Coed Boarding 11-16)

STOCKTON-ON-TEES

Billingham

Ash Trees Academy
Bowes Road, BILLINGHAM, Stockton-on-Tees TS23 2BU
Tel: 01642 563712
Headteacher: Ms Yvonne Limb
Category: SLD PMLD AUT (Coed 4-11)

Thornaby-On-Tees

Horizons Specialist Academy Trust, Westlands School
Eltham Crescent, THORNABY-ON-TEES TS17 9RA
Tel: 01642 883030
Principal: Mr Pete Ewart
Category: BESD (Coed Residential 11-16)

SUFFOLK

Bury St Edmunds

Priory School
Mount Road, BURY ST EDMUNDS, Suffolk IP32 7BH
Tel: 01284 761934
Head: Mr Lawrence Chapman
Category: MLD (Coed Day & boarding 8-16)

Ipswich

Stone Lodge Academy
Stone Lodge Lane West, IPSWICH, Suffolk IP2 9HW
Tel: 01473 601175
Head: Mr Rick Tracey
Category: MLD ASD (Coed Day 5-16)

Thomas Wolsey School
Defoe Road, IPSWICH, Suffolk IP1 6SG
Tel: 01473 467600
Head: Ms Rupinder Hosie
Category: PD/Comunication (Coed Day 3-16)

Lowestoft

The Ashley School Academy Trust
Ashley Downs, LOWESTOFT, Suffolk NR32 4EU
Tel: 01502 565439
Head: Mrs Sally Garrett
Category: MLD (Coed Day & boarding 7-16)

SURREY

Chobham

Wishmore Cross School
Alpha Road, CHOBHAM, Surrey GU24 8NE
Tel: 01276 857555
Head: Mr J Donnelly
Category: BESD (Boarding & day 11-16)

EAST SUSSEX

Bexhill-On-Sea

Glyne Gap School
Hastings Road, BEXHILL-ON-SEA, East Sussex TN40 2PU
Tel: 01424 217720
Head: Ms Kirsty Prawanna
Category: CLD/ASD (Coed 2-19)

Eastbourne

The Lindfield School
Lindfield Road, EASTBOURNE, East Sussex BN22 0BQ
Tel: 01323 502988
Head: Ms Kirsty McIlhargey
Category: ACLD (Coed 11-16)

The South Downs Community Special School
(West Site), Beechy Avenue, EASTBOURNE, East Sussex BN20 8NU
Tel: 01323 730302
Head: Ms Sharon James
Category: ACLD (Coed 3-11)

Hastings

Torfield School
Croft Road, HASTINGS, East Sussex TN34 3JT
Tel: 01424 428228
Head: Ms Natalie Shuttleworth
Category: ACLD (Coed 3-11)

Heathfield

St Mary's School Horam
Maynards Green, Horam, HEATHFIELD, East Sussex TN21 0BT
Tel: 01435 812278
Head: Mr Paul Murphy
Category: LD EBSD (Boys 9-16)

Seaford

Cuckmere House School
Eastbourne Road, SEAFORD, East Sussex BN25 4BA
Tel: 01323 893319
Head: Ms Lorraine Myles
Category: SEBD (Boys 6-16)

St Leonards-On-Sea

New Horizons School
Beauchamp Road, ST LEONARDS-ON-SEA, East Sussex TN38 9JU
Tel: 01424 858020
Head: Ms Simone Hopkins
Category: SEBD (Coed 7-16)

Saxon Mount School
Edinburgh Road, ST LEONARDS-ON-SEA, East Sussex TN38 8HH
Tel: 01424 426303
Head: Ms Elaine Gardner
Category: ACLD (Coed 11-16)

THURROCK

South Ockendon

Beacon Hill Academy (Main Site)
Erriff Drive, SOUTH OCKENDON, Essex RM15 5AY
Tel: 01708 852006
Head: Mrs Sue Hewitt
Category: PNI PMLD SLD (Coed 3-16)

TORBAY

Torquay

Combe Pafford School
Steps Lane, Watcombe, TORQUAY TQ2 8NL
Tel: 01803 327902
Head: Mr Michael Lock

TYNE & WEAR

Gateshead

The Cedars Academy
Ivy Lane, Low Fell, GATESHEAD, Tyne & Wear NE9 6QD
Tel: 01914 874595
Head: Mrs Jane M Fraser
Category: PD (Coed 2-16)

Sunderland

Barbara Priestman Academy
Meadowside, SUNDERLAND, Tyne & Wear SR2 7QN
Tel: 01915 536000
Head: Mrs C Barker
Category: ASD CLD (Coed Day 11-19)

North View Academy
St Lukes Road, SUNDERLAND, Tyne & Wear SR4 0HB
Tel: 01915 534580
Head: Mr G Mellefont
Category: EBD ASD (4-11)

Portland Academy
Weymouth Road, Chapelgarth, SUNDERLAND, Tyne & Wear SR3 2NQ
Tel: 01915 536050
Head: Mrs M Carson
Category: SLD (Coed Day 11-19)

The New Bridge Academy (Lower Site)
Swindon Road, SUNDERLAND, Tyne & Wear SR3 4EE
Tel: 01915 536067
Head: Mr G Shillinglaw
Category: EBD (Coed Day 11-16)

The New Bridge Academy (Upper School)
Craigshaw Road, Hylton Castle, SUNDERLAND, Tyne & Wear SR5 3NF
Tel: 01915 535335
Head: Mr G Shillinglaw
Category: SEBD (Coed Day 11-18)

WARWICKSHIRE

Nuneaton

Discovery Academy
Vernons Lane, NUNEATON, Warwickshire CV11 5HJ
Tel: 07494 457314
Head: Mr Matthew Pike
Category: (Coed 9-19)

WEST MIDLANDS

Birmingham

Calthorpe Teaching Academy
Darwin Street, Highgate, LADYWOOD, Birmingham B12 0TP
Tel: 01217 734637
Head: Mr Richard Chapman
Category: SLD MLD CLD PD MSI AUT (Coed Day 2-19)

James Brindley Hospital School
Bell Barn Road, Edgbaston, LADYWOOD, Birmingham B15 2AF
Tel: 01216 666409
Acting Head: Mr John Bradshaw
Category: HS (Coed Day 2-19)

Wilson Stuart School
Perry Common Road, ERDINGTON, Birmingham B23 7AT
Tel: 01213 734475
Head: Mr Stephen Hughes
Category: PD (Coed Day 2-19)

Coventry

RNIB Three Spires Academy
Kingsbury Road, COVENTRY, West Midlands CV6 1PJ
Tel: 02476 594952
Head: Mr Robert Jones
Category: MLD (Coed Day 3-11)

Wolverhampton

Broadmeadow Special School
Lansdowne Road, WOLVERHAMPTON, West Midlands WV1 4AL
Tel: 01902 558330
Head: Miss K Warrington
Category: SLD ASD PMLD (Coed Day 2-6)

Northern House School
Cromer Gardens, Whitmore Reans, WOLVERHAMPTON, West Midlands WV6 0UB
Tel: 01902 551564
Acting Head: Mrs T Whitehouse
Category: BESD ADHD (Coed Day 8-16)

Westcroft School
Greenacres Avenue, Underhill, WOLVERHAMPTON, West Midlands WV10 8NZ
Tel: 01902 558350
Head: Ms A Brown
Category: CLD (Coed Day 4-16)

WILTSHIRE

Salisbury

**Exeter House
Special School**
Somerset Road, SALISBURY,
Wiltshire SP1 3BL
Tel: 01722 334168
Head: Mr Richard Chapman
Category: SLD PMLD SPLD
Del (Coed Day 2-19)

NORTH YORKSHIRE

Scarborough

The Woodlands Academy
Woodlands Drive, SCARBOROUGH,
North Yorkshire YO12 6QN
Tel: 01723 373260
Head: Mrs Annette Fearn
Category: MLD (2-16)

SOUTH YORKSHIRE

Doncaster

Pennine View School
Old Road, Conisbrough,
DONCASTER, South
Yorkshire DN12 3LR
Tel: 01709 864978
Head: Mrs Luci Windle
Category: MLD (Coed Day 7-16)

WEST YORKSHIRE

Huddersfield

Joseph Norton Academy
Busker Lane, Scissett,
HUDDERSFIELD, West
Yorkshire HD8 9JU
Tel: 01484 868218
Head: Ms Sarah Wilson
Category: SEMH (Coed Day 7-16)

SCOTLAND

GLASGOW

Hollybrook Academy
135 Hollybrook Street,
GLASGOW G42 7HU
Tel: 01414 235937
Head: Ms Jaqueline Newell
Category: MLD (Secondary)

Linburn Academy
77 Linburn Road,
GLASGOW G52 4EX
Tel: 01418 832082
Head: Ms Lorna Wallace
Category: CLD (Secondary)

GREENOCK

Lomond View Academy
Ingleston Street, GREENOCK,
Inverclyde PA15 4UQ
Tel: 01475 714414
Head: Mr David Peden

Useful associations
and websites

Action for Sick Children

10 Ravenoak Road,
Cheadle Hulme,
Stockport SK8 7DL.
Tel: 0161 486 6788
Helpline: 0800 0744 519
Email: enquiries@actionforsickchildren.org
Website: www.actionforsickchildren.org
Twitter: @Action4SickCh
Facebook: @ActionforSickChildren

A charity specially formed to ensure that sick children receive the highest standard of care possible.

Action on Hearing Loss

19-23 Featherstone Street
London EC1Y 8SL
Tel: 0808 808 0123 (freephone)
Textphone: 0808 808 9000 (freephone)
SMS: 0780 0000 360
Email: informationline@hearingloss.org.uk
Website: www.actiononhearingloss.org.uk
Twitter: @ActionOnHearing
Facebook: @actiononhearingloss

Action on Hearing Loss, formerly the Royal National Institute for Deaf People, is the largest national charity representing the 11 million confronting deafness and hearing loss in the UK.

Action on Hearing Loss Cymru

Ground Floor,
Anchor Court (North)
Keen Road
Cardiff
CF24 5JW
Tel: 02920 333 034
Text: 02920 333 036
Fax: 02920 333 035
Email: cymru@hearingloss.org.uk

See main entry above.

Action on Hearing Loss Northern Ireland

Harvester House
4-8 Adelaide Street
Belfast
BT2 8GA
Tel: 028 9023 9619
Fax: 028 9031 2032
Textphone: 028 9024 9462
Email: information.nireland@hearingloss.org.uk
Twitter: @hearinglossNI

See main entry above.

Action on Hearing Loss Scotland

Empire House
131 West Nile Street
Glasgow
G1 2RXJ
Tel: 0141 341 5330
Textphone: 0141 341 5347
Fax: 0141 354 0176
Email: scotland@hearingloss.org.uk

See main entry above.

ADDISS – National Attention Deficit Disorder Information & Support Service

PO Box 340
Edgware
Middlesex HA8 9HL
Tel: 020 8952 2800
Fax: 020 8952 2909
Email: info@addiss.co.uk
Website: www.addiss.co.uk

ADDISS provides information and assistance for those affected by ADHD.

Advisory Centre for Education – (ACE)

72 Durnsford Road,
London
N11 2EJ
Tel: 0300 0115 142
Email: enquiries@ace-ed.org.uk
Website: www.ace-ed.org.uk
Twitter: @ACEducationUK

ACE is an independent national advice centre for parents/carers of children aged 5 to 16. Advice booklets can be downloaded or ordered from the website. Training courses and seminars for LA officers, schools and governors are available. As well as a training package for community groups advising parents on education matters. Has Facebook page and you can follow them on Twitter.

AFASIC – Unlocking Speech and Language

20 Bowling Green Lane
London EC1R 0BD
Tel: 020 7490 9410
Fax: 020 7251 2834
Helpline: 0300 666 9410
Website: www.afasicengland.org.uk
Twitter: @Afasic
Facebook: @Afasic.Charity

Helps children and young people with speech and language impairments. Provides: training/conferences for parents and professionals; a range of publications; support through local groups; and expertise in developing good practice. Has a Facebook page.

AFASIC – Cymru

Titan House
Cardiff Bay Business Centre
Lewis Road
Ocean Park
Cardiff CF24 5BS
Tel: 029 2046 5854
Fax: 029 2046 5854
Website: www.afasiccymru.org.uk

See main entry above.

AFASIC – Northern Ireland

Cranogue House
19 Derry Courtney Road
Caledon
County Tyrone BT68 4UF
Tel: 028 3756 9611 (M-F 10.30am-2.30pm)
Email: mary@afasicnorthernireland.org.uk
Website: www.afasicnorthernireland.org.uk

See main entry above.

AFASIC – Scotland

42-44 Castle Street,
Dundee, DD1 3AQ
Tel: 01382 250060
Fax: 01382 568391
Email: info@afasicscotland.org.uk
Website: www.afasicscotland.org.uk

See main entry above.

Association of Blind and Partially-Sighted Teachers and Students (ABAPTAS)

BM Box 6727
London
WC1N 3XX
Tel: 0117 966 4839
Website: www.abapstas.org.uk

National organisation of visually impaired people that focuses on education and employment issues.

Association of Sign Language Interpreters (ASLI)

Derngate Mews
Derngate
Northampton
NN1 1UE
Tel: 01604 320834
Textphone: 18001 0871 474 0522
Fax: 08451 70 80 61
Email: office@asli.org.uk
Website: www.asli.org.uk
Twitter: @ASLIuk
Facebook: @ASLIuk

Has a useful online directory of sign language interpreters.

Asthma UK

18 Mansell St
London E1 8AA
Tel: 0300 222 5800
Email: info@asthma.org.uk
Website: www.asthma.org.uk
Twitter: @AsthmaUK
Facebook: @AsthmaUK

Charity dedicated to helping the 5.2 million people in the UK who are affected by asthma.

Ataxia (UK)

12 Broadbent Close
London N6 5JW
Tel: 020 7582 1444
Helpline: 0845 644 0606
Email: office@ataxia.org.uk
Website: www.ataxia.org.uk
Twitter: @AtaxiaUK
Facebook: @ataxiauk

Aims to support all people affected by ataxia. Has a Facebook page and you can follow them on Twitter.

BCS – IT Can Help

c/o Information Technologists
39a Bartholomew Close
London EC1A 7JN
Freephone & text phone helpline: 0800 269 545
Email: enquiries@abilitynet.org.uk
Website: www.itcanhelp.org.uk
Twitter: @AbilityNet
Facebook: @AbilityNet

Provides onsite volunteers to help individuals with disabilities who have computer problems

BIBIC (British Institute for Brain Injured Children)

Old Kelways
Somerton Road
Langport
Somerset TA10 9SJ
Tel: 01458 253344
Fax: 01278 685573
Email: info@bibic.org.uk
Website: www.bibic.org.uk
Twitter: @bibic_charity

BIBIC helps children with a disability or learning difficulty caused by conditions such as cerebral palsy, Down's syndrome and other genetic disorders; acquired brain injury caused by trauma or illness; and developmental disorders such as autism, ADHD, Asperger syndrome and dyspraxia.

All children are assessed by a multi-professional team who put together a report and a therapy plan that is taught to the family by the child's key worker. This provides support for the family to learn about their child and how they can make a positive difference to their development. Sections of the plan are designed to be shared with the child's school and social groups to ensure a consistent approach in areas such as communication, behaviour and learning. Families return on a regular basis for reassessments and updated therapy programmes.

Brain and Spine Foundation

LG01, Lincoln House
Kennington Park
1-3 Brixton Road
London SW9 6DE
Tel: 020 7793 5900
Helpline: 0808 808 1000
Fax: 020 7793 5939
Fax helpline: 020 7793 5939
Email: info@brainandspine.org.uk
Website: www.brainandspine.org.uk
Twitter: @brainspine
Facebook: @brainandspine

A charity founded in 1992 to help those people affected by brain and spine conditions.

British Blind Sport (BBS)

Pure Offices
Plato Close
Tachbrook Park
Leamington Spa
Warwickshire CV34 6WE
Tel: 01926 424247
Fax: 01926 427775
Email: info@britishblindsport.org.uk
Website: www.britishblindsport.org.uk
Twitter: @BritBlindSport
Facebook: @BritishBlindSport

BBS provide sport and recreation for blind and partially sighted people.

British Deaf Association England

356 Holloway Road
London N7 6PA
Tel: 020 7697 4140
Textphone: 07795 410724
Fax: 01772 561610
Email: bda@bda.org.uk
Website: www.bda.org.uk
Twitter: @BritishDeafNews
Facebook: @BritishDeafAssociation

The BDA is a democratic, membership-led national charity campaigning on behalf of deaf sign language users in the UK. It exists to advance and protect the interests of the deaf community, to increase deaf people's access to facilities and lifestyles that most hearing people take for granted and to ensure greater awareness of their rights and responsibilities as members of society. The association has several main service areas, with teams covering education and youth, information, health promotions, video production and community services, offering advice and help. There is a national helpline that provides information and advice on a range of subjects such as welfare rights, the Disability Discrimination Act (DDA) and education.

British Deaf Association Northern Ireland

Unit 5c, Weavers Court
Linfield Road
Belfast BT12 5GH
Tel: 02890 437480
Textphone: 02890 437486
Fax: 02890 437487
Email: northernireland@bda.org
Website: www.bda.org.uk

See main entry under British Deaf Association England.

British Deaf Association Scotland

1st Floor Central Chambers, Suite 58
93 Hope Street
Glasgow G2 6LD
Tel: 0141 248 5565
Fax: 0141 248 5554
Email: scotland@bda.org.uk
Website: www.bda.org.uk

See main entry under British Deaf Association England.

British Deaf Association Wales

GAVO Offices
Church Road
Newport NP19 7EJ
Email: bdm.waleseng@bda.org.uk
Website: www.bda.org.uk

See main entry under British Deaf Association England.

British Dyslexia Association

Unit 8, Bracknell Beeches
Old Bracknell Lane
Bracknell RG12 7BW
Tel: 0333 405 4567 (Helpline) or
0333 405 4555 (Admin)
Fax: 0845 251 9005
Email: helpline@bdadyslexia.org.uk
Website: www.bdadyslexia.org.uk
Twitter: @BDAdyslexia
Facebook: @bdadyslexia

Helpline/information service open between 10am and 4pm (M-F) also open late on Wednesdays 5-7pm. Has a Facebook page.

British Institute of Learning Disabilities (BILD)

Birmingham Research Park
97 Vincent Drive
Edgbaston
Birmingham B15 2SQ
Tel: 0121 415 6960
Fax: 0121 415 6999
Email: enquiries@bild.org.uk
Website: www.bild.org.uk

BILD are committed to improving the quality of life of people with learning disabilities. They do this by advancing education, research and practice and by promoting better ways of working with children and adults with learning disabilities. BILD provides education, training, information, publications, journals, membership services, research and consultancy. Has a Facebook page and you can follow them on Twitter.

British Psychological Society

St Andrews House
48 Princess Road East
Leicester LE1 7DR
Tel: 0116 254 9568
Fax: 0116 227 1314
Email: enquiries@bps.org.uk
Website: www.bps.org.uk
Twitter: @BPSofficial
Facebook: @OfficialBPS

The representative body for psychology and psychologists in the UK. Has search facility for details on psychologists.

Brunel Able Children's Education (BACE) Centre

Brunel University
School of Sport & Education,
Kingston Lane
Uxbridge, Middlesex UB8 3PH
Tel: 01895 267152
Fax: 01895 269806
Email: catherina.emery@brunel.ac.uk
Website: www.brunel.ac.uk/cbass/education/research/bace

Conducts research into all aspects of identification and provision for able and exceptionally able children. The centre has been involved in supporting the education of able children in inner city schools for a number of years. A number of courses are run for teachers to train them to make effective provision for able pupils.

Butterfly AVM Charity

Unit C2 Crispin Industrial Centre,
Angel Road Works
Advent Way
London
N18 3AH
Tel: 07811 400633
Fax: 0208 8037600
Email: support@butterflyavmcharity.org.uk
Website: www.butterflyavmcharity.org.uk
Twitter: @Butterfly080666
Facebook: @ButterflyAvmCharity

Offers advice and support to anyone affected by an AVM

CALL Scotland

University of Edinburgh
Paterson's Land
Holyrood Road
Edinburgh
Midlothian EH8 8AQ
Tel: 0131 651 6235
Fax: 0131 651 6234
Email: call.scotland@ed.ac.uk
Website: www.callcentrescotland.org.uk
Twitter: @CallScotland
Facebook: @CallScotland1983

CALL Scotland provides services and carries out research and development projects across Scotland for people, particularly children with severe communication disabilities, their families and people who work with them in augmentative communication techniques and technology, and specialised computer use.

Cambian Group

Helpline: 0800 138 1418
Email: education@cambiangroup.com
Website: www.cambiangroup.com
Twitter:@Cambian_Group
Facebook: @cambiangroup

Cambian Group is one of the UK's leading providers of specialist services in education, care, mental health and learning disabilities. Works with 140 public authorities.

Capability Scotland (ASCS)

Osborne House
1 Osborne Terrace
Edinburgh EH12 5HG
Tel: 0131 337 9876
Textphone: 0131 346 2529
Fax: 0131 346 7864
Website: www.capability-scotland.org.uk
Twitter: @capability_scot
Facebook: @CapabilityScotland

ASCS is a national disability advice and information service, which provides free confidential advice and information on a range of disability issues including advice on cerebral palsy.

Carers UK

20 Great Dover Street
London SE1 4LX
Tel: 020 7378 4999
Fax: 020 7378 9781
Adviceline: 0808 808 7777 or Email: advice@carersuk.org
Email: info@carersuk.org
Website: www.carersuk.org
Twitter: @CarersUK
Facebook: @carersuk

For carers run by carers.

Carers Northern Ireland

58 Howard Street
Belfast BT1 6PJ
Tel: 028 9043 9843
Email: info@carersni.org
Website: www.carersuk.org/northern-ireland
Twitter: @CarersNI
Facebook: @carersuk

See main entry under Carers UK.

Carers Scotland

The Cottage
21 Pearce Street
Glasgow G51 3UT
Tel: 0141 445 3070
Email: info@carersscotland.org
Website: www.carersuk.org/scotland
Twitter: @CarersScotland
Facebook: @carersuk

See main entry under Carers UK.

Carers Wales

Unit 5
Ynys Bridge Court
Cardiff
CF15 9SS
Tel: 029 2081 1370
Email: info@carerswales.org
Website: www.carersuk.org/wales
Twitter: @carerswales
Facebook: @carersuk

See main entry under Carers UK.

Centre for Studies on Inclusive Education (CSIE)

The Park
Daventry Road
Knowle
Bristol BS4 1DQ
Tel: 0117 353 3150
Fax: 0117 353 3151
Email: admin@csie.org.uk
Website: www.csie.org.uk
Twitter: @CSIE_UK
Facebook: @csie.uk

Promoting inclusion for all children in restructured mainstream schools.

Challenging Behaviour Foundation

c/o The Old Courthouse
New Road Avenue
Chatham
Kent ME4 6BE
Tel: 01634 838739
Family support line: 0300 666 0126
Email: info@thecbf.org.uk
Website: www.challengingbehaviour.org.uk
Twitter: @CBFdn
Facebook: @thecbf

Supports families, professionals and stakeholders who live/work with people with severe learning disabilities who have challenging behaviour.

Child Brain Injury Trust (CBIT)

Unit 1, The Great Barn
Baynards Green Farm
Bicester
Oxfordshire OX27 7SG
Tel: 01869 341075
Email: info@cbituk.org
Website: www.childbraininjurytrust.org.uk
Twitter: @CBITUK
Facebook: @childbraininjurytrust

Formerly known as the Children's Head Injury Trust (CHIT) this organisation was originally set up in 1991. It offers support to children and families affected by brain injuries that happen after birth. Registered charity nos. 1113326 & SCO39703. Has Facebook page and you can follow them on Twitter.

Communication Matters

Leeds Innovation Centre
103 Clarendon Road
Leeds LS2 9DF
Tel/Fax: 0845 456 8211
Email: admin@communications.org.uk
Website: www.communicationmatters.org.uk
Twitter: @Comm_Matters
Facebook: @communicationmattersuk

Support for people who find communication difficult.

Contact a Family

209-211 City Road
London EC1V 1JN
Tel: 020 7608 8700
Helpline: 0808 808 3555 Textphone: 0808 808 3556
Fax: 020 7608 8701
Email: helpline@cafamily.org.uk
Website: www.cafamily.org.uk
Twitter: @ContactAFamily
Facebook: @contactafamily

A charity that provides support, advice and information to families with disabled children. Has a Facebook page and you can follow them on Twitter.

Coram Children's Legal Centre

Riverside Office Centre
Century House North, North Station Road
Colchester,
Essex CO1 1RE
Tel: 01206 714 650
Fax: 01206 714 660
Email: info@coramclc.org.uk
Website: www.childrenslegalcentre.com
Twitter: @CCLCUK
Facebook: @CCLCUK

The Children's Legal Centre is an independent national charity concerned with law and policy affecting children and young people. The centre runs a free and confidential legal advice and information service covering all aspects of law and the service is open to children, young people and anyone with concerns about them. The Education Legal Advocacy unit provides advice and representation to children and/or parents involved in education disputes with a school or a local education authority.

Council for Disabled Children

8 Wakley Street
London EC1V 7QE
Tel: 020 7843 1900
Fax: 020 7843 6313
Email: cdc@ncb.org.uk
Website: www.councilfordisabledchildren.org.uk
Twitter: @CDC_tweets
Facebook: @councilfordisabledchildren

The council promotes collaborative work and partnership between voluntary and non-voluntary agencies, parents and children and provides a national forum for the discussion, development and dissemination of a wide range of policy and practice issues relating to service provision and support for children and young people with disabilities and special educational needs. Has a particular interest in inclusive education, special education needs, parent partnership services, play and leisure and transition.

Council for the Registration of Schools Teaching Dyslexic Pupils (CReSTeD)

Old Post House
Castle Street
Whittington
Shropshire SY11 4DF
Tel: 01691 665783
Email: admin@crested.org.uk
Website: www.crested.org.uk

CReSTeD's aim is to help parents and also those who advise them choose an educational establishment for children with Specific Learning Difficulties (SpLD). It maintains a register of schools and teaching centres which meets its criteria for the teaching of pupils with Specific Learning Difficulties.

All schools and centres included in the Register are visited regularly to ensure they continue to meet the criteria set by CReSTeD. CReSTeD acts as a source of names for educational establishments which parents can use as their first step towards making a placement decision which will be critical to their child's educational future.

Cystic Fibrosis Trust

One Aldgate
Second floor
London EC3N 1RE
Tel: 020 3795 1555
Helpline: 0300 373 1000 or 0203 795 2184
Fax: 020 8313 0472
Email: enquiries@cftrust.org.uk
Website: www.cftrust.org.uk
Twitter: @CFtrust
Facebook: @cftrust

The Cystic Fibrosis Trust is a national charity established in 1964. It offers information and support to people with cystic fibrosis, their families, their carers and anyone affected by cystic fibrosis. It funds research, offers some financial support to people with cystic fibrosis and campaigns for improved services. It provides a wide range of information including fact sheets, publications and expert concensus documents on treatment and care for people with cystic fibrosis.

Disabled Living Foundation

Unit 1, 34 Chatfield Road
Wandsworth
London SW11 3SE
Tel: 020 7289 6111
Helpline: 0300 999 0004
Email: info@dlf.org.uk
Website: www.dlf.org.uk
Twitter: @DLFUK
Facebook: @dlfuk

This foundation provides free, impartial advice about products for disabled people.

Down's Syndrome Education International

6 Underley Business Centre
Kirkby, Lonsdale
Cumbria LA6 2DY
Tel: 0300 330 0750
Fax: 0300 330 0754
Email: enquiries@downsed.org
Website: www.dseinternational.org
Twitter: @dseint
Facebook: @dseinternational

Down's Syndrome Education International works around the world to improve the development, education and social achievements of many thousands of people living with Down's syndrome. We undertake and support scientific research and disseminate quality information and advice widely through our websites, books, films and training courses.

Our education services support families and professionals to help people with Down's syndrome achieve sustained gains in all areas of their development.

For 30 years, we have disseminated the latest research findings in practical and accessible formats to the widest audiences, from birth to adulthood. Please visit our website for more information. We have a Facebook page and you can follow us on Twitter.

Down's Syndrome Association

Langdon Down Centre
2a Langdon Park
Teddington TW11 9PS
Tel: 0333 1212 300
Email: info@downs-syndrome.org.uk
Website: www.downs-syndrome.org.uk
Twitter: @DSAInfo
Facebook: @downsyndromeassociation

We provide information and support for people with Down's syndrome, their families and carers, and the professionals who work with them. We strive to improve knowledge of the condition. We champion the rights of people with Down's syndrome.

Down's Syndrome Association Northern Ireland

Unit 2, Marlborough House
348 Lisburn Road
Belfast BT9 6GH
Tel: 028 90666 5260
Fax: 028 9066 7674
Email: enquiriesni@downs-syndrome.org.uk

See main entry above.

Down's Syndrome Association Wales

Suite 1, 206 Whitchurch Road
Heath
Cardiff CF14 3NB
Tel: 0333 1212 300
Email: wales@downs-syndrome.org.uk

See main entry above.

.

Dyslexia Scotland

2nd floor – East Suite
Wallace House
17-21 Maxwell Place
Stirling FK8 1JU
Tel: 01786 446 650
Helpline: 0344 800 8484
Fax: 01786 471235
Email: info@dyslexiascotland.org.uk
Website: www.dyslexiascotland.org.uk
Twitter: @DyslexiaScotlan

Scottish association set up to support and campaign on behalf of people affected by dyslexia. They have a useful and easy to use website.

Dyspraxia Foundation

8 West Alley
Hitchin
Hertfordshire SG5 1EG
Tel: 01462 455016
Helpline: 01462 454 986
Fax: 01462 455052
Email: dyspraxia@dyspraxiafoundation.org.uk
Website: www.dyspraxiafoundation.org.uk
Twitter: @DYSPRAXIAFDTN
Facebook: @dyspraxiafoundation

The foundation exists to support individuals and families affected by dyspraxia; to promote better diagnostic and treatment facilities for those who have dyspraxia; to help professionals in health and education to assist those with dyspraxia; and to promote awareness and understanding of dyspraxia. As well as various publications, the Dyspraxia Foundation organises conferences and talks and supports a network of local groups across the United Kingdom.

Education Scotland

Denholm House
Almondvale Business Park
Almondvale Way
Livingston EH54 6GA
Tel: 0131 244 4330
Textphone: 18001+ 0131 244 4330
Email: enquiries@educationscotland.org.uk
Website: www.education.gov.scot
Twitter: @EducationScot
Facebook: @EducationScot

Education Scotland is an executive non-departmental public body sponsored by the Scottish government. It is the main organisation for the development and support of the Scottish curriculum and is at the heart of all major developments in Scottish education, moving education forward with its partners.

ENABLE Scotland

Inspire House
3 Renshaw Place
Eurocentral
Lanarkshire ML1 4UF
Tel: 01698 737 000
Helpline: 0300 0200 101
Email: enabledirect@enable.org.uk
Website: www.enable.org.uk
Twitter: @ENABLEScotland
Facebook: @enablescotland

Contact the ENABLE Scotland Information Service about any aspect of learning disability. They offer jobs, training, respite breaks, day services, supported living, housing and support for people with learning disabilities in different parts of Scotland. Its legal service can assist families with wills and trusts.

English Federation of Disability Sport

Sport Park, Loughborough University
3 Oakwood Drive
Loughborough
Leicestershire LE11 3QF
Tel: 01509 227750
Fax: 0509 227777
Email: info@efds.org.uk
Website: www.efds.co.uk
Twitter: @Eng_Dis_Sport
Facebook: @EnglishDisabilitySport

A charity that creates opportunities for disabled people to participate in sporting activities.

Epilepsy Action

New Anstey House
Gate Way Drive,
Yeadon
Leeds LS19 7XY
Tel: 0113 210 880
Helpline: 0808 800 5050
Fax: 0113 391 0300
Email: epilepsy@epilepsy.org.uk
Website: www.epilepsy.org.uk
Twitter: @epilepsyaction
Facebook: @epilepsyaction

Epilepsy Action is the UK's leading epilepsy organisation and exists to improve the lives of everyone affected by the condition. As a member-led association, it is led by and represent people with epilepsy, their friends, families and healthcare professionals.

Epilepsy Society

Chesham Lane
Chalfont St Peter
Gerrards Cross,
Buckinghamshire SL9 0RJ
Tel: 01494 601300
Helpline: 01494 601400
Fax: 01494 871927
Website: www.epilepsysociety.org.uk
Twitter: @epilepsysociety
Facebook: @EpilepsySociety

The Epilepsy Society provides information and support to those affected by epilepsy.

GIFT

7 Tower Road
Writtle
Chelmsford
Essex CM1 3NR
Tel: 01245 830321
Email: enquiries@giftcourses.co.uk
Website: www.giftcourses.co.uk
Twitter: @giftcourses
Facebook: @giftcourses

GIFT aims to offer a value-for-money education consultancy of quality, which meets the needs of gifted and talented children and those working to support them in the excitement and challenge of achieving their full potential as human beings. Residential and non-residential courses are organised for exceptionally able children aged five to 18 throughout the year (see our website). INSET courses for schools on provision, identification and school policy are provided with a special emphasis on workshops for practical activities.

Haringey Association for Independent Living (HAIL)

Tottenham Town Hall
Town Hall Approach Road
Tottenham
London N15 4RY
Tel: 020 8275 6550
Fax: 020 8275 6559
Email: admin@hailltd.org
Website: www.hailltd.org
Twitter: @HAIL_tweets
Facebook: @HAIL6650

Haringey Association for Independent Living is a support service for adults with learning difficulties moving towards independent living. You can follow them on Twitter.

Headway

Bradbury House
190 Bagnall Road
Old Basford
Nottingham NG6 8SF
Tel: 0115 924 0800
Helpline: 0808 800 2244
Fax: 0115 958 4446
Email: enquiries@headway.org.uk
Website: www.headway.org.uk
Twitter: @HeadwayUK
Facebook: @headwayuk

A charity that supports people with brain injuries and their carers.

Helen Arkell Dyslexia Centre

Arkell Lane
Frensham
Farnham
Surrey GU10 3BL
Tel: 01252 792400
Email: enquiries@arkellcentre.org.uk
Website: www.arkellcentre.org.uk
Twitter: @ArkellDyslexia

A registered charity providing comprehensive help and care for children with specific learning difficulties, including assessment, specialist tuition, speech and language therapy, summer schools and short courses. Initial consultations can be arranged in order to give advice on options for support. Professional teacher-training programmes and schools' support. Financial help available in cases of need.

Huntington's Disease Association

Suite 24
Liverpool Science Park IC1
131 Mount Pleasant
Liverpool L3 5TF
Tel: 0151 331 5444
Fax: 0151 331 5441
Email: info@hda.org.uk
Website: www.hda.org.uk
Twitter: @HDA_tweeting
Facebook: @hdauk

Registered charity offering support to people affected by Huntington's Disease (HD); which is sometimes referred to as Huntington's Chorea. Has a Facebook page.

Independent Panel for Special Education Advice (IPSEA)

24 Gold Street
Saffron Walden CB10 1EJ
Tel: 01799 582030
Adviceline: 0800 018 4016
Email: info@ipsea.org.uk
Website: www.ipsea.org.uk
Twitter: @IPSEAcharity

IPSEA offers free and independent advice and support to parents of children with special educational needs including: free advice on LAs' legal duties towards children with free accompanied visits where necessary, free support and possible representation for those parents appealing to the Special Educational Needs Tribunal, free second opinions on a child's needs and the provision required to meet those needs.

Institute for Neuro-Physiological Psychology (INPP)

1 Stanley Street
Chester
Cheshire CH1 2LR
Tel: 01244 311414
Fax: 01244 311414
Email: mail@inpp.org.uk
Website: www.inpp.org.uk
Twitter: @INPPLtd
Facebook: @INPPLtd

Established in 1975 to research into the effect central nervous system (CNS) dysfunctions have on children with learning difficulties, to develop appropriate CNS remedial and rehabilitation programmes, and to correct underlying physical dysfunctions in dyslexia, dyspraxia and attention deficit disorder (ADD).

Ivemark Syndrome Association

18 French Road
Poole
Dorset BH17 7HB
Tel: 01202 699824
Email: marcus.fisher@virgin.net

Support group for families with children affected by Ivemark Syndrome (also know as right atrial isomerism).

Jeans for Genes

199 Victoria Street
London SW1E 5NE
Tel: 0800 980 4800
Email: hello@jeanforgenes.com
Website: www.jeansforgenes.com
Twitter: @JeansforGenes
Facebook: @JeansforGenesUK

The first Friday of every October is Jeans for Genes Day. Their aim is to raise money to fund research into genetic disorders and their target figure is £3million each year.

KIDS

7-9 Elliott's Place
London, N1 8HX
Tel: 020 7359 3635
Website: www.kids.org.uk
Twitter: @KIDScharity
Facebook: @KIDScharity

KIDS was established in 1970 to help disabled children in their development and communication skills. Has a Facebook page and you can follow them on Twitter.

Leonard Cheshire Disability England

66 South Lambeth Road
London SW8 1RL
Tel: 020 3242 0200
Fax: 020 3242 0250
Email: info@lcdisability.org
Website: www.lcdisability.org
Twitter: @LeonardCheshire
Facebook: @LeonardCheshireDisability

Leonard Cheshire – the UK's largest voluntary-sector provider of support services for disabled people. They also support disabled people in 52 countries around the world.

Leonard Cheshire Disability Northern Ireland

Unit 5, Boucher Plaza
Boucher Road
Belfast BT12 6HR
Tel: 028 9024 6247
Fax: 028 9024 6395
Email: northernirelandoffice@lcdisability.org

See main entry – Leonard Cheshire Disability England.

Leonard Cheshire Disability Scotland

Murrayburgh House
17 Corstorphine Road
Edinburgh EH12 6DD
Tel: 0131 346 9040
Fax: 0131 346 9050
Email: scotlandoffice@lcdisability.org

See main entry – Leonard Cheshire Disability England.

Leonard Cheshire Disability Wales

Llanhennock Lodge
Llanhennock
Nr Caerleon
NP18 1LT
Tel: 01633 422583
Email: walesoffice@leonardcheshire.org

See main entry – Leonard Cheshire Disability England.

Leukaemia Care UK

1 Birch Court
Blackpole East
Worcester WR3 8SG
Tel: 01905 755977 Careline: 08088 010 444
Fax: 01905 755 166
Email: care@leukaemiacare.org.uk
Website: www.leukaemiacare.org.uk
Twitter: @LeukaemiaCareUK
Facebook: @LeukaemiaCARE

Registered charity that exists to provide care and support to anyone affected by leukaemia.

Leukaemia Care Scotland

Regus Management
Maxim 1, Maxim Office Park
2 Parklands Way, Eurocentral
Motherwell ML1 4WR
Tel: 01698 209073
Email: scotland@leukaemiacare.org.uk

See main entry on Leukaemia Care UK.

Listening Books

12 Lant Street
London SE1 1QH
Tel: 020 7407 9417
Fax: 020 7403 1377
Email: info@listening-books.org.uk
Website: www.listening-books.org.uk
Twitter: @ListeningBooks
Facebook: @ListeningBooks12

A charity that provides a postal and internet based audio library service to anyone who is unable to read in the usual way due to an illness, disability or learning difficulty such as dyslexia.

Has a range of educational audio material to support all aspects of the National Curriculum, as well as thousands of general fiction and non-fiction titles for all ages. There is no limit to the number of titles you may borrow during the year.

Manx Dyslexia Asociation

Coan Aalin
Greeba Bridge
Greba
Isle of Man IM4 3LD
Tel: 07624 315724
Email: manxdyslexia@gmail.com
Website: www.manxdyslexia.com

Charity (no. IM706) founded in 1993 to help raise the awareness of dyslexia on the Isle of Man.

MENCAP England

123 Golden Lane
London EC1Y 0RT
Tel: 020 7454 0454
Helpline: 0808 808 1111
Fax: 020 7608 3254
Email: information@mencap.org.uk
Website: www.mencap.org.uk
Twitter: @mencap_charity
Facebook: @Mencap

The Royal MENCAP Society is a registered charity that offers services to adults and children with learning disabilities. We offer help and advice in benefits, housing and employment via our helpline.

Helplines are open from Monday to Friday 9.30am-4.30pm; Wednesday – subject to change: (open am-closed pm). Language line is also used. Our office is open Monday-Friday 9-5pm.

We also offer help and advice to anyone who has any other issues or we can signpost them in the right direction. We can also provide information and support for leisure, recreational services (Gateway Clubs) residential services and holidays.

MENCAP Northern Ireland

5 School Road
Newtownbreda
Belfast BT8 6BT
Tel: 028 9069 1351
Email: helpline.ni@mencap.org.uk
Twitter: @Mencap_NI

See main entry – MENCAP England.

MENCAP Cymru

31 Lambourne Crescent
Cardiff Business Park
Llanishen, Cardiff CF14 5GF
Helpline: 02920 747588
Email: helpline.wales@mencap.org.uk
Twitter: @MencapCymru

See main entry – MENCAP England.

MENSA

British Mensa Ltd
St John's House
St John's Square
Wolverhampton WV2 4AH
Tel: 01902 772771
Fax: 01902 392500
Email: enquiries@mensa.org.uk
Website: www.mensa.org.uk
Twitter: @BritishMensa
Facebook: @BritishMensa

MENSA aims to bring about awareness that giftedness in a child is frequently a specific learning difficulty and should be recognised and treated as such, train teachers to recognise giftedness in a child, train teachers to teach gifted children, establish mutually beneficial relationships with other organisations having similar aims to our own and to devise and implement strategies aimed, at ministerial and senior civil servant levels, at bringing about recognition of the importance of catering for the needs of gifted children.

Mind, the National Association for Mental Health

15-19 Broadway
Stratford
London E15 4BQ
Tel: 020 8519 2122
Fax: 020 8522 1725
Email: suppoterservices@mind.org.uk
Website: www.mind.org.uk
Twitter: @MindCharity
Facebook: @mindforbettermentalhealth

Mind (the National Association for Mental Health) is the leading mental health charity in England and Wales. Mind works for a better life for everyone with experience of mental or emotional stress. It does this by: advancing the views, needs and ambitions of people experiencing mental distress; promoting inclusion and challenging discrimination; influencing policy through effective campaigning and education; providing quality services that meet the expressed needs of people experiencing mental distress and which reflect the requirements of a diverse community; achieving equal legal and civil rights through campaigning and education.

With over 60 years of experience, Mind is a major national network consisting of over 200 local Mind associations, which cover most major towns and rural areas in England and Wales. These are separately registered charities operating under the Mind brand. The Mind network is the largest charitable provider of mental health services in the community. The work of the local associations is strengthened and supported by staff and activities through its many offices in England and Wales. This ensures that, as a national charity, Mind keeps a distinct local perspective to their work.

Mind believes in the individual and equipping them to make informed choices about options open to them. Mind's mental health telephone information service (Mindinfoline) deals with thousands of calls each year. We offer a vital lifeline to people in distress, their relatives and carers, as well as providing mental health information to members of the public, professionals and students.

Mind Cymru

3rd Floor, Quebec House
Castlebridge
5-19 Cowbridge Road East
Cardiff CF11 9AB
Tel: 029 2039 5123
Fax: 029 2034 6585
Email: contactwales@mind.org.uk

See main entry above.

Motability

City Gate House
22 Southwark Bridge Road
London SE1 9HB
Tel: 0300 4564566
Minicom/textphone: 0300 037 0100
Fax: 01279 632000
Website: www.motability.co.uk
Facebook: @motabilityevents

Motability helps disabled people to use their mobility allowance to obtain new transport.

MS Society

MS National Centre
372 Edgware Road
London NW2 6ND
Tel: 020 8438 0700
Fax: 020 8438 0701
Website: www.mssociety.org.uk
Twitter: @MSSocietyUK
Facebook: @MSSociety

Multiple Sclerosis Society.

MS Society Cymru

Temple Court
Cathedral Road
Cardiff CF11 9HA

Tel: 029 2078 6676
See main entry above.

MS Society Northern Ireland

The Resource Centre
34 Annadale Avenue
Belfast BT7 3JJ
Tel: 02890 802 802

See main entry above.

MS Society Scotland

National Office, Ratho Park
88 Glasgow Road
Ratho Station
Newbridge EH28 8PP
Tel: 0131 335 4050
Fax: 0131 335 4051

See main entry on MS Society.

Muscular Dystrophy Campaign

61A Great Suffolk Street
London SE1 0BU
Tel: 020 7803 4800
Helpline: 0800 652 6352
Email: info@musculardystrophyuk.org
Website: www.musculardystrophyuk.org
Twitter: @TargetMD
Facebook: @musculardystrophyuk

Provides information and advice for families affected by muscular dystrophy and other neuromuscular conditions.

NAS – The National Autistic Society – England

393 City Road
London EC1V 1NG
Tel: 020 7833 2299
Helpline: 0800 800 4104
Fax: 020 7833 9666
Email: nas@nas.org.uk
Website: www.autism.org.uk
Twitter: @Autism
Facebook: @NationalAutisticSociety

The National Autistic Society is the UK's leading charity for people who are affected by autism. For more than 50 years we have worked to support children and young people with autism (including Asperger syndrome) to reach their goals. A well-rounded education, tailored to the needs of the individual, can help people to reach their full potential.

NAS Cymru

6/7 Village Way,
Greenmeadow Springs Business Park
Tongwynlais
Cardiff CF15 7NE
Tel: 02920 629 312
Fax: 02920 629 317
Email: wales@nas.org.uk

See main entry NAS – England.

NAS Northern Ireland

59 Malone Road
Belfast BT9 6SA
Tel: 02890 687 066
Fax: 02890 688 518
Email: northern.ireland@nas.org.uk

See main entry NAS – England.

NAS Scotland

Central Chambers
1st Floor
109 Hope Street
Glasgow G2 6LL
Tel: 0141 221 8090
Fax: 0141 221 8118
Email: scotland@nas.org.uk

See main entry NAS – England.

Nasen

4/5 Amber Business Village
Amber Close
Amington
Tamworth
Staffordshire B77 4RP
Tel: 01827 311500
Fax: 01827 313005
Email: welcome@nasen.org.uk
Website: www.nasen.org.uk
Twitter: @nasen_org
Facebook: @nasen.org

nasen promotes the interests of children and young people with exceptional learning needs and influences the quality of provision through strong and cohesive policies and strategies for parents and professionals.

Membership offers a number of journals, professional development and publications at a reduced cost, and provides a forum for members to share concerns and disseminate expertise and knowledge.

National Association for Able Children in Education (NACE)

NACE National Office
The Core Business Centre
Milton Hill
Abingdon
Oxfordshire OX13 6AB
Tel: 01235 828280
Fax: 01235 828281
Email: info@nace.co.uk
Website: www.nace.co.uk
Twitter: @naceuk

NACE works with teachers to support able children in schools. The organisation also provides, publications, journals, booklets, courses and conferences.

National Association of Independent Schools and Non-Maintained Special Schools (NASS)

PO Box 705
York YO30 6WW
Tel: 01904 624446
Email: krippon@nasschools.org.uk
Website: www.nasschools.org.uk
Twitter: @NASSCHOOLS

NASS is a voluntary organisation that represents the interests of those special schools outside the maintained sector of the education system.

Our commitment is to achieve excellence and to attain the highest professional standards in working with unique children and young people who have physical, sensory and intellectual difficulties. We exist to promote, develop and maintain the highest professional standards for non-maintained and independent special schools. We offer free information and advice on our member schools to families and professionals.

National Federation of the Blind of the UK

Sir John Wilson House
215 Kirkgate
Wakefield
Yorkshire WF1 1JG
Tel: 01924 291313
Fax: 01924 200244
Email: admin@nfbuk.org
Website: www.nfbuk.org
Twitter: @NFBUK

A charity that was set up to better the understanding between blind and sighted people.

NDCS – The National Deaf Children's Society

Ground Floor South, Castle House
37- 45 Paul Street
London
EC2A 4LS
Tel: 020 7490 8656
Minicom: 020 7490 8656
Fax: 020 7251 5020
Email: ndcs@ndcs.org.uk
Website: www.ndcs.org.uk
Twitter: @NDCS_UK
Facebook: @NDCS.UK

Leading provider of information, advice, advocacy and support for deaf children, their parents and professionals on all aspects of childhood deafness. This includes advice and information on education, including further and higher education, and support at Special Educational Needs Tribunals.

NDCS also provides advice on equipment and technology for deaf children at home and at school.

NDCS Cmyru

Ty-Nant Court, Morganstown, Cardiff, South Glamorgan CF15 8LW
Tel: 029 2037 3474
Minicom: 029 20811861
Fax: 029 2081 4900
Email: ndcswales@ndcs.org.uk

See main entry above.

NDCS Northern Ireland

38-42 Hill Street
Belfast BT1 2LB
Tel: 028 9031 3170
Text: 028 9027 8177
Fax: 028 9027 8205
Email: nioffice@ndcs.org.uk

See main entry above.

NDCS Scotland

Second Floor, Empire House
131 West Nile Street
Glasgow G1 2RX
Tel: 0141 354 7850
Textphone: 0141 332 6133
Fax: 0141 331 2780
Email: ndcs.scotland@ndcs.org.uk

See main entry above.

Network 81

10 Boleyn Way
West Clacton
Essex CO15 2NJ
Tel: 0845 077 4056 (Admin)
Helpline: 0845 077 4055
Fax: 0845 077 4058
Email: Network81@hotmail.co.uk
Website: www.network81.org.uk

Network 81 offers practical help and support to parents throughout all stages of assessment and statementing as outlined in the Education Act 1996. Their national helpline offers an individual service to parents linked to a national network of local contacts.

NIACE – National Learning and Work Institute

Chetwynd House
21 DeMontfort Street
Leicester LE1 7GE
Tel: 0116 204 4200
Fax: 0116 204 6988
Email: enquiries@learningandwork.org.uk
Website: www.learningandwork.org.uk
Twitter: @LearnWorkUK
Facebook: @festivaloflearning

Works across sectors and age groups to raise national standards and encourage adults in achieving literacy, numeracy and language skills. You can follow them on Twitter.

NOFAS – UK (National Organisation for Fetal Alcohol Syndrome)

022 Southbank House
Black Prince Road, Lambeth
London SE1 7SJ
Tel: 0208 458 5951
Email: info@nofas-uk.org
Website: www.nofas-uk.org
Twitter: @NOFASUK

Offers advice, support and information about Foetal Alcohol Spectrum Disorder.

Paget Gorman Signed Speech

PGS Administrative Secretary
43 Westover Road
Fleet GU51 3DB
Tel: 01252 621 183
Website: www.pagetgorman.org

Advice and information for parents and professionals concerned with speech and language-impaired children.

Parents for Inclusion (PI)

336 Brixton Road
London SW9 7AA
Tel: 020 7738 3888
Helpline: 0800 652 3145
Email: info@parentsforinclusion.org
Website: www.parentsforinclusion.org

A network of parents of disabled children and children with special needs.

Physically Disabled and Able Bodied (PHAB Ltd)

Summit House
50 Wandle Road
Croydon
CR0 1DF
Tel: 020 8667 9443
Fax: 020 8681 1399
Email: info@phab.org.uk
Website: www.phab.org.uk
Twitter: @phab_charity
Facebook: @PhabCharity

A charity that works to promote and encourage people with and without physical disabilities to work together to achieve inclusion for all in the wider community.

Potential Plus UK

Suite 1-2
Challenge House
Sherwood Drive
Bletchley
Milton Keynes MK3 6DP
Tel: 01908 646433
Fax: 0870 770 3219
Email: amazingchildren@potentialplusuk.org
Website: www.potentialplusuk.org
Twitter: @PPUK_
Facebook: @PotentialPlusUK

A mutually supportive self-help organisation offering services both through local branches and nationally. Membership is open to individuals, families, education professionals and schools.

Royal National Institute of Blind People (RNIB)

105 Judd Street
London WC1H 9NE
Tel: 020 7388 1266
Helpline: 0303 123 9999
Email: helpline@rnib.org.uk
Website: www.rnib.org.uk
Twitter: @RNIB
Facebook: @rnibuk

We're RNIB (Royal National Institute of Blind People) and we're here for everyone affected by sight loss. Whether you're losing your sight or you're blind or partially sighted, our practical and emotional support can help you face the future with confidence.

We raise awareness of sight problems, and how to prevent sight loss, and we campaign for better services and a more inclusive society.

We offer a wide range of services for blind and partially sighted children and young people, their families and the professionals who work with them. This includes children and young people with additional disabilities and multiple complex needs.

As well as our specialist schools, college and residences we offer:

- Equipment, toys and games
- Accessible books
- Family support
- Teaching and learning guidance and resources
- Information and networks for young people
- Research and campaigns

Scope

6 Market Road
London N7 9PW
Helpline: 0808 800 3333 (Scope response)
Tel: 020 7619 7100
Text SCOPE plus message to 80039
Email: helpline@scope.org.uk
Website: www.scope.org.uk
Twitter: @Scope
Facebook: @Scope

Scope is a national disability organisation whose focus is people with cerebral palsy. We provide a range of support, information and campaigning services both locally and nationally in addition to providing opportunities in early years, education, employment and daily living. For more information about cerebral palsy and Scope services, contact Scope Response, which provides free information, advice and initial counselling. Open 9am-7pm weekdays and 10am-2pm Saturdays.

Scope Cymru

4 Ty Nant Court
Morganstown
Cardiff CF15 8LW
Tel: 029 20 815 450
Email: helpline@scope.org.uk

See main entry above.

Scottish Society for Autism

Hilton House,
Alloa Business Park
Whins Road
Alloa FK10 3SA
Tel: 01259 720044
Advice line: 01259 222022
Twitter: @scottishautism
Email: autism@scottishautism.org
Website: www.scottishautism.org
Twitter: @scottishautism
Facebook: @scottishautism

The Scottish Society for Autism is a registered charity established in 1968. They aim to work with individuals of all ages with autism spectrum disorder (ASD), their families and carers, to provide and promote exemplary services and training in education, care, support and life opportunities.

Sense – The National Deafblind Charity

101 Pentonville Road
London N1 9LG
Tel: 0300 330 9250
Textphone: 0300 330 9252
Fax: 0300 330 9251
Email: info@sense.org.uk
Website: www.sense.org.uk
Twitter: @Sensetweets
Facebook: @sensecharity

Sense is the leading national charity that supports and campaigns for children and adults who are deafblind. They provide expert advice and information as well as specialist services to deafblind people, their families, carers and the professionals who work with them. They support people who have sensory impairments with additional disabilities.

Services include on-going support for deafblind people and families. These range from day services where deafblind people have the opportunity to learn new skills and Sense-run houses in the community – where people are supported to live as independently as possible. They provide leading specialist advice, for example on education options and assistive technology.

Shine

42 Park Road
Peterborough PE1 2UQ
Tel: 01733 555988
Fax: 01733 555985
Email: info@shinecharity.org.uk
Website: www.shinecharity.org.uk
Twitter: @SHINEUKCharity
Facebook: @ShineUKCharity

The new name for the Association for Spina Bifida and Hydrocephalus (ASBAH). Europe's largest organisation dedicated to supporting individuals and families as they face the challenges arising from spina bifida and hydrocephalus. Advisers are available to explain the problems associated with spina bifida and or hydrocephalus and may be able to arrange visits to schools and colleges to discuss difficulties. Has a Facebook page and you can follow them on Twitter.

Signature

Mersey House
Mandale Business Park
Belmont
Country Durham DH1 1TH
Tel: 0191 383 1155 Text: 07974 121594
Fax: 0191 3837914
Email: enquiries@signature.org.uk
Website: www.signature.org.uk
Twitter: @SignatureDeaf
Facebook: @SignatureDeaf

Association promoting communication with deaf and deafblind people.

SNAP-CYMRU

Head Office
10 Coopers Yard
Curran Road
Cardiff CF10 5NB
Tel: 02920 348 990
Helpline: 0845 120 3730
Textphone: 0345 120 3730
Fax: 029 2034 8998
Email: enquiries@snapcymru.org
Website: www.snapcymru.org
Twitter: @SNAPcymru
Facebook: @SNAPCymru

An all-Wales service for children and families, which provides: accurate information and impartial advice and support for parents, carers, and young people in relation to special educational needs and disability; disagreement resolution service; casework service; independent parental support service; advocacy for children and young people in receipt of services; training for parents, carers, young people; training for professionals in relation to SEN/disability. Has a Facebook page.

Spinal Injuries Association

SIA House
2 Trueman Place
Oldbrook
Milton Keynes MK6 2HH
Tel: 01908 604 191
Adviceline: 0800 980 0501
Text: 81025
Email: sia@spinal.co.uk
Website: www.spinal.co.uk
Twitter: @spinalinjuries
Facebook: @SpinalInjuriesAssociation

Set up to provide services for people with spinal cord injuries.

The ACE Centre

Hollinwood Business Centre,
Albert Street
Oldham OL8 3QL
Tel: 0161 358 0151
Fax: 0161 358 6152
Helpline: 0800 080 3115
Email: enquiries@ace-north.org.uk
Website: www.ace-north.org.uk
Twitter: @ACECentre
Facebook: @ACECentre.UK

The centre offers independent advice and information, assessments and training in the use of assistive technology for individuals with physical and communication disabilities across the north of England.

The Alliance for Inclusive Education

336 Brixton Road
London SW9 7AA
Tel: 020 7737 6030
Email: info@allfie.org.uk
Website: www.allfie.org.uk
Twitter: @ALLFIEUK
Facebook: @ALLFIEUK

National network campaigning for the rights of disabled children in education.

The Association of National Specialist Colleges (NATSPEC)

Robins Wood House
Robins Wood Road
Aspley
Nottingham NG8 3NH
Tel: 0115 854 1322
Email: info@natspec.org.uk
Website: www.natspec.org.uk

NATSPEC represents independent specialist colleges across England, Wales and Northern Ireland, providing for over 3000 learners with learning difficulties and/or disabilities, often with complex or additional needs. Most colleges offer residential provision. Member colleges support learners in their transition to adult life, participation in the community and where possible, employment.

NATSPEC acts as a national voice for its member colleges and works in partnership with a range of other providers, agencies and organisations. You can contact colleges directly, via the website, or through your connexions/careers service.

The Brittle Bone Society

Grant-Paterson House
30 Guthrie Street
Dundee DD1 5BS
Tel: 01382 204446
Fax: 01382 206771
Email: bbs@brittlebone.org
Website: www.brittlebone.org
Twitter: @BrittleBoneUK
Facebook: @brittlebonesociety

A UK registered charity providing support for people affected by Osteogenesis Imperfecta (OI).

The Disability Law Service

The Foundry, 17 Oval Way,
London, SE11 5RR
Tel: 020 7791 9800
Fax: 020 7791 9802
Email: advice@dls.org.uk
Website: www.dls.org.uk
Twitter: @DLS_law
Facebook: @disabilitylawservice

The Disability Law Service (DLS) offers free, confidential legal advice to disabled people in the following areas: benefits; children; community care; consumer/contract; discrimination; further and higher education; and employment.

In some cases they are able to offer legal representation. The Disability Law Service is made up of solicitors, advisers and trained volunteers who provide up-to-date, informed legal advice for disabled people, their families, enablers and carers.

The Fragile X Society

Rood End House
6 Stortford Road
Great Dunmow,
Essex CM6 1DA
Tel: 01371 875 100
Fax: 01371 859 915
Email: info@fragilex.org.uk
Website: www.fragilex.org.uk
Twitter: @fragilexuk
Facebook: @thefragilexsociety

The aims of The Fragile X Society are to provide support and comprehensive information to families whose children and adult relatives have fragile X syndrome, to raise awareness of fragile X and to encourage research. There is a link network of family contacts, national helplines for statementing, benefits and family support for epilepsy. They publish information booklets, leaflets, a publications list, video and three newsletters a year. There are also national conferences four times a year. Family membership (UK) is free. Welcomes associate membership from interested professionals.

The Guide Dogs for the Blind Association

Hillfields
Burghfield Common
Reading
Berkshire RG7 3YG
Tel: 0118 983 5555
Fax: 0118 983 5433
Email: guidedogs@guidedogs.org.uk
Website: www.guidedogs.org.uk
Twitter: @guidedogs

Blind Children UK and Guide Dogs have fully integrated into one charity to become The Guide Dogs for the Blind Association, building on their existing services to support more children with sight loss and the issues they face. The Guide Dogs for the Blind Association provides guide dogs, mobility and other rehabilitation services to blind and partially sighted people.

The Haemophilia Society

Willcox House,
140 – 148 Borough High Street
London, SE1 1LB
Tel: 0207 939 0780
Email: info@haemophilia.org.uk
Website: www.haemophilia.org.uk
Twitter: @HaemoSocUK
Facebook: @HaemophiliaSocietyUK

Founded in 1950, this registered charity has over 4000 members and a network throughout the UK providing information, advice and support services to sufferers of haemophilia, von Willebrand's and related bleeding disorders. You can follow them on Twitter.

The Hyperactive Children's Support Group (HACSG)

71 Whyke Lane
Chichester
Sussex PO19 7PD
Tel: 01243 539966
Email: hacsg@hacsg.org.uk
Website: www.hacsg.org.uk

Support group. Will send information pack if you send a large SAE.

The London Centre for Children with Cerebral Palsy

143 Coppetts Road
London
N10 1JP
Tel: 020 8444 7242
Fax: 020 8444 7241
Email: info@cplondon.org.uk
Website: www.cplondon.org.uk
Twitter: @C_Potential
Facebook: @CPotentialTrust

Provides education for young children with cerebral palsy using the system of Conductive Education.

The Makaton Charity

Westmead House
Farnborough
Hampshire GU14 7LP
Tel: 01276 606760
Fax: 01276 36725
Email: info@makaton.org
Website: www.makaton.org
Twitter: @MakatonCharity
Facebook: @TheMakatonCharity

Makaton vocabulary is a language programme using speech, signs and symbols to provide basic means of communication and encourage language and literacy skills to develop in children and adults with communication and learning difficulties. Training workshops, courses and a variety of resource materials are available and there is a family support helpline too.

The Planned Environment Therapy Trust (PETT)

Archive and Study Centre
Church Lane
Toddington
Cheltenham
Gloucestershire GL54 5DQ
Tel: 01242 621200
Fax: 01242 620125
Website: www.pettrust.org.uk
Twitter: @pettconnect

Founded to promote effective treatment for those with emotional and psychological disorders.

The Social, Emotional and Behavioural Difficulties Association (SEBDA)

c/o Goldwyn School
Godinton Lane
Great Chart
Ashford
Kent TN23 3BT
Tel: 01233 622958
Twitter: @SebdaOrg
Email: admin@sebda.org
Website: www.sebda.org
Twitter: @SebdaOrg

SEBDA exists to campaign on behalf of and to provide information, training and a support service to professionals who work with children and young people with social, emotional and behavioural difficulties. Please note: they do not provide any services to parents.

The Stroke Association

Stroke House
240 City Road
London EC1V 2PR
Tel: 020 7566 0300
Helpline: 0303 3033 100
Fax: 020 7490 2686
Email: info@stroke.org.uk
Website: www.stroke.org.uk
Twitter: @thestrokeassoc
Facebook: @TheStrokeAssociation

More than 250,000 people in the UK live with the disabilities caused by a stroke. The association's website provides information and advice for free.

The Thalidomide Society

Tel: 020 8464 9048
Email: info@thalidomidesociety.org
Website: www.thalidomidesociety.org
Twitter: @ThalSociety

Created in 1962. A support group for impaired adults whose disabilities are a result of the drug Thalidomide.

Together for Short Lives

New Bond House,
Bond Street
Bristol, BS2 9AG
Tel: 0117 989 7820
Helpline: 0808 8088 100
Email: info@togetherforshortlives.org
Website: www.togetherforshortlives.org.uk
Twitter: @Tog4ShortLives
Facebook: @togetherforshortlives

The new name for the Association for Children's Palliative Care (ACT). Helps families with children who have life-limiting or life threatening conditions.

Tourette's Action

The Meads Business Centre,
19 Kingsmead, Farnborough,
Hampshire, GU14 7SR
Tel: 0300 777 8427
Email: admin@tourettes-action.org.uk
Website: www.tourettes-action.org.uk
Twitter: @tourettesaction
Facebook: @TourettesAction

Registered charity offering support and information about Tourette's.

U Can Do IT

1 Taylors Yard
67 Alderbrook Road
London SW12 8AD
Tel: 020 8673 3300
Fax: 020 8675 9571
Website: www.ucandoit.org.uk
Twitter: @ucdit

U CAN DO IT is a London charity providing blind, deaf and physically disabled children and adults with the skills they need to utilise the internet. Tuition is one to one at home with costs starting from £1 per lesson.

WheelPower – British Wheelchair Sport

Stoke Mandeville Stadium
Guttman Road
Stoke Mandeville
Buckinghamshire HP21 9PP
Tel: 01296 395995
Fax: 01296 424171
Email: info@wheelpower.org.uk
Website: www.wheelpower.org.uk
Twitter: @wheelpower
Facebook: @wheelchairsport

The British Wheelchair Sports Foundation is the national organisation for wheelchair sport in the UK and exists to provide, promote and develop opportunities for men, women and children with disabilities to participate in recreational and competitive wheelchair sport.

Young Minds

Suite 11
Baden Place
Crosby Row
London SE1 1YW
Tel: 020 7089 5050
Parent Hotline: 0808 802 5544
Fax: 020 7407 8887
Website: www.youngminds.org.uk
Email: ymenquiries@youngminds.org.uk
Twitter: @youngmindsuk
Facebook: @youngmindsuk

National charity committed to improving the mental health of young people and children in the UK. Their website has advice, information and details of how you can help.

WEBSITES

www.abilitynet.org.uk

Ability Net is a charity that provides impartial, expert advice about computer technology for disabled people. You can follow them on Twitter.

www.abilityonline.net

Disability information and news and views online.

www.actionondisability.org.uk

Formerly HAFAD – Hammersmith and Fuham Action for Disability. Campaigning for rights of disabled people, the site is managed and controlled by disabled people.

www.amyandfriends.org

Website set up to support those families affected by Cockayne Syndrome in the UK.

www.cae.org.uk

Centre for Accessible Environments is the leading authority on providing a built enviroment that is accessible for everyone, including disabled people.

www.choicesandrights.org.uk

CRDC – Choices and Rights Disability Coalition. Run for and by disabled people in the Kingston upon Hull and East Riding of Yorkshire area.

www.deafcouncil.org.uk

UK Council on Deafness. Has interesting list of member websites.

www.disabilitynow.org.uk

Disability Now – award winning online newspaper for everyone with an interest in disability.

www.direct.gov.uk/disabledpeople

The UK government's web page for disabled people..

www.focusondisability.org.uk

Focus on Disability – resource of general information regarding disability in the UK.

www.heartnsoul.co.uk

Heart 'n' Soul Music Theatre – a leading disability arts group. Has a Facebook page.

www.ncil.org

National Centre for Independent Living. A resource on independent living and direct payments for disabled people and others working in the field.

www.peoplefirstinfo.org.uk

WELDIS – an online information resource of services in and around Westminster for older people, adults and children with disabilities and their carers.

www.qefd.org.uk

Queen Elizabeth's Foundation – a national charity supporting over 20,000 physically disabled people annually.

www.ssc.education.ed.ac.uk

Scottish Sensory Centre – for everyone who is involved in the education of children and young people with sensory impairment.

www.theark.org.uk

A registered charity set up to enhance the lives of people with multi-sensory impairment, learning difficulties and physical disabilities.

www.tuberous-sclerosis.org

Tuberous Sclerosis Association of Great Britain. Website provides information and support for people and families affected by TSC.

www.vitalise.org.uk

Vitalise (formerly The Winged Fellowship Trust) provides respite care for disabled children, adults and their carers.

www.youreable.com

Information, products and services for the disabled community including news, shopping, pen pals and discussion forums.

Glossary

ACLD	Autism, Communication and Associated Learning Difficulties
ADD	Attention Deficit Order
ADHD	Attention Deficit and Hyperactive Disorder (Hyperkinetic Disorder)
AdvDip SpecEduc	Advanced Diploma in Special Education
AFBPS	Associate Fellow of the British Psychological Society
ALAN	Adult Literacy and Numeracy
ALCM	Associate of the London College of Music
ALL	Accreditation of Lifelong Learning
AOC	Association of Colleges
AQA	Assessment and Qualification Alliance/ Northern Examinations and Assessment Board
ASC	Autistic Spectrum Conditions
ASD	Autistic Spectrum Disorder
ASDAN	Qualifications for 11-16 age range
ASP	Asperger syndrome
AUT	Autism
AWCEBD	now SEBDA
BA	Bachelor of Arts
BDA	British Dyslexic Association
BESD	Behavioural, Emotional and Social Difficulties
BMET	Biomedical Engineering Technologist
BPhil	Bachelor of Philosophy
BSc	Bachelor of Science
BSL	British Sign Language
BTEC	Range of practical work-related programmes; which lead to qualifications equivalent to GCSEs and A levels (awarded by Edexcel)
C & G	City & Guilds Examination
C(Ed) Psychol	Certificate in Educational Psychology
CACDP	Council for the Advancement of Communication with Deaf People
CAMHS	Child and Adolescent Mental Health Service
CB	Challenging Behaviour
CD	Communcation Difficulties
CertEd	Certificate of Education
CF	Cystic Fibrosis
CLAIT	Computer Literacy and Information Technology
CLD	Complex Learning Difficulties
CNS	Central Nervous System
COPE	Certificate of Personal Effectiveness
CP	Cerebral Palsy

CPD	Continuing Professional Development
CRB	Criminal Records Bureau
CReSTeD	Council for the Registration of Schools Teaching Dyslexic Pupils
CSSE	Consortium of Special Schools in Essex
CSSIW	Care and Social Services Inspectorate for Wales
CTEC	Computer-aided Training, Education and Communication
D	Deaf
DDA	Disability Discrimination Act
DEL	Delicate
DfE	Department for Education
DIDA	Diploma in Digital Applications
DipAppSS	Diploma in Applied Social Sciences
DipEd	Diploma of Education
DipSEN	Diploma in Speial Educational Needs
DipSpEd	Diploma in Special Education
DT	Design and Technology
DYC	Dyscalculia
DYSL	Dyslexia
DYSC	Dyscalculia
DYSP	Dyspraxia
EASIE	Exercise and Sound in Education
EBD	Emotional, Behavioural Difficulties
EBSD	Emotional, Behavioural and/or Social Difficulties
ECDL	European Computer Driving Licence
ECM	Every Child Matters (Government Green Paper)
EdMng	Educational Management
ELC	Early Learning Centre
ELQ	Equivalent or Lower Qualification
EPI	Epilepsy
EQUALS	Entitlement and Quality Education for Pupils with Learning Difficulties
FAS	Foetal Alcohol Syndrome
FLSE	Federation of Leaders in Special Education
FXS	Fragile X Syndrome
GLD	General Learning Difficulties
HA	High Ability
HANDLE	Holistic Approach to Newuro-DEvelopment and Learning Efficiency
HEA	Higher Educaiton Authority/Health Education Authority
HI	Hearing Impairment
HS	Hospital School
ICT	Information Communication Technology

Glossary

IEP	Individual Education Plan
IIP	Investors in People
IM	Idiopathic Myelofibrosis
ISI	Independent Schools Inspectorate
IT	Information Technology
KS	Key Stage
LA	Local Authority
LD	Learning Difficulties
LDD	Learning Difficulties and Disabilities
LISA	London International Schools Association
MA	Master of Arts
MAPA	Management of Actual or Potential Aggression
MBA	Master of Business Administration
MD	Muscular Dystrophy
MDT	Multidisciplinary Team
MEd	Master of Education
MLD	Moderate Learning Difficulties
MS	Multiple Sclerosis
MSc	Master of Science
MSI	Multi-sensory Impairment
NAES	National Association of EBD Schools
NAS	National Autistic Society
NASEN	Northern Association of Special Educational Needs
NASS	National Association of Independent Schools & Non-maintained Special Schools
NATSPEC	National Association of Specialist Colleges
NOCN	National Open College Network
NPQH	National Professional Qualification for Headship
NVQ	National Vocational Qualifications
OCD	Obsessive Compulsive Disorder
OCN	Open Course Network
ODD	Oppositional Defiant Disorder
OT	Occupational Therapist
P scales	method of recording the achievements of SEN students who are working towards the first levels of the National Curriculum
PACT	Parents Association of Children with Tumours
PACT	Parents and Children Together
PCMT	Professional and Clinical Multidisciplinary Team
PD	Physical Difficulties
PDA	Pathological Demand Avoidance
PE	Physical Education

PECS	Picture Exchange Communication System
PGCE	Post Graduate Certificate in Education
PGCertSpld	Post Graduate Certificate in Specific Learning Difficulties
PGTC	Post Graduate Teaching Certificate
PH	Physical Impairment
PhD	Doctor of Philosophy
Phe	Partially Hearing
PMLD	Profound and Multiple Learning Difficulties
PNI	Physical Neurological Impairment
PRU	Pupil Referral Unit
PSHCE	Personal Social Health, Citizenship and Economics
RE	Religious Education
SAT	Standard Asessment Test
SCD	Social and Communication Difficulties
SCLD	Severe and Complex Learning Difficulties
SEAL	Social and Emotional Aspects of Learning
SEBD	Severe Emotional and Behavioural Disorders
SEBDA	Social, Emotional and Behavioural Difficulties Association
SEBN	Social, Emotional and Behavioural Needs
SHB	Sexually Harmful Behaviour
SLCN	Speech, Language and Communicational Needs
SLD	Severe Learning Difficulties
SLI	Specific Language Impairment
SLT	Speech and Language Teacher
SP	Special Purpose/Speech Processing
SpEd	Special Education
SPLD	Specific Learning Difficulties
SP&LD	Speech and Language Difficulties
STREAM	Strong Therapeutic, Restoring Environment and Assesssment Model
SWALSS	South and West Association of Leaders in Special Schools
SWSF	Steiner Waldorf Schools Foundation
TAV	Therapeutic, Academic and Vocational
TEACCH	Treatment and Education of Autistic and related Communication Handicapped Children (also sometimes written as TEACHH)
TCI	Therapeutic Crisis Intervention
ToD	Teacher of the Deaf
TOU	Tourette syndrome
VB	Verbal Reasoning
VIS	Visually Impaired
VOCA	Voice Output Communication Aid

Index

Index